The Presbyterian Controversy

RELIGION IN AMERICA SERIES

Harry S. Stout

GENERAL EDITOR

A Perfect Babel of Confusion:
Dutch Religion and English Culture in the Middle Colonies

Randall Balmer

The Presbyterian Controversy:
Fundamentalists, Modernists, and Moderates

Bradley J. Longfield

Mormons and the Bible:
The Place of the Latter–day Saints in American Religion

Philip L. Barlow

The Rude Hand of Innovation:
Religion and Social Order in Albany, New York 1652–1836

David G. Hackett

Seasons of Grace:
Colonial New England's Revival Tradition in Its British Context

Michael J. Crawford

The Muslims of America
Edited by Yvonne Yazbeck Haddad

THE PRESBYTERIAN CONTROVERSY

Fundamentalists, Modernists, and Moderates

BRADLEY J. LONGFIELD

New York   Oxford
OXFORD UNIVERSITY PRESS

Oxford University Press

Oxford   New York   Toronto
Delhi   Bombay   Calcutta   Madras   Karachi
Kuala Lumpur   Singapore   Hong Kong   Tokyo
Nairobi   Dar es Salaam   Cape Town
Melbourne   Auckland   Madrid

and associated companies in
Berlin   Ibadan

Copyright © 1991 by Bradley J. Longfield

First published in 1991 by Oxford University Press, Inc.
200 Madison Avenue, New York, New York 10016

First issued as an Oxford University Press paperback, 1993.

Oxford is a registered trademark of Oxford University Press, Inc.

Library of Congress Cataloging-in-Publication Data
Longfield, Bradley J.
The Presbyterian controversy:
fundamentalists, modernists, and moderates /
Bradley J. Longfield.
p. cm.—(Religion in America series)
Includes bibliographical references.
ISBN 0-19-506419-4   ISBN 0-19-508674-0 (pbk.)
1. Modernist-fundamentalist controversy.
2. Presbyterian Church in the U.S.A.—History—20th century.
3. Presbyterian Church—United States—History—20th century.
I. Title. II. Series: Religion in America series (Oxford University Press)
BX8937.L65 1991 285'.1'09042—dc20 90-33625

2   4   6   8   10   9   7   5   3

Printed in the United States of America

Acknowledgments

I have incurred numerous debts in working on this project that I gratefully acknowledge. George M. Marsden, mentor and friend, offered advice and encouragement from start to finish. Others who have read all or part of the manuscript in various stages of development and have made valuable suggestions include: Dennis M. Campbell, Harry E. Farra, Stuart C. Henry, Irving B. Holley, Jr., John M. Mulder, John F. Piper, Jr., David C. Steinmetz, Grant Wacker, and Geoffrey Wainwright.

I am thankful for permission to quote from papers in the collections of the following institutions: the Henry Sloane Coffin Papers, Burke Library, Union Theological Seminary in the City of New York; the Charles R. Erdman Papers and the Robert E. Speer Papers, Speer Library, Princeton Theological Seminary, Princeton, New Jersey; the Clarence E. Macartney Papers, McCartney Library, Geneva College, Beaver Falls, Pennsylvania; the J. Gresham Machen Papers, Montgomery Library, Westminster Theological Seminary, Philadelphia, Pennsylvania; and the Department of History, Presbyterian Church (U.S.A.), Philadelphia, Pennsylvania.

The efforts of Cynthia Read, Paul Schlotthauer, and Michael Lane of Oxford University Press have made this a better book.

Finally, my deepest appreciation goes to my family, who fill my life with joy. I hope that Stephen and Sarah, when they are able to read, may find this work worthy of their time. Linda, my wife and companion, has contributed to this book in more ways than I can say. For her wisdom, patience, and love I am profoundly grateful.

Durham, North Carolina   B. J. L.
September 1990

To Linda

Contents

The Presbyterian Controversy

Introduction

The mainstream churches in America today face a serious crisis. For over two decades now mainline communions—such as the Presbyterian Church (U.S.A.), the United Methodist Church, the Episcopal Church, and the United Church of Christ—have faced staggering membership declines that threaten the continued vitality of these bodies.[1] The Presbyterian Church (U.S.A.), for example, lost over 1.2 million members from 1966 to 1987, and the membership of the United Methodist Church declined from over 10.6 million in 1970 to under 9.2 million in 1986.[2] Though the reasons for this hemorrhage in membership are many and complex, one contributor to the decline noted by analysts is the nebulous doctrinal identity of the churches. In a quest for inclusiveness and relevance to the increasingly secular American culture, the mainstream churches have adopted a policy of doctrinal pluralism, thereby blurring their theological identities. Thus Wade Clark Roof and William McKinney recently argued: "A crucial challenge for liberal Protestantism is to recapture some sense of particularity as a community of memory and not merely as a custodian of generalized cultural values. This will require among other things a countering of the secular drift that has had a disproportionate impact on its traditional constituency."[3] Without clear theological boundaries distinct from the ideals of the surrounding culture, the churches have been increasingly subject to cultural currents. Moreover, in the absence of a clearly articulated faith, many individuals can see little reason to join or stay in the mainline churches.

The roots of this nebulous identity lie, at least in part, in the fundamentalist–modernist controversy of the 1920s. The churches in the 1920s, in response to the growth of liberal theology and the resultant reaction of fundamentalism, chose to allow for diverse doctrinal views in order to preserve institutional unity. Though the theological movement dubbed neo-orthodoxy at least provided the appearance, if not the reality, of a theological consensus until the 1960s, the past two decades have witnessed the theological fragmentation encouraged by

3

doctrinal pluralism. The doctrinal diversity in the churches makes it difficult for the mainstream bodies to articulate clearly their theological beliefs. Adherence to doctrinal pluralism, while maintaining institutional unity, has left the churches devoid of a clear theological voice.

The factors that led the mainstream churches to accept doctrinal pluralism are shown perhaps nowhere more clearly than in the Presbyterian Church in the U.S.A. in the 1920s and 1930s.[4] There, a church that had maintained a strong doctrinal position opted to widen its boundaries to preserve the mission of the church to the culture. In many ways the Presbyterian Church can be seen as representative of the mainstream denominations in America. It is one of three churches (the other two being the Episcopal Church and the United Church of Christ) that "lie at the heart of the old historic Protestant mainline."[5] Moreover, though never the largest denomination in the United States, it has had theological and social influence out of all proportion to its size. Its membership and leadership, as educated, articulate members of the middle and upper classes, have played a formidable role in shaping American Protestantism. By examining the views and motivations of the leadership of the Presbyterian Church in the 1920s and 1930s, it is possible to see precisely what factors encouraged the church to embrace doctrinal inclusiveness as a policy and thereby better understand how the Presbyterian Church, and perhaps other mainstream churches, have arrived at their present situation.

From 1922 until 1936 the Presbyterian Church in the U.S.A. was wracked by conflict. Sparked by a sermon of Dr. Harry Emerson Fosdick, a liberal Baptist preaching in a Presbyterian pulpit, the Presbyterian controversy raged for fourteen years over such issues as ordination requirements, the mission of Princeton Seminary, and the orthodoxy of the Board of Foreign Missions. Though at the height of the conflict in the mid-1920s the church managed to hold together, the controversy resulted in a loosening of the church's ordination standards, the reorganization of Princeton Theological Seminary, the creation of Westminster Theological Seminary, and the eventual founding of the Presbyterian Church of America.[6]

The Presbyterian controversy was one major aspect of the wider fundamentalist–modernist controversy of the era. In the cultural crisis that followed World War I, differences within the church, which had been developing for over fifty years, exploded. Numerous factors contributed to this disruption. In the intellectual arena, the advent of Darwinism, historicism, higher criticism of the Scriptures, and comparative religion all strained traditional modes of thought. These intellectual changes were aggravated by massive social alterations in America. The rise of the city, vast immigration, rapid industrialization, and the gradual secularization of the culture changed the face of the nation. In the wake of World War I growing labor tensions, bombings, and the Russian Revolution spurred a fanatical fear of bolshevism. Moreover, the war accelerated the secularization of America and precipitated a "revolution in morals." Jazz became popular, women smoked, sex was openly discussed, the Charleston dominated the dance floor, and the divorce rate skyrocketed.[7] Such a climate exacerbated the differences between liberals or modernists and conservatives in the church.[8] Differing theologies and differing visions of the church's role in the culture resulted in the eruption of the Presbyterian controversy.

Stewart Cole, in his early study of the fundamentalist–modernist conflict, astutely observed that "the controversy may be characterized mainly as a conflict between types of church leaders."[9] The Presbyterian controversy was, by and large, a conflict among generals; it was they who prosecuted the war and they who worked to galvanize a constituency. By examining the lives and thought of six of the major protagonists in the conflict—J. Gresham Machen, William Jennings Bryan, Henry Sloane Coffin, Clarence E. Macartney, Charles R. Erdman, and Robert E. Speer—this study seeks to provide a fuller understanding of the religious and cultural issues in the struggle.

One aspect of the conflict becomes immediately apparent on even a cursory examination of this group of individuals. All the leaders studied here were economically secure and educated members of the dominant cultural tradition in America. Within this main cultural tradition, however, the characters under examination represent various theological and cultural subgroups; and these divisions affected the roles each would play in the controversy.

J. Gresham Machen, a militant conservative who eventually became the focus of much of the controversy, was born in Baltimore, Maryland, to parents devoutly loyal to the South. Raised in the Southern Presbyterian Church, he attended Princeton Seminary, concentrating in New Testament. A year's study in Germany precipitated a profound spiritual crisis for Machen, which was ultimately resolved in his adoption of the Princeton Theology and its philosophical foundation of Scottish Common Sense Realism. He received ordination into the Northern Presbyterian Church in 1914.

Machen's role as a leader of the militant conservatives or fundamentalists in the Presbyterian conflict, though determined primarily by his dedication to the Princeton tradition, was also influenced by his Southern heritage.[10] As heir of a tradition that looked back to an earlier day of spirituality and high culture, Machen abhorred the secularizing tendencies working their way in the Northern United States. In the course of the conflict Machen fought doggedly to preserve orthodox Calvinist doctrine, first because he believed it was true but also because he was convinced that only orthodox ideas could provide the basis for a new Reformation, which would restore the culture to its former glory.

Clarence Macartney, Machen's ally throughout most of the controversy, was born in Ohio into the Reformed Presbyterian Church. Macartney experienced a period of religious doubt in late adolescence but resolved his questions, attended Princeton Seminary, adopted its theology, and became a pastor in the Presbyterian Church. The Reformed Presbyterian Church, which had led the effort of the National Reform Association to christianize America, instilled in Macartney a dedication to moral reform as well as to orthodox doctrine. He was a zealous Sabbatarian, an advocate of Prohibition, and an opponent of lax divorce laws. It was Macartney who, in response to Harry Fosdick's sermon "Shall the Fundamentalists Win?" mounted a conservative counteroffensive. Dedicated to the preservation of orthodox Calvinism and to the church's mission to America, Macartney struggled throughout the controversy to defend supernatural Christianity and the church's evangelical witness to a culture that seemed to be drifting rapidly away from its Christian moorings.

William Jennings Bryan, an ally of Machen and Macartney until 1925, represented yet a different heritage. Born on America's "Middle Border," he inherited a broad evangelical theology. As an adolescent he joined the Cumberland Presbyterian Church and migrated from there to the larger Presbyterian Church later in life. Though conservative in theology, his actions in the conflict were dictated not so much by theological as by social concerns. In the aftermath of World War I he became convinced that Darwinist might-makes-right philosophy had inspired German aggression and atrocities and now threatened to undo the moral underpinnings of American civilization. His fight against Darwinism, in and out of the church, was his last great moral crusade. By preserving the fundamentals of the faith in the church, Bryan sought to preserve the mission of the church and the Christian mission of America.

Charles Erdman, on the other hand, was a moderating force throughout the conflict and provided critical leadership for the traditionalist inclusivists.[11] Son of William J. Erdman, a Presbyterian clergyman who was a leader in the Premillennialist and Holiness movements of the late nineteenth century, Charles entered the ministry as a matter of course.

Deeply influenced by Dwight L. Moody, the leading revivalist of the Gilded Age, Erdman's theology was conservative but tolerant, emphasizing evangelism and Christian living rather than precise doctrine. Erdman was concerned about the cultural turmoil in the 1920s, but his response to the disorder of the society was notably different from that of his fundamentalist brethren. To Erdman's mind, the church provided the moral adhesive for the nation. But a church torn apart by doctrinal controversy could never bind the nation together. In working to maintain the unity of the church, Erdman sought, primarily, to preserve the evangelical mission of the church. But additionally, he worked to maintain the stabilizing influence of the church in a culture that looked increasingly out of control.

Erdman's efforts to preserve peace in the church were greatly aided by the work of his friend, Robert E. Speer. Speer, a layman, had been raised in central Pennsylvania in a Presbyterian home. Converted by the premillennialist Arthur T. Pierson, he became a recruiter for the nascent Student Volunteer Movement and thus came under Moody's conservative, evangelical influence. Speer matriculated at Princeton Seminary, intending to pursue a calling as a foreign missionary, but never finished his seminary course. Instead, he was tapped by the Presbyterian Church to serve as a secretary of the Board of Foreign Missions, where he labored for forty-six years. In the course of his career Speer became one of the leading missionary statesmen in the world. In time Speer's involvement with missionary and ecumenical agencies broadened his theological outlook. His mature thought, in fact, reflected many of the themes of the theology of Horace Bushnell. He always affirmed the historical accuracy of the Gospels and such traditional doctrines as the virgin birth and the "real Resurrection" of Christ. But like Christians theologically more liberal than he, Speer came to adopt a Social Gospel that envisioned a world society unified in the power of the Kingdom of God. In working for church unity in the Presbyterian conflict, Speer sought first to preserve the united evangelical mission of the church. But in doing so, he also strove to ensure the creation of a new world order, unified in the One Lord Jesus Christ.

Speer's social views placed him very close to the ideals of the final character in this study, Henry Sloane Coffin. Coffin, who became a good friend of Speer, was the most prominent liberal in the Presbyterian Church. A native of New York City, the epitome of the urban culture that was coming to dominate the Northern United States, Coffin embraced modern culture and its intellectual trends, most notably historicism. Born into the Presbyterian Church, he early decided to pursue a ministerial calling and adopted the liberal theology he learned at New College, Edinburgh and Union Seminary in New York. The church, he insisted, had to accommodate to modern thought or perish for irrelevance. But more than freedom of thought and the preservation of the church were at stake in the conflict. Like Speer, Coffin believed that the church was called to build a new world order in the aftermath of World War I. Inasmuch as the effort to transform the world into God's Kingdom required the participation of all persons of Christian spirit, Coffin's struggle to preserve doctrinal liberty was also a struggle to further the hope of a world family living in peace and goodwill.

The Presbyterian controversy was fought primarily over questions of theology and ecclesiology. But the leading protagonists in the conflict were not concerned simply to defend their particular theological viewpoint. Underneath and behind these struggles lay vital concerns about the role of Christianity in the culture and how that role was to be expressed. Matters of religion and culture were inextricably intertwined. While the leaders of the conflict fought on the battlefields of doctrine, polity, and administration, cultural concerns dramatically affected the controversy and its outcome.

1

The Conflict Erupts: Harry Emerson Fosdick and the Presbyterian Church

On Sunday morning, 21 May 1922, Harry Emerson Fosdick mounted the pulpit of the First Presbyterian Church in the City of New York to preach the most famous sermon of his career, "Shall the Fundamentalists Win?"[1] Described by Fosdick as a "plea for good will," the sermon fell like a bombshell on the Presbyterian Church and set in motion a series of explosions that would rock the church until well into the next decade.[2] A liberal Baptist preaching by special arrangement in the Presbyterian Church, Fosdick had become increasingly dismayed by conservative intolerance of liberal Christians. Since the close of the war, liberals and conservatives had been sparring on such issues as biblical authority, evolution, and foreign missions. In response to the escalating militancy of the fundamentalists, Fosdick launched a counteroffensive and thereby precipitated the Presbyterian controversy.[3]

The sermon contrasted the differences between liberal and fundamentalist theology and proposed a solution to the tensions that threatened to tear the Baptist and Presbyterian churches apart. Liberals, Fosdick maintained, were sincere evangelical Christians who were striving to reconcile the new knowledge of history, science, and religion with the old faith. Fundamentalists, on the other hand, were intolerant conservatives determined "to shut the doors of Christian fellowship" against all who would modify any traditional doctrines. Most powerful among Baptists and Presbyterians, the fundamentalists had decided to draw the line at certain doctrines such as the virgin birth of Christ, the inerrancy of Scripture, the substitutionary atonement, and the literal second coming of the Lord upon the clouds of heaven. Fosdick specifically addressed all but the third of these "opinions," contrasting the "points of view" of fundamentalist Christians with those of their more progressive counterparts.[4]

Fosdick allowed that many devout Christians believed that the virgin birth was an historical event, that "it actually happened; there was no other way for a personality like the Master to come into this world except by a special biological miracle." But, he argued, many others within the evangelical churches accepted another point of view. These Christians held that "those first disciples adored Jesus—as we do; when they thought about his coming they were sure that he came specially from God—as we are; this adoration and conviction they associated with God's special influence and intention in His birth—as we do; but they phrased it in terms of a biological miracle that our modern minds cannot use."[5] Likewise, while many evangelical Christians affirmed the inerrancy of the Scriptures and the literal second coming of Christ on the clouds of heaven, others believed the Scriptures were "the progressive unfolding of the character of God" and that development, not supernatural intervention, was God's way of working out his will in the world.[6]

Given this division in the church, Fosdick declared, only tolerance and Christian liberty would make for peace. If the church was to attract the young men and women of the day and address the great needs of the world, it would have to end its narrow-minded bickering. The liberals would not be driven from the church, he averred. For the sake of the peace and mission of the church, therefore, both liberals and conservatives needed to assume a posture of courtesy, kindliness, humility, and fairness.[7]

Had the sermon remained within the walls of the First Presbyterian Church, reaction might have been minimal; but such was not to be the case. In a slightly modified version and under a new title—"The New Knowledge and the Christian Faith"—Fosdick's plea for tolerance was quickly published in three religious journals and distributed in pamphlet form to every Protestant clergyman in the country.[8] Conservative reaction was swift and strong.

Though Fosdick had refrained from specifically endorsing any of the liberal doctrines he had described, he clearly indicated his sympathy for modernist viewpoints. Moreover, conservatives had long been aware of Fosdick's liberal leanings. As early as 1916 J. Gresham Machen, who was soon to become a leader of the militant conservatives, had condemned Fosdick's preaching as "dreadful! ... undogmatic Christianity."[9] Fosdick's books and a recent debate with

William Jennings Bryan over evolution published in the *New York Times* made his theological position clear enough to conservative opponents.[10] When Fosdick boldly proclaimed that liberal interpretations of such doctrines as the virgin birth and the inspiration of Scripture should be tolerated within the church, many traditionalist Presbyterians could bear no more.

Clarence Edward Macartney, prominent preacher and pastor of the Arch Street Presbyterian Church in Philadelphia, led the response. He answered Fosdick's sermon with one of his own entitled "Shall Unbelief Win?" which was published in a pamphlet and in *The Presbyterian.*[11] Macartney contended that the naturalistic views described by Fosdick were simply irreconcilable with the doctrinal position of the Presbyterian Church. It was therefore the duty of the church and all evangelical Christians to make this incompatability known, to fight for the faith— "earnestly and intelligently and in a Christian spirit" but nevertheless to fight.[12]

Macartney answered Fosdick's sermon point by point. The virgin birth, he maintained, far from being myth or rubbish, was historical fact; the Bible was the inspired and authoritative Word of God; and premillenarians, though mistaken in their exegesis, were at least loyal to the "Person and claims of Jesus Christ."[13] Liberal preaching, on the other hand, was "slowly secularizing the Church." The minority of modernists and rationalists in the church, Macartney argued, depended on the tolerance of evangelicals to let them spread their message. But tolerance could only end in an emasculated gospel. The future was clear. If left unchecked, liberalism would lead the church to a new type of Christianity, "a Christianity of opinions and principles and good purposes, but a Christianity without worship, without God, and without Jesus Christ."[14]

Having rallied the troops, Macartney sounded the call to charge. Led by Macartney, the Presbytery of Philadelphia requested the General Assembly to "direct the Presbytery of New York to take such action as will require the preaching and teaching in the First Presbyterian Church of New York City to conform to the system of doctrine taught in the Confession of Faith."[15] The issue was thus joined. Fosdick had thrown down the gauntlet, challenging conservatives to tolerate liberal teachings. Militant traditionalist Presbyterians took up the challenge with a vengeance. More tolerant conservatives, drawn into the battle by those on either extreme, would eventually be forced to choose sides. There was no turning back.

Causes of Conflict: Intellectual and Social Change
in the Gilded Age

The circumstances that led to this confrontation had been developing for over fifty years. Americans awoke from the nightmare of the Civil War only to encounter revolutions in the intellectual, social, and religious life of the nation. Commenting on these vast changes, Henry Adams observed that "in essentials like religion, ethics, philosophy; in history, literature, art; in the concepts of all science, except perhaps mathematics, the American boy of 1854 stood nearer the year 1 than to the year 1900."[16] In the intellectual arena, Darwin's evolutionary hypothesis and the new "higher criticism" of the Scriptures challenged cherished notions about the Bible's accuracy and authority. Moreover, developments in the infant fields of psychology, sociology, and comparative religions questioned the possibility of absolute truth. Many colleges, long a stronghold of evangelical Protestantism, were becoming secular universities with specialized faculty. These challenges to the culture were aggravated by unprecedented social changes. Massive immigration added new hues, languages, and religions to the American landscape. Industrialization changed the way Americans earned their livings and where they lived. Cities swelled as foreigners and natives moved to urban areas while millionaire entrepreneurs, proclaiming a gospel of wealth, became America's heroes. By 1900 the United States was the world's industrial leader. In all areas of life, change occurred at an unprecedented pace. The United States was coming face to face with modernity.

Though scientists like Benjamin Silliman and Edward Hitchcock had managed to reconcile Genesis with the findings of geology in the nineteenth century, the publication of Charles Darwin's *Origin of Species* in 1859 set off another round of controversy.[17] Darwin's theory of natural selection not only challenged the biblical account of creation and the fall but also denied God's providential design. To the vast majority of Christians in America who still believed that God created the world in six days and placed humans in it by an act of special creation, this whole scheme seemed incredible. As Bert Loewenberg has noted, "Darwinism attacked the whole American *Weltanschauung*."[18] Lengthy and heated debate followed inevitably.

At the time of the publication of the *Origin of Species* most Americans were preoccupied with the rumblings of war. Nevertheless, both the scientific and religious communities began to address the implications of Darwin's work before long. Renowned paleontologist and glacial theorist Louis Agassiz led the scientific assault on the theory of organic evolution. Darwinism was, he claimed, a "mere mine of assertions," a "scientific mistake, untrue in its facts, unscientific in its method, and mischievous in its tendency."[19] Many naturalists, eager to guard their reputations, and clergy, eager to protect their faith, were quick to agree.[20]

Asa Gray, Agassiz's colleague at Harvard, proffered a different evaluation. Gray, the foremost botanist in America and an orthodox Christian, became Darwin's leading scientific apologist in North America. He attempted to reconcile his faith with natural selection by maintaining that God could work in the world through the evolutionary process. There was nothing in Darwin's theory, Gray maintained, that necessitated the rejection of the Christian faith. Rather, he contended, "agreeing that plants and animals were produced by Omnipotent fiat does not exclude the idea of natural order and what we call secondary causes."[21] Many would follow Gray down this path of harmonization.

The religious community responded to Darwin's theory in diverse ways. The distinguished Princeton theologian Charles Hodge found it utterly impossible to reconcile the scriptural understanding of God's providential design with the idea of natural selection. Darwinism was, Hodge declared, synonymous with atheism.[22] President James McCosh of Princeton University responded more moderately that Darwin's theory likely contained a "large body of important truths."[23] Still others in the religious community, such as Henry Ward Beecher and Lyman Abbott, became enthusiastic interpreters of evolutionary thought to the faithful, echoing the philosopher John Fiske's claim that evolution was "God's way of doing things."[24]

For the most part the idea of theistic evolution won the day. Although the well-known clergyman T. DeWitt Talmage denounced Darwinism and the Southern Presbyterians skirmished over the issue in the 1880s, most late-Victorian Americans seemed unconcerned with the threats perceived by Hodge. Rather, reconcilers like Asa Gray, John Fiske, and Lyman Abbott preached an optimistic evolutionism to willing believers.[25] Even A. A. Hodge and B. B. Warfield, successors to Charles Hodge at Princeton Seminary, came to endorse the idea of theistic evolution.[26] This popular acceptance of evolutionary thought would be severely tested after World War I by conservatives who were convinced that German atrocities had been inspired by a Darwinist might-makes-right philosophy.

While scientists, philosophers, and preachers were busy finding ways to interpret evolution to America, changes in historical studies posed problems on another front. In the early nineteenth century scholars in German universities began applying literary analysis, comparative linguistics, and archaeological findings to the study of the Hebrew Scriptures. Employing such methods, Julius Wellhausen and others questioned the Mosaic authorship of the Pentateuch, the dating of Daniel, and the historical accuracy of Job. In New Testament studies, David Friedrich Strauss arrived at equally revolutionary conclusions about the Gospel narratives. Though popular American response to these ideas was delayed by language barriers, the Civil War and Reconstruction, and cultural lag, by 1880 educated Americans were coming to realize that some dearly held notions were under severe attack. As theologians at Oberlin College, Union Theological Seminary (New York), and the University of Chicago adopted higher criticism, fervent debate and heresy trials ensued.[27] Inasmuch as the vast majority of evangelicals retained a traditional view of the Scriptures, tension over historical criticism did not abate.[28] In the 1920s this dispute exploded into full-scale war.

The advent of the study of comparative religions, stimulated by innovations in communications and transportation, provided another area of contention. Rather than demonstrating the superiority of Christianity to other faiths, the study of comparative religions seemed to place Christianity on a par with all religions. This was perhaps most clearly demonstrated at the 1893 World's Parliament of Religions, which sought to "unite all religion against irreligion and to make the basis of this union rest on the principle of the Golden Rule." To many American Christians this kind of syncretism equalled apostasy. Christianity was either true or false and if true, then not open to compromise. In opening the question of the relativity of Christian truth, the study of comparative religions further agitated the already-troubled waters of Protestant America.[29]

In all of these intellectual innovations, as well as in the infant fields of sociology and psychology of religion, historical relativity attacked the deeply held belief in absolute truth. The truth of the Bible, personal and social moral standards, and the teachings of the church all came under fire, condemned as historically conditioned.[30] Historical consciousness, as historian Grant Wacker has argued, was the force that finally destroyed the edifice of Victorian culture.[31]

Adjustments to the intellectual shocks of the Gilded Age were made more difficult by unprecedented alterations in the economic and social life of the United States. Technological advances in the generation of power and manufacturing drove economic growth at a furious pace. The improvement of the steam engine and steam turbine and the development of the internal combustion engine dramatically increased the power available for production. Innovations in transportation and communications such as the invention of the typewriter and telephone, and improvements in rail and ocean transport spurred industrialization and opened vast new markets for American products. Additionally, the mechanization of American industry, encouraged by favorable legislation, European capital, and natural resources, fueled the economic revolution.[32] These factors, organized by the chief entrepreneurs of the day—Andrew Carnegie, John D. Rockefeller, Cornelius Vanderbilt, James B. Duke—made the United States the leading industrial nation in the world by the turn of the century.[33]

The startling rise in the wealth of America benefited some more than others. In an effort to bring order out of the chaotic economic environment of late-nineteenth-century America, the industrial barons of the period created vast monopolies.[34] By 1901 Standard Oil, U.S. Steel, International Harvester, and Armour and Company each had captured over half of the total market in their fields, and the 305 largest companies in America controlled almost 40 percent of the nation's manufacturing capital.[35]

The leaders of these monopolies made unprecedented sums of money. On his death in 1877, Vanderbilt left an estate worth ninety million dollars and by 1900 Andrew Carnegie claimed an annual income of twenty-three million dollars.[36] In diametric opposition to these businessmen, millions of laborers, including women and children, worked sixty to seventy hours a week for five hundred dollars per year. One-eighth of America was, as Robert Hunter found, "underfed, underclothed, and poorly housed."[37]

The economic revolution occasioned equally revolutionary social transformation. At the time of the Civil War barely one-fifth of the population lived in "cities" of over 25 hundred people. By 1900 city dwellers made up 40 percent of the population, and in 1920 this figure passed 50 percent. Even more illustrative of the changes rocking America was the astronomical growth of the largest urban centers. In the four decades from 1860 to 1900 Chicago's population skyrocketed from 109 thousand to 1.7 million; Pittsburgh grew from 67 thousand to 450 thousand; and New York increased from slightly over 1 million to 3.4 million inhabitants.[38] The sense of community, accountability, and homogeneity, so familiar to nineteenth-century rural Americans, gave way to the heterogeneity and anonymity of the city.[39]

The rise of the city was the result not only of rural migration to the metropolis but also of immigration from abroad.[40] Improved transportation and economic opportunity encouraged massive immigration in the years following Appomattox. Approximately fourteen million Europeans came to America's shores in the last forty years of the century, so that in 1900 immigrants and their children made up over one-third of America's population. As the pace of immigration climbed even higher in the twentieth century, the makeup of the immigrants began to change. While most immigrants before 1900 were from Northern or Western Europe, the bulk of the newcomers from 1900 to 1914 were natives of the Southern and Eastern areas of the continent. Different languages, features, and religions distinguished this wave of immigrants from the mass of Americans and accelerated nativist trends.[41]

A number of factors led to a revival of antiforeign sentiment. Not least, the older Americans believed the immigrants would lower wages by expanding the labor pool. Beyond this, they worried that the newcomers, with no experience of democracy, would corrupt the American political system. Finally—and perhaps most importantly—the old stock feared for the future of American culture. The new immigrants observed a continental Sabbath that to devout Protestants was no Sabbath at all. They drank and danced and, more frequently than not, carried the stigma of poverty in a land where poverty evidenced sinfulness.[42] The foreigners threatened to destroy the white, Anglo-Saxon, Protestant vision of the United States.

Industrialization, urbanization, and immigration combined with changes in the intellectual world to encourage the secularization of American culture. Though the major Protestant denominations tripled in membership from 1860 to 1900 (from five to sixteen million), religion was having a smaller and smaller impact on large areas of American life.[43]

The secularization of American culture was visible nowhere more clearly than in the nation's colleges.[44] Since their inception, American colleges had been nurseries not only of learning but of piety. In 1850 the overwhelming majority of colleges were church-related and had clergymen as their presidents. Education sought to develop sound faith and moral integrity as well as intellectual acumen. After the Civil War the importation of the German university model, the advent of professionalism, and the rise of scientific positivism and historicism combined to turn many evangelical colleges into secular centers of scientific research. An integrated classical curriculum slowly gave way to specialization and growing antagonism between science and faith moved religion even further from the academic mainstream. Especially in the years after 1900, more and more professors, like William Graham Sumner at Yale, simply awoke one day to find their faith had vanished.[45]

These trends were accelerated as state governments and industrial tycoons replaced the churches as major contributors to higher education.[46] This movement culminated in the Carnegie Foundation's offer to provide large grants for professorial pensions to private, nondenominational colleges. Given the choice between funding or faith, many colleges—Bowdoin, Wesleyan, and Rochester among them—chose to sever their denominational ties.[47] Henceforth, in the words of Richard Hofstadter, "sectarianism was left mainly with the rearguard of American education."[48]

These changes in education were reflected in the secularization of the culture at large. In the face of a booming economy, materialistic values gained popular acceptance. More and more Americans became not so much antireligious as simply areligious. Outings, ball games, and the Sunday theater inspired an increasing apathy to attendance at Sunday worship. The advent of the Sunday newspaper, growing use of a seven-day work week, a noticeable rise in the use of trains on Sunday, and the establishment of country clubs all demonstrated a move away from traditional Protestant values.[49]

As the nineteenth century waned, the business world extruded the last vestiges of religious influence from the boardroom. Although John D. Rockefeller could claim that "The good Lord gave me my money," the economic philosophy of most all businessmen at the turn of the century was a secular laissez-faire capitalism.[50] Economic values tended to encourage maximum profit with minimum interference: "survival of the fittest" and economic expediency—not biblical principle—ruled in the marketplace.[51] To be sure, the Social Gospel movement attempted to impose the moral precepts of the Christian faith onto business practices, but the results frequently looked more like "secular social service" than Christian economics.[52] Despite the attempts of many to christianize the business world, the economic order moved further and further from Christian influences. America was gradually becoming a profane nation.

Religious Responses to Cultural Change

Among the diverse religious responses to these profound social and intellectual changes, perhaps none was so American as the revival, and no revivalist was more in tune with the times than Dwight L. Moody.

A portly, bearded, ex–shoe salesman, Moody applied the best entre-preneurial practices of his day to the business of winning souls and became the nation's foremost evangelist.[53] He traveled from city to city with his musical companion Ira D. Sankey, preaching a message of "Ruin by sin, Redemption by Christ, and Regeneration by the Holy Ghost" to thousands of urban Christians.[54] Conservative in theology, Moody saw little value in the results of the new higher criticism. "What's the use of telling people there were two Isaiahs," he asked, "so long as most of them don't even know there was one?"[55] Nonetheless, he was not averse to cooperating with his more progressive brothers if it fur-thered the evangelical cause. Above all else, Moody sought to rescue the perishing from the "wrecked vessel" of this world.[56]

In addition to campaigns in America and England, Moody started a series of summer conferences near his home in Northfield, Massachusetts that were to have far-reaching effects. At the 1886 conference a mis-sionary "gusher" of about one hundred students—the "Mount Hermon Hundred"—committed themselves to foreign missionary service after graduating from college. In the following year this number swelled to two thousand; the Student Volunteer Movement had been born. In-spired by a premillennial zeal to spread the gospel and the indefatigable labors of their leader, John R. Mott, the students strove to fulfill their motto, *The evangelization of the world in this generation.*[57]

The Student Volunteer Movement, closely connected with the Young Men's Christian Association, provided an accurate reflection of much of the spirit of turn-of-the-century Protestantism. Although the move-ment did not act as a sending agency, it recruited over thirteen thousand missionaries for other societies between 1886 and 1936. Other foreign mission ventures, which grew in popularity with the rise of imperialist sentiment, were the Laymen's Missionary Movement and the Foreign Missions Conference of North America.[58]

The crusade for foreign missions was but one of the numerous efforts of the churches to advance the Christian cause. At home, Protestants responded to the cultural and social crises with new or revitalized or-ganizations. The Sunday School movement found new life under the leadership of men like B. F. Jacobs and John H. Vincent.[59] Secular tendencies to make the Sabbath more of a holiday than a holy day were attacked by zealous Sabbatarians. Likewise, Protestants of almost every stripe united to combat the evils of alcohol. As Robert T. Handy has shown, "evangelicals were convinced that theirs was a Christian civili-zation on the way to victory and perfection."[60] Propelled by such a vision, Christians joined together to fulfill their destiny.

All was not well, however. While Victorian Protestants were busy uniting to evangelize America and the world, seeds of division were being planted that would bear fruit in the dramatic polarization of the 1920s. Differing responses to the intellectual and cultural crises of post–Civil War America would eventually lead to what historian Sydney Ahlstrom has called "the most fundamental controversy to wrack the churches since the age of the Reformation."[61]

By 1880 it was clear that a nascent theological movement, billed as the New Theology, was making a serious bid for the hearts and minds of American Christians. Drawing on the earlier traditions of Unitarianism, transcendentalism, and the evangelicalism of Horace Bushnell, theologians such as Newman Smyth, Theodore Munger, Washington Gladden, and Henry Ward Beecher set out to reconcile the Christian tradition with evolutionary thought and the results of biblical criticism. In *The Freedom of the Faith* (1883) Munger argued for a broader use of reason, a view of the solidarity of the human race, and the elimination of the distinction between the sacred and the secular. Popularized by the likes of Henry Ward Beecher and Lyman Abbott and systematized by William Newton Clarke and William Adams Brown, liberal theology had, by 1900, achieved parity with the more conservative parties in most major denominations.[62]

Although liberalism, or modernism, as it came to be called, was a diverse movement, certain doctrinal tendencies can be perceived. As William Hutchison has shown, the modernist impulse was guided by the "conscious, intended adaptation of religious ideas to modern culture."[63] This led to a persistent accent on the immanence of God in human culture, the goodness and value of humanity, the moral interpretation of the atonement, and the importance of experience, feeling, and ethics in religion. Moreover, the adoption of evolutionary thinking and historical criticism resulted in an understanding of the Bible as the account of the progressive revelation of God fulfilled in the life of Jesus. Inasmuch as evolution was equated with progress, an optimistic view of history lent a roseate glow to almost all liberal thought. Liberals were postmillennialists, convinced that history was a nonstop journey to the Kingdom of God. Though misery and suffering were not yet eradicated, the advances of technology and Christian civilization made perfection only a matter of time.[64]

Within the liberal camp many proponents of a Social Gospel arose to encourage the advance of God's Kingdom on earth.[65] The rapid urbanization and mechanization of American society had left industrial war, class hatred, political corruption, poverty, crime, and intemperance in its wake.[66] In 1876 Washington Gladden published *Working People and Their Employers* contending that Christian principles needed to control inhuman economic forces.[67] Following Gladden, Josiah Strong, William Stead, Charles Stelzle, and Walter Rauschenbusch, among a host of others, declared that social injustice could be eliminated—the Kingdom of God could come on earth—if only men and women of goodwill would work together for social amelioration.[68] Having accepted most of the tenets of liberal Christianity, Social Gospelers held that society could be saved only by collective action, not by converting individuals one at a time.[69] Social and individual salvation could not be divorced.

The Social Gospel received broad-based ecclesiastical endorsement with the founding of the Federal Council of Churches of Christ in 1908. Though the council was concerned with ecumenical cooperation on all levels, social and economic issues dominated its agenda. At its first meeting the council adopted a "Social Creed of the Churches," which called for the abolition of child labor and improvements in the wages and working conditions for industrial laborers. Moreover, the federal council gave adherents of the Social Gospel an important means of influencing national labor policy in the early part of the century.[70] Though the program of progressive social reform advocated by proponents of the Social Gospel gradually won the support of many church-goers, a large number of the laity refused to surrender their more conservative nineteenth-century theology for the tenets of liberalism.[71] For many, like prominent Presbyterian layman William Jennings Bryan, progressive politics and progressive theology did not necessarily go hand in hand.

While some Christians were trying to make peace with modernity through liberal adaptation, others developed more conservative innovations.[72] As the country was struggling through the era of Reconstruction, a new type of millennial thought, dubbed dispensational premillennialism, was winning adherents. Developed primarily by the Englishman John Nelson Darby around 1840, dispensationalism asserted that the history of the world was divided into seven dispensations including the historical "parenthesis" of the current church age. Grounding his theology on a complex literal interpretation of the prophetic Scriptures, Darby maintained that the present era would steadily deteriorate until it ended with the secret rapture of the church and the return of Christ.[73] Popularized by Darby on seven missionary journeys to the United States and Canada from 1862 to 1877, dispensationalism received its greatest impetus from annual Prophetic and Bible Conferences initiated in 1875 and from the publication of the dispensationalist *Scofield Reference Bible* in 1909. The founding of the Moody Bible Institute in 1886, the Bible Institute of Los Angeles in 1907, and numerous Bible schools, gave dispensationalists institutional bases from which to propagate their doctrine.[74]

The rise of the Holiness movement lent further support to conservative Christianity in the late nineteenth century. Springing mainly from Wesleyan roots, the Holiness teachings were also propagated in America by adherents of the more Reformed Keswick and Oberlin movements.[75] Despite the resultant doctrinal variations, all Holiness teaching stressed a literal biblicism, emotional fervor, strict moral conduct, and, most important, sanctification through the work of the Holy Spirit.[76] Disseminated through camp meetings, conferences, and Holiness denominations such as the Church of God and the Nazarenes, perfectionism became a pervasive theme in conservative theology. Holiness doctrines inspired a dramatic concern for social work among the poor, resulting in the establishment of nurseries, diet kitchens, relief programs, and employment bureaus to help the needy.[77] Through at least the early part of the twentieth century, therefore, conservative evangelicalism and social concern were wedded in an effort to christianize America.

Between 1910 and 1915 conservatives of various shades joined forces to publish a series of twelve volumes entitled *The Fundamentals: A Testimony to the Truth*.[78] Financed by California oil magnates Lyman and Milton Stewart, the works contained a series of essays by British, Canadian, and American theologians on such issues as scriptural authority, sin, salvation, the virgin birth, missions, and Sabbatarianism. Approximately three million volumes were distributed to "every pastor, missionary, theological professor, theological student, YMCA and YWCA secretary, college professor, Sunday school superintendent, and religious editor in the English-speaking world."[79] These works were more important for their symbolic value than for their contributions to theology: as historian George Marsden has argued, when the term *fundamentalist* was coined in 1920, "it called to mind the broad, united front of the kind of opposition to modernism that characterized these widely known, if little studied, volumes."[80] In contradistinction to post–World War I fundamentalism, however, the majority of the articles in *The Fundamentals* manifested a nonbelligerent tone. In the midst of postwar polarization many moderates who wrote articles for *The Fundamentals*, like Presbyterians Charles Erdman and Robert Speer, would find their position almost impossible to maintain.[81]

Developments within the Presbyterian Church

Developments within the Presbyterian Church during this period set the stage for the conflict that would plague the church in the 1920s and 1930s. As higher critical interpretations of the Bible increasingly threatened the traditional understanding of the scriptures as God's infallible Word, Presbyterian conservatives, especially at Princeton Seminary, built an almost impregnable apologetic for scriptural "inerrancy." The Princeton Theology, grounded in the philosophy of Scottish Common-Sense Realism and the doctrines of the Westminster Confession, held that the Bible was a record of truth in all it reported. This view found its classic expression in 1881, when Archibald Alexander Hodge and Benjamin Breckinridge Warfield argued that "the Scriptures not only contain, but ARE, THE WORD OF GOD, and hence that all their elements and all their affirmations are absolutely errorless and binding the faith and obedience of men."[82] While many Presbyterian clergy responded to the words of Hodge and Warfield with a resounding *amen!* a significant minority viewed this doctrine of inerrancy with amazed incredulity. The most prominent and articulate opponent of Princeton's doctrine of Scripture was the professor of Hebrew and cognate languages at Union Seminary in New York, Charles Augustus Briggs.

In the late nineteenth century Charles Briggs was the foremost biblical scholar in the nation. Born in New York City in 1841, he had been educated at the University of Virginia, Union Theological Seminary in New York, and the University of Berlin. After brief service as a Presbyterian pastor, he accepted a call to Union Seminary in New York where, in 1876, he assumed the chair of Hebrew and cognate languages.[83] Briggs became coeditor, with Archibald A. Hodge of Princeton, of the newly founded *Presbyterian Review* in 1880. Before long, this journal proved to be a source of tension as Briggs's higher critical views conflicted sharply with the more traditional doctrine of Scripture held by his peers at Princeton. This, combined with irreconcilable differences over proposed confessional revisions in the Presbyterian Church, led to the journal's demise in 1889.[84]

Throughout the 1880s Briggs published works that championed the higher critical method and questioned the orthodoxy of Princeton Theology, particularly its doctrine of biblical inerrancy.[85] Additionally, Briggs was a major proponent of revision of the Westminster Confession of Faith to bring its section on creation in line with the discoveries of modern natural science.[86] These positions notwithstanding, Briggs was no radical. He fully accepted the infancy narratives of Matthew and Luke and the doctrine of the virgin birth.[87]

Despite already-strong opposition to many of Briggs's positions in the church, it was Briggs's inaugural address, "The Authority of Holy Scripture," delivered upon his induction into the chair of Biblical Studies at Union in 1891 that finally precipitated his long and bitter heresy trial. Reiterating his established views on the Bible, Briggs declared that "there are errors in the Scriptures that no one has been able to explain away; and the theory that they were not in the original text is sheer assumption."[88] He went on to deny the Mosaic authorship of the Pentateuch, the unitary authorship of the book of Isaiah, and the conception of prophecy as a detailed prediction of the future. Moreover, his belligerent tone did nothing to soothe the nerves of those who took the speech as a frontal attack on Presbyterian orthodoxy. In rapid succession, sixty-three presbyteries called on the 1891 General Assembly to address Briggs's heretical statements.[89]

As a result, the 1891 General Assembly, exercising power granted to it by Union in 1870, vetoed Briggs's appointment to the chair; and the 1892 assembly, in a statement that came to be known as the Portland Deliverance, specifically endorsed the doctrine of biblical inerrancy, claiming, "Our church holds that the inspired Word, as it came from God, is without error."[90] In October of 1892, Union Seminary, determined to appoint Briggs to the new position, unilaterally rescinded the assembly's veto power over professorial appointments while simultaneously professing loyalty to the church's government and doctrine.[91] The controversy came to a head in 1893 when, after extensive appeals and judicial maneuvers, the trial came before the General Assembly.[92]

By an overwhelming majority the 1893 assembly voted to suspend the belligerent professor from the ministry for propagating "views, doctrines, and teachings" contrary to the doctrine of Holy Scripture and the standards of the church and in violation of his ordination vows.[93] On the same day the assembly adopted a report that disavowed responsibility for the teaching at Union and reaffirmed the previous year's deliverance on biblical inerrancy.[94] Moreover, Lane Seminary professor Henry Preserved Smith also lost his ministerial status for defending Briggs and his view of Scripture.[95] In no uncertain terms, the Presbyterian Church had placed itself squarely on the side of biblical inerrancy.

The theology of Charles Briggs was not the only item on the minds of Presbyterian clergy in the early 1890s. Many within the church had been agitating for revision of the Westminster Confession to bring it in

line with intellectual trends of the late nineteenth century. In 1903 this
effort bore fruit when the presbyteries approved eleven confessional
changes emphasizing such items as God's love for all humanity and the
salvation of all who die in infancy.[96] Though perhaps the majority of
Presbyterians understood these changes to be consistent with their Calvinistic heritage, the revisions were read by some, especially by many
in the Cumberland Presbyterian Church, as an abandonment of the
doctrines of reprobation and limited atonement.[97]

In 1813 the Cumberland Presbyterians had separated from the larger
Presbyterian communion because of, among other issues, disagreements
over the "fatalism" of the Westminster Confession.[98] This difficulty,
many Cumberlanders felt, had been removed by the confessional revisions of 1903, thus clearing the way for reunion with their parent
church.[99] At the request of the Cumberland Presbyterians the two
churches entered into union discussions. Many in the Presbyterian
Church were wary of reunion lest it imply that the confessional revision
allowed an Arminian understanding of the church's creed.[100] Likewise,
many in the Cumberland Church opposed reunion for fear of marrying
a communion full of unrepentant Calvinists.[101] Despite such opposition,
by 1905 both churches had approved a plan of union based on "the
Confession of Faith of the Presbyterian Church in the U.S.A. as revised
in 1903, and of its other doctrinal and ecclesiastical standards; and the
Scriptures of the Old and New Testaments . . . as the inspired Word of
God, the only infallible rule of faith and practice."[102] The union was
consummated in 1906 with almost ninety thousand Cumberland Presbyterians joining in the ranks of the Presbyterian Church in the U.S.A.[103]

This union had significant ramifications for later Presbyterian history.
Though doctrinal interpretation can always be a matter of debate, it
seems clear that the confessional revision of 1903 hardly made the Presbyterian Church an Arminian body. By all but the broadest interpretations, the Presbyterian Church still held to its Calvinistic heritage.
Nevertheless, many Cumberland clergy were willing to enter the Presbyterian Church because they maintained a loose understanding of
confessional subscription. While it is impossible to tell exactly how many
Cumberland ministers agreed to enter the larger church because of a
lenient view of confessional subscription, it is safe to claim that the
"broad-subscriptionist" party in the Presbyterian Church gained sub-
stantially as a result of the union of 1906. When in the 1920s liberals
pressed for wide latitude in interpreting the confession they received
significant support from former Cumberland ministers.[104]

A final development within the Presbyterian Church that influenced the battles in the twenties was the adoption of a five-point declaration of "essential and necessary" doctrines by the General Assemblies of 1910 and 1916. Troubled by the liberal tendencies of some ministerial candidates, the assembly declared that all candidates for ordination should be able to affirm the inerrancy of Scripture and the virgin birth, substitutionary atonement, bodily resurrection, and miracle-working power of Christ.[105] These doctrines in no way exhausted the Reformed system of doctrine but did provide something of a hedge around the confession, allowing conservatives to test candidates by a few simple questions.

By the second decade of the twentieth century, therefore, the Presbyterian Church included most of the ingredients necessary for a major battle. Strict conservatives, determined to maintain the orthodox faith, had won significant victories in the expulsion of Briggs and Smith and in the adoption of the Portland Deliverance and the five fundamentals. Having come thus far, they were not about to tolerate any liberal advances. Even so, liberal sentiment, aided by the Cumberland reunion, was growing apace. Liberals, feeling more powerful, were becoming increasingly assertive in their demands. The two factions were on a collision course. Before the advent of World War I, theological moderates in the church helped keep the ecclesiastical peace. In the aftermath of the cultural crisis that swept across the nation after the war, peacekeeping would become a well-nigh-impossible task.

The War and the Cultural Crisis

World War I marked a turning point in U.S. history. Although, as Henry May has shown, many were "cheerfully laying dynamite" in the hidden cracks of nineteenth-century culture before the war, it was the experience of military confrontation that detonated these explosives.[106] In the postwar years the walls of Victorian America came crashing down.

America entered the war with all the fervor of a religious crusade. "The world must be made safe for democracy," President Wilson declared, "Its peace must be planted upon the tested foundations of political liberty."[107] In this effort to extend American Christian civilization around the globe, the nation sacrificed its sons and its liberties. Citizens scrimped and saved to support the mission. The Sedition and Espionage Acts curtailed freedom of speech. As the Selective Service System determined the fate of draft-age men, the War Industries Board, the Fuel Administration, and the Railroad Administration determined the course of the country's industry.[108] In the eyes of America, the European confrontation became nothing less than a holy war. It was, in the words of the Creel Committee, "a Crusade not merely to re-win the tomb of Christ, but to bring back to earth the rule of right, the peace, goodwill to men and gentleness he taught."[109]

This crusading passion of the war did not abate with the cessation of hostilities in November 1918. Having won the war, Wilson campaigned for his dream of a League of Nations. Though the majority of the American people supported entrance into the league, Congressional opposition and presidential obstinacy made ratification impossible.[110] The war, undertaken with optimistic visions of the triumph of the American democratic faith, ended in disillusioned isolationism.

The "religious counterpart to the League of Nations" appeared with the creation of the interdenominational Interchurch World Movement (IWM) in 1918. Ecclesiastics, delirious over the unprecedented success of the United War Work Campaign, which had netted over two hundred million dollars, set about to realize the dream of "a united church uniting a divided world."[111] The movement sought to consolidate all of the missionary agencies of American Protestantism into a single effort to fulfill their common task. Despite these grandiose plans—or perhaps because of them—the movement never gained altitude. Conservative opposition, a resurgence of denominational loyalty, and a general weariness with idealistic campaigns condemned the IWM to the same fate as the League of Nations. By 1921 the movement had collapsed.[112]

On the domestic front, idealism gave way to bitterness, intolerance, and a quest for "normalcy." Fear of bolshevism, mounting labor unrest, urban riots, and terrorist bombings fueled an anticommunist hysteria in 1919 and 1920. Moreover, as European immigrants began spilling onto America's shores once again, racist and nativist tendencies rose to meet them. The Ku Klux Klan, preaching hatred of blacks, Catholics, and Jews, experienced phenomenal growth. Congress, faced with the prospect of unrestrained immigration, quickly restricted entrance into the country. Responding to citizens' fears of the dilution of the Anglo-Saxon stock, the 1924 National Origins Act sought to ensure white hegemony by pegging immigration quotas to the ethnic makeup of the United States in 1890.[113]

The war also accelerated the secularizing tendencies that had been altering American life for over two generations. America experienced a "revolution in morals." Newly franchised women competed for jobs and the title of Miss America. Freud became a household name; sex came to dominate headlines, movies, and conversations; and the divorce rate soared. The waltz gave way to the Charleston; jazz moved north from New Orleans; and Sabbath worship succumbed to Sunday golf. On almost every count the civilization Americans had fought to save was coming apart at the seams.[114]

To many conservative Christians, one reason for the dissolution of American culture was all too apparent. For the past thirty years liberal ministers, relying on German historical criticism and Darwinian thought, had been, in the words of Clarence Macartney, "slowly secularizing the church."[115] Clearly, a secularized church could not halt the apostasy of the culture. Within the Presbyterian Church efforts to halt this decline had been, by in large, successful. Militant traditionalists were well aware, however, that a pure faith was bought only at the price of eternal vigilance. When Harry Emerson Fosdick challenged the fundamentals of the faith, therefore, the only option for men like Clarence Macartney was active prosecution. The battle lines were being drawn, and no one was to draw them more sharply than a professor at Princeton Theological Seminary named John Gresham Machen.

2

J. Gresham Machen:
Princeton Theology
and Southern Culture

Young, energetic, and aggressively conservative, J. Gresham Machen had been watching the Fosdick–Macartney duel with rapt attention. For more than a decade Machen, assistant professor of New Testament at Princeton Theological Seminary, had been warning the church of the destructive consequences of modernist theology. In November 1921 he distilled his ideas into a brief, poignant address entitled "Liberalism or Christianity." As the title implied, Machen had concluded that the liberal religion preached by Fosdick and his kind was not simply a variety of Christianity but a different faith altogether. "At every point," he declared, "the liberal movement is in opposition to the Christian message."[1] Encouraged by positive responses to the article and, no doubt, by Fosdick's sermon, Machen expanded the essay into a landmark volume, *Christianity and Liberalism*, published in 1923.[2]

Machen set the theological debate of the church squarely within its historical and cultural context. "The past one hundred years," he stated, "have witnessed the beginning of a new era in human history." Changes in the economic and intellectual arenas—in industry, science, psychology, and sociology—had, he contended, flung hallowed tradition to the wind. Concurrent with these changes, the modern world, though aided by material advance, had become a spiritual wasteland. He lamented, "No great poet is now living to celebrate the change. . . . Gone, too, are the great painters, and the great musicians, and the great sculptors." The advance of utilitarian education and socialistic government endangered the soul of America. "The materialistic paternalism of the present day, if allowed to go on unchecked," he warned, "will rapidly make of America one huge 'Main Street,' where spiritual adventure will be discouraged and democracy will be regarded as consisting in the reduction of all mankind to the proportions of the narrowest and least gifted of the citizens."[3]

The cause of spiritual decline was clear to all who cared to see. The "glories of the past" had vanished with the rise of naturalistic, materialistic thought and the consequent advent of liberal theology. Liberalism, which to Machen's mind was rooted in naturalism, denied any supernatural intervention of God into history. In an effort to accommodate the faith to culture, liberal theology had sacrificed "everything distinctive of Christianity," leaving nothing but a "sordid life of utilitarianism."[4]

The question of the church's role in modern culture was therefore the most important issue before the faithful. If the church continued to abandon Christian teaching in the face of materialistic naturalism, Christianity would vanish. Only the rebirth of Christianity could stop the spiritual decline of the age. Here Machen found hope: a "new Reformation" could "bring light and freedom to mankind." But such a Reformation required honest and courageous soldiers, soldiers willing to maintain the truth of the Christian faith in the face of a hostile culture. The time had come, Machen declared, to proclaim that modern liberalism was not only a different religion from Christianity but belonged in a totally different class of religion altogether.[5]

Liberalism not only departed from the historic Christian tradition on every fundamental doctrine but, most important, denied the value of doctrine itself. Having accepted the premises of modern historicism, liberals believed that creeds were "merely the changing expression of a unitary Christian experience."[6] Fosdick was a perfect example of this tendency: "All theology," he said, "tentatively phrases in current thought and language the best that, up to date, thinkers on religion have achieved; and the most hopeful thing about any system of theology is that it will not last."[7] In contradistinction to this relativism, Machen argued, historic Christianity had always held that creeds were not merely expressions of Christian experience but statements of the facts on which experience was based. Doctrines, composed of historical "facts" plus the meaning of the facts, were the very foundation of the Christian message. The modernist derogation of doctrine, Machen insisted, separated it from any legitimate claim to the title Christian.[8]

Christianity and liberalism maintained radically different views of God and humanity. While modernism stressed God's immanence in history, Christianity emphasized the "awful transcendence" of the Creator. The modernist stress on divine immanence, Machen argued, led inevitably to a complete loss of the consciousness of human sinfulness. Christianity, on the other hand, was "the religion of the broken heart." Rather than ignoring the fact of sin, the Christian faith acknowledged sin's power and rejoiced in the forgiveness delivered in Christ's substitutionary atonement.[9] Religious authority provided another point of contention. The Bible, God's inspired and inerrant Word, authorized all genuinely Christian doctrine; but "Christian consciousness" or "Christian experience" provided the touchstone for the claims of liberalism. Machen agreed that experience did have a place in the Christian life; but it was secondary, not primary. Though experience confirmed, it could never replace the biblical witness and could "never enable us to be Christians whether the events occurred or not."[10] The facts of the Bible, not Christian consciousness, stood as the foundation of the faith.

Machen subscribed wholeheartedly to the Princeton doctrine of inspiration; that is, he held that "the Holy Spirit so informed the minds of the Biblical writers that they were kept from falling into the errors that mar all other books." Nevertheless, he allowed some leeway on the question of biblical inspiration. "There are many who believe that the Bible is right at the central point, in its account of the redeeming work of Christ," he claimed, "and yet believe that it contains many errors. Such men are not really liberals, but Christians; because they have accepted as true the message upon which Christianity depends." Though such a mediating view was logically inconsistent, it did not preclude the possibility of orthodox belief.[11]

Liberalism's Christology fell far short of the Christian view of Jesus. Modernists denied the miracles, the virgin birth, the substitutionary atonement, and the deity of Christ. While Christians accepted Jesus as the divine Savior who had paid the price of sin on the cross, liberals looked on him as simply an example of moral perfection. But sinful humanity could not be redeemed by the example of a man. To deny the supernatural and the substitutionary atonement was to deny Christianity.[12]

Not all liberals, Machen allowed, held all of the doctrines he had described. A "salutary lack of logic" often prevented "the whole of a man's faith being destroyed when he has given up a part." But Machen insisted that the only way to examine liberalism was not by its actual manifestation but by its logical implications. Sooner or later those who accepted the naturalistic premises of liberalism would follow them to paganism. The time to contend for the faith had long since passed.[13]

A "separation between the two parties in the Church" was "the crying need of the hour." The most honest and responsible solution to the theological division, Machen maintained, would be for the liberals to admit their apostasy and withdraw. Failing this, true Christians might be forced to secede. Above all, theological pacifism could not be countenanced. The future of the evangelical churches depended on the courage and determination of Christian soldiers willing to fight for the faith.[14]

The Southern Roots of J. Gresham Machen

Machen's analysis of the theological crisis in America reflected not only his allegiance to Princeton Theology but also to his Southern heritage. The second of three sons, John Gresham Machen had been born to Arthur Webster Machen and Mary Gresham Machen on 28 July 1881. Arthur Machen was a Southerner by ancestry and inclination. A native of Washington, DC, he received his education at a private academy, Columbian College (later George Washington University), and Harvard Law School. In 1853 he passed the Maryland bar exam and opened an office in Baltimore.[15]

On settling in Baltimore, he rented a pew in the Central Presbyterian Church, but around 1862 broke his Presbyterian ties to attend Christ Protestant Episcopal Church. In 1863 Machen changed his religious habits yet again to accommodate his mother and sister, who had moved to Baltimore and become members of the Franklin Street Presbyterian Church.[16] This church, pastored by Dr. J. J. Bullock, a staunch supporter of the Confederacy, would, under Bullock's leadership, leave the Northern Church in 1866 to unite with the Presbyterian Church in the United States.[17] It appears that though a frequent worshiper, Arthur Machen failed to become a communicant of any church through this period.[18]

Machen's sympathies during the War Between the States rested with the Confederacy. In 1861 he declined an appointment to become District Attorney for Maryland because it "might have required him to prosecute those who adhered openly to the Southern cause."[19] Nevertheless, Arthur chose not to follow his brother James into the ranks of the Confederate Army. He waited out the war in Baltimore, avoiding the Union draft and caring for his family after they moved from Virginia to Maryland in 1862.[20]

After the cessation of hostilities Machen's law practice flourished, raising his income and prestige. In 1870 he met a Georgian belle, Mary Gresham, who had stopped at her aunt's home in Baltimore on her way to Europe. Though twenty-two years her senior, Arthur was taken by

Mary's charms and pursued a long-distance romance. He proposed marriage in 1872; and they wedded in 1873, settling in Baltimore.[21]

Like her husband, Mary Gresham Machen descended from English ancestors who had made their home in the South. Her father, John Gresham, a successful attorney and businessman, was one of the leading citizens of Macon, Georgia, a thriving commercial center before the war. A devout Old School Presbyterian, he served the church as a ruling elder for forty-four years, from 1847 until his death in 1891.[22]

Mary, or Minnie (as she came to be called), grew up with all the advantages of antebellum Southern aristocracy. In 1899 J. Gresham Machen, reflecting on his childhood experiences, described his mother's homestead: "On College Street, in Macon, Georgia, stands a typical Southern mansion, almost hidden by luxuriant shrubs and tall magnolia trees. The house is built of wood in the colonial style, and is painted white. In front of the house, supporting the roof, stand four tall fluted pillars. These pillars are hollow, and were used during the war to hide the family silver from the Yankees."[23] Polished by a college education and European travel, Minnie Gresham became one of the "charming and accomplished young women who adorned the social and literary life" of Macon.[24]

Evangelical Christianity pervaded the life of high culture enjoyed by Mary Gresham. She embraced the faith of her father, joined the Franklin Street Presbyterian Church on her arrival in Baltimore and, it appears, successfully encourged Arthur Machen to do the same.[25] Although Arthur eventually became a dedicated and influential member of the Presbyterian Church, Mary was the undisputed spiritual leader in the Machen household.[26]

The faith Mary Gresham received as a child and the faith she bequeathed to her sons was the Old School Calvinism preached by the Southern Presbyterian Church. As a young boy Machen began memorizing the Westminster Shorter Catechism, and by early adolesence he had a firm command of the Scriptures and Reformed doctrine.[27] In 1896, at age fourteen, he joined the Franklin Street Church.[28] Significantly, the faith Machen inherited was no unalloyed Calvinism. Rather, he, like the entire Southern Presbyterian Church, reflected the theological tradition of their patron saint, James Henley Thornwell.

The Legacy of James Henley Thornwell

Old School Presbyterianism, which subscribed strictly to the Westminster Confession of Faith, found its principal support in the descendants of the doctrinally oriented Scottish and Scotch–Irish Presbyterians. In the first third of the nineteenth century, a sizable number of Presbyterians in the North, dubbed New School, moved away from the Westminster standards to embrace the more "Pelagian" teachings then being propagated by Nathaniel W. Taylor of the newly founded Yale Divinity School. These doctrinal differences, aggravated by disagreements over the import of strict confessionalism, church polity, the relation of the church to voluntary societies, revivalism, and slavery, had led to a division between the Old and New School parties in 1837.[29]

New School theology had never made much headway in the South.[30] Rather, Southern Presbyterians, insisting on the importance of doctrine, stood fast by the Westminster standards, particularly as mediated by James Henley Thornwell. Described by his contemporaries as the "Calhoun of the [Southern] Church" and the "most learned of the learned," Thornwell was the undisputed leader of antebellum Southern Presbyterianism.[31] Henry Ward Beecher, no conservative, credited Thorwell with being "the most brilliant minister in the Old School Presbyterian Church, and the most brilliant debater in the General Assembly."[32]

In the course of his career Thornwell served as a pastor, professor, and president of South Carolina College and professor of didactic and polemic theology at Columbia Theological Seminary. He won election to the position of moderator of the General Assembly in 1847, the youngest ever to hold that post; and in 1861, shortly before his death, led the Old School Southern Presbyterians in the formation of the Presbyterian Church of the Confederacy.[33] The Southern Presbyterian Church was unquestionably the lengthened shadow of James Henley Thornwell.[34]

In the 1857 inaugural address of Columbia Theological Seminary, Thornwell, then professor of didactic and polemic theology in the seminary, revealed the philosophical system that undergirded his thought. Theology, he argued, was a "positive science grounded in observation and induction, consisting of facts 'arranged and classified according to the necessary laws of the human mind.'"[35] He continued, "The great work of seminaries and theological professors now is to meet the altered aspects of infidelity; and not only to vindicate the external evidences of Christianity, but the internal, by showing the complete harmony of sound philosophy and theology."[36] As Thornwell spoke his listeners must have nodded in agreement; for his emphasis on facts, the inductive method, and the harmony of philosophy and religion demonstrated his devotion to the dominant philosophy in the nation, Scottish Common Sense Realism.

The Scottish philosophy of Common Sense had been developed primarily by Thomas Reid (1710–1796) and Dugald Stewart (1753–1828) in Glasgow and Edinburgh to refute the idealism of Bishop Berkeley and skepticism of David Hume.[37] Contrary to the thinkers who had followed Locke in claiming that "ideas," not external realities, are the objects of our thought, Common Sense philosophers maintained that we can and do know the real world directly through our senses. Ideas, Reid argued, were mental acts, not mental objects. Therefore, to have an idea of any object was to perceive the object itself, not just a mental image.[38] Anyone in right mind (except, perhaps, a few skeptical philosophers) knew that the objective world, the self, causal relationships, and moral principles existed.[39] Without this *common* sense, life would be quite literally impossible.

Truth, these philosophers maintained, was a single entity, absolute, permanent, and discoverable by all people through all ages. Following seventeenth-century thinker Francis Bacon, they argued that the one sure way to arrive at the truth was through the inductive scientific method. Flights into the fanciful world of metaphysical speculation and hypotheses could never lead to certainty. Rather, by observing the "facts" perceptible to common sense and classifying these "facts" scientists in every field could arrive at irrefragable conclusions.[40]

This philosophy, so well suited to the democratic ethos in America, was brought from Scotland in its most complete form by John Witherspoon, president of the College of New Jersey (Princeton) from 1768 to 1794.[41] By the early nineteenth century, Scottish Common Sense Realism had become the dominant philosophical school in America and was unquestionably the prevailing philosophy in the South.[42] Long before Thornwell had decided on a career in theology, he had discovered the philosophy of Dugald Stewart and adopted it as his own.[43]

The Scottish tradition, in maintaining the reliability of knowledge, provided a firm foundation for Thornwell's efforts to reconcile the claims of science and religion. Like his Northern contemporary Charles Hodge, Thornwell refused to concede the impossibility of Natural Theology. Truth was one and the method of discovering truth—observation and induction—was single. Given such realities, science could be nothing but the "handmaid of theology."[44]

Thornwell's epistemological convictions buttressed his doctrine of scriptural authority. Though he allowed that there might be errors of geography, politics, customs, or manners in the Scriptures, he insisted that the Bible was "an adequate and perfect measure of faith."[45] Scripture provided "facts" to the theologian in the same way that nature provided "facts" to the physical scientist. The task of the theologian was simply to organize these facts into a systematic whole reflecting God's truth.[46] Thornwell's biblical hermeneutic and philosophical proclivities provided support for his social views. In defense of slavery, the predominant social issue of his day, Thornwell turned to the Scriptures and discovered that "no direct condemnation of slavery can anywhere be found in the Sacred Volume." He continued,

> The Scriptures not only fail to condemn slavery, they as distinctly sanction it as any other social condition of man.... Our argument then is this: If the Church is bound to abide by the authority of the Bible, and that alone, she discharges her whole office in regard to slavery when she declares what the Bible teaches, and enforces its laws by her own peculiar sanctions. Where the Scriptures are silent, she must be silent too.... To this she is shut up by the nature of her Constitution.[47]

Those who condemned slavery as a sin did so only by going beyond the facts of Scripture. True exegesis, like any true science, prohibited just this type of speculation.

Thornwell's attitude toward slavery reflected the doctrine with which his name became most closely associated, the *spirituality of the church*. Just as the church had no right to meddle in slavery, he argued, so "it is not the distinctive province of the Church to build asylums for the needy or insane, to organize societies for the improvement of the penal code, or for the arresting of the progress of intemperance, gambling or lust."[48] The church and state as distinct bodies had no right to usurp each others' jurisdiction. Individual Christians had a right and a responsibility to strive to effect the common life of the nation; but the church, as a spiritual institution, was constrained to remain within its own sphere.[49]

In the years before the Civil War, as secession sentiment grew, Thornwell attempted to provide a moderating tone. Separation should be, he argued, a solution of last resort to be pursued only when all other avenues had been exhausted. Nevertheless, constitutionally guaranteed liberties were not to be conceded. After the election of Lincoln he lamented that the "good faith" that bound the sovereign states of the Union together had been broken by the North. He continued, "If the non-slaveholding States cannot in conscience redeem their faith, they are bound in honour to take back their pledges, to withdraw from the Union, and to release their confederates from all the conditions of the contract."[50] The North, by its breach of faith, had dissolved the Union. The only road open to the South, therefore, was to withdraw. Secession would not be easy, but a question of principle was at stake. The nation split in two; and in this split, the church could not remain united. In 1861 Thornwell led his fellow Southern Presbyterians in the organization of the Presbyterian Church in the Confederate States of America.[51]

When the War Between the States came to a close the infant church was in shambles. Church buildings lay in ruins; missionary activity and religious publication had ceased; congregations could not support pastors; and the endowments of the theological seminaries, based on Confederate investments, had largely evaporated.[52] Moreover, with Thornwell's premature death on 1 August 1862, the church had lost her foremost theologian. In the face of new realities Southern Presbyterians took a new name, the Presbyterian Church in the United States, but refused to adopt a new theology. Old School Presbyterianism, primarily as interpreted by James H. Thornwell, remained the theology of the Southern Church, of Mary Gresham Machen, and thus of her middle son, John Gresham.[53]

Minnie Machen's legacy to her son included more than the religious tradition of James Henley Thornwell, however. She was a devoted daughter of the Old South and, with the aid of her husband, instilled a passionate devotion to Southern culture and Southern values in her children. The extremely close ties Machen would maintain with his mother throughout her life would reinforce his understanding of himself as heir not only to orthodox Christianity but to the noble civilization of the Old South.[54]

The Legacy of the Lost Cause

In 1861 the Confederate States of America had severed its ties with the Union in the name of liberty. Four years later the South lay devastated by the ravages of war. Visions of a Confederate nation had been smashed. The Southern economy was a wreck. Railroads had been decimated, bridges were cut, rivers had been blocked, ocean ports were destroyed. Once-bustling cities—Jackson, Atlanta, Selma, Columbia—were in ruins; once-productive fields lay barren. As surging industrial growth spurred the booming economy of the North, the South languished in unrelenting poverty.[55]

In the face of humiliating military defeat and debilitating indigence,

Southerners found sustenance and identity in the myth of the Lost Cause. As various scholars have shown, a "cult of chivalry," emphasizing "manners, women, military affairs, the ideal of Greek democracy, and Romantic oratory," developed in the South prior to the Civil War.[56] By the 1830s Southerners, convinced that they were the descendants of English cavaliers, had begun to see themselves as comprising a "chivalric society, embodying many of the agrarian and spiritual values that seemed to be disappearing in the industrializing North."[57] When the political Confederacy was crushed by Yankee aggressors, Southerners turned to their mythic past for meaning and redemption. The cult of chivalry gave birth to the cult of the Lost Cause.[58]

Early in 1866 a group of women in Columbus, Georgia initiated the idea of a Southern Memorial Day to honor "those who died, defending the life, honor and happiness of the SOUTHERN WOMEN."[59] Then, in 1867, the women of Cheraw, South Carolina dedicated the first monument in memory of the Confederate casualties, beginning a movement that would run the length and breadth of Dixie.[60] By 1880 the myth of the Lost Cause was coming to dominate the Southern mind and landscape. Museums, statues, celebrations, songs, pictures, periodicals, books, and poems perpetuated the memory of Old South's glory.[61]

The United Daughters of the Confederacy (UDC), founded in Atlanta in 1894, institutionalized the cult of the Lost Cause.[62] The UDC built hundreds of memorial monuments across the South to tell the story "of a glorious past, of heroic deeds, and of unfailing loyalty to a beloved Cause."[63] They also lent their full support to the *Confederate Veteran*, a major journalistic voice of the Lost Cause. In prose, poetry, and oratory the UDC glorified the South's love of liberty, gallant men, gentle women, noble institutions, and proud people.[64] Having been overcome by the materialistic Yankees, postwar Southern women cultivated the memory of a better time and a superior civilization. Mary Gresham Machen became, of course, a member of the Baltimore chapter of the UDC.[65]

In the last twenty years of the nineteenth century the values of the Lost Cause blended with those of late Victorianism to create what Paul Gaston has called the "New South Creed."[66] To the Victorian mind, as David Hall has noted, "things spiritual ranked higher than things material"; and for the Southerner, "things spiritual" equaled the chivalry of the Old South.[67] Indeed, to the Southern mind, spirituality was one of the major traits that distinguished Southern and Yankee civilization.[68] While the Northern states were rushing toward the industrial, urban, secular culture that would come to dominate twentieth-century America, Southerners clung to the ideal of a genteel society dominated by spiritual beliefs and values.

Although the prophets of the New South encouraged their people to industrialize, the defeated Confederacy "set itself with determination against change" in lifestyle and government.[69] The Old South, the chivalrous, spiritual civilization imagined by postwar Southerners, became the measure of all culture. The war, Southerners insisted, was fought not over slavery but for the preservation of constitutional liberty.[70] The North and South had been divided on a question of principle. Having lost on the field of battle, Southerners were determined to maintain true civilization, true religion, and a true love of liberty against the secularizing trends of Yankee culture. Late-nineteenth-century Baltimore, the home of the Machens, proved to be a perfect environment for the cultivation of both Southern Presbyterian orthodoxy and the cult of the Lost Cause.

J. Gresham Machen: The Early Years

Postwar Baltimore was, as historian C. Vann Woodward has noted, "the last refuge of the Confederate spirit in exile."[71] A surge of Southern immigrants in the years after Appomattox had strengthened the city's long-standing cultural and economic ties to the South.[72] Both William H. Browne's *Southern Magazine* and Albert T. Bledsoe's *Southern Review* made Baltimore their home, and in 1876 the Johns Hopkins University opened its doors in the city to become the "dispenser of the higher learning to Southern scholars in the last quarter of the nineteenth century."[73]

Though the "queen city of the South" mirrored the culture and political values of the land south of the Potomac, it did not endure the debilitating poverty of the former Confederacy. The city flourished as a commercial center, becoming the third largest port in America by 1900. Massive shipments to the South by rail and water earned Baltimore the sobriquet Gateway to the South by the turn of the century.[74] The *Manufacturers' Record* declared that "Baltimore's business interests present and prospective depend almost wholly upon the South" and dubbed the city the "metropolis of the South."[75] Advantageously situated between the North and South, Baltimore profited from northern prosperity yet maintained a culture with a distinctly Southern flavor. For Southern aristocracy, it provided the best of both worlds.[76]

J. Gresham Machen benefited from all that Baltimore had to offer. Scion of Southern parents, raised in the most affluent Southern city of his day, surrounded by Southern culture and weaned on Southern Presbyterian orthodoxy, J. Gresham Machen was destined to reflect Southern cultural, political, and theological ideals all his life. Machen's Southern roots were nourished particularly by the extraordinarily close ties he maintained with his mother. Machen was a lifelong bachelor. He and his mother often vacationed together and corresponded continually, frequently several times a week, until her decline and death in 1931. Even while he lived in the North, therefore, Machen maintained deep Southern sympathies.[77] In correspondence Machen referred admiringly to the values embodied in Robert E. Lee and identified himself with the cause of the Confederacy.[78] Machen's Southern perspective and values would profoundly influence the role he would eventually play in the Presbyterian controversy.

Following the tradition of most wealthy Southerners, Machen attended a local private academy, where he acquired a solid classical education. During his early childhood young Gresham enjoyed summer visits to relatives in Virginia and Georgia; in later years the family vacationed in the cooler climes of New England.[79]

With one of the foremost universities in the nation next door, it was only natural that Gresham would follow his older brother to Johns Hopkins. He was awarded a Hopkins scholarship in 1898 and matriculated in classics. While an undergraduate he attended the summer conferences at Northfield, Massachusetts founded by Dwight Moody, where he likely heard his future ecclesiastical opponent, Robert E. Speer.[80] In 1901, with a Phi Beta Kappa key in his pocket, Machen delivered the class valedictory and received the bachelor of arts degree with highest honors.[81]

Following graduation, Machen, in the throes of vocational indecision, studied classics at Hopkins under Basil Gildersleeve and tried his hand at banking and international law at the University of Chicago. Finding neither of these satisfactory, he decided to enter Princeton Theological Seminary for a trial year of theological training in 1902.[82]

Though affiliated with the Northern Presbyterian Church, Princeton had much to recommend it. At the turn of the century the seminary was without peer in the nation as a center of scholarly Old School Presbyterianism. Since its founding in 1812, a parade of eminent divines—Archibald Alexander, Charles Hodge, Archibald Alexander

Hodge, and Benjamin Breckinridge Warfield—had established a formidable theological tradition of conservative Calvinist thought at Princeton.[83] Southern Presbyterian schools, still suffering from the effects of the war and Reconstruction, could not even approach Princeton's stature in the theological world.[84] Moreover, Princeton had strong Southern ties, revealed most clearly in the Southern roots of Alexander and Warfield; and Francis Landey Patton, an intimate friend of the Machens, had recently been elected to the newly created office of president of the seminary.[85] Finally, as Machen's biographer has suggested, in avoiding the seminaries of his own church Machen may have felt less pressure to commit himself to a career in the ministry. Whatever the reason, Machen settled in at Princeton and quickly distinguished himself as one of the most able students in the seminary.[86]

The education Machen received at Princeton complemented and refined the religious heritage of his boyhood.[87] Like the Thornwellian theology of the Southern Presbyterians, Princeton held tightly to the doctrines of the Westminster divines undergirded by Common Sense philosophy and the Baconian method. For Princetonians theology was a matter of systematizing "the facts of the Bible" and ascertaining "the principles or general truths which these facts involve."[88] The Princeton Theology insisted on the primacy of ideas in religion and stood firmly for a strict doctrine of biblical inerrancy.[89] Additionally, Princeton adhered to the traditional Reformed belief that Christians must strive to bring all of culture under God's rule.[90] Despite these vast similarities, the traditions were not identical. Most notably, Southern Presbyterians insisted that the spiritual mission of the church precluded church involvement of any sort in civil affairs.[91] Moreover, the Southern church, following Thornwell, was adamantly opposed to the concentration of power in church boards.[92] Nevertheless, the similarities far outweighed the differences; and Princeton, a bastion of Calvinist orthodoxy in an increasingly hostile world, provided Machen a haven in the midst of his own intellectual and professional struggles.

In the final year of his study at Princeton Machen entered and won the fellowship competition in New Testament studies. Though still undecided about a vocation, the award convinced him to spend a year of study in Germany. Graduate work, he thought, would give him further time to consider his professional options while he honed his skills as a New Testament scholar.[93] Little did Machen expect the impact that his confrontation with German thought and culture would have. For far from providing a calm retreat for reflection, Machen's year abroad precipitated an intellectual and personal crisis of unprecedented proportions. In resolving that crisis, Machen would determine his life's agenda.

A Conflict of Cultures

At Marburg and Göttingen, Machen sat at the feet of some of the leading biblical scholars in the world: Adolf Jülicher, Johannes Weiss, and Wilhelm Bousset. But none of these men impressed Machen nearly as much as the Marburg systematic theologian Wilhelm Herrmann. Machen arrived in Germany disturbed by doubts about the truth of Christianity and the depth of his own piety; Herrmann's attractive personality and liberal theology threw Machen into complete turmoil. In letter after letter home Machen sang Herrmann's praises and despaired of his own uncertainties. To his mother he declared, "The first time that I heard Herrmann may almost be described as an epoch in my life";[94] and to his father he confessed, "Herrmann refuses to allow the student to look at religion from a distance as a thing to be *studied* merely. He speaks right to the heart; and I have been thrown into all confusion by what he says—so much deeper is his devotion to Christ than anything I have known in myself during the past few years."[95] Two weeks later he wrote to his brother Arthur stating, "Herrmann affirms very little of that which I have been accustomed to regard as essential to Christianity; yet there is no doubt in my mind but that he is a Christian, and a Christian of a peculiarly earnest type."[96]

Wilhelm Herrmann was the most prominent theologian at Marburg and probably the leading liberal theologian in the world.[97] Contrary to those who would endorse orthodox theology or philosophy of religion, Herrmann maintained that metaphysics had no place in theology. Reliance on doctrines or the teachings of Jesus, he asserted, was no more than legalism and could never make one a Christian or bring a person to "that reality which gives faith its certainty."[98] Since the Scriptures were liable to be refuted by historical research, Herrmann argued, they could not provide a sure foundation for Christian faith.[99] Moreover, in direct contradiction to the orthodox, Common Sense tradition of Thornwell and Princeton, Herrmann asserted that the domains of science and faith were completely separate.[100]

The realm of faith was not found in metaphysics or natural science or revelation. Rather, inner consciousness alone gave the assurance faith required. Self-verifying faith found its ground in the experience of "a communion of the soul with the living God through the mediation of

Christ," which was tied to the historical fact of the "inner life of Jesus." Though Jesus was not and could not be present to mankind through the merely probable findings of historical investigation, the Bible did present a picture of Jesus' inner life that was able to transform individuals and free them forever from the mediation of the Scriptures. True faith was grounded in an encounter with the inner life of Jesus—an experience unassailable by history or science.[101]

Herrmann's disparagement of the biblical witness and emphasis on the personal experience of the inner life of Jesus cut at the very root of Machen's Old School Presbyterian heritage. The letters that crossed the Atlantic from Germany reflected increasing intellectual and vocational doubts inspired by Herrmann's appeal. To his friend and mentor William P. Armstrong he wrote that his unsettled theological convictions prohibited him from accepting Princeton's fellowship award. In an epistle to his brother he lamented that he had "made a failure of things so far," and conceded, "For me to speak of the Christian ministry in one breath with myself is hypocrisy."[102] Although he continued to consider himself an orthodox Christian and attended a local Baptist church, his faith had been shaken to its roots.[103]

Though some of Machen's vocational struggles resulted from questions about the depth of his piety, the central and determinative struggle that he faced in Germany was intellectual. Machen found Herrmann and the liberal Jesus he proclaimed extremely appealing. Moreover, Machen's dedication to intellectual honesty and logical consistency made a thorough investigation of liberalism a necessary prerequisite to any final decision regarding religious truth. In a letter to his mother he outlined the heart of his struggle: "There is just exactly one thing for a man that feels himself getting into such a position to do—namely to go forward honestly and find out exactly how things stand (remember it is an intellectual question not a moral one that is to be decided). Only when he has done that can he attain anything like certainty."[104]

Questions of personal identity were inextricably entwined in this struggle for intellectual certainty. For over four years Machen had been plagued by vocational indecision. Now, in Germany, separated from his family and friends, he hung midway between two worlds. On one side stood the world of his parents, the Southern, aristocratic Christian culture based on an inerrant Bible and rooted in the values of spirituality and liberty. On the other side stood early-twentieth-century Germany, the epitome of modern secular culture grounded in the values of naturalism and materialism.[105] Machen's rigorously logical mind would not allow him to create some kind of synthetic compromise between these two worlds. They were mutually exclusive; if one was founded on truth the other had to be counterfeit. The question was, therefore, not simply intellectual but intensely personal: In which world would he stand? As he returned home from Germany he hung suspended between two cultures, two worlds, and two faiths.[106]

The Crisis Resolved: The Adoption of the Princeton Tradition

Despite serious reservations about returning to Princeton as an instructor in New Testament, Machen received assurances that he would not have to subscribe to a statement of faith and accepted a one-year appointment for 1906–1907. Princeton proved, once again, to be a safe port in the midst of Machen's inner storm. He easily slipped back into the life he had known as a student: eating at the Benham Club, fraternizing with the students, and spending hours in study. Gradually Machen's dream of returning to Germany faded; and, almost by default, he remained at Princeton year after year. The seminary's familiar surroundings and congenial atmosphere slowly alleviated the trauma of his year abroad; as the seasons rolled by, he quietly resolved the crises of belief, identity, and vocation that had plagued his life.[107] Most important, Machen thoroughly adopted the Princeton tradition as his own and became a staunch defender of the scholarly, Old School Calvinism Princeton espoused.

Three individuals in particular—William P. Armstrong, Francis L. Patton, and Benjamin B. Warfield—drew Machen securely into the Princeton fold.[108] Armstrong, a Southerner only slightly older than Machen, not only served as Machen's mentor in New Testament studies but became an intimate friend. Armstrong had convinced Machen to return to Princeton after his traumatic year in Germany and encouraged him throughout his intellectual and vocational struggles. Moreover, Armstrong's firm command of the "modern scientific method" combined with a "supernaturalistic view of the New Testament" provided a model for Machen's scholarship.[109]

Francis Patton influenced Machen on a different and deeper level. Patton's close friendship with Machen's parents had attracted Machen to Princeton in 1902. In the ecclesiastical realm Patton had distinguished himself as the prosecutor of David Swing in the famous 1874 heresy trial and as one of the youngest men ever to win election as moderator of the General Assembly. Appointments to the Presbyterian Theological Seminary of the Northwest (McCormick), Princeton University, and

Princeton Theological Seminary had allowed him to exercise his talents in the academy. Patton's untiring defense of orthodoxy in church and classroom and his unstinting support of Machen during his years of indecision earned Machen's deepest affection. Patton was, as Machen claimed, Machen's "spiritual father."[110]

Nevertheless, Benjamin Breckinridge Warfield exceeded all other Princetonians in his influence on the young Machen.[111] Warfield, a New Testament scholar turned theologian, embodied the Princeton tradition. He had studied under the renowned Princeton theologian Charles Hodge and was a close friend of Archibald Alexander Hodge, Warfield's predecessor at Princeton.[112] Warfield, naturally, subscribed wholeheartedly to the Reformed theology of his teacher, Charles Hodge, and to the Common Sense philosophy and Baconianism that undergirded Hodge's system.[113] Though Machen came to accept most every facet of the Princeton Theology as mediated by Warfield, Warfield's emphases on apologetics, scriptural inerrancy, supernaturalism, and the relationship of Christianity and culture seem to have had an especially profound impact on the young scholar.

Warfield insisted that apologetics stood "at the head of the departments of theological science."[114] This focus on apologetics was not new with Warfield in the Princeton tradition.[115] Nevertheless, Warfield accentuated and expanded the role of apologetics in his work, demanding that it was the primary and preeminent task of the Christian theologian.[116] Indeed, for Warfield, apologetics was not simply a concern to the systematic theologian but played a critical role in Christianity's mission in the world. The Christian faith, he maintained, "has come into the world clothed with the mission to *reason* its way to its dominion. Other religions may appeal to the sword, or seek some other way to propagate themselves. Christianity makes its appeal to right reason and stands out among all religions, therefore, as distinctively "the Apologetic religion.'"[117] Machen would mirror both Warfield's emphasis on the ability and need for Christianity to defend itself at the bar of reason and the importance of intellectual defense to the evangelical mission of the church.

As noted above, the Princeton tradition, like Machen's native religious heritage, had always maintained a high view of Scripture. In reaction to higher critical attacks on the traditional doctrine of scriptural inspiration, A. A. Hodge and Warfield refined and expanded the doctrine of biblical inspiration held by their predecessors. "All the affirmations of Scripture," they wrote, "are without any error when the *ipsissima verba* of the original autographs are ascertained and interpreted in their natural and intended sense."[118] In the course of his career at Princeton, Warfield worked tirelessly to defend his doctrine of inerrancy against the increasingly prevalent liberal views of the Bible.[119] Machen eventually came to subscribe completely to Warfield's doctrine of the Bible and defended it as the doctrine of inspiration held by the church throughout the ages.

Another key emphasis in Warfield's theology that clearly influenced Machen's thinking was Warfield's defense of supernaturalism in the face of the increasing power of naturalistic thought. In numerous articles and reviews Warfield took liberal biblical critics to task for imposing their naturalistic assumptions on the Scriptures. In the words of W. Andrew Hoffecker, Warfield countered "the radical [biblical] critics' claim that Christianity was merely another natural religion by demonstrating that such assertions arose not from an examination of the Bible itself, but from the naturalistic presuppositions that critics brought to their study of Scripture."[120] Machen, who contended that the chief mark of modernism was its rejection of the supernatural, would level similar criticisms at his opponents throughout the 1920s and 1930s.

Finally, Warfield's Reformed understanding of the role of Christianity in culture reinforced the heritage Machen carried with him from his Southern Presbyterian upbringing. Warfield maintained that the primary means by which Christians influenced the surrounding culture was by cultivating correct doctrine. God was, he insisted, "saving the world and not merely one individual here and there out of the world."[121] Neither art, science, literature, or politics fell outside of the proper purview of Christian influence. Rather, Christians were called to consecrate all of life to the cause of Christ.[122] In resolving his intellectual and vocational crises, Machen would come to agree, in large part, with Warfield's views.

Though Machen arrived at Princeton well versed in the Old School theology of the Southern Presbyterian Church, it was at Princeton—especially, it seems, in the years following his study in Germany—that he refined his theological position and came to appreciate fully the scholarly Calvinist heritage embodied in Princeton Seminary.[123] In the course of resolving the crisis precipitated by his experience in Germany, he incurred an immense debt to the Princeton tradition in general and to Benjamin B. Warfield in particular. Despite some profound differences in social and academic matters, Machen sincerely praised Warfield as the "greatest man" he had known.[124]

In 1912 Machen delivered a speech—later published as "Christianity and Culture"—that not only revealed the resolution of his crises but in large measure set the agenda for the remainder of his career. The church, he maintained, was facing a desperate emergency precipitated by the secularization of modern culture. Sabbath desecration and declining attendance at worship signaled a seriously diseased society. These, however, were but symptoms of the true illness, which was the secular intellectual atmosphere of the day. The defection from Christianity was rooted in modern culture's apathy or outright hostility to the gospel. Since the universities were the intellectual greenhouses of the nation, the cultural apostasy had to be stopped there or it would not be stopped at all. "What is to-day matter of academic speculation," he warned, "begins to-morrow to move armies and pull down empires. In that second stage, it has gone too far to be combatted; the time to stop it was when it was still a matter of impassionate debate."[125]

The answer to this crisis, Machen argued, was to consecrate modern culture to the service of God. This was the Reformed tradition Machen had learned in Baltimore and Princeton. "As Christians," he wrote, "we should try to mould the thought of the world in such a way as to make the acceptance of Christianity something more than a logical absurdity." For this task evangelization was not enough. He wrote, "We may preach with all the fervor of a reformer, and yet succeed only in winning a straggler here and there, if we permit the whole collective thought of the nation or of the world to be controlled by ideas which, by the resistless force of logic, prevent Christianity from being regarded as anything more than a harmless delusion. Under such circumstances, what God desires us to do is to destroy the obstacle at its root."[126] Like Warfield, Machen insisted that Christianity influenced culture primarily by the furtherance of right doctrine.[127] If the church succumbed to intellectual sloth, Christianity, overrun by secular ideals and ideas, would lose all influence. Certainly, God would preserve the church; but the "labor of centuries" would be destroyed. What the church needed more than anything were intellectual soldiers willing to subdue modern culture on the intellectual battlefield. Neutrality was no longer an option. The battle was on, and Christians had to take a stand.[128]

Here, in 1912, Machen broached an issue that would come to dominate the fundamentalist–modernist conflict of the 1920s. In the wake of the cultural crisis following World War I, the secularization of America became a major conservative concern. But Machen, earlier than most, clearly saw the immense implications of secular trends transforming America. His Southern heritage, it appears, played no little part in his ability to perceive the beginnings of the cultural revolution that would culminate in the 1920s. Machen was, significantly, an outsider in Yankee society, a member of a culture whose ideals sharply conflicted with the values of the urban, industrial North. The South, surrounded by an ideological curtain, had largely avoided the intellectual, social, and economic forces that had been relegating religion to a more and more narrowly defined place in Northern life. Additionally, the cult of the Lost Cause, continually nurtured by Machen's mother, accentuated the real and imagined differences between Northern and Southern culture. This heritage, combined with Machen's confrontation with the secular culture of turn-of-the-century Germany, brought the ideological transformation of America into sharp focus for Machen. While many of Machen's Northern peers had been gradually acculturating to the secular trends in Yankee life and were thus oblivious to the implications of secularization until the postwar years, Machen viewed the changing Northern society against the background of an older culture pervaded by explicitly religious values. Better than most, therefore, he could see the power of secularism and its pervasive impact on the course of civilization.

Machen's unique Southern perspective, when combined with his Old School Presbyterian insistence on the importance of ideas, had momentous implications for the role he would play in the Presbyterian controversy. In maintaining the preeminence of ideas in Christianity, Machen not only demonstrated his Old School heritage but sharply separated himself from the "soul-winning" emphasis of nineteenth-century evangelicalism. While not wanting to derogate the import of evangelism, he insisted that the primary battleground of Christianity in the modern world was in the academy: there ideas were formed, and there the intellectual foundations of the culture were laid. The future impact of Christianity on culture would be determined not in the pulpits but in the university and seminary. In the 1920s and 1930s Machen's passionate belief in the primacy and power of ideas would not only lead him into serious controversy with his more liberal and pietistic peers but would drive him to abandon Princeton, found a new seminary, and finally organize a new church.

While the thoughts Machen developed in "Christianity and Culture" had a critical impact on his future course of action, the lecture's immediate implications were no less significant. After years of struggle, Machen had found his vocation and his faith. For nearly a decade he had wrestled with the messengers of modern culture who threatened to destroy the faith and culture of his boyhood. The battle had required all the intellect, courage, and honesty he could muster; but in the end orthodoxy had triumphed. He now realized that his personal struggle was but a microcosm of the battle engulfing the church and the culture. To Machen there was no middle ground. If Christian orthodoxy did not harness the intellectual powers of the day, it would perish. Having won the struggle for his soul, he now set forth to win the soul of the church. Here was a vocation worthy of an intellectual knight. Armed with a sharp mind and a legacy that valued principle, logical consistency, constitutional liberty, and the scholarly defense of right doctrine, Machen was ready to do battle for his Lord.

In 1913 Machen reconciled himself to the prospect of ordination to the ministry, which allowed his promotion to the rank of assistant professor. Since he would be laboring within the bounds of the New Brunswick Presbytery, ordination required that he sever his formal ties with the Southern Presbyterian Church and submit to ordination by its Northern sister. Though unenthusiastic about this change, he realized that he had no other options if he intended to remain at Princeton. Machen received ordination in June 1914 and was installed as an assistant professor of New Testament in May 1915. His inaugural address, "History and Faith," complemented "Christianity and Culture" by focusing on the chief intellectual struggle of the day—the role of history in the Christian faith.[129]

Though not billed as such, the lecture was clearly Machen's response to his former teacher, Wilhelm Herrmann. Herrmann, in seeking "certainty" for faith, had argued that the experience of the "inner life of Jesus," not the scriptural record, provided assurance for Christians. The Bible, subject to the criticisms of scientific history, could never provide a foundation for faith.[130] Machen was now, at long last, ready to reply. To an admiring audience he proclaimed, "Give up history, and you can retain some things. You can retain a belief in God. . . . You can retain a lofty ethical ideal. But be perfectly clear about one point—you can never retain a gospel. For gospel means 'good news,' tidings, information about something that has happened. In other words, it means history. A gospel independent of history is simply a contradiction in terms."[131] The Bible as historical narrative was not, as Herrmann had claimed, disposable, but was absolutely essential for the faith.

Committed to Common Sense philosophy and Baconian induction, Machen believed that the "facts" of the past were immediately available to people without "interpretation."[132] The task of the historian was merely to examine the facts and classify them in complete objectivity. He granted that history could not give certainty; experience was needed to confirm the truth of the faith. But contrary to Herrmann, Machen insisted that the biblical witness could not be ignored once Christ was known; if the Bible could be proven false, faith would crumble. History and faith could not be divorced.[133] To Machen's mind, liberalism was intellectually bankrupt.

Clearly, the clouds in Machen's life had lifted. He had resolved the questions that had plagued him for years, received ordination, and found an intellectual and professional home at the foremost conservative theological seminary in the country. An adopted son of Princeton, he would become one of the tradition's staunchest defenders. Life, for Machen, had turned a corner; his future looked bright with promise. The same could not be said for the future of Europe.

Prepared for Battle

As the faculty and students of Princeton Seminary listened to their brilliant young professor, most of the country was listening with growing concern to the sounds of war from across the Atlantic. Though Machen's sympathies rested at first with Germany, he was quick to volunteer with the YMCA when the United States entered World War I. He had hoped to serve in a religious capacity but was assigned to duty in Belgium and France as a canteen director. Only after the signing of the armistice was he able to preach to camps at Tours, Samur, and LeMans, among others, before returning home in March of 1919.[134]

Inspired by the tremendous success of the church's United War Work Campaign, a wave of ecumenical desire swept over church bureaucrats, clergy, and laity after World War I. The 1918 General Assembly of the Presbyterian Church received thirty-five overtures requesting the church to pursue union negotiations with other evangelical churches in America. In response, the 1920 General Assembly received and passed a proposal to enter into the "United Churches of Christ in America."[135] Two of Machen's colleagues at Princeton, J. Ross Stevenson and Charles Erdman, were among the most vocal proponents of the plan. But Machen, seeing this endeavor as a threat to pure doctrine and ecclesiastical liberty, set out to battle the proposal in the presbyteries. In letters, speeches, and articles he lambasted the plan as omitting "not some, but practically all, of the great essentials of the Christian faith."[136] This concern, along with a belief that the Federal Council of Churches was already fulfilling the purpose of the plan, led to the proposal's overwhelming defeat in 1921.[137]

The fight over church union was only a warm-up for the battles Machen would wage for the next fifteen years. In the face of an in-

creasingly secularizing culture and ever more aggressive liberal church-
men, he would work indefatigably to defend Old School orthodoxy and
Princeton Seminary. Like his chief role models—J. H. Thornwell, Francis Patton, and Benjamin Warfield—Machen was devoutly committed
to principle and unafraid to fight for his beliefs.[138] Indeed, combat was,
to Machen, a sure sign of the value of an ideal. "The really important
things," he wrote in 1923, "are the things about which men will fight."[139]

While the battles Machen would wage in the Presbyterian controversy
were primarily inspired by his devotion to true doctrine, Machen was
also motivated by what he perceived to be the secular destruction of
liberty in the modern world. As has been shown, Machen, with many
other conservative Christians in the postwar era, deplored the increasing
secularization of American culture. But Machen's response to secularization was nothing short of unique. To Machen's mind the rise of
"paganism" in America resulted in one paramount social crisis: the loss
of liberty. All other manifestations of secularization were subordinate
to this, and none other deserved equal attention. "The real indictment
against the modern world," he declared in 1931, "is that by the modern
world human liberty is being destroyed."[140] Machen's concern for loss
of individual liberty was not unfounded. World War I had inspired a
dramatic acceleration in the centralization and bureaucratization of the
government that peaked in the years after 1930.[141] Here, as in the rise
of secularization in general, Machen's keen perception of societal trends
seems to be at least partially attributable to his Southern heritage. Mach-
en's deep-seated devotion to constitutional liberty, inherited from his
Southern forebears, led him not only to see the changes consequent to
the increasing centralization of power better but also to react forcefully
against any restriction of individual liberties in the society. Especially
after World War I, Machen would battle tirelessly to defend civil and
spiritual liberties.[142]

A radical civil libertarian, Machen addressed social issues in articles,
speeches, and letters to major papers.[143] Fearing the "soul-killing collectivism," "materialistic paternalism," standardization, and centralization of modern government, Machen denounced the national parks
system for forcing forests "into the commonplace mold of a city park,"
opposed the creation of a Federal Department of Education, and decried
the compulsory draft, enrollment of aliens, and child labor legislation
as violations of states and personal rights. Indeed, in the name of individual freedom he stood almost alone among leaders of the Presbyterian Church against the Volstead Act.[144] On state and local issues he
spoke out against legislation in New York, Oregon, and Nebraska that

regulated public education and, in 1933 and 1934, even championed the liberties of Philadelphia's pedestrians against the tyranny of a jaywalking ordinance.[145] While Machen's conservative peers were battling secularization by opposing the evils of divorce, alcohol, contraception, crime, Sabbath desecration, and the decline of the family altar, Machen's guns were leveled at any legislation, no matter how trivial, that might infringe on the freedoms of states and individuals.

The battles Machen fought outside the church were intimately related to his ecclesiastical concerns. To Machen liberty was not—indeed could not be—merely a civil concern, for ultimately the gospel was the only guarantor of freedom.[146] In a 1924 article in the *New York Times*, Machen drew the connection: "If liberty is to be preserved against the materialistic paternalism of the modern state, there must be something more than courts and legal guarantees; freedom must be written not merely in the constitution but in the people's heart. And it can be written in the heart, we believe, only as a result of the redeeming work of Christ."[147] The liberty of the gospel, of course, was much more profound and far more important than civil liberty, but they were not unrelated; all true freedom was rooted in the freedom from sin purchased by Christ's sacrifice on the cross.[148] The choice, as Machen perceived it, was between a mechanistic civilization rooted in naturalism and a free civilization based on supernaturalism and the Word of God.[149] At one level, then, Machen's fights in the church for pure doctrine and in society for civil liberties were but two different manifestations of a single offensive to preserve Christian freedom. If the true faith was abandoned in the church, civilization would succumb to the bondage of secular thought. Against such a possibility, Machen dreamed of a Reformation, a "mighty revival of the Christian religion," that would both improve the "conditions in this world" and "bring mankind into the glorious liberty of communion with the living God."[150] This dream would compel Machen's actions throughout the controversy.

Machen also brought to the Presbyterian conflict a profound respect for a particularly Southern solution to disagreement: secession. Like Thornwell, Machen's devotion to logic, principle, and freedom led him to view separation as a perfectly legitimate means of settling disputes. As early as 1851, Thornwell had maintained that secession from the Union would be a right and duty of the South if the North abrogated the Constitution by violating states' rights.[151] Likewise, when the Old School Presbyterian Church passed the Spring resolution supporting the Union cause in 1861, Thornwell argued that the consequences of the unconstitutional proceedings merited separation. If the models of the Confederacy and the Southern Presbyterian Church were not sufficient to impress Machen with the legitimacy of separation as a solution to differences, he had the example of Joseph J. Bullock, who, while pastor of the Franklin Street Presbyterian Church of Baltimore, led a schism from the Northern Church to unite with the Southern denomination.[152] Secession, in Machen's heritage, provided not only an acceptable, but, in many respects, an honorable solution to irreconcilable disagreements of principle.

Machen expressed his high view of separatism perhaps nowhere more clearly than in a statement he made in 1927 to the General Assembly's special committee to visit Princeton. In response to a statement made by J. Ross Stevenson, president of Princeton Seminary, Machen maintained,

> Dr. Stevenson objects to the League [of Evangelical Students] because it brings our students into connection with "secession bodies," with "small institutions and sects which are committed to separation and secession." . . . I confess, gentlemen, that at no point is my disagreement with Dr. Stevenson more profound than here. His attitude at this point seems to me to be hostile to the very foundations of Christian liberty, . . . "Forbid him not" said our Lord, with regard to a secessionist of the early days, who was objected to because he did not follow with the company of the other disciples; and so from that day to this He has had in His care those who follow the dictates of their conscience in the worship and service of Him. We Protestants are all secessionists; and if, in the interests of organizational conformity, we fail to honor liberty of conscience, our high heritage has been lost.[153]

When, in the years between 1922 and 1936, Machen called for a separation of Christians and liberals he was drawing, in large part, on a tradition unavailable to many of his Northern sympathizers. This tradition would provide a key rationale for Machen's eventual break with his longtime ally and friend, Clarence Macartney.

The part Machen would play in the Presbyterian controversy was a function both of his Southern upbringing and of his adoption of the heritage of Princeton Seminary. Machen unquestionably saw himself as heir to the Princeton tradition, and in the 1920s and 1930s he was determined to defend it against all opponents. Not only had Princeton provided his formal theological training, but it had given him the intellectual and emotional support he needed to overcome the trauma of his year in Germany. Princeton was Machen's theological home. But this alone fails to explain his peculiar emphases and the final path he would follow in the Presbyterian controversy. Wedded with the Princeton tradition were deep-seated principles derived from his Southern heritage. As his biographer noted, he "carried with him into an atmosphere dominated by distinctly Northern political views his own passionately-held Southern perspectives and sympathies."[154] In large part, Machen felt at home at Princeton because its tradition meshed so well with the legacy of his native church. The theological positions espoused by the Southern Presbyterian Church and by Princeton theologians found common ground in their doctrinal emphasis, confessional heritage, philosophical foundations, strict biblicism, and understanding of Christianity's role in culture. Nevertheless, Machen's "Southernness" gave him a perspective and a set of values that in certain ways were unique among the leaders of Northern Presbyterians; and these differences would play a major role in determining the final outcome of the Presbyterian controversy.

In January of 1921 Machen delivered the James Sprunt Lectures at Union Theological Seminary in Virginia, published in a well-received volume under the title *The Origin of Paul's Religion*. In the fall of 1921 he delivered the address "Liberalism or Christianity," and in February 1923 *Christianity and Liberalism* rolled off the presses.[155] Machen, a little-known assistant professor at the end of World War I, had, in the course of five years, established himself as a respected scholar and polemicist. By all accounts he was a formidable intellectual and ecclesiastical foe.

The spring of 1923 brought no time for Machen to rest on his well-deserved laurels. As he had so eloquently explained, liberal theology threatened to destroy the witness of the church and with it all true liberty and culture. Only a "rebirth of Christianity" founded on a solid intellectual defense of orthodox doctrines could stop the spiritual decline of the age. The battle in the Presbyterian Church, though "only one battle in a mighty world-wide war," was a crucial front.[156] If the fight were lost here it could very well be lost everywhere.

The next major test would come at the 1923 General Assembly. If the Presbyterian Church was to be saved, if Fosdick was to be silenced and the faith preserved, an orthodox Christian knight would have to be elected moderator. For better or for worse, William Jennings Bryan, three-time presidential contender and Presbyterian elder *extraordinaire*, thought he was just the man for the job.

3

William Jennings Bryan
and the 1923 General Assembly

In 1923 William Jennings Bryan stood unchallenged as "the most widely influential layman in the church."[1] Three presidential campaigns, two years as secretary of state, a nationally syndicated newspaper column, and over twenty-five years on the Chautauqua lecture circuit ensured his fame.[2] Though religion and politics were never far removed in Bryan's mind, religious issues, especially the threat of Darwinism to Christianity and Christian civilization, had come to dominate Bryan's agenda after the war.[3] In 1921 Bryan described the danger: "I believe that the Darwinian doctrine leads people into agnosticism and pantheism, plunged the world into the worst of wars, and is dividing society into classes that fight each other on a brute basis. It is time that the Christian church should understand what is going on and array itself against these enemies of the church, Christianity, and civilization."[4] In direct contradiction to the law of love proclaimed by Christianity, Darwinism taught a materialist doctrine of "survival of the fittest." An invitation from Union Theological Seminary in Virginia to deliver the James Sprunt Lectures in October 1921 gave Bryan the opportunity to expand, organize, and further publicize his thoughts. The lectures, published under the title *In His Image*, provided the most comprehensive statement of the faith and ideas that motivated Bryan's last great crusade.[5]

The nine lectures were vast in scope if not in depth. Bryan ranged from a defense of the Bible, the virgin birth of Christ, and the substitutionary atonement to a discussion of Prohibition, labor relations, and woman's suffrage. The heart of the series was a talk entitled "The Origin of Man," in which Bryan addressed "the problem which underlies all others," the question of humanity's place in the universe and the end for which mankind was created.[6]

Religion, or belief in God, Bryan claimed, was the mainspring of life, absolutely necessary if life was to be what it should be, "a real life and not a mere existence." Moral responsibility, prayer, belief in personal immortality, and the spirit of brotherhood rested on faith in the Almighty. But Darwinism, by enfeebling faith in God, sabotaged the cause of righteousness. "By putting man on a brute basis and ignoring spiritual values," Bryan insisted, evolutionism weakened the underpinnings of Christianity. It transformed the Bible into a "storybook" and repudiated the doctrine of the deity of Christ, giving Jesus "an ape for an ancestor on His mother's side at least and, as many evolutionists believe, on His Father's side also." Evolutionists denied the fundamental Christian truths of biblical inspiration, the virgin birth, and the resurrection, thereby kicking the props out from under the Christian life. Bryan thundered, "The [Darwinian] instructor gives the student a new family tree millions of years long, with its roots in the water (marine animals) and then sets him adrift, with infinite capacity for good or evil but with no light to guide him, no compass to direct him and no chart of the sea of life!"[7]

Evolutionary theory inspired hatred and struggle at every level. Friedrich Nietzsche's atheistic and amoral philosophy, the "ripened fruit of Darwinism," Bryan argued, had provided the philosophical basis for German military atrocities. By denying God and the spiritual life based on faith in God, Darwinism had laid "the foundation for the bloodiest war in history." Likewise, the brute doctrine of the survival of the fittest had transformed the industrial world into a "slaughter-house"; it eliminated sympathy and the spirit of brotherhood from the economic realm, driving labor and management into a life-and-death struggle.[8] By glorifying the battle for self-preservation, Darwinist theory authorized any and all efforts for military and economic conquest, removing the very basis of civilization.

Finally, Darwinism stole hope from the reformer. The materialistic Darwinist would "improve the race by 'scientific breeding.'" "A few hundred years may be required," Bryan scoffed, "possibly a few thousand—but what is time to one who carries eons in his quiver?" The Christian reformer possessed an alternate and more efficient plan: "A man can be born again; the springs of life can be cleansed instantly so that the heart loves the things that it formerly hated and hates the things that it once loved. If this is true of *one*, it can be true of *any number*. Thus, a nation can be born in a day if the ideals of the people can be changed."[9] New life in Christ was the one true avenue to social progress.

Bryan's belief that Darwinist theory would cut the nerve of moral reform points to the essentially pragmatic character of his war against evolution. He was determined to demonstrate both the truth and need of Christianity, but the usefulness of Christianity often took precedence. "There has not been a great reform in a thousand years," Bryan argued, "that was not built about [Christ's] teachings; there will not be in all the ages to come an important movement for the uplift of humanity that will not be inspired by His thought and words."[10] "A groundless hypothesis—even an absurd one—would be unworthy of notice if it did no harm," Bryan maintained. But, he insisted, Darwinism did do "incalculable harm."[11] Ever a politician and social reformer, the harm Bryan was concerned with was not primarily the injury of false ideas per se but the results consequent of acting on untruth.[12]

Bryan found it incredible that people would accept the destructive Darwinian philosophy when it was based on nothing more than a "guess." Revealing his debt to Common Sense philosophy and Baconian induction, Bryan maintained that "science to be truly science is classified knowledge; it is the explanation of facts." Instead of basing his conclusions on "facts," however, Darwin had built upon "presumptions, probabilities and inferences." True to the tenets of Common Sense Realism, Bryan also held that true science and the Bible could not disagree. "There should be no conflict between the discoverers of *real* truths because real truths do not conflict," Bryan wrote. "Every truth harmonizes with every other truth." Christianity had nothing to fear from genuine scientists addressing established facts. It was the "*guessing* by scientists and so-called scientists" that undermined the Bible and threatened to undo the advances of culture.[13]

Bryan's condemnation of evolutionary philosophy frequently bordered on antiintellectualism.[14] In marked contrast to Machen, who could see only intellectual decadence in modernist theology, Bryan condemned Darwinism, and with it modernism, as encouraging "mind-worship."[15] "The natural and inevitable tendency of Darwinism," he wrote, "is to exalt the mind at the expense of the heart, to overestimate the reliability of the reason as compared with faith and to impair confidence in the Bible."[16] But, he warned, "All the intellectual satisfaction that Darwinism ever brought to those who have accepted it will not offset the sorrow that darkens a single life from which the brute theory of descent has shut out the sunshine of God's presence and the companionship of Christ." Though both a developed mind and a good heart were desirable, the good heart was unquestionably of higher value.[17]

Evolutionary thought conflicted with the Scriptures on point after point: Darwin assumed life on earth; the Bible revealed the source of life, Darwin emphasized man's similarity to the brute; the Bible emphasized man's reflection of God, Darwin's teachings led to war; the Bible revealed the Prince of Peace, Darwin placed God far away; the Bible brought God close at hand, Darwin gave no reason for life; the Bible offered purpose and the promise of abundant life here and hereafter. By contradicting the Bible, evolution undermined Christianity and the hope of Christian civilization. "The great need of the world today," Bryan declared, "is to get back to God—back to a real belief in a living God." No progeny of the brute, "man was made in the Father's image." God beckoned man upward, and the Bible pointed the way. The law that controlled the universe was not the survival of the fittest but love of God and neighbor. "In His Image:" Bryan concluded, "in this sign we conquer."[18]

The words of Bryan had barely stopped echoing through the halls of Union Seminary before his lectures rolled off the presses. Advertised as "Bryan's Answer to Darwin," the work won plaudits as "one of the most influential religious books of recent years."[19] The success of *In His Image*, which sold over one-hundred thousand copies, was supplemented by the separate publication of "The Origin of Man" under the title *The Menace of Darwinism*, which also enjoyed huge sales. Evolution was becoming the chief concern of the fundamentalist crusade, and William Jennings Bryan had established himself as the leader of the anti-evolutionists.[20]

In February of 1922 the *New York Times* offered Bryan another forum to express his views, and he replied with an article entitled "God and Evolution." Bryan reiterated his charges against evolution: it was a guess, contradicted the Scriptures, and destroyed the Christian faith. Additionally, he proffered two programmatic proposals he had suggested in his earlier talks. First, he wrote, ministers who were unable to accept the biblical witness "should be honest enough to separate themselves from the ministry and not attempt to debase the religion which they profess."[21] There was not room in one church, Bryan held, for those who believed in evolution and those who did not. The majority—and Bryan believed most Christians rejected evolution—should take control of their churches.[22] Likewise, atheistic and agnostic teachers should not be allowed "to use the public schools as a forum for the teaching of their doctrines." Neither of these propositions denied freedom of speech; they merely demanded fairness and truthfulness. "As religion is the only basis of morals," Bryan concluded, "it is time for Christians to protect religion from its most insidious enemy,"[23] that is, Darwinism.

Bryan's indignant opposition to the spread of evolutionary philosophy in church and school resonated with many Americans bewildered by the social and intellectual changes rocking America in the early 1920s. The nation was succumbing to the forces of secularization, and Bryan seemed to know why: Darwinism was destroying America's Christian foundations. Supporters encouraged Bryan to make the antievolution movement his life's work. One enthusiast wrote, "You are the first to fundamentally assume the offensive against evolution and you have triumphantly demolished it forever as a rational system."[24] Propelled by the praise of his admirers and certain that this campaign was the will of God, Bryan, in the spring of 1923, thought the time had come to take the fight to his own denomination, the Presbyterian Church in the U.S.A.[25]

A long-standing Presbyterian elder and frequent attender of General Assemblies, Bryan queried some Presbyterian friends in March and April of 1923, soliciting their opinions on a possible moderatorial campaign. Though far from unanimous, the response was generally positive and must have lifted Bryan's spirits.[26] Never able to lead the nation, perhaps he was predestined to lead his church.

Despite the widespread opinion that Bryan would run for moderator, he refused to toss his hat into the ring until the night before the assembly convened on 17 May 1923.[27] Three brave clergy decided to oppose the seasoned campaigner: Charles F. Wishart, president of the College of Wooster; Hugh K. Walker, pastor of the First Presbyterian Church of Los Angeles; and Frank M. Silsley, pastor of the First Presbyterian Church of Oakland, California. Since Wooster tolerated the teaching of evolution, Wishart's candidacy was especially significant.[28] Though the Fosdick controversy had promised to ignite the most fireworks at the assembly, the moderatorial candidates suddenly thrust the battle over evolution onto center stage. In the words of a reporter for the *New York Times*, the Presbyterian Church was "being divided into evolutionists and anti-evolutionists."[29]

William Jennings Bryan: "Son of the Middle Border"

Bryan's run for the moderatorial office was but one part of a larger campaign of moral reform that stretched back to the nineteenth century. Since the 1890s Bryan had been a leader of progressive politics, struggling for the rights of the less fortunate, for "free silver," a federal income tax, temperance, a minimum wage, the popular election of senators, government regulation of business and industry, and world peace.[30] In all of these efforts Bryan, who became known as the "Great Commoner," pursued the ideal of a Christian America that he had adopted as a boy in the nation's heartland. Bryan was, in the words of historian Paul Glad, a "son of the Middle Border."[31]

William Jennings Bryan was born to Silas and Mariah Bryan on 19 March 1860.[32] Silas Bryan, born in 1822, descended from Irish stock who had settled in Virginia. At age eighteen he followed his siblings west by walking to Troy, Missouri to reside with his elder brother.[33] Silas worked his way through McKendree College in Lebanon, Illinois, earning a bachelor's degree in 1849 and eventually a master's degree. Following graduation he taught at the Walnut Hill School in Illinois and prepared for the Illinois bar exam. During his brief tenure as a teacher, one of his students, Mariah Elizabeth Jennings, captured his heart. She possessed all the qualities Silas could ask for in a wife: "modesty, simplicity in dress, capacity for household management, particular devotion to the church, and a family of some political influence."[34] A courtship ensued; and in 1852 Silas, now an attorney, married his former pupil and built a home in Salem, Illinois, a county seat in the south-central portion of the state.[35]

A staunch Jacksonian Democrat, Silas parlayed his legal skills into a political office, winning election to the state senate shortly after his wedding. During his eight years in the legislature, Senator Bryan witnessed the growing hostility over slavery and rubbed elbows with such political giants as Abraham Lincoln and Stephen Douglas.[36] He lost his seat to a Republican in 1860 but rebounded by capturing the office of state circuit judge. In 1872, after twelve years on the bench, Bryan ran for the House of Representatives. Though supported by the Democratic and Greenback parties, Silas could not overcome the strong Republican sentiment that persisted in the wake of the Civil War and felt the sting of defeat yet again.[37] While he maintained a passionate interest in politics after this loss, he refused to enter the public arena again and finished his career as a respected trial lawyer.[38]

In the spring of 1866, when Willy was six years old, Silas moved the family from town to a 520-acre farm northwest of Salem.[39] The income from his practice of law as judge and attorney had allowed him to build a ten-room house that was the envy of Marion County.[40] William grew up knowing the joys and labors of farm life; the tasks of chopping wood, stoking the fire, feeding the livestock, and milking the cows found pleasant interruption in hunting, sleigh rides, and swimming.[41] Silas, much too busy with his legal affairs to concern himself with agriculture, was a gentleman farmer, "as close to being an aristocrat as rural conditions permitted." As one of Bryan's biographers noted, "Few families in Salem owned five hundred acres unencumbered, hired Negro servants, used silver at table, and had a piano in the parlor."[42] Silas and Mariah Bryan, both devout Christians, belonged to different churches for their first twenty years of life together.[43] Mariah held membership in a local Methodist Church until 1872 when she joined her husband among the Salem Baptists. As a result, young William's Sabbath ritual included Sunday school with the Methodists in the morning and the Baptists in the afternoon.[44] Despite the doctrinal differences between the denominations, the Bryan household was marked by a nonsectarian evangelicalism. William Jennings later recalled that "there was never the slightest religious discord in the family and I never heard a word said in regard to the differences between denominations. Both of them were firmly wedded to the fundamentals of Christianity, but charitable on all nonessentials."[45] Every year Judge Bryan hosted a dinner party for the town clergy, including the Catholic priest; and each fall he gave every minister a bale of hay.[46] The judge, who paused thrice daily to lift his concerns to God, drilled his children on various catechisms and led them in prayer around the family altar.[47] He regularly read to his children from the book of Proverbs and instilled a profound antipathy for drinking, smoking, dancing, and gambling in all his offspring.[48]

Salem township, which by 1870 boasted 2,041 inhabitants, supported eight Protestant churches.[49] After Mariah joined the Baptist Church, William started attending the Cumberland Presbyterian Church on Sunday afternoons. When he was fourteen, he attended a revival hosted by the Cumberland Church. Moved by the evangelistic preaching and the momentum of his peers, Bryan joined seventy of his schoolmates in affiliating with the Presbyterians. His baptism as a Cumberland Presbyterian caused scarcely a ripple in his religious consciousness. "Having been brought up in a Christian home," he noted, "conversion did not mean a change in my habits of life or habits of thought."[50] Nevertheless, Bryan later called the day of his conversion the most important day of his life, adding, "the Book to which I swore allegiance on that day has been more to me than any party platform."[51]

That Bryan entered the Presbyterian fold through the Salem Cumberland Church rather than its larger sister communion was no accident.[52] The Cumberland Presbyterians were in many ways archtypical of the broad-minded evangelicalism that dominated the nineteenth century in general and the Bryan household in particular. The Cumberland Church had been born on the Kentucky frontier in 1813 as a result of irreconcilable differences between New Side revivalist Presbyterians and Old Side antirevivalists.[53] The tensions that culminated in the schism were not new to American Presbyterians. Since its inception the Presbyterian Church had been composed of two distinct parties: a doctrinally oriented Old Side (or Old School) party primarily of Scottish and Scotch–Irish descent and a revivalistic New Side tradition heir to the Puritanism of England and New England.[54] The Great Awakening that swept through the American colonies in the eighteenth century precipitated a break between these two parties lasting from 1741 to 1758. Though the different schools maintained a cordial relationship after their reconciliation, the advent of the Second Awakening aggravated these differences once again.[55]

At the turn of the century Presbyterians on the frontier found their evangelical efforts handicapped by the church's stringent educational requirements and strict confessional theology.[56] While Baptists and Methodists commissioned preachers with little or no education, Presbyterians required their clergy to possess a college degree and formal theological training. As a result, numerous Presbyterian pulpits sat vacant and many Presbyterian converts lacked pastoral care and oversight.[57] In order to remedy this situation, the Cumberland Presbytery in Kentucky, with precedent from former New Side brethren, began to license and ordain men deficient in classical knowledge. Not surprisingly, this transgression of the church's standards did not sit well with many of the Old Side clergy.[58]

Perhaps even more important than laxness in clerical education as a cause of contention was the Cumberland Presbytery's casual attitude toward doctrinal orthodoxy.[59] The Westminster divines may have found comfort in the immutable decrees of God, but the doctrine of election failed to make sense to many frontier people building a nation on the foundation of human freedom and ability. In order to avoid disputes over Reformed teachings, the Cumberland Presbytery allowed its candidates to subscribe to the Westminster Confession only "so far as they deemed it agreeable to the Word of God."[60] Old School clergy stood aghast at this flagrant disregard of the Reformed system of faith. These two issues, in addition to conflict over questions of ecclesiastical authority, eventually led the Synod of Kentucky to dissolve the presbytery. Consequently, a number of the suspended ministers founded the Cumberland Presbyterian Church in 1813.[61]

Cumberland Presbyterians were fervent believers in the mission of America. The future of the world, they held, depended on the future of America and the future of America depended on the triumph of the evangelical message. "Save America to save the world," the Cumberland Board of Missions declared in 1887.[62] The church stood foresquare against such evils as liquor, tobacco, dancing, gambling, card playing, Sabbath desecration, and the Catholic Church.[63] The blessing God had bestowed on Christian America made the export of its civilization, as well as its religion, a divine imperative. The 1890 General Assembly proclaimed,

> The strength of our own national life, the providential environments, the Heaven-bestowed blessings through which we are the inheritors and the favored possessors of personal liberty and the beneficiaries of the purest spiritual Christianity, through which we are to-day the most powerful and wealthy of nations, make us pre-eminently debtors to all the less favored portions of humanity, and bid us be the leaders in race elevation. Of Christian civilization we are the Western exponents.[64]

No wonder one of the Cumberland Church's chief theologians could boast that his church was "properly called an American church, if not the only one."[65]

Though Bryan later joined the more traditionally Calvinistic Presbyterian Church in the U.S.A., his theology always reflected the revivalistic heritage embodied in the Cumberland Presbyterians. One scholar correctly observed that Bryan "wore the mantle of Calvinism lightly."[66] While he defended the "fundamentals of the faith," Bryan allowed that he had never studied the differences between Baptists, Methodists, and Presbyterians.[67] Christianity to Bryan was not so much a system of doctrine as a way of life; the heart, not the mind, was the most important religious organ. Christian living, not doctrinal disputation, was therefore the most effective method of Christian apologetics. "A speech may be disputed," Bryan declared, "even a sermon may not convince, but no one has yet lived who could answer a Christian life; it is the unanswerable argument in support of the Christian religion."[68]

Bryan's evangelical faith was perfectly complemented by the education he received at his mother's knee. Mariah Bryan directed young William's studies at home until his tenth birthday. As a child he would learn his lessons and then, while standing on a small table, recite them to his mother. Bryan recalled, "Webster's spelling book and McGuffey's reader, then a geography, whose author I cannot recall, formed the basis of my education and furnished the themes for my earliest declamations."[69] The McGuffey readers were second only to the Bible in influence on the culture of the Middle Border, and as such on the values of the Great Commoner.[70]

William Holmes McGuffey—Presbyterian clergyman, professor, author, editor, and sometime college president—was a child of the Ohio frontier.[71] After acquiring a college education, he became professor of ancient languages at Miami University, Ohio and was eventually ordained by the Presbyterian Church. Between 1836, when his first eclectic reader rolled off the presses, and 1920 publishers sold over 120 million copies of his schoolbooks.[72] A proponent of "religion, morality, and education," McGuffey sought to use his readers to "bolster midwestern civilization against the dangers inherent in pioneering new frontiers."[73] To do so, he preached a gospel of Christianity, morals, and patriotism.[74]

Church, school, and home were the three principal custodians of the ideals preached by McGuffey.[75] Belief in God, sin, and salvation through Christ were central tenets of his faith; but religion was valued as much for its benefits to society as for its truth.[76] In a passage that adumbrated Bryan's criticism of Darwinism, McGuffey wrote, "If you can induce a community to doubt the genuineness and authenticity of the Scriptures; to question the reality and obligations of religion; to hesitate, undeciding, whether there be any such thing as virtue or vice; whether there be an eternal state of retribution beyond the grave; or whether there exists any such being as God, you have broken down the barriers of moral virtue, and hoisted the floodgates of immorality and crime."[77] Public education was a must, but McGuffey warned against concentrating so much on developing the mind that the heart went unattended. Again, in words Bryan would echo years later, McGuffey advised that "God's grace in the heart will render the knowledge of the head a blessing; but without this, it may prove to us no better than a curse."[78] Likewise, a good family life drove home the value of virtue. Cooperation, respect for elders, obedience, humility, and honesty benefited not only the family but the entire nation. It could not be otherwise, for the morally upright reaped the rewards of following God's fundamental law.[79]

A passionate devotion to the nation completed the constellation of values preached by McGuffey. John Westerhoff, pointing out the religious basis of patriotism in the McGuffey readers, claimed, "Love of country is understood as a religious act. America is a gift from God. We are God's holy nation, his blessed people."[80]

Belief in the unity of evangelicalism and American civilization preached by the Cumberland Church and the McGuffey reader found no more devoted disciples than Silas Bryan and his eldest son. In his *Memoirs* William Jennings Bryan wrote that his father "saw no necessary conflict—and I have never been able to see any—between the principles of our government and the principles of Christian faith."[81] Bryan explained to his audiences that "a good Democratic speech and a good sermon are so much alike that one will get them mixed,"[82] and enthusiastically described the mission of Christian America: "For nineteen hundred years the gospel of the Prince of Peace has been making its majestic march around the world, and during these centuries the philosophy of the Sermon on the Mount has become more and more the rule of daily life. It only remains to lift that code of morals from the level of the individual and make it real in the law of nations, and this, I believe is the task that God has reserved for the United States."[83] This merger of Christianity and culture lay at the root of Bryan's reform activities and would inspire his campaign against evolution. The Darwinist contradiction of the Scriptures and Christian morals, he would later contend, threatened the church and Christian civilization.

Well indoctrinated in the harmonic philosophies of his parents, his church, and McGuffey, Bryan left the familiar surroundings of Salem for Whipple Academy in Jacksonville, Illinois in 1874. Though only fourteen years of age, the young man's character and values were, for the most part, set. Bryan's education at Whipple Academy, Illinois College, and Union Law College no doubt broadened his knowledge and sharpened his mind; but his devotion to the faith of the Middle Border never changed.[84] In the words of Richard Hofstadter, "Intellectually, Bryan was a boy who never left home."[85]

William Jennings Bryan: Moral Crusader

In 1900, after a brief career as an attorney, two terms in the House of Representatives, and two unsuccessful bids for the White House, Bryan, still only forty years old, concluded that his passion for politics had obscured his calling as a Christian.[86] Determined to redress the imbalance, Bryan prepared a number of speeches defending Christian faith and morals and hit the lecture trail. Though he preached to almost all who would give him a forum, Bryan was nowhere more at home than on the Chautauqua circuit.[87] For over twenty-five years Bryan dominated the Chautauqua, and the Chautauqua dominated the culture of the Middle Border.[88]

Chautauquas took their name from "The Chautauqua Sunday School Assembly" at Chautauqua Lake, New York, founded by John H. Vincent in 1874.[89] The Chautauqua combined Bible study, entertainment, and exercise in a beautiful outdoor environment.[90] Over time, Vincent broadened the strictly religious fare available to participants by adding classes in arts and crafts, literature, and home economics. The Chautauqua's combination of religion, education, and recreation realized immediate success and almost immediate imitation. By 1900 over two hundred copies of the New York venture had sprung up from Maine to California. Having pirated the idea, directors of these offspring did not hesitate to borrow the name. By the turn of the century Chautauqua was becoming a household word.[91]

In 1904 an innovative entrepreneur, Keith Vawter, decided to try a variation on the theme and initiated the traveling Chautauqua.[92] These peripatetic shows, mirroring the optimism and pietistic moralism of the times, provided the perfect food for a people hungry for culture.[93] Talent of every stripe—singers, bell ringers, instrumentalists, ventriloquists, yodelers, storytellers, and sculptors—peopled their platforms. But entertainment alone was not enough. As one performer stated, "The essential of any Chautauqua programme was its 'message.' . . . A platform performance might be excellent from an artistic or informative point of view, but it wasn't up to Chautauqua standards unless it taught a moral lesson."[94] The more the entertainment resembled a sermon, the more successful it was on the Chautauqua circuit.[95]

Despite the popularity of the various acts, lectures remained the mainstay of the Chautauqua.[96] Like the entertainment, lectures were meant to inspire and inform.[97] "Buoyant prophets of hope and morality" pleased the crowds with such perennial favorites as "The Man Who Can," "The Secret of Power," "Take the Sunny Side," and "The Silver Lining."[98] Ralph Parlett's "University of Hard Knocks" and Russell Conwell's "Acres of Diamonds" were heard thousands of times. But no speaker came close to William Jennings Bryan as the favorite of the Chautauqua.[99] Summer after summer, year after year, even when serving as secretary of state, Bryan traveled the back roads of the great Midwest to be with his people. There, under the canvas, he was at home. Mrs. Bryan reminisced, "When Mr. Bryan stood in the Chautauqua tent at night under the electric lights and the starlight, with practically every adult and most of the children from miles around within sound of his voice, he could forget the hardships and weariness of travel. His voice would grow deep and solemn, for he knew he was speaking to the heart of America."[100]

In his speeches Bryan expounded the faith he had learned as a boy at home, church, and school. In "The Prince of Peace," his most popular and favorite lecture, Bryan declared his religious posture. "I am interested in the science of government," he admitted, "but I am more interested in religion than in government. I enjoy making a political speech . . . but I would rather speak on religion than on politics." Bryan's predilection for religion rested on his belief that "government affects but a part of the life which we live here and does not deal at all with the life beyond, while religion touches the infinite circle of existence as well as the small arc of that circle which we spend on earth."[101] To Bryan politics was no more, and no less, than the means of fulfilling his calling as a Christian statesman.

Bryan emphasized the ethical aspects of religion in his lectures. "Religion is the foundation of morality," he declared, "in the individual and in the group of individuals." As early as 1905 he warned Chautauquans of the dangers of Darwinism, claiming, "The Darwinian theory represents man as reaching his present perfection by the operation of the law of hate—the merciless law by which the strong crowd out and kill off the weak. If this is the law of our development then, if there is any logic that can bind the human mind, we shall turn backward toward the beast in proportion as we substitute the law of love. I prefer to believe that love rather than hatred is the law of development." In marked opposition to Darwinism, belief in the resurrection had a salutary effect on morality:

> A belief in immortality not only consoles the individual, but it exerts a powerful influence in bringing peace between individuals. If one actually thinks that man dies as the brute dies, he will yield more easily to the temptation to do injustice to his neighbor when the circumstances are such as to promise security from detection. But if one really expects to meet again, and live eternally with, those whom he knows today, he is restrained from evil deeds by the fear of endless remorse.[102]

The command of Jesus *Love thy neighbor as thyself* provided the solution to all human difficulties. Only by following the Prince of Peace, Bryan insisted, could the world finally know true peace.[103]

Christians, Bryan told his auditors, could not help but live a life of service to others. "Service is the measure of greatness," he asserted. "It always has been true; it is true today and it always will be true, that he is greatest who does the most good."[104] In "The Value of an Ideal," another of Bryan's renowned Chautauqua orations, he demanded, "What we need today is an ideal of life that will make people as anxious to render full service as they are to draw full pay—an ideal that will make them measure life by what they bestow upon their fellows and not by what they receive."[105]

Bryan did not limit his efforts for moral reform to the Chautauqua circuit alone. In marked contrast to his fellow Presbyterian, J. Gresham

Machen, Bryan campaigned tirelessly within the church for social, political, and economic reform. "What is a church for," he asked in 1909, "if it is not to stand for morality in all things and everywhere?"[106] A prophet of personal and national piety, Bryan manifested unswerving loyalty to the nineteenth-century evangelical heritage that married revivalistic fervor and dedication to social reform. The church could not neglect its calling to christianize America.

Bryan was, in fact, a theologically conservative Social Gospeler. The social agenda that Bryan set before the church included "taxation, trust regulation, labor, the monetary system, peace and disarmament, temperance, anti-imperialism, woman's suffrage."[107] "These questions are before us," Bryan insisted. "They cannot be avoided; they must be settled, and church members must take their part in the settlement; ministers also must have a voice in this work."[108] Bryan served on the temperance committee of the Federal Council of Churches and the general committee of the Interchurch World Movement.[109] In 1919 he praised the Federal Council of Churches—no group of conservatives—as "the greatest religious organization in our nation," noting, "It gives expression to the conscience of more than seventeen million members of the various Protestant churches; its possibilities for good are limitless; its responsibilities are commensurate with its opportunities."[110] Though committed to traditional Christianity, Bryan willingly cooperated with those who differed from him theologically in order to further his crusade to build a Christian nation.[111]

Bryan's Christian faith and trust in the people buoyed his reforming zeal with an inexhaustible optimism. He believed he was born into "the greatest of all the races" in the "greatest of all lands" during the "greatest of all ages."[112] In 1911 he itemized the progress that marked his era's superlative character: "Intelligence and intellectual capacity were increasing; educational standards were rising; moral standards were improving; people were studying ethics as never before; the spirit of brotherhood was abroad in the land; there was more altruism than ever before; the tide was running in favor of democracy; the peace movement was spreading; reason was asserting itself; and moral forces were taking control."[113] To Bryan only one conclusion was possible: "The morning light is breaking. Day is at hand."[114]

The advent of the World War beclouded Bryan's sunny forecast. The horror of Christians slaughtering one another with the blessings of their Christian nations damaged but did not destroy the Commoner's faith. Christian civilization had gone mad; Bryan set out to determine the cause of its disease.[115]

In "The Prince of Peace" Bryan had warned against the consequences of Darwinism but moderately allowed, "While I do not accept the Darwinian theory I shall not quarrel with you about it; I only refer to it to remind you that it does not solve the mystery of life or explain human progress."[116] The war impelled Bryan to reevaluate Darwinism as a possible cause of the hostilities.[117]

Two books that Bryan read during the war, *Headquarters Nights* by Vernon Kellogg and *The Science of Power* by Benjamin Kidd, convinced Bryan that evolutionary theory was at the root of the world's problems. Kellogg's work demonstrated the influence of Darwin on German military officers; and Kidd attempted "to trace a straight line from Darwin through Nietzsche to the growth of German nationalism, militarism, and materialism."[118] For Bryan the connection was sealed. The civilized world had gone to war because it had turned away from the philosophy of the Prince of Peace to a philosophy of *Might makes right* based on the Darwinian hypothesis.[119] In 1920 Bryan told the World Brotherhood Congress that Darwinism was "the most paralyzing influence with which civilization has had to contend during the last century." Nietzsche, who merely carried Darwinian theory to its logical conclusion, had "promulgated a philosophy that condemned democracy . . . denounced Christianity . . . denied the existence of God, overturned all standards of morality . . . and endeavored to substitute the worship of the superman for the worship of Jehovah."[120] In short, Darwinism was the antithesis of everything Bryan held dear. Nevertheless, the Commoner's attacks on Darwin remained sporadic until he realized that the atheistic philosophy that drove Germany to war was threatening to capture the soul of America.[121]

In the spring of 1921 Bryan launched an all-out offensive against Darwinism with the publication and distribution of an essay entitled "The Menace of Darwinism." This work—which in a slightly modified form became the heart of *In His Image*—announced the anti-Darwinian arguments that Bryan would repeat endlessly throughout the next four years. As one scholar summarized, "Bryan had fought plutocracy and imperialism, war and liquor because they dehumanized man; because they were more worthy of the brute. Now he found in the quiet, unhurried atmosphere of the classroom a group of teachers promulgating the thesis that man after all *was* a brute!"[122] By substituting the law of hate for the law of love, Darwinism was secularizing American culture and ruining the last, best hope of the world. The fight against evolution became Bryan's final, and greatest, crusade. Surely, he thought, it was a mission worthy of the Presbyterian Church.

Varying Views of Evolution in the Church

The Presbyterian Church was far from being of one mind on the question of evolution. As would be expected, liberals, like Henry Sloane Coffin, had no difficulty accepting a theistic view of evolution. The idea of evolution had been a central emphasis of liberal theology for years, and Coffin's thought was no different.[123] More moderate leaders in the church, though perhaps not as vocal as the likes of Coffin, also subscribed to a theistic interpretation of evolution. For example, Charles Erdman, who would play a major role in bringing peace to the church in 1925, asserted, "Evolution theory is all right so long as it does not deny God or God's creative action."[124] Unfortunately, for Bryan, there was not even unanimity of opinion on the topic of evolution in the most conservative wing of the church. Machen and Macartney provide an interesting case in point.

Machen was, at least in the 1920s, hesitant to discuss the question of evolution in public because, as he said, "I have some objection to discussing subjects that I know little or nothing about."[125] It was for this reason, at least in part, that Machen, when asked to pen an article on evolution for the *New York Times* on the eve of the Scopes Trial in 1925, chose to confine himself to questions of doctrine in an essay entitled, "What Fundamentalism Stands for Now."[126] This coyness notwithstanding, Machen did hold some views about evolution, which he revealed in private correspondence.

In a 1926 letter Machen denied that the idea of *creative evolution* had any viability. He wrote,

> "Creative [corrected from theistic] evolution" is, I think, a contradiction in terms. Evolution is God's way of working in certain spheres at least through nature, while creation means creation out of nothing. Evolution, by its very idea, cannot explain the origin of the world, and the origin of the world, with those creative acts of God that we call miracles, alone is produced by creation. Nothing is more absolutely fundamental to Christianity I think, than this sharp distinction between God's works of providence and his work of creation, for upon that sharp distinction the uniqueness of redemption in Christianity rests.[127]

Here, notably, while rejecting creative evolution, Machen did accept a form of *theistic evolution:* it was God's way of working in the world through natural processes. But this notion could not possibly be merged with creation, which was God's supernatural intervention into history.

Indeed, the key issue for Machen in discussing evolution was that of the supernatural; for, Machen believed, some versions of evolutionary theory denied the possibility of the supernatural entrance of God into history. As such, Machen repeatedly linked the question of special creation with the question of the virgin birth.[128] "The bodily structure of Jesus," he wrote, "was no doubt similar to the bodily structures of those men who had lived before him, yet it was not derived from those previous men by evolution. On the contrary there was a tremendous break—the Virgin Birth."[129] Likewise, similarities between the human race and other beings did not disprove special creation.[130] Though Machen was not specific on how God intervened in history in the creation of humanity, he wanted to insist that mankind was not simply the product of natural forces.[131]

Machen's adherence to a view of theistic evolution helps to account for his reticence on the topic of evolution during the 1920s. In the first place, biological evolution was not to Machen's mind the chief, or even a major, problem for church and culture. The rise of naturalistic thought in general and the spread of liberal theology were the prime enemies in the modern world. To concentrate on biological evolution was therefore to deflect the energy of Christians away from the central battle. Moreover, Machen was probably astute enough to realize that to speak out explicitly on evolution might alienate part of the constituency he was trying to galvanize.

Finally, two other factors, Machen's spiritual view of the church and his Southern libertarianism, almost certainly played into his reluctance to address the topic of evolution publicly. Unlike Bryan, Machen would have seen questions about the teaching of evolution as completely beyond the bounds of proper ecclesiastical concern. Likewise, a strident defender of academic freedom, he could never accept a legislative solution to an academic problem.[132] Given this variety of motivations, it is hardly surprising that Machen simply avoided the topic of evolution as best he could throughout the Presbyterian controversy.

In contrast to Machen, Macartney did not hesitate to approach the topic of evolution in the 1920s. In 1926 he debated Dr. Harry F. Osborne, president of the American Museum of Natural History, on the subject "Does the Teaching of Evolution Menace Religion?"[133] Macartney, who in his youth had apparently accepted Darwinism without difficulty, scored the hypothesis of evolution as "a vast, but fascinating, mistake on the part of science."[134] Like Machen, Macartney acknowledged that the theory of natural selection denied the supernatural entrance of God into history. But, unlike his ecclesiastical ally, Macartney did so by drawing a sharp contrast that precluded any possibility of a

Christian view of evolution. Macartney wrote, "More and more it becomes evident that what confronts us is a choice between out and out evolution, man in the totality of his nature produced from the brute creation under him, and that long process set in motion by some power of which we know, and can know, absolutely nothing; or, creationism, that the species came into existence not through dim aeons of change and growth, but by the fiat of the Almighty."[135] Moreover, Macartney pursued the discussion (as Machen never would have) by showing the devastating effects of the theory of evolution on theology and morality. In this, Macartney revealed a strain of thought much closer to Bryan's than to Machen's.

"Intelligent Christians," Macartney charged, "are more awake to the de-Christianizing influences of evolution today than they were in the eighties. They have had an opportunity to see its terrible fruitage." Evolution put God far off, submerging "Him in a germ of protoplasm." It withered "worship, faith, devotion"; left no room for revelation or miracles; and contradicted the biblical teachings on man, sin, and the incarnation, atonement, and resurrection. In undermining the Christian faith, Macartney argued, evolution imperiled the moral order of society. In a passage that rivaled Bryan himself, Macartney asserted,

> The world today, and a large portion of the Church, is running on the spiritual and moral capital of past generations. But even now we see much of the terrible fruitage from the sowing of the dragon's teeth of evolution. We see it in the growing conviction among our young people that the moral ideals and principles of the older generation have no binding authority. We see it in the ghastly ravages of divorce, slowly disintegrating the American home. We see it in the appalling laxity of the relationship between the sexes, the sure forerunner of the breakdown of civilization. We see it in the nation-wide renaissance [of] paganism, the worship of pleasure and power, well named in the Apocalypse, the Worship of the Beast. We see it in the almost complete de-Christianization of our great universities, a more truly pagan institution than which it would be hard to imagine. We see it in the sad secularization of our Protestant Churches. And if all this we can see today, in our own generation, a decline of faith in God and the hereafter, a crumbling in the public morality, then what will it be fifty years hence, when the leaven of evolution has had another half century in which to work? If this has happened in the green tree, what will it be in the dry? After us, the deluge!

Finally, Macartney concluded, evolution quashed all hope of progress here and of life hereafter. "Evolution is the death of hope," Macartney warned. It was "fatal to our great social hopes of progress and the coming of the Kingdom of God" and "dims, if it does not altogether quench, the hope of life after death."[136] Given these realities, any compromise between Christianity and evolution was impossible. "The Christian who accepts evolution," Macartney charged, "invariably is one who holds in a very loose and vague way the grand doctrines of the Gospel." Against those who allowed evolutionary thought to determine their Christian faith, Macartney insisted, "Christianity is not to be moulded and controlled by the thought of the world, but to control it and dominate it."[137]

Macartney's views on evolution reveal strains of both the Old School tradition of Princeton and of the broader evangelical heritage that had come to dominate America in the nineteenth century. True to the Princeton tradition, Macartney believed that Christian ideas were to mold the thought of the world. But unlike Machen, Macartney manifested the Northern evangelical concern for social reform and the christianization of America. Christianity had a responsibility not just to preserve true doctrine but to save the family and the nation from the breakdown of morality inspired by evolution. In this he was much closer to Bryan than to Machen. In 1923 this difference had little influence on the relationship between Machen and Macartney, bound together, as they were, by the fight against a common enemy. Before the end of the Presbyterian controversy, however, the differences disclosed by these variant responses to evolution would help to inspire a break in the fundamentalist alliance.

The 1923 General Assembly

The moderatorial battle at the 1923 Assembly in Indianapolis possessed all of the ingredients of a classic political confrontation. Though four men were nominated for the post—Bryan, Wishart, Walker, and Silsley—Bryan and Wishart were the two leading contenders. The choice was clear-cut. On one side stood Bryan, who for over two years had been castigating colleges that wrecked the faith of students by teaching Darwinism as a fact. On the other side stood Wishart, president of the College of Wooster, a Presbyterian school that unapologetically taught evolutionary theory as a part of the science curriculum.[138] Bryan believed that the church could not long endure with a membership divided on the question of evolution.[139] Wishart desired a church tolerant enough to embrace those with a variety of doctrinal views.[140] Though Bryan clearly failed to inspire confidence in all of the commissioners, he was, the *New York Times* reported, "the favorite and his election was deemed almost certain."[141]

Bryan led in the first two ballots but by the third round of voting Walker and Silsley had dropped out of the race, dramatically altering the complexion of the contest. As such, Bryan, who had been confident of victory, narrowly lost the election, 451 to 427.[142] When the results were announced the assembly "went wild," breaking into thunderous applause.[143] Bryan silently acquiesced to the will of the people.[144]

Wishart broached Bryan on his preference for an appointed position; and although it was known that Bryan wanted to chair the Bills and Overtures Committee, which would handle the Fosdick affair, Bryan requested time to consider his options. In an apparently strategic move, the moderator took advantage of Bryan's hesitation and appointed Bryan chair of the Committee on Home Missions. The Commoner declined the offer, explaining, "I think that the fight against the brute doctrine of evolution is more important than any work I can do as chairman of any committee."[145]

Bryan was not long in confronting the assembly with his program. After winning the backing of the church for a resolution endorsing total abstinence from alcoholic beverages, he turned his guns on Darwinism.[146] Unable to convince the Committee on Education, on which he sat, to endorse a motion opposing the teaching of evolution in Presbyterian schools, Bryan took the issue to the floor of the assembly and offered the resolution:

> That no part of the Educational Fund of the Presbyterian Church of the United States of America, shall be paid to any school, college, university, or theological seminary that teaches, or permits to be taught as a proven fact, either Darwinism or any other evolutionary hypothesis that links men in blood relationship with any other form of life.[147]

Speaking to the motion, Bryan lambasted Darwinism for over an hour, inspiring raucous applause, screams, and laughter.[148] Substitute motions, amendments, amendments to amendments, motions to refer to committee and motions to table filled the air.[149] Opponents argued that the assembly's approval of the resolution would "drive young people from the church" and tell the world that the Presbyterian Church denied the possibility of a Christian evolutionist.[150] After three hours of stormy debate Bryan offered a summation. Turning to the assembly he took aim and fired his best shot. "There has not been a reform for twenty-five years that I did not support, and I am now engaged in the biggest reform of my life," he thundered. "I am trying to save the Christian Church from those who are trying to destroy her faith. We have preachers in this audience who don't believe in the virgin birth . . . in the resurrection of Christ's body . . . in the miracles"; and all of this apostasy, Bryan argued, was the direct result of Darwinist philosophy.[151] The time had come for Christians to stand up and defend their faith.

The assembly was not convinced. Apparently dominated by the likes of Erdman and even Machen (who accepted evolution to some degree), the assembly approved a much milder substitute motion that instructed church judicatories to "withhold their official approval from such academies, colleges, and training schools where any teaching or instruction is given which seeks to establish a materialistic evolutionary philosophy of life or which disregards or attempts to discredit the Christian faith."[152] "When Mr. Bryan realized that he was defeated," one observer noted, "he sank into his chair and looked so pale as to appear almost ill."[153]

The debate over evolution turned out to be no more than a warm-up for the battle concerning Fosdick. The Committee on Bills and Overtures, which addressed the memorial from the Philadelphia Presbytery, brought two reports to the floor of the assembly on the afternoon of 23 May.[154] The majority report, signed by twenty-two of the twenty-three committee members, declared the church's continuing commitment to the standard of the Westminster Confession but recommended that since the New York Presbytery was investigating the complaint, no action be taken against First Church. The minority report, signed solely by A. Gordon MacLennen of Philadelphia, specifically reaffirmed the five fundamentals of the faith first declared by the 1910 General Assembly and directed the Presbytery of New York "to take such action . . . as will require the preaching and teaching in the First Presbyterian Church of New York City to conform to the system of doctrines taught in the Confession of Faith."[155]

A vigorous, sharp, and often acrimonious debate followed, consuming five hours of the assembly's docket. Supporters of the majority report argued that assembly action on the matter would be redundant, intrusive, and presumptive, given the New York Presbytery's pending investigation. Backers of the minority report, ever suspicious of the liberal New York Presbytery, were in no mood to leave Fosdick's fate in the hands of his friends. Fosdick had, beyond doubt, publicly denied doctrines of the Presbyterian Church; the situation demanded a response.[156]

Although there was no love lost between Bryan and Fosdick—indeed, they had debated the issue of evolution in the *New York Times* a year earlier—it appears that Bryan attempted to encourage a compromise measure in the midst of the debate.[157] Bryan refused to endorse a false peace based on a repudiation of the fundamentals. But, he maintained, "I am a harmonizer. Why not, then, add the statement of faith contained in the minority report to the proposal of action in the majority report, and make it a unanimous action? If you vote down the minority report, you vote down the assembly action of 1910 which is contained therein."[158] Bryan, no student of Presbyterian polity, history, or doctrine, was more concerned with the assembly's reaffirmation of the five fundamentals than prosecution of Fosdick. As Bryan had suggested in the earlier debate, defending the fundamentals was but another way of preserving the Christian church from the inroads of Darwinism and thereby one more way of ensuring the future of Christian civilization. The "unproven hypothesis of evolution" was "the root cause of nearly all the dissension in the church over the five points under discussion," Bryan argued. "The evolutionary hypothesis is the only thing that has seriously menaced religion since the birth of Christ and it menaces all other religions as well as the Christian religion and civilization as well as religion."[159] When the assembly failed to agree with Bryan's compromise, he had no choice but to come down firmly on the side of the minority report, against the evolutionists.[160]

Clarence Macartney, who was a commissioner to the assembly, concluded the debate for the minority. After thanking the moderator for his parliamentary abilities, he warned that the coming storm could not be stopped by compromise.[161] Macartney then raised the stakes. The issue before the church was not merely a denominational squabble. Rather,

> the eyes of the whole church and the whole nation are upon this Assembly. They are waiting to hear what you will say. If you answer the Philadelphia overture in the affirmative you rejoice the hearts and strengthen the arms of thousands of followers of Christ throughout the land. . . .
>
> But if you answer the overture in the negative, you disappoint thousands of praying men and women, you discourage them in their battle for Christ and his kingdom.[162]

When the question was called, Bryan, insisting that this was, "the most important issue before the Assembly" demanded a roll call vote.[163] The minority report passed by a vote of 439 to 359.[164]

Though Bryan had lost the election for moderator and failed to convince the assembly of the imminent threat of Darwinism, he counted his loss but gain. To his daughter Grace he wrote, "I think my defeat for Moderator was providential. I did far more on the floor than I could have done in the chair. . . . It was a great victory for orthodox Christianity—other churches will follow. It means a new awakening for the church."[165] Bryan fought his battles in the Presbyterian Church for the preservation of evangelical Christianity and thereby the preservation of American Christian civilization.[166] Above all, he was concerned that Darwinism be prevented from destroying the Christian basis of America. By reaffirming the fundamentals, the Presbyterian Church had, Bryan believed, struck a serious blow to the evolutionist "mind worshipers" and upheld the basis of American Protestant culture. Lifted by his unquenchable optimism, Bryan convinced himself that Bible-based Christianity would regain its lost ground in the church and in the culture at large. America was on the road to recovery; the future of Christian civilization looked bright.

Bryan's assessment may have been a bit too sanguine; for on the closing day of the assembly eighty-five commissioners, led by William P. Merrill of New York, filed an official protest against the assembly's action in the Fosdick case. The protest argued that the assembly's decision was based on unsubstantiated allegations, addressed a matter not properly before the body, and sought to impose on church officers "doctrinal tests other than, or in addition to, those solemnly agreed upon in the Constitution of our Church."[167] Concurrently, Henry Sloane Coffin, pastor of the Madison Avenue Presbyterian Church in New York, issued a statement declaring that he did not accept the five fundamentals as stated in the report and claiming, "I feel that I owe it to my congregation and to the Presbytery to state plainly that if any action is taken which removes Dr. Fosdick from the pulpit of the First Church on account of his interpretation of the Christian Gospel, I cannot honestly be allowed to remain in the pulpit of Madison Avenue Church, for I share fully his point of view."[168] Far from settling the controversy, the assembly's action had only added fuel to the fire. The church was clearly splitting into factions. Modernists, convinced that they had as much right to remain in the church as their fundamentalist peers, refused to be silenced without a fight. In the course of the battle, Henry Sloane Coffin would emerge as one of the most able and articulate defenders of the liberal cause.

4

Henry Sloane Coffin
and the Auburn *Affirmation*

Liberal theology had been gaining strength within American Protestantism in general and the Presbyterian Church in particular since the late nineteenth century. Though the Presbyterian Church had unequivocally rejected the tenets of modernism in the Portland Deliverance of 1892 and in the doctrinal declarations of 1910 and 1916, some presbyteries, most notably that of New York City, had continued to ordain men who accepted the higher critical method and the assumptions of liberalism.[1] That eighty-five commissioners would publicly protest the assembly's endorsement of the five fundamentals was a mark of how adamant many were in defending the rights of modernists within the church.

Even before the assembly of 1923 had convened, one member of the liberal party, Robert Hastings Nichols, a professor at Auburn Theological Seminary, had initiated preemptive action to rebuff the fundamentalist offensive. In early 1923 he distributed a paper that defended the doctrinal liberty of Presbyterian clergy within the bounds of evangelical Christianity. Nichols argued that the Adopting Act of 1729 (one of the foundational documents of American Presbyterianism), the Old School–New School reunion of 1870, and the 1906 merger with the Cumberland Presbyterians all allowed for doctrinal diversity within the church. Moreover, he maintained that the Westminster Confession did not assert scriptural inerrancy and that the Holy Spirit, not the church, was the final authority for Protestant ministers. Though his close friend Henry Sloane Coffin suggested he solicit signatures and publish the statement before the Indianapolis convention, those who cautioned restraint prevailed. With luck, many liberals hoped, the storm would blow over and peace return of its own accord.[2]

The assembly failed to fulfill the liberals' wishes. In the wake of the church's pronouncement concerning the Fosdick situation, liberal leaders quickly set out to mobilize their constituency. Not more than two weeks after the assembly's adjournment, five clergy from upstate New York distributed a letter to sixty-eight ministers protesting the Fosdick pronouncement and calling a meeting to discuss possible responses. Thirty-three of the recipients answered by attending the meeting on 19 June in Syracuse, New York.[3]

Using Nichols' preassembly paper as a base, the committee adopted a three-part statement condemning the assembly's decision on ecclesiastical and theological grounds. During the next six months this paper evolved into a declaration, entitled *An Affirmation Designed To Safeguard the Unity and Liberty of the Presbyterian Church in the United States of America* and commonly called the Auburn Affirmation. In the course of the Presbyterian controversy this document became the chief symbol of the liberal movement within the church.[4]

The Affirmation opened with a statement declaring the evangelical orthodoxy of its signatories and affirming the system of the Westminster Confession of Faith. In an effort to defend broad doctrinal liberty within the church, the statement briefly recounted the history of Presbyterianism in America, stressing the historical freedom of interpretation of the Scriptures and the Confession within the church. In addition the Affirmation asserted that since doctrine could be "declared only by concurrent action of the General Assembly and the presbyteries" in the Presbyterian Church, doctrinal declarations such as those of the 1923 assembly were unconstitutional. Echoing the protest issued by the commissioners at the assembly, the Affirmationists declared that the assembly's action against First Church, New York was irresponsible, unpastoral, and unconstitutional.[5]

Though these statements alone raised a number of points of contention, the brief theological statement included in the declaration inspired the greatest response from conservative opponents. The Affirmationists argued,

> Furthermore, [the endorsement of the five fundamentals] attempts to commit our church to certain theories concerning the inspiration of the Bible, and the Incarnation, the Atonement, the Resurrection, and the Continuing Life and Supernatural Power of our Lord Jesus Christ. *We all hold most earnestly to these great facts and doctrines; we all believe from our hearts that the writers of the Bible were inspired of God; that Jesus Christ was God manifest in the flesh; that God was in Christ, reconciling the world unto Himself, and through Him we have our redemption; that having died for our sins He rose from the dead and is our ever-living Saviour; that in His earthly ministry He wrought many mighty works, and*

*by His vicarious death and unfailing presence He is able to save to the
uttermost.* Some of us regard the particular theories contained in the
deliverance of the General Assembly of 1923 as satisfactory explanations
of these facts and doctrines. But we are united in believing that these are
not the only theories allowed by the Scriptures and our standards as
explanations of these facts and doctrines of our religion, and that all who
hold to these facts and doctrines, whatever theories they may employ to
explain them, are worthy of all confidence and fellowship.[6]

The signers maintained that they did not desire to exceed the boundaries
of "evangelical Christianity" but insisted that in order to "more effectively preach the gospel of Jesus Christ" they were obliged to defend
their "liberty of thought and teaching." In closing, the Affirmation
deplored ecclesiastical infighting "*in the face of a world so desperately
in need of a united testimony to the gospel of Christ.*" The church needed
to preserve freedom and unity within the bounds of a broadly construed
evangelical Christianity.[7]

The drafters of the Affirmation began seeking subscriptions for the
document in November 1923, and by the end of the year 174 signatories
had endorsed the statement. It was officially released through the church
and secular press in early January 1924, appended by 150 signatures.
The modernist counteroffensive was under way.[8]

Henry Sloane Coffin: New York Native

In 1924 no presbytery in the church was more aggressively liberal than
the Presbytery of New York, and no Presbyterian liberal in New York
was more prominent than Henry Sloane Coffin. Coffin was pastor of
the Madison Avenue Presbyterian Church and associate professor of
pastoral theology at Union Theological Seminary in New York. For
years he had been defending the liberal gospel in pulpit and print. He
was one of the first and most adamant supporters of Fosdick and a major
force in the development of the Auburn Affirmation. Articulate, determined, tall, and handsome, Coffin became, by the mid-1920s, the
unquestioned national leader of liberal Presbyterians.[9]

Coffin was heir to the urban aristocratic culture of late-nineteenth-
century New York. The first child of Edmund and Euphemina Coffin,
he was born on 5 January 1877 in Manhattan. He loved New York and
enthusiastically accepted the patrician responsibility of advancing its
welfare.[10] The influences Coffin encountered in New York—his home

for all but a few years of his life—had a profound effect on the theology and cultural views he came to accept and defend.

In 1877 New York City was, in most every way, the modern capital of the nation.[11] The sociological, technological, and cultural developments that were transforming America were nowhere more apparent than in America's largest urban center. Between 1850 and 1880 waves of foreign immigrants helped to swell New York's population from five hundred thousand to over one million two-hundred thousand; by 1900 the city would number close to 3.5 million.[12] These vast demographic changes were mirrored by physical alterations spurred by advances in engineering. High-rise buildings, symbols of the triumph of technology, began to challenge church steeples for control of the city's skyline. Additionally, the completion of the Brooklyn Bridge in 1883—then the world's longest suspension bridge—and the advent of the elevated railroads testified to the seemingly limitless possibilities of scientific progress.[13]

New York stood at the center of the economic revolution that was changing America from an agricultural to a manufacturing nation. In 1880 the city boasted over eleven thousand factories creating goods worth nearly 450 million dollars. Large department stores, pioneered by Alexander T. Stewart and Rowland Macy, revolutionized retail marketing and helped make New York the advertising center of the country. The city's ports controlled half of the nation's foreign trade; the New York Stock Exchange surpassed all competitors in volume of business; and New York bankers dominated the financial world.[14] In short, New York became the monetary hub of the nation.

The years after the Civil War also witnessed New York's rise to cultural dominance. The Metropolitan Opera Company and the Metropolitan Museum of Art advanced the musical and visual arts. Attracted by the wealth, freedom, and stimulation offered by the country's largest city, painters, sculptors, authors, poets, vocalists, instrumentalists, and actors thronged to New York. Many of the nation's leading publishing houses were based in the city, as were the majority of the nation's top periodicals. Theatre—drama, comedy, musicals—thrived, making performers the idols of America. Though New York produced few celebrated classical musicians, European talent filled its concert halls. New ideas, new art, and new life-styles flourished in New York and spread from there to the rest of the country. By the turn of the century New York was the undisputed cultural pacesetter of the nation.[15]

This was the city in which Henry Sloane Coffin matured. Henry's father, Edmund Coffin, was himself a native New Yorker descended from English settlers who arrived with the seventeenth-century Puritan migration.[16] A graduate of Yale, he developed a lucrative law practice in New York, providing counsel for a number of distinguished individuals and corporations. The fact that Edmund Coffin never joined a church must have had a profound influence on Henry. A man of deep principle and honesty, the elder Coffin could never reconcile new scientific findings with traditional Christian beliefs and therefore found it impossible to offer a public affirmation of faith. Nevertheless, he was a pewholder and a regular worshiper in the Fifth Avenue Presbyterian Church and, in time, a trustee of the Brick Presbyterian Church. As counsel to Union Theological Seminary, he introduced his elder son to the world of ecclesiastical conflict. In 1893 Edmund Coffin attended the heresy trial of Charles A. Briggs of Union to provide legal advice to the seminary. Henry, then sixteen, accompanied his father to the trial and thereby witnessed the most celebrated heresy trial in the annals of American church history.[17] As noted earlier, Briggs, who had denied the inerrancy of the Scriptures and challenged other doctrines dearly held by many Presbyterians, was suspended from the ministry for violating his ordination vows.[18] Moreover, the trial occasioned the severing of Union's official relationship with the church.[19]

Attendance at the Briggs trial left an "indelible impression" on the young Henry Coffin, who was already considering the ministry as a career.[20] In later years Coffin claimed it was the "less educated and more intolerant elements" that had attacked and driven Briggs out of the church and maintained that the Briggs trial had inspired Union to accept "a mission under God to champion the freedom of Christian scholars."[21] By inviting his son to accompany him to the Briggs trial, Edmund Coffin, intentionally or not, helped to instill in Henry a profound devotion to broad-minded ecclesiastical tolerance.

Henry's mother, Euphemina Sloane Coffin, was the true religious leader in the Coffin household. Daughter of Scottish immigrants, she was a devout Presbyterian who led the family in daily prayers. Euphemina's mother, also a pious Presbyterian, lived with the Coffins throughout Henry's boyhood and taught him the Westminster Shorter Catechism.[22] Though Henry grew to appreciate his Scotch Presbyterian heritage he would not hold the doctrines of the Confession as his own. In 1926 he said of the catechism, "Many of its formulations are obsolete, and I am not passing it on to another generation, but its purpose, to supply Christians with definite convictions and to make them think for themselves, is part of the inheritance worth striving to maintain."[23]

Like his ecclesiastical rival, J. Gresham Machen, Coffin maintained extremely close ties with his mother, writing to her almost daily while he was away at college and seminary. She was undoubtedly a major influence in his decision to enter the ministry and rejoiced at the prospect of her elder son's pursuing a clerical career. But their relationship was not without disagreement. Euphemina was of the mind that aristocracy and plebians should maintain a respectable distance, while her son became an outspoken advocate of social and ecclesiastical democracy. In the course of his career, Coffin would convince the Madison Avenue Church to abolish pew rents, encouraging rich and poor to join in worship in one church.[24]

As a boy Coffin benefited from all the accoutrements of wealth. The Coffin home, at the center of the midtown residential area, was properly maintained by domestic help. Henry attended a private boys school in the city, took piano lessons, and spent his summers at the Atlantic shore and touring Europe with his family. He enjoyed sailing, swimming, bicycling, and walking and could occasionally be found playing a game of baseball.[25]

Henry regularly attended worship and Sunday school at the Fifth Avenue Presbyterian Church with his family, becoming a communicant at the age of fourteen. An active participant in the life of the church, he played the organ, taught at a local mission Sunday school, and rose to the office of president of the Young People's Association.[26] The pastor of the Fifth Avenue Church, Dr. John Hall, was one of the most renowned leaders in the church.[27] Hall was a conservative thinker and a director of Princeton Seminary, who opposed efforts to revise the Westminster Confession and rejected the arguments of higher criticism and Darwinism.[28] Although Coffin's theology would develop along lines radically different from those of his pastor, Coffin's ecclesiastical activities inspired in him a strong devotion to the church and a leaning toward ministry as his chosen profession.[29]

There seems to have been little question concerning Henry's path after graduation from preparatory school. He followed a long line of relatives to New Haven, Connecticut to matriculate at Yale in 1893.[30] In the last decade of the nineteenth century Yale was experiencing something of a renaissance. The trustees had only recently responded to the changes revolutionizing higher education by rebaptizing Yale College as Yale University. In the six years prior to Coffin's arrival, the university enrollment had almost doubled—to 1,969—and the income, buildings, property, and faculty of the school had realized substantial gains. Rightly or not, Yale prided itself on maintaining the most rigorous admissions and degree standards of any school in the country.[31]

Coffin enthusiastically joined into the life of the college. Taking full advantage of the electives that had been recently introduced into the Yale curriculum, he supplemented his traditional coursework with the study of economics, sociology, and drama.[32] He excelled in the classroom and was early recognized as one of the top scholars in the college. Coffin was also an eager participant in extracurricular activities. The young man led Bible studies and won election as a deacon in the Church of Christ in Yale and as president of the Yale Christian Association.[33] In the summers he attended the Northfield Summer Conferences and cultivated a relationship with the aging evangelist, Dwight L. Moody.[34] In addition, Coffin was elected to the fraternities of Kappa Psi, Delta Kappa Epsilon, and the prestigious Skull and Bones. Notably, his later rivalry with William Jennings Bryan was foreshadowed in 1896 when Coffin "led cheers for McKinley" at a New Haven rally for the Great Commoner. Skilled in the social graces, he frequently invited young ladies from New York (properly chaperoned of course) to the teas, dances, and parties at the college.[35] He enjoyed the annual Yale–Harvard football game and the fall regatta on nearby Lake Whitney.[36] Despite his active life-style, Coffin maintained his high academic record and graduated near the top of his class, winning membership in Phi Beta Kappa.[37]

Coffin's decision to enter the ministry appears to have been a foregone conclusion. During his college years he considered pursuing a life in business but believed the merchant's life to be too dull and pedestrian for his liking. Completely oblivious to the kinds of intellectual and professional struggles that assailed the likes of Machen, Coffin embraced the liberal accommodation of Christianity and culture. He ignored his father's pleas for patience in the matter of choosing a vocation and early made up his mind to seek ordination in the church. The only real question for Coffin was where he would pursue his theological work.[38] Coffin was advised by friends and mentors to consider New College (Edinburgh), Auburn, Yale, Andover, and Union Seminary in New York. He decided on New College, and, after spending the summer of 1897 with his parents on the Continent, settled into life in Scotland.[39]

By the time Coffin arrived at Edinburgh, the faculty had accepted and were actively propagating biblical higher criticism. In a letter home he wrote,

> If I am not a deep dyed higher critic it will be no fault of New College for you get it everywhere in most attractive form and I must say whatever more conservative ideas I had have been rudely blown away. . . . The remarkable thing is that these advanced views are held not only by theological professors but by nearly all the ministers and by a large majority

of the ordinary listeners. You have advanced theology from almost every pulpit and all Scotland with very few exceptions is in the same boat with Professor Briggs.[40]

Coffin's subscription to higher critical views was not greeted with complete approval by those back home. In 1898 he tried to allay the fears of his family, writing, "Do not worry about the heresy of New College. The Scotch Church seems to stand it and preach better sermons than the bluest Princetonians. . . . I am getting plenty of good Calvinism and lots of the Confession of Faith only with a new interpretation."[41] Coffin attributed the differences between the theology of the Scottish and American Presbyterians to a difference in education and expected that with time and study Americans would catch up with the more advanced views taught in Edinburgh.[42] He would echo this analysis of conservative–liberal differences repeatedly during the controversy of the twenties.[43]

Inasmuch as Coffin planned to pursue his calling in America, he thought it wise to finish his education in the United States and decided to complete his work at Union Seminary in New York. Before returning home, however, he wanted to improve his command of German and made plans to study for three months at the University of Marburg. In April 1899 he said good-bye to his Scottish friends and crossed the English Channel to begin his stay on the Continent.[44]

Like Machen, who would follow Coffin to Marburg a few years later, Coffin sat at the feet of Adolf Jülicher and Wilhelm Herrmann. Coffin realized that his more conservative mother did not look on Herrmann's theology favorably and teased her, "You will find among my books a copy of Prof. Herrmann's book "Communion with God." . . . It is in English and very good. You can see by it what particular learning I am now imbibing and get some antidotes ready against[?] my home coming. I have not got much yet however that will stand comparison with the Shorter Catechism."[45] Coffin was impressed with the zeal and missionary spirit of Herrmann's disciples and believed that American Presbyterians would be more tolerant of German theology if only they could see its practical results.[46]

While Coffin was in Germany, the General Assembly of the Presbyterian Church engaged in a theological struggle of measurable import to the budding scholar. In 1897 Arthur Cushman McGiffert, professor of church history at Union Seminary, published *A History of Christianity in the Apostolic Age,* which contained controversial conclusions regarding the authenticity and inerrancy of the Scriptures. In 1898 the General Assembly received an overture from the Pittsburgh Presbytery charging that McGiffert's book denied the inspiration and authority of the Scriptures.[47] In response the General Assembly pleaded for peace in the church and counseled McGiffert "to reconsider the questionable views set forth in his book" and to withdraw from the ministry if he could not "conform his views to the Standards of our Church."[48]

McGiffert stood by his conclusions, and in 1899 the General Assembly received memorials from ten presbyteries requesting action in response to his views. The assembly addressed the matter in a declaration stating that the inerrancy of Scripture, the inerrancy of all statements of Jesus, the belief that the Lord's Supper was instituted by the direct act of Jesus, and justification through faith alone were "fundamental doctrines" of the Word of God and the Confession of Faith and by referring the McGiffert case back to the New York Presbytery for action.[49]

Coffin, who remained abreast of the situation through his mother's correspondence, reacted strongly to this activity. In a letter to his mother he expressed disgust and disappointment at the assembly's deliverance claiming, "Any man of brains and familiar with modern ways of looking at things will feel that its assertions are just[?] untenable."[50] The matter for Coffin was not simply academic. He had set his sights on ordination by the Presbytery of New York, but the McGiffert case gave him pause for serious reconsideration: "Unless very decided changes occur in a year or so," he wrote home, "I don't intend to go up before that august body."[51] He worried that if men like McGiffert could not be tolerated, he might not be accepted either.

Nevertheless, Coffin returned home from Germany to finish his theological education at Union Seminary. Having been well schooled in the liberal theology of Edinburgh and Marburg, Coffin was comfortable with the views of the Bible and theology propagated at Union. Though he lived at home, he developed close relationships with many of the faculty and students. Most significant was the intimacy he shared with Charles Cuthbert Hall, the president of the seminary, who would call Coffin to the position of part-time instructor of pastoral theology in 1904. In the spring of 1900 Coffin finished his formal education, receiving the Bachelor of Divinity summa cum laude.[52]

Coffin's earlier fears concerning his possible rejection by the Presbytery of New York proved to be unfounded. He appeared before the presbytery, passed without controversy, and on 2 May 1900 was ordained in the University Place Presbyterian Church.[53]

In subscribing to the Westminster Confession of Faith Coffin did not believe that he was accepting the doctrines stated in the Confession. Rather, as he later maintained, "The formula [of subscription] means to me that under the supreme authority of Christ I receive the confession as setting forth in seventeenth century thought and language the principal doctrines which have grown out of and foster the religious experience of protestant evangelical Christians, and which it is my privilege to teach in the best thought and speech at my command for those to whom I minister."[54] This interpretation of the subscription vow obviously gave Coffin a great deal of leeway in accepting the Confession. Unlike Machen, he saw no difficulty in a loose adoption of the creed. Indeed, Coffin seemed to intimate that no creedal affirmations at all should be required for ordination when he wrote, "To acknowledge that a man possesses the Spirit of God and is equipped to serve the Kingdom, but to hold him unfit to minister in our select theological club because he does not wholly share the views of the majority, seems to me perilously like blasphemy against the Holy Ghost."[55] In any event, Coffin did not believe that creedal differences should bar one from ministry. There was no inconsistency, he maintained, "in worshipping and working, or even in occupying a position of leadership, in a communion with whose creed, or ritual, or methods one is not in full sympathy."[56]

In June, Coffin was called to the position of stated supply pastor of the Bedford Park Presbyterian Church, a small mission church in the Bedford Park section of the Bronx. Years later he described his first pastorate, writing, "The pulpit was a former oyster counter in a fish shop attached to the butcher enterprise. Everything in the hall was primitive so that it was difficult to have orderly services, but the people were in earnest." Not shy about using his contacts, Coffin appealed to his wealthy friends and relatives for funds to assist in building a sanctuary for the young fellowship. By December of 1900 he was preaching in a handsome new edifice to a swiftly growing congregation, and in January 1901 the church called Coffin as their regular pastor.[57] Coffin's ministry won the plaudits of his parishioners and attracted the attention of the local press. On 22 December 1901 the *New York Journal and American,* in its edition for Harlem and the Bronx, highlighted the young man's flourishing ministry with the banner headline: "MILLIONAIRES HEAR THEIR WEALTHY COUSIN PREACH: REVEREND HENRY SLOANE COFFIN, A YOUNG RELATIVE OF THE SLOANES AND VANDERBILTS, IS THE IDOL OF HIS PARISHIONERS."[58] Given such publicity, Coffin's talents were not long confined to Bedford Park. He accepted an offer to serve as a part-time faculty member of Union Seminary in 1904 and regularly traveled to colleges— Amherst, Barnard, Princeton, and Union among them—to proclaim the gospel. In the summers he refreshed himself with travel to New England and Europe.[59]

Though Coffin received a variety of calls to churches in other cities, not until the Madison Avenue Presbyterian Church offered him a position in 1905 did he decide to leave his first pastorate. Coffin's arrival at Madison Avenue marked the beginning of his rise to ecclesiastical prominence. A skilled pastor, he worked to break down the social and economic barriers in the church. The Sunday school membership, the physical plant, and the program of the church all grew apace. Unable to maintain his teaching responsibilities at Union and oversee the expanding activities of the church, Coffin hired an associate pastor and secured the help of a bevy of Union seminarians.[60]

In 1906 Coffin married Dorothy Ells, the daughter of family friends. A native of California and an Episcopalian, Dorothy had first met Henry during a stay in New York in 1902. Though she was ten years younger than Coffin, their friendship grew until, during a visit to San Francisco, Coffin proposed marriage. The two wedded in September and eventually moved into a house they built on East Seventy-first Street. Bright, skilled in the social graces, and devoted to the arts, she admirably complemented the interests and activities of her new husband. They began every day kneeling in prayer together and frequently gathered around the piano to sing hymns. In time the family was blessed by two children, Ruth and David, who, with visitors and the family servants, kept the Coffin household astir.[61]

Over the years Coffin's ideas became well known through the publication of a number of books, most of them collections of sermons. In 1907 *The Creed of Jesus* rolled off the presses followed by works such as *Social Aspects of the Cross* (1911), *Some Christian Convictions* (1915), *The Ten Commandments* (1915), and *In a Day of Social Rebuilding* (1918). Coffin's accomplishments in pulpit and print were recognized by a number of universities—Yale, Harvard, Princeton, Glasgow, and Marburg among them—by the conferring of honorary doctorates upon him.[62] During World War I he spoke at home and abroad to American troops under the auspices of the YMCA.[63] When he returned stateside from his overseas ministry, he found not only a changed nation but himself in the role of a leading warrior in the cause of modernism.[64]

Henry Sloane Coffin: Liberal Theologian

Henry Sloane Coffin was a self-proclaimed "liberal evangelical." In the closing address of Union Seminary in May 1915, he insisted that though he and his sympathizers were unapologetic liberals, they were, most fundamentally, evangelical Christians. Coffin declared,

> We are first and foremost evangelicals—evangelicals to the core of our spiritual beings. We own ourselves redeemed by and we worship God in Jesus Christ. . . . Any attempt to belittle Jesus, to reduce Him to a mere Teacher, a sage superior to other sages but one among many, not the unique Saviour of the world; to substitute any other standard for the Bible as the authoritative expression of God's life with men; to regard the cross as anything less than the power of God and the wisdom of God for a world's redemption; to trust to human effort alone for salvation, personal or social; runs counter to our deepest instincts and convictions, and seems to us, as such attempts have seemed to our fathers in the faith, to depreciate the Christian religion and to rob it of its vital force.[65]

Liberal evangelicals, Coffin argued, cultivated freedom not for its own sake but for the gospel's sake. If the church was to maintain its appeal to the thinking men and women of his day it had to accommodate the Christian message to the intellectual changes that had swept over America in the late nineteenth and early twentieth centuries. Here Coffin pointed to the conservative impulse behind modernist theology. The choice faced by Christianity, liberals believed, was accommodation or irrelevance. By reinterpreting the faith in light of modern thought forms, liberals sought to preserve the core of the faith and maintain its vitality in the modern world.[66]

In a telling passage of *Some Christian Convictions* Coffin revealed the epistemological presuppositions of his theology. He wrote,

> The life of men with Christ in God preserves its continuity through the ages; it has to interpret itself to every generation in new forms of thought. Under old monarchies it was the custom on the accession of a sovereign to call in the coins of his predecessor and remint them with the new king's effigy. The silver and the gold remain, but the impress on them is different. The reminting of our Christian convictions is a somewhat similar process: the precious ore of the religious experience continues, but it bears the stamp of the current ruling ideas in men's view of the world. . . . The remolding of the forms of its convictions does more than conserve the same quantity of experience; a more commodious temple of thought enables the Spirit of faith to expand the souls of men within.[67]

Unlike Machen and Bryan, who both adhered to a view of history based on Common Sense Realism, Coffin had adopted the historicist assumptions which had been gaining ground in America in the preceding generation. While for Machen history was a record of facts that remained true for all time, historicist thinkers understood history to be profoundly colored by the historian's perspective. All the historian possessed in the present was a memory of the past, not the past itself. As such, history was primarily a matter of interpretation, not the compilation of data.[68] Moreover, for Machen, unlike Coffin, historical facts were not open to a variety of interpretations all of which might be valid in a given time and place. Events had only one proper interpretation and that was the meaning given to them by God in the Scriptures. True doctrines, like true facts, did not change. These variant views of history lay at the root of much of the controversy that eventually split the church.[69]

Coffin had learned his historicism not only at Edinburgh and Marburg but also at Union. In 1892 Arthur McGiffert, Coffin's teacher and then colleague, delineated the assumptions of the modern church historian, stating, "A sharp distinction must be drawn between divine truth and our conceptions of that truth; that, though the former is always and eternally the same, unchanged and unchangeable, in our conceptions of it—in other words in our *doctrines*—there has been as real a development as in our institutions."[70] Later in the same speech he asserted, "The historical study of Christian doctrine reminds us that human notions and conceptions change from age to age, that even the categories of thought undergo more or less of a revision, and it thus teaches us, that, if we will be true to the truth as it has been revealed unto us, we must from time to time adjust our statements to the new conditions."[71] To McGiffert's mind and to his student Coffin's, the shifting patterns of thought throughout history required constant reinterpretation of doctrines. Creeds were only "man's attempt in the best thought and language at his command to express his religious experience."[72]

This view of history did not lead Coffin to a thoroughly relativistic view of Christianity. For Coffin there was an eternal essence of the faith that remained throughout history, that merely needed periodic reformulation. True to the tradition of Friedrich Schleiermacher, *religious experience* provided the ahistorical bedrock of the Christian faith for Coffin. "Religion is experience," Coffin believed. "It is the response of man's nature to his highest inspirations. It is his intercourse with Being above himself and his world." Under the rubric of experience Coffin included feeling, intellect, and will, but warned of exalting one of these elements to the detriment of the whole.[73]

Inasmuch as experience provided the foundation of religion it necessarily had to be the basis of preaching. The minister of God was "not to repeat what others have said in Scripture or out of it; he is to say what he is sure of, because he has experienced it and believes it as he believes himself."[74] Likewise, Coffin advised his congregations, "If any man here is trying to make himself believe anything about God, or Christ, or the Bible, or the Christian life, let him be sure that he is looking at some man-made view of the Divine, a mere idol. When God's truth comes along, it does its own convincing. . . . Its inescapableness is the test of its divineness."[75] Although grounding religious truth in experience may have satisfied many modernists, traditionalists believed this view denied history any religious import.

Significantly, Coffin, like Machen, placed his theology on an empirical base; but the "facts" used by the two theologians were dramatically different. Machen, arguing from a Common Sense belief that the facts of history (namely, events) could to some degree be known with certainty, insisted that the facts of the Bible were the preeminent data for determining Christian belief.[76] For Coffin, however, the prime data for Christians was their contemporary experience, which conditioned their interpretations of the past.[77] The truth of any doctrine could be determined empirically. "Try the doctrine by using it," Coffin advised his congregation. "If it is of no service, let it go. If it opens our eyes, thank God for it."[78]

Given this understanding of religion, the Bible, for Coffin, was not the inerrant Word of God but "the record of the progressive religious experience of Israel culminating in Jesus Christ." He mocked the Princeton doctrine of the inerrancy of Scripture, claiming,

> Certain recent scholars, acknowledging that no version of the Bible now existing is free from error, have put forward the theory that the original manuscripts of these books, as they came from their authors' hands, were so completely controlled by God as to be without mistake. Since no man can ever hope to have access to these autographs, and would not be sure that he had them in his hands if he actually found them, this theory amounts to saying with the nursery rhyme:
>
> > Oats, peas, beans, and barley grows,
> > Where you, nor I, nor nobody knows.[79]

Because the Bible was not the inerrant Word of God but an historically limited record of the ever-evolving religious experience of the Hebrew people, the less well developed portions of Scripture had to be interpreted in terms of the climax of the "faith of Jesus." As the authoritative collection of writings recognized by Christians, the Bible was "*a standard of religious experience.*" But this did not mean that it could be used as "a treasury of proof texts for doctrines, or of laws for conduct, or of specific provisos for Church government and worship." Rather, it was "the norm of our life with God" revealing "the spirit we should manifest towards God and towards one another as individuals, and families, and nations."[80]

Two views of the Scripture's authority were contending for supremacy. One claimed that the Bible contained "mysteries beyond our reason" and the other that the Scriptures were "the revelation of self-evidencing truth." The latter view—which, Coffin alleged, was held by Luther and Calvin—resulted in a carefully circumscribed authority for Scripture. In direct opposition to the likes of Machen who insisted on the historical truth of the biblical narrative, Coffin believed that Scripture could only determine the veracity of religious experience, not of historical events. Coffin wrote,

> We can verify spiritually the truth of a religious experience by repeating that experience; but we cannot verify spiritually the correctness of the report of some alleged event, or the accuracy of some opinion. . . . Our own knowledge of Jesus Christ as a living Factor in our careers confirms the experience His disciples had of His continued intercourse with them subsequent to His crucifixion; but the manner of His resurrection and the mode in which *post mortem* He communicated with them must be left to the untrammelled study of historical students.[81]

He enthusiastically endorsed the pursuit of historical criticism: "To found a 'Bible Defence League' is as unbelieving as to inaugurate a society for the protection of the sun. Like the sun the Bible defends itself by proving a light to the path of all who walk by it." Finally, he maintained the Bible was not the ultimate authority for the Christian. Jesus alone was the Word of God; the Bible simply contained the Word. Thus, every Scripture had to be tested by "the Spirit of Christ in us."[82]

Coffin rejected the views of scholars who claimed either that Jesus was not a historical person or that he was simply another man. In the current age, he argued, Christians were most interested in three particular aspects of Jesus: his "*singular religious experience*," his "*singular character*," and his "*singular victory*" over sin and death. Jesus had embodied the God he trusted and gave faith new power.[83] As with all modernists, the Jesus Coffin saw revealed in the Bible made no distinction between the natural and supernatural. Coffin contended, "One might say that Jesus did not believe in miracles, were it not much truer to say, that to Him everything was a miracle."[84] Though Coffin seemed to allow for Jesus' supernatural power in his writings, Jesus' power in the moral sphere eclipsed his control of physical forces.[85]

Of course, Coffin did not insist that Christians accept every account in Scripture as historical. For example, he argued that the virgin birth was not an essential tenet of the faith. "The question of Jesus' origin is not of primary importance," Coffin maintained. "No man, today, should be hindered from believing in Christ, because he does not find a particular statement in connection with His origin credible." Rather, "to know Him is not to know how He came to be, but what He can do for us."[86] One suspects that despite Edmund Coffin's refusal to join the church, he would have easily slipped into the fold by his son's definition of a Christian as "one who clings to Him in whom Jesus trusted, one who responds to the highest inspirations of Jesus of Nazareth."[87]

The historical Jesus was authoritative for Christians because his consciousness of God was corroborated by their own religious experience. Inasmuch as Jesus led believers to God, he was the revelation of God; inasmuch as he believed in the "divine possibilities of divinely changed men," he was the *revelation of what man may become.*"[88] Jesus was "the divinest life we know," "the Best we can imagine, the Loveliest we can conceive."[89] As such Jesus was the criterion by which all thought of God had to be tested. "Anything attributed to God in past, present or future," Coffin wrote, "which a Christian is convinced is unlike Jesus, he must refuse to believe, or he ceases to be a Christian."[90]

The cross of Christ revealed the "unchristlikeness" of the world, the "marvellous conscience" of Jesus, and the "incomparable sympathy of the Victim" for mankind. Coffin rejected the traditional understanding of the substitutionary atonement but maintained that "in the sense of suffering sin's force, of conscientiously accepting its burden, of sensitively sympathizing with the guilty, Jesus bore sin in His own body on the tree." Most important was the moral influence of the cross: "there is a direct line of ancestry from the best principles in the lives of nations, and of men and women about us, running back to Calvary," which was a revelation of the love and forgiveness of God.[91]

This doctrine of the atonement suggests the high view of humanity held by Coffin. Jesus, as the supreme moral example, inspired in liberals a sublime confidence in the ability of mankind. "We believe in the capacities of ordinary men and women," Coffin wrote, "because we have seen what a man can be in Jesus, the Son of God."[92] As has been noted, Coffin, along with all other turn-of-the-century liberals, subscribed to a theistic view of biological evolution. This led in turn to a faith in moral evolution, with "each age surpassing its predecessor in its standards of duty, [and] its conceptions of man's obligations to man in home and industry and commerce and government."[93] Though in later life Coffin abandoned his sanguine religious progressivism, he was able to claim, even in the wake of World War I, "The day will come when the nations shall be bound in the all-comprehending Kingdom of God."[94]

The God whom Jesus revealed gave the Christian hope for the life everlasting. For Coffin this faith was not based primarily on a historical resurrection but on an "inevitable inference from what we know His and our God to be."[95] The proof of the resurrection lay primarily in "the re-embodiment of His spirit, in lives useful, forceful, beautiful with His faith and hope and self-sacrifice."[96] Because the faithful knew what God had done in their lives, they were convinced of what he would do. Death could not separate believers from God's love.[97]

The God revealed in Jesus was a "Christlike Father," "the Lord of heaven and earth." Though God might not be absolutely sovereign, he was, Coffin argued, "sufficiently in control over all things to accomplish through them His will." Most prominently, God was an immanent, "indwelling Spirit." "He is," Coffin wrote, "the Conscience of our consciences, the Wellspring of motives and impulses and sympathies."[98]

God was revealed not only in Jesus and the Scriptures but in non-Christian faiths and in a sense of duty and beauty. The God known in these ways Christians had experienced in the grace of Jesus, the fatherhood of God, and the fellowship of God's Spirit. Though the Scriptures did not expound on the precise nature of this threefold experience, later Christians developed the doctrine of three Persons in one Godhead to explain their religious experience. This doctrine had been useful in the past, Coffin believed; but it was not of great help to his contemporaries. As such, he recommended that those who had difficulty with the doctrine of the Trinity simply remember that "it is only a man-made attempt to interpret Him who passeth understanding" and that "each age must revise and say in its own words what God means to it." "The important matter," Coffin said, "is not the orthodoxy of our doctrine, but the richness of our personal experience of God."[99]

Coffin looked to the ideas of Jesus for an ecclesiology and determined that Jesus was not ultimately concerned with the constitution, worship, or doctrine of the Jewish church but "was primarily interested in the religious experience that lay back of government, worship and creed." Thus the church was not determined by polity, liturgy, or doctrine but by "oneness of purpose with Christ."[100] It was "the company of those who share the purpose of Jesus and possess His Father's Spirit for its accomplishment."[101] The only criterion for membership Coffin perceived in the New Testament church was the "possession of the Spirit of Jesus"; thus, nothing more should be required in the twentieth century.[102]

In marked contrast to Machen, who believed the early church manifested doctrinal agreement, Coffin discovered doctrinal diversity among the first Christians. This former freedom within the church invited freedom in all times. While the "continuity of the Spirit" maintained the identity of the church, it was always changing in polity, doctrine, and worship. Modern Christians were therefore not bound "by the precedents of bygone centuries in our organization," but were at liberty to take what was helpful from the past and "let the rest go."[103]

Within the unity of the Spirit, church unity became not only a possibility but an obligation.[104] Throughout his ministry Coffin worked tirelessly for the abolition of what he considered to be anachronistic denominational divisions.[105] In 1910 he attended the World Missionary Conference at Edinburgh and in 1929 represented his church at the reunion of the Church of Scotland and the United Free Church of Scotland. Undoubtedly his marriage to an Episcopalian gave special impetus to his efforts to unite the Presbyterian and Episcopal Churches in the 1930s and 1940s. When he was elected moderator of the Presbyterian General Assembly in 1943, he made reunion of the Northern and Southern branches of the church a top priority but to no avail.[106]

Division of the church was, Coffin insisted, "a flat denial of the will of Christ for his people." The continued maintenance of denominations was nothing short of "a sin against Christ, a denial of our obedience to him."[107] Moreover, church unity was essential if the church was to accomplish its task of transforming the world into the Kingdom of God.

A disciple of the Social Gospel, Coffin cherished a grand vision of the salvation of the world worked out by the unified people of God. In 1912 he lifted up his dream to the students and faculty of Union Seminary:

> The Christian who is trying to transform the City of Destruction into the City of God needs the cooperation of every fellow-Christian. He has too vast and too urgent an undertaking on his hands to inquire closely into his brother's doctrinal orthodoxy, or his view of the mode of administering some sacrament, or the validity of his ecclesiastical order. . . . The sense of obligation for the world-wide Kingdom of justice, mercy, and faithfulness renders denominationalism both ridiculous and intolerable. In preparation for the United Christian Church that is to be God's instrument for world-redemption it behooves us to rid our existing communions of every barrier which prevents any man, layman or minister, from fulfilling in them the work for which we recognise that he has been spiritually endowed.[108]

The crisis of World War I only deepened Coffin's resolve to work for the redemption of the world through the unified society of the redeemed.

As the custodian of the Spirit of Jesus, the church held the key to the salvation of the world. Unity was a must if the church was to fulfill its task of transforming the "earth into a household of brethren dwelling together in peace and goodwill."[109]

The Social Gospel of Henry Sloane Coffin

As a proud proponent of the Social Gospel, Henry Sloane Coffin insisted that salvation was not just a matter for individuals. Rather, he argued, "the life of God enters our world by two paths—personally, through individuals whom it recreates, and by whom it remakes society; socially, through a new communal order which reshapes the men and women who live under it."[110] In 1926 Coffin chastised the church for focusing too closely on the individual aspects of the gospel to the detriment of its social component. The church, he declared, had "preached Christ apart from the kingdom of God which He preached and for which He died."[111] Truly Christian evangelism had to incorporate both the individual and social dimensions of the gospel. The full evangel included a message of salvation for industry, education, and government—all of life—as well as for the individual.[112] The church existed, Coffin urged, "to make the world the Kingdom of God."[113]

Coffin spelled out many of the social dimensions of the gospel in the Lyman Beecher lectures that he delivered at Yale in 1918. Though the war placed the very future of Western civilization in jeopardy, the gospel, he argued, provided the hope for a redeemed society. Coffin told the Yale students and faculty, "Our sole hope of social rebuilding along lines that will endure is the proclamation of the Gospel of God, and the making of men and nations disciples of His Son." The greatest need of the world in the aftermath of the war was "a regenerated social order in which saved souls shall be safe." Such transfomation would require "the combined effort of every Christian." In the face of the undoing of Western civilization, a united church was more necessary than ever. "A national Church is demanded for a nation's renewing," Coffin declared, "and a universal Church for a world's reconstruction." Only a united church could generate the power necessary to transform a divided world into the one Kingdom of God.[114]

If the Kingdom was to come, "families, nations, and races" would need to be redeemed. Coffin, like many Christians in the postwar decade, grew deeply concerned about the state of the Christian family. In 1926 he painted the grim picture: "Today the Christian home is in jeopardy. The permanence of the marriage tie is widely flouted. In the United States several hundred thousands are living in a legalised consecutive concubinage, marrying, divorcing and marrying again. . . . There are situations where it is inhuman to forbid the separation of man and wife; but these occur rarely, and heroic souls, with a loyal love like Hosea's, can often hold on, despite the impossible, and work redemption."[115] Yet Coffin's concern was not so much with the prohibition, as with the prevention, of divorce.[116] Though the church could not ignore questions about its responsibility to those already divorced, its first task was to educate Christians in such a way that divorce would never need to be an option.[117]

Like families, the relations in industry required christianization.[118] Coffin insisted on the need for economic and industrial reform in America, declaring, "Our commercial order stimulates the competitive motive, holds our personal gain as the incentive to effort, and sanctions selfish possession as the reward of labor. As a result it produces men and women diametrically opposite in mind and heart to Jesus Christ, and moulds nations after the pattern of bellicose sons of Belial."[119] In such a situation the preacher was to proclaim "the Kingdom of God in protest against existing industrial relations."[120] Coffin was an ardent defender of the Labor Temple, an institutional effort by the Presbyterian Church in New York to address economic and social problems of the day.[121] But he was no social radical. He opposed all grand schemes for the reorganization of economic structures, maintaining instead that Christians were called to permeate the social order with the Spirit of Jesus in order to form "a more Christian industrial order." "Christianity," he wrote, "is not dynamite but leaven."[122]

An industrial order fashioned after the mind of Christ would, at least, provide a job for every worker and a living wage with every job.[123] He allowed that the government would probably have to play a role in maintaining full employment, but this was permissible in order that "luxury and want" not exist side by side. As a Christian society, America had to set a minimum standard of living and ensure that no one was deprived of the opportunity to maintain that standard.[124]

Concerned for more than simply guaranteeing a living wage, Coffin also argued that "it is the community's duty to see that every member of society is a property owner."[125] Eschewing communistic schemes, Coffin argued that all property is God's, given to the community and individuals in the community in trust.[126] Ownership of property was a blessing not just to the individual but to the society as well. A propertyless individual, Coffin held, was incomplete and unable to "feel himself a full member of society." Seemingly just as important, however, was Coffin's assumption that the propertyless were a threat to society; for, he argued, "when . . . a man is without property, it is difficult to-day to educate him in a Christian sense of obligation. . . . The propertyless are restless. They do not consider the community does much for them, and they do not feel bound to do aught for it."[127]

The spiritual principle of Christianity held the key to struggles between management and labor. Just as slavery was abolished when Americans accepted the principle of "Christian brotherhood," so industrial peace, Coffin argued, would come when employer and employee finally adopted a "Christian mind."[128] Though industry conducted in the Spirit of Jesus would succeed financially, success would not be measured "primarily in terms of profits or of wages . . . but in terms of the brotherhood of the workers in the enterprise with one another and with the public which they serve."[129] Bound together in the Spirit of Christ, employer and employee would realize that true fulfillment came in service to the community, not in concern for personal gain.[130]

Coffin's interest in industrial relations shows marked similarities with the concerns of his ecclesiastical opponent, William Jennings Bryan. Though Bryan was primarily a spokesman for rural America, he addressed labor issues, calling for "shorter working hours, minimum wage laws, the right to bargain collectively, and the curbing of the use of the injunction in labor disputes."[131] In 1919 Bryan charged the churches with "having too little sympathy for those who toil" and penned an open letter to the churches in America demanding that they address the issue of labor relations.[132] Likewise, in 1920, he encouraged the General Assembly of the Presbyterian Church to drive all "profiteers" from the fellowship so that "when they go to the penitentiary they will not go as Presbyterians."[133] Though Bryan's version of the Social Gospel was populist and Coffin's was essentially elitist, both maintained an interest in the reformation of America's economic structures. Theological differences did not prevent them from holding similar views on some social issues.

Coffin's concern for economic fellowship was inseparably connected with the larger question of the salvation of the nations of the world. In the postwar era the most important mission of the church was to lead in the world's rebuilding. Ministers were to work for social redemption through the community of God's people. "The sorest need of a world in pieces," Coffin declared, "is fellowship—the fellowship of nations, of races, of producers and distributers of the world's wealth. The Church of Christ, whose distinctive note is fellowship, is the divinely created company for the world's reconstruction into a universal fellowship." While Coffin had supported America's entrance into World War I, he insisted that Christians were called to transcend national allegiances in their faith and thereby bind up the wounds of the world. "It is intolerable," Coffin wrote, "that national hostilities should set brother against brother in the one household of faith—the Church, which exists to embody and create the world-wide community of God." The war taught Coffin that "the world moves in no steadily advancing evolution," but he still anticipated the day when all nations would be united in the Kingdom of God.[134]

In the realm of international relations, as in industrial relations, Coffin and Bryan manifested similar views. Bryan had been an indefatigable champion of world peace since the turn of the century and encouraged the church to take a lead in repairing international divisions after World War I.[135] In 1919 he wrote, "Now that peace has been restored, the Christian church faces a supreme duty, the duty of healing the wounds of war and uniting all the nations in an universal brotherhood."[136] Though Bryan worked on various fronts for peace, he insisted that Christianity provided the only sure foundation for global brotherhood.[137] "If the Church cannot end war," Bryan declared, "there is no organization on earth who can."[138] In marked contrast to Coffin, however, Bryan took up the battle against Darwinism in order to combat a philosophy that he believed had led to the tragedy of World War I. Though both Coffin and Bryan insisted that the church had an important mission in world reconciliation, their strategies for fulfilling that mission were dramatically different.

Key to the church's mission of reconciliation, Coffin believed, was the need for doctrinal openness in the church. He wrote, "The building of a new world-order is so titanic an undertaking that the Church must have within her ranks all men of Christian purpose. Upon her leaders rests the duty of so stating her convictions that no man of Christian goodwill will feel that he cannot be heartily loyal to the truth and in fullest sympathy with the Church, and that no believer of maturest experience will complain that our restatements omit aught of the wealth of the life with Christ in God of the Church's heritage."[139] Christians had to broaden their sympathies, to "learn to tolerate those who do not wish to tolerate us," in order to create a united force for the upbuilding of the Kingdom.[140]

Moreover, if the church was to fulfill its calling of uniting the world, it had to break down the economic segregation within the Christian fellowship. "The Church that wishes to preach brotherhood to the nations and embody it in the social order," Coffin declared, "must first exemplify it in her own fellowship. Her congregations must be such families as she wishes the race to become."[141] Coffin had long been a proponent of the "democratic church" incorporating members of every social stratum and had worked for such equality in his own church.[142] In 1912 he had noted that one special duty of the church was "the reconstruction of its congregations, so that they cease to be the exclusive class groups they now almost invariably are." Then, as after the war, he was convinced that if the church could not bring rich and poor together around the Lord's table, she could never build brotherhood in the world.[143] A unified church, theologically and socially, was the necessary model for a unified world.[144]

Ministers of the church had a special calling in this endeavor to build the Kingdom on earth. Pastors were to reshape society by seeking to "develop Christians of enlightened and sensitive consciences," who would strive to transform the church and the world under God's guidance. The clergy's task was therefore "to teach people how to live together in God in families, industries, nations, and in the earth-wide brotherhood of mankind." Even as the war raged on in Europe, Coffin elevated a vision of hope for a new day. "We are to lead the Church," he told the students at Yale Divinity School, "in a day when it cannot have less than a world outlook nor a smaller purpose than the regeneration of the entire social order."[145]

Here was the hope and the calling that carried Coffin into the ecclesiastical battles of the 1920s. In the Presbyterian conflict Coffin would fight for doctrinal liberty in the church, for the freedom to rethink Christian convictions in present-day categories. This was essential if the church was to survive in the modern world.[146] But beyond that, Coffin was fighting to preserve the hope of a social and economic order redeemed through the people of God. The church existed "to embody and create the world-wide community of God," "to conquer all the kingdoms of this world—art, science, industry, education, politics—for God and for His Christ." Such an endeavor required the efforts of men and women of "Christian goodwill" the world around.[147] The attacks of fundamentalists like Machen and Macartney on liberal evangelicals therefore threatened both the freedom of Christians and the future of the world. Only a universal church, a "re-united world-wide Church of Christ, supernational," could marshal the power to remake the world according to Christ's mind. In fighting for freedom in the church, Coffin was fighting for nothing less than the advent of God's Kingdom on earth.[148]

Activities: 1923–1924

In response to the assembly mandate of 1923, Coffin and his modernist allies in the New York Presbytery addressed the Fosdick situation. In February the Presbytery adopted a report that essentially exonerated Fosdick of any wrongdoing and proposed no change in his status.[149] If this were not enough to ruffle conservative feathers, two other events further agitated the situation. First, in June 1923 the New York Presbytery voted to license two Union students, Henry P. Van Dusen and Cedric O. Lehman, who refused to affirm the truth of the virgin birth.[150] Then, on 31 December 1923, Dr. Henry van Dyke, former pastor of the Brick Street Church in New York and then professor at Princeton University, publicly relinquished his pew at First Presbyterian Church, Princeton because of disagreement with the preaching of Machen, who was serving as stated supply preacher of First Church.[151] Fundamentalists, of course, took offense at all of these actions and responded in the press and church courts.

In the months before the 1924 assembly Coffin and his allies worked to convince the church of the legitimacy and propriety of their theological and political positions. They continued to dig into ecclesiastical records to find precedent for their claims and gathered more signatures for the Affirmation. They decided to republish the Affirmation with all of the additional signatures before the opening of the assembly and therefore released in May a pamphlet including the document, supplementary material, and 1,274 signatures.[152]

Realizing that the publication of the Affirmation alone would not carry their cause, modernists sought additional means to further their program. Led by R. H. Nichols, they planned a "pre-Assembly conference" in Detroit and formulated an elders' overture to the assembly in support of the views of the Affirmation. Nichols, acknowledging that a forthright liberal could not possibly win election as moderator, thought that Robert Speer, a respected, broad-minded layman serving as secretary of the Board of Foreign Missions, would be the liberals' best hope. But Speer refused to run; and with all other options exhausted, liberals approached the assembly willing to give their unenthusiastic backing to Charles R. Erdman, professor of practical theology at Princeton Seminary.[153]

While liberals were busy composing the Auburn Affirmation and designing other defensive strategies, fundamentalists engaged in political actions of their own. In October 1923 the first in a series of "mass meetings" was held in New York to buoy the fundamentalist cause.

About three hundred "ministers, elders, and devout women" listened to Machen and Macartney describe the perilous condition of the Presbyterian Church. To Macartney's mind the battle was not simply a denominational affair. Indeed, it had reached global proportions. Macartney declared,

> They who love the gospel of Christ dare not sin by silence. In this critical day, they must be ready to endure the reproaches of the world for the sake of Jesus Christ. The eyes of the whole Christian world are fixed upon the Presbyterian Church. They wait to see if the Presbyterian Church will haul down its flag and join the long procession of creedless churches. By reason of its grand confessional declarations, and its noble history, the Presbyterian Church has come to the kingdom for such an hour as this.[154]

The Presbytery of New York's exoneration of Fosdick only served to stir up the already-troubled waters of the church. At a mass meeting held in Pittsburgh on 5 February 1924 Macartney sounded the battle cry yet again. Echoing the thesis of Machen's *Christianity and Liberalism*, he declared that the root cause of the controversy lay in "the presence in the Protestant churches of two groups, calling and professing themselves Christians, who hold views as to Christ and the Scriptures so divergent and so irreconcilable as to constitute two different religions. With two such groups in the same church, collision and conflict are inevitable."[155] Macartney lambasted the theological and constitutional assumptions of the Affirmationists. In response to the argument of the liberals that there are many acceptable theories of biblical inspiration, the incarnation, atonement, resurrection, and miracles of Jesus he asserted that the church had always held to one understanding of each of these tenets, the understanding held by the conservatives.[156] Likewise, he dismissed the liberal contention that the Adopting Act of 1729 gave ministers wide liberty in subscribing to the Westminster standards.[157] Ultimately, however, the controversy was not a matter of constitution or creed. Rather, the issue was the integrity of the gospel: "The question now before the Presbyterian Church is not merely, Have ministers a right to interpret the Confession of Faith to suit themselves, rejecting and accepting what they please? But something far more than that. It is this (think of it! this in the Presbyterian Church!): Can the minister of the Presbyterian Church deny with impunity the most carefully recorded facts of the Gospel about the Lord Jesus Christ?"[158]

In many respects, then, the debate, as noted earlier, was aggravated by diverse epistemologies. In article after article Machen pressed this difference before the church. In April 1924 he wrote,

At this point we find the most fundamental divergence between modernism and the Christian faith; the modernist assertion that doctrine springs from life, and may be translated back into the life from which it came, really involves the relinquishment of all objective truth in the sphere of religion. If a thing is merely useful it may cease to be useful in another generation; but if it is true, it remains true to the end of time. . . . It makes little difference how much or how little of Christian doctrine the modernist affirms since whatever he affirms, he affirms as a mere expression of an inner experience, and does not affirm any of it as fact.[159]

To the likes of Machen, Bryan, and Macartney, the Gospels recorded facts unconditioned by their historical setting. To Coffin and his allies, who had accepted historicist views, the Scriptures embodied timeless truths in historically limited language. Conservatives were convinced that liberal assumptions would lead inevitably to a bottomless relativism, while the liberals pondered how intelligent moderns could possibly insist on the verity of the biblical worldview.

That the issue did not hinge simply on doctrinal and epistemological issues, however, was evident from a resolution adopted at a fundamentalist mass meeting in December 1923. Then the conservatives stated, "We are met together in critical and anxious days. The great facts upon which the Christian revelation rests are openly questioned and rejected, and the very foundations of the moral order among men and nations are imperiled."[160] Not doctrine alone but, with doctrine, the moral underpinnings of Christian civilization were threatened by the spread of modernist theology. While Coffin and his ilk were striving for tolerance and open-mindedness for the sake of the construction of God's Kingdom, conservatives were marshaling their forces in order to preserve the basis of Christian civilization. Both believed the moral order of the world was at stake. Both had radically different ideas of how to save that order.

Conservative activities were not limited to pulpit and press. In March of 1924 the Presbytery of Philadelphia adopted an overture to the assembly recommending that no one who could not affirm the "five fundamentals" be allowed to "serve as a member or paid officer of any Board or the General Council of the Presbyterian Church."[161] Additionally, the Presbytery of Cincinnati passed an overture calling the Affirmation and its signers to the attention of the assembly, and conservatives in the Presbytery of New York appealed the Fosdick case to the church's highest judicatory.[162] Perhaps most importantly, fundamentalists turned to Clarence E. Macartney to lead them to victory as moderator of the 1924 General Assembly. Macartney, the man who had first called the church to arms against Fosdick's preaching, would be given the opportunity to finish what he started. As the 1924 assembly approached, the church prepared for yet another round in the ongoing controversy.

5

Clarence E. Macartney and the 1924 General Assembly

As at every General Assembly, the first item of business for Presbyterians gathered in Grand Rapids in May 1924, was the election of a moderator. Both candidates were conservative; but one, Clarence Macartney, was the acknowledged leader of the fundamentalist party, while the other, Charles Erdman, was more tolerant of diverse views within the church. William Jennings Bryan placed Macartney's name in nomination stating, "His election to the office of chief executive of our militant Church will be accepted as an announcement of the Church's unshaken adherence to the impregnable Rock of the Holy Scriptures."[1] The vote could hardly have been closer. Out of 910 ballots cast Macartney garnered 464; and Erdman, supported by moderates and modernists, won 446. Fundamentalists thereby won an important victory.[2]

Liberals, who had supported Erdman en masse, despaired at Macartney's victory. Henry Sloane Coffin, writing home to his wife, bewailed, "Here the dreaded worst has happened. On Bryan's nomination Macartney has been elected by a close majority." Nevertheless, Coffin and other liberals were determined not to give up without a struggle. "My fighting blood's up," he added, "and I am rather glad that the issue can be clearly drawn."[3] Of course, fundamentalists, too, wanted nothing more than to draw the lines as sharply as possible. As the battle came to a head, liberals, led by Henry Sloane Coffin, and fundamentalists, directed by Clarence Macartney, stood eye to eye, toe to toe. Both refused to budge. In such a situation, the moderate majority could not long remain neutral.

Clarence E. Macartney: Scion of Scottish Covenanters

Clarence Edward Noble Macartney had come to the Presbyterian Church by way of the Reformed Presbyterian Church, an offspring of the Scottish Covenanters. Macartney, who altered the spelling of his surname from that of his parents, was born in September 1879 in North-wood, Ohio to John L. and Catherine R. McCartney. At the time of Clarence's birth, John McCartney, then fifty-one, was pastor of the Reformed Presbyterian Church in Northwood and professor of Natural Science in Geneva College, a Reformed Presbyterian institution.[4] Having graduated from Jefferson College in 1851, John McCartney had worked as a teacher, editor, and professor before feeling the call to ministry. In 1856 he enrolled in the Reformed Presbyterian Theological Seminary in Allegheny, Pennsylvania and in 1858 set sail for Scotland to further his theological training.[5]

One Sabbath, while preaching in Rothesay on the Isle of Bute, John happened to spy a young woman by the name of Catherine Robertson sitting in the congregation.[6] Daughter of a wealthy mill owner, Catherine had been educated in Europe and possessed "a unique mixture of deep piety and refined secular taste."[7] The two met after worship, were immediately attracted to one another, and courted during John's stay in Scotland. Her father's opposition to his daughter's marrying a poor American pastor seemed to consign the relationship to inevitable defeat, however; and when John returned to Ohio in 1861, Catherine remained in Scotland. But the lovers were not to be denied. The obstacles of distance and time did not dull their affection for each other; and finally, in 1868, Catherine was allowed to marry her sweetheart of ten years.[8]

On her arrival in Northwood, Catherine Robertson McCartney stood in shock. Though the region had undoubtedly been described to her numerous times, she had no way of anticipating the primitive conditions of the American Midwest. As Clarence would relate years later, "the unpaved streets, the uncultivated manners of the people, the lack of servants—all this made Northwood a tremendous contrast to the beautiful and well-appointed home at Blairbeth in Scotland."[9] But Northwood was not without its redeeming qualities. Like Catherine, the Covenanters of the region took education and religion earnestly. Moreover, John McCartney built a house modeled after Catherine's Scottish home.[10] Nevertheless, it took years for Catherine to adjust to life in America.

Catherine dominated the McCartney's family life. A woman of high intellect, profound spirituality, and broad learning, she brought up her children in the fear of the Lord, teaching them to be diligent in prayer and Bible reading.[11] Not content to serve God by the Christian upbringing of her flock alone, Catherine encouraged other mothers through various pamphlets on childrearing. In a booklet entitled "A Word to Mothers," she advised her readers to protect their children from the evil influences of gossiping nurses and school playgrounds. Mothers, she wrote, should examine the books their children read, ensure modest and simple dress, and speak frankly with their sons and daughters. Promiscuous dancing and the use of tobacco and alcohol should be strictly prohibited, she warned, inasmuch as these led inevitably to "the swamps of impurity." Most important, mothers had to bring their children up in the Christian faith; only in the blood of the Lamb could boys and girls "wash and be clean."[12]

When Clarence was nine months old Geneva College was moved from Northwood to Beaver Falls, Pennsylvania to be more accessible to its Covenanter constituency. A bustling industrial town, Beaver Falls offered new opportunities for the college and the McCartney clan.[13] John and Catherine built a handsome fourteen-room home overlooking the Beaver River and bordering the college campus.[14] The pleasant surroundings, domestic help, and intellectual stimulation provided by Beaver Falls gave Catherine a new outlook on life.[15] Here she could raise her family with culture and piety. At last she began to settle into life in the new world.

The Reformed Presbyterian Church, to which John and Catherine belonged, was a small denomination opposed to oath taking, hymn singing, and secret societies. Important for the future course of Clarence Macartney's life was the church's strong opposition to church division, believing that "schism and sectarianism are sinful in themselves, and inimical to true religion."[16] Before the Civil War, the church's strident opposition to slavery had led many of its members, including John McCartney, to serve as conductors on the Underground Railroad.[17]

The most distinctive teaching of the Reformed Presbyterians, rooted in the controversies of the Scottish church, was their doctrine of "political dissent." Since the Constitution of the United States did not recognize God and Christianity, the Covenanters insisted, church members could not vote or serve in government office.[18] This conviction, however, had not stopped the Reformed Presbyterians from throwing their weight solidly behind the Union cause during the Southern rebellion. The church had vowed in 1862 to do all within its means to "promote the welfare of the nation, and sustain it in the conflict against the Southern Confederacy."[19]

After the war, Reformed Presbyterians took the lead in organizing the National Reform Association (NRA), a movement to christianize America.[20] Spurred especially by the increasing secularization of state and society in the late nineteenth century, the association sought to array "the friends of Christian government on the defensive against ... [the] aggressions of secularism."[21] Chief among the remedies proposed by the NRA was the adoption of a new preamble to the U.S. Constitution that would make the government explicitly Christian.[22] Additionally, the NRA worked to halt the spread of secular culture by encouraging legislation supporting Sabbath enforcement, religion in the schools, stricter divorce laws, and Prohibition.[23]

The NRA's efforts to build a Christian America garnered support from members of a number of denominations. Northern Presbyterians, Episcopalians, Congregationalists, and Methodists all donated their time and energy to the cause. Nonetheless, it was the church of John and Catherine McCartney that did most of the organization's legwork. Reformed Presbyterians edited the movement's journal, *The Christian Statesman*, developed most of its promotional material, and delivered numerous addresses at the annual conventions. David McAllister, a colleague of John McCartney at Geneva College, became a—if not the— leading spokesman of this effort to christianize the nation. Notably absent from this consortium of Christians were representatives of the Southern Presbyterian Church. As staunch advocates of the spirituality of the church, the forebears of J. Gresham Machen refused to participate in an effort that so blatantly mingled the affairs of church and state.[24]

The faith Clarence Macartney learned as a child thus consisted of strict Calvinist doctrine fortified by the message that true believers in America must strive mightily to make their country a Christian nation. Having helped rid the country of the scourge of slavery, it was now the task of the faithful to weave Christianity into the very fabric of government and society. Raised in the home of a Reformed Presbyterian minister beside the campus of the Reformed Presbyterian college, Clarence Macartney imbibed the faith of the Scottish Covenanters for the first fifteen years of his life.

The McCartney family began and ended each day with prayer at the family altar. The morning of the Lord's day was, of course, devoted to worship at the Beaver Falls Covenanter Church, while Sabbath afternoons often found Catherine reading Bible stories to her children at home or out-of-doors. Although by tradition Covenanters sang only the Psalms, Catherine would sometimes break with convention and lead her children in some favorite hymns. As the children went off to school, their mother offered them a Bible verse to guide them along life's way.[25] In Clarence's eleventh year his pious upbringing bore fruit and he joined the church.[26] Though his adherence to Christianity would be sorely tested later in life, Macartney's mature thought mirrored the faith of his parents, in devotion both to the Westminster theology and to the quest for a Christian America.

In Beaver Falls the McCartneys enjoyed a comfortable and cultured life.[27] The children played in the family's orchard and on the college campus. In the winter they skated on the Beaver River; in the summer they enjoyed boating, swimming, and duck hunting; and every autumn the family would make excursions to surrounding farms to pick nuts.[28] At Christmas John McCartney bundled up the children and took them on a sleigh ride to cut a Christmas tree. The family would place their evergreen in the drawing room, decorate it with candles, and "romp" (though never dance) around their yuletide decoration.[29]

Clarence received his formal education at various public and private schools in the vicinity of Beaver Falls.[30] Seemingly as important as this classroom instruction was the less-structured learning that took place at home and at the college. The future pastor attended the speeches, debates, and concerts offered at Geneva College and plundered his father's library for literary entertainment. Additionally, Catherine McCartney frequently took her offspring on nature hikes and instructed them in the wonders of botany.[31]

The McCartneys spent fourteen happy years in Beaver Falls. But by 1894 John McCartney's deteriorating health forced the family to move to a more favorable clime. In September 1894 they packed their belongings and headed west on a journey that would broaden Clarence's intellectual, theological, and cultural horizons. The family settled in Redlands, California for a year before moving on to Claremont to take advantage of Pomona College. At Redlands High School and Pomona Preparatory School Clarence's coursework included Latin, Greek, mathematics, English, modern languages, science, and rhetoric.[32] There is evidence that although, as seen, Macartney later rejected the theory of biological evolution, he accepted it without difficulty at this juncture of his life.[33] Outside of the classroom Clarence enjoyed baseball, football, basketball, track, and mountain climbing. Separated from a close-knit community of Covenanters, the McCartney's worshiped with Presbyterians, thereby becoming familiar with the wider Reformed community in America.[34]

Though the McCartney clan enjoyed California, it provided no relief for John McCartney's respiratory problems, and so in 1896 the family moved again, this time to the higher altitude of Denver. Clarence, only a year shy of high school graduation, opted to remain in Claremont to finish his course at Pomona and followed his family to Colorado in 1897. He matriculated at the University of Denver but studied there for only one year before his parents, unhappy with life in the mountains, decided to pack their bags once more.[35]

By 1898 the two eldest McCartney sons, Robertson and Ernest, were pastors of Presbyterian churches in Wisconsin. Aware of their parents' discontent with Denver, they recommended Madison as a possible home. Not only would such a move reunite the family, they held, but the University of Wisconsin could supply Albert and Clarence with a superior college education.[36] The family was convinced and headed back east.

Despite a streak of shyness that Macartney manifested throughout his life, he pledged the Beta Theta Pi fraternity and became an accomplished member of the Athena Debating Society at Wisconsin.[37] When preparing for a major oratorical contest, he solicited the help—and earned the admiration—of the future senator, Robert M. LaFollette.[38] Macartney chose not to pursue his interest in history, majoring instead in English literature, and graduated from the university in 1901.[39]

During these years of pilgrimage the religious life of the McCartneys in general, and Clarence in particular, was eclectic at best. The family, which had not been consistently connected with any particular church since leaving Beaver Falls, was later described by Clarence's sister as "neither fully convinced Covenanters, nor Methodists, nor Presbyterians." Along the way Clarence had drifted slowly from the orthodox moorings of his early upbringing. In obedience to family tradition he practiced "the outward forms of religion." But, his sister observed, "to an outsider there was no evidence of a deep emotional experience." "The trend of thought at both Pomona and Wisconsin," she related, "while not anti-religious, was decidedly not rigorously orthodox." Clarence's move away from the orthodox faith, initiated at Pomona, gained momentum during his studies at the University of Wisconsin.[40] Though he affiliated with Christ Presbyterian Church in Madison, Clarence frequently attended a local Congregationalist church, whose minister possessed "decidedly advanced views."[41] By the time of his graduation, Macartney's move to the religious Left had reached its furthest extreme. He was struggling with questions of the verity of the faith and found the idea of following his three brothers into the ministry, at the very least, problematic.[42]

Adrift on the sea of vocational and theological indecision, upon graduation Clarence returned home to Beaver Falls to sort out his thoughts.[43] In the fall of 1901 he headed for Harvard to pursue graduate work but on his arrival in Cambridge thought better of this plan and decided to travel in Europe. He boarded a steamer to Liverpool and spent the remainder of the year wandering through Scotland, England, and France. When he returned stateside, he stopped off at Princeton to visit his brother Albert, who was a student at the seminary, before landing once more in Beaver Falls. Unable to secure a teaching position, Clarence took a job with the *Beaver Times* and tried his hand at reporting.[44]

Clarence's tenure as a journalist was short-lived, for by the fall of 1902 he was on the road again, this time to Connecticut to enroll at Yale Divinity School. Though this move indicated his resolve at least to explore the pastorate as a vocation, Clarence had yet to determine his theological identity.[45] Years later he wrote, with marked understatement, that he went to Yale, "partly, perhaps, because my brother was already at Princeton and partly because of a degree of something akin to revolt against the orthodox position."[46] But his revolt against the faith of his boyhood had nearly run its course; after one class Clarence abandoned the halls of Yale and crossed the Hudson to join his brother at Princeton Seminary.[47] At Princeton Clarence resolved whatever religious questions remained. In the words of his sister, "Gradually the peace of the cloisters entered his troubled spirit. The study of the Scriptures under wise guidance restored the faith which the University had nearly wrecked. The comradeship he needed was found with congenial associates; and best of all, the close relationship of early days between the two brothers was renewed. He was home at last."[48]

Concurrent with Macartney's arrival at Princeton, a young Southerner by the name of J. Gresham Machen, himself plagued by theological and vocational doubts, also arrived at the seminary to test its theological waters. The similarity of the struggles Machen and Macartney endured is striking. Both men were raised in devout Calvinist homes, both experienced profound vocational and theological crises in their postcollege years, and both eventually became adopted sons of Princeton and ardent defenders of the faith. Machen's militant defense of the Princeton tradition stemmed, at least in part, from the intense theological and cultural battles he had waged to reach his convictions. The personal struggle he endured in coming to his beliefs made him all the more adamant in his defense of Princeton orthodoxy in the course of the Presbyterian controversy.

Macartney's period of religious and vocational indecision seems to have played a similar role in his life. Having breathed the liberal atmosphere of Pomona and Wisconsin, he developed serious questions about the validity of Reformed orthodoxy. Compounding these doubts was his career indecision, reflected in his anxious geographical wanderings. The faith Macartney learned as a child had been severely undermined at Wisconsin, and only a year of deep searching brought him to the place where he could embark on seminary education at Princeton. Like Machen, the price Macartney paid in coming to his convictions made him that much more strident in defending those beliefs in the 1920s.

Despite the similarities between the personal battles of these two young men, Macartney's struggle lacked the intensity and extent of the crisis Machen endured. Compared to his Southern comrade, Macartney resolved his difficulties rather quickly. At least part of this difference, it seems, can be attributed to the different context of each man's battle. The liberalism Macartney was exposed to in America was, by all accounts, of a less radical variety than that Machen met in Germany under Herrmann. The lines between orthodoxy and liberalism were thus not as stark for Macartney as for Machen and the struggle, therefore, less intense. Added to this difference was the question of culture. The secularism of the culture Machen had seen in Germany, particularly against the backdrop of his Southern upbringing, was decidedly more pronounced than that Macartney knew in the Northern United States. The worries of the National Reform Association notwithstanding, turn-of-the-century America still had the distinct aura of a Christian nation. The cultural concerns that impinged on Machen's struggle were, therefore, much less conspicuous for Macartney. Though Macartney's bout with liberalism was clearly important to his development, the arena in which he fought that battle allowed him to resolve his difficulties with a greater facility than Machen would know. One suspects that inasmuch as Macartney's personal crisis over liberal religion was not as deep as Machen's, he perceived the conflict in the church in the 1920s and 1930s in slightly less radical tones than did his Southern colleague. This may help to explain Macartney's more moderate stance in the church controversy of the 1930s.

Macartney was impressed by several of the Princeton faculty, B. B. Warfield, Francis Patton, and Robert Dick Wilson among others. None, apparently, had a greater impact on Macartney than an instructor in church history named Frederick Loetscher. "Dr. Loetscher," Macartney later recalled, "did more than any other to open for me the thrill, romance and majesty of the long history of the Christian Church. This proved to be of the highest importance for me in my work as a minister."[49] Loetscher, who had served as a pastor and professor of homiletics at Princeton before assuming the chair of church history, played a moderating role during the church fights of the 1920s.[50] He maintained a powerful influence over Macartney throughout the latter's career. In 1925, when Macartney was offered the chair of apologetics and Christian ethics at Princeton, Loetscher successfully advised Macartney to remain in the pastorate, and in 1952 Loetscher preached at Macartney's twenty-five-year anniversary celebration at First Presbyterian Church, Pittsburgh.[51]

Macartney's concerns, like Loetscher's, revolved around the two hubs of preaching and history. Before turning to the ministry, Macartney had seriously considered pursuing a career as a professor of history,[52] but having decided on a clerical calling, he devoted most of his energy to preaching. Nevertheless, he became an accomplished historian and used his love of history to enhance his ministry. Macartney cultivated the art of biographical preaching—telling the personal histories of biblical characters—and published dozens of sermons on the men and women of the Bible.[53] Inspired, no doubt, by the strong abolitionist views of his Covenanter forebears, Macartney also developed a keen interest in the Civil War, visiting many of its battlefields and writing numerous studies of the war.[54] Additionally, Macartney made "following the footsteps of the Apostle Paul" a lifelong project and, in fifteen trips to the Near East, succeeded in tracing most of Paul's journeys.[55]

Though Macartney was a diligent student at Princeton, his days were not filled with uninterrupted study. Occasionally he took trips to New York's museums, galleries, and concert halls.[56] In the summers he supplied a small church in Prairie du Sac, Wisconsin, where he developed the discipline of preaching without notes. Amidst the rolling hills of Wisconsin he received a valuable complement to the scholastic training he received at Princeton. "There," he later wrote, "I came in close touch with the joys, the trials, the sorrows, and the beautiful affections of the common people. There I heard, and have never forgotten, the deep, glad, sad, sweet music of the human heart."[57]

As noted, Macartney's ties to the Covenanter Church had suffered serious erosion since early adolescence. The McCartneys' travels in the 1890s had exposed them to a wide range of ecclesiastical traditions, and Clarence's three older brothers had all left the Covenanter fellowship to become pastors in the larger Presbyterian Church. Clarence himself had joined the local Presbyterian Church in Wisconsin, opted to attend the flagship Presbyterian seminary in the nation, and in 1904 affiliated with the Princeton Presbyterian Church in Philadelphia.[58] It was certainly no surprise that on graduation from Princeton in 1905 he sought ordination in the Presbyterian Church in the U.S.A.

In October 1905 the Presbytery of Jersey City ordained Macartney to the pastorate of the First Presbyterian Church of Paterson, New Jersey. A downtown congregation in a city of 120,000, the church had been struggling for a number of years. In time, Macartney's energetic and imaginative leadership reversed this trend and the congregation began to flourish. Following the tradition of the Reformed Presbyterian

Church, he became an outspoken advocate of Prohibition, even attending hearings before the state legislature.[59]

During his pastorate in Paterson, Macartney received numerous calls to other churches.[60] Not until 1914, though, when the Arch Street Presbyterian Church in Philadelphia offered him their pulpit, did he decide to move. Charles R. Erdman, who would be his opponent in the 1924 moderatorial contest, preached the installation sermon.[61] Like his previous pastorate, the Arch Street Church was located in a deteriorating neighborhood and suffered from declining attendance. The congregation still boasted a number of wealthy members, though; and after Macartney's arrival the church started to show signs of new life. The sanctuary was completely redecorated and a new pipe organ installed. Macartney made a special effort to attract students from the surrounding medical schools and in time began broadcasting sermons on the radio.[62] He renewed his ties with Princeton, delivering weekly lectures on homiletics, and eventually earned a reputation as "Philadelphia's foremost preacher."[63]

Unlike many of his ministerial colleagues, Macartney did not serve as a chaplain during World War I. Even so, he was deeply influenced by the war. The Allied victory, he insisted, was a magnificent vindication of the cause of righteousness. "The most 'monstrous assault' upon the freedom of the world and the majesty of God we have seen meet with disaster and engulfed in overwhelming defeat and judgment," he proclaimed. "We know now that the stars in their courses fought against Germany."[64] But the outcome of the war was not all glory. Macartney perceived ominous religious changes in the wake of the conflict. Most particularly, he was concerned by a tendency among American soldiers to view their sufferings on the battlefield as ample atonement for their sins. Such a belief, Macartney asserted, was flatly un-Christian and needed to be staunchly opposed.[65]

Macartney's stance led to a minor confrontation with Harry Fosdick in 1919. Fosdick, in an analysis of the war entitled "The Trenches and the Church at Home," warned that soldiers, having experienced the ravages of war, would never accept the traditional doctrines and mores of yesterday's Christianity. The church therefore needed to adjust its doctrines to the spirit of the age.[66] Macartney absolutely refused to subscribe to this logic. In a response published in *The Presbyterian* he claimed that despite the crisis of the war Christian truth held firm. He wrote,

If men like Dr. Fosdick have ceased to feel the grip of Christian truth, we shall be sorry because of that fact; we regret their falling out of the ranks. But when they call upon the church to reform herself by abandoning all that is distinctively Christian in her teaching, and put this demand of their own into the mouth of lads returning home from the battlefields of Europe, it is the privilege and the duty of those who love the church and would be loyal to their Master to let men know what they think and feel.[67]

In the coming years Macartney did not hesitate to let the church know what he thought and felt. Though he became ever more vocal in his opposition to liberalism, not until he came forward to lead the conservative response to Fosdick in 1922 did he attain national recognition. By then he was convinced that Christianity was in greater peril "than ever before in its long history."[68] A dignified and gracious pastor of impeccable conservative pedigree, Macartney seemed just the man to direct the fundamentalist counteroffensive at the 1924 assembly.

The Theology of Clarence Macartney

Though Clarence Macartney had memorized and accepted the faith of the Westminster Catechism as a boy, it was at Princeton, after his crisis of faith, that he arrived at a final conviction regarding the truth of Reformed orthodoxy. In the course of his career, Macartney published numerous books, most of them collections of sermons, that testify eloquently to his faith.

Like Machen, Macartney, in adopting the Princeton tradition, accepted not simply the theology of the Westminster divines but the epistemology of Scottish Common Sense Realism and the Baconian method as well. Truth, to Macartney, was concrete and eternal. "Any truth spoken in one age," he maintained, "is applicable to man in every age, and truth spoken in one age will still be truth in every other age."[69] The "teachings of Jesus" were "not subject to the limitations of any one period, or any age" but suited every era.[70] Truth, however, was not simply propositional; it was to be lived as Christ lived God's truth.[71] "We get into the habit," Macartney declared, "of thinking of Christianity as a grand proposition; but the true grandeur of Christianity, its never-failing and tragic interest, is its conquest over the enemies of men's souls and its bringing them up out of the land of bondage."[72] With Machen, Macartney insisted that Christianity was neither a life nor a doctrine but a life founded upon doctrine.

Of course, the Bible was the chief repository of religious truth. Macartney fully accepted the Princeton doctrine of Scripture. In 1924 he approvingly noted the stance adopted by the 1923 General Assembly:

the General Assembly "did not declare that every extant copy and version of the Scripture is without error, but 'that the Holy Spirit did so inspire, guide and move the writers of the Holy Scriptures as to keep them free from error.' Not that all scribes and copyists were kept from every slightest error, but that the original writers were so kept, and that the original autographs of the Scriptures were without error."[73] With the Princeton theologians he maintained that this teaching had been the general doctrine of the church through history. While Macartney insisted that the truth of Christianity did not depend on the inspiration of the Scriptures, the faith did rest upon the Bible's accuracy. "The Bible is true and credible," he wrote, "the great acts and words of God therein recorded are true. This is a foundation belief of the Christian religion. Ultimately Christianity stands or falls with the truth or falsehood of the Bible."[74]

The Bible was inspired by God in three different senses. First, God guided "the narration of facts" to be related; second, the Holy Spirit worked on the minds of the authors to elevate their thought; and finally, God suggested the predictions of the Bible to the minds of the prophets.[75] As the inspired and inerrant word of God, the Scriptures were the ultimate religious authority and the ground of all preaching. Unlike Coffin, who demanded that sermons be rooted in personal religious experience, Macartney claimed that throughout history the church had dared to speak only on the ground "that it possessed and declared the Word of the Living God."[76]

The God revealed in Scripture was, above all, sovereign and transcendent. In a personal declaration of faith Macartney wrote, "I believe in Almighty God, Who created all things, and Who by his wise and just providence rules all men and nations, and is infinite in His being, wisdom, power, holiness, justice, goodness, and truth."[77] He subscribed to the traditional Calvinistic understanding of providence and predestination, holding that "the decrees of God are His eternal purpose, whereby for His own glory He hath foreordained whatsoever cometh to pass." Closely tied to this was a view of life as a period of probation; that is, he believed that "life here is not a cruise of selfish pleasure nor a desperate leap in the dark, but a wise and beneficent probation where all things work together for our good, and where with fear and trembling we are to work out the secrets of our predestination."[78]

Macartney's Christology focused on the virgin birth, the crucifixion, and the bodily resurrection of Christ. The virgin birth, he held, was a fundamental doctrine of Christianity not only because the Bible recorded it as an historical fact but because Christ's divinity rested on this fact.[79]

Nevertheless, it was Christ's substitutionary atonement on the cross rather than his birth that stood at the center of the Christian faith.[80] The cross of Christ, he insisted, was not "a part of our salvation . . . but it is *the* gospel, without which there is no gospel."[81] Here, on the doctrine of the atonement, Macartney found modernism's greatest apostasy. He protested,

> Use terms as loosely as they may, they who now pride themselves as liberals and modernists will have great difficulty in persuading any one that they really accept and believe and preach the Christianity which must be defined as the "revelation of a way of salvation from sin through the incarnation and blood-shedding of the Son of God." Their Christianity is a Christianity of ethics, of ideals, of development, of inspiration, of education; and not a Christianity which stands or falls with one grand redemptive act by Jesus Christ.[82]

Macartney never tired of claiming that the "empty grave is the cradle of the church."[83] Easter confirmed the message of the forgiveness bought by the cross. It was "the great proof and seal that Christ died for our sins, and that he has overcome the power of sin in human life."[84] The evidence for the resurrection lay not only in Jesus' repeated predictions of his rising and the testimony of the apostles but also "upon the impossibility of accounting for the belief in the resurrection in any other way than on the ground of the *fact* of the resurrection."[85]

Like his friend Bryan, Macartney emphasized the salutary effect of belief in the afterlife on morals. In a work entitled *Putting on Immortality* he alleged that "one of the greatest calamities which could befall the human race would be a serious decline in faith in the life after death. Such a decline would destroy one of the great motives for moral living."[86] Indeed, in 1940 he echoed Bryan's language writing, "Belief in a future destiny is the mainspring of the moral government of God. It is this conviction which gives dignity to human nature, and . . . gives a meaning and purpose to our life."[87]

This concern for right living points to the Northern evangelical strain running throughout Macartney's thought. Wedded to his Old School emphasis on doctrine was a deep passion for moral reform and Christian civilization derived largely from his Reformed Presbyterian heritage. Reformed Presbyterians had not only been strong abolitionists and the major backers of the National Reform Association's effort to christianize America, but worked diligently in support of poor relief, temperance, and labor reform.[88]

Macartney's adherence to the cultural tradition of the Reformed Pres-

byterians appears nowhere more clearly than in his interest in and interpretation of the Civil War. In his statements about the war Macartney
demonstrated a deep commitment to the "holy purpose" of the Union
cause.[89] Though Clarence abandoned the Reformed Presbyterian prohibition on voting, a letter to his parents in 1900 must have made his
father swell with pride. "I expect to vote the Republican ticket," he
wrote. "The choice of one's political party is a serious matter. I think
that I have chosen the right one: the party which came into being that
slavery might be abolished, and which, ever since, has stood for the
best government, *the truest* liberty, and the highest statesmanship."[90]
As if to reinforce these sentiments, Macartney kept a picture of Lincoln's
birthplace in his church study.[91]

Amplifying Macartney's adherence to the social vision of his parents'
faith was his appreciation of the broader tradition of Northern revivalism. In a sermon to the 1926 General Assembly Macartney declared,

> The great service of the Church to a nation is not its witness in council
> or battlefield, nor its contribution to education, but what it does for the
> moral and spiritual life of the people. The greatest event in the religious
> history of America was the Great Awakening in the middle of the eigh-
> teenth century and the Great Revival of the first decade of the nineteenth
> century. . . . [The Great Awakening] split churches, as did the later revival,
> but it left behind it, as did the second revival, something more important
> than organic unity—a love for Christ and consuming zeal for his kingdom.[92]

The revivals, especially the Second Great Awakening, not only brought
the message of salvation to individuals but redeemed American civilization and inspired a passion for moral reform. Macartney waxed eloquent about the inevitable results of the Great Revival:

> Ere long the flames began to subside. *But a mighty work had been done,
> never to be undone. The nation was saved from barbarism and irreligion,
> and the Church from apostasy and unbelief.* Instead of a godless, mater-
> ialistic civilization being built up in the east and the southwest, there was
> founded a civilization which with all its crudities and shortcomings, was
> rich in the fear of God, the only solid foundation of those nations which
> endure. *Those great movements of grace gave the Churches the study of
> the Bible, the prayer-meeting and the evangelistic meetings. There was born
> the missionary movement, the agitation against slavery, and the temperance
> reform.* "It wrought in fact a social revolution, whose extent is hidden
> from us by the fact that we have always lived among its results and do
> not realize with what a price they were bought for us."[93]

This concern for moral reform and for the preservation of Christian
civilization, rooted in the Northern evangelical tradition in general and

in Macartney's Reformed Presbyterian heritage in particular, determined, in large part, Macartney's response to the cultural crisis of the
1920s and his role in the Presbyterian controversy.[94]

Preserving a Christian America: The Social Thought of Clarence Macartney

In 1924 Macartney, echoing the concerns of William Jennings Bryan,
warned of the increasing apostasy not only of America but of all of
Western civilization. He wrote,

> Today the Christian theory of life is menaced by what may be called a
> world-wide revival of paganism. Man is taught to exalt himself instead of
> to humble himself, to gratify himself instead of to deny himself. God the
> Creator, the immortal soul of man, his responsibility to God, principles
> of the spiritual kingdom, the unseen life and the life after death with its
> rewards and punishments, all these have commenced to fade from the
> horizon of human thought. The light of the soul burns low and the influ-
> ence of the unseen world becomes fainter and fainter, as our civilization
> drifts towards paganism again.[95]

Convinced that the future of his nation was intimately connected with
the future of his faith, Macartney worried about the soul of America.
His country was, he believed, the greatest nation in the world; but she
was faltering in her mission.[96] In a 1927 Memorial Day address he
cataloged the decline of morality brought on by the encroachments of
secularization. Widespread murder, rampant divorce, the decline of
family religion, rising hemlines, blatant hedonism, and apostate preachers all signaled a seriously diseased society.[97]

Many of Macartney's fears centered on the decline of the Christian
home. "The home," he believed, was "the most important school, the
most important church, the most important club or organization."[98] He
warned his congregation that unless America's homes were "reclaimed
for God" the "spiritual fibre of the Church and the moral fibre of the
nation" would inevitably weaken.[99] But the Christian understanding of
the home as "the cradle of the race and the nation, the nursery of virtue
and piety" was crumbling under the secular onslaught that viewed the
home as "a place of convenience and indulgence."[100] All of the programs, studies, and movements the church might initiate could never
substitute for the role of God-fearing parents who "in the home and in
the presence of their children, pray for their eternal salvation."[101] The

home had to march beside the church if the gospel was to permeate the culture.

Macartney focused his concern for the family most intensely on the issue of divorce. In response to the skyrocketing divorce rates of the early twentieth century, he authored an overture on divorce that the Philadelphia Presbytery sent to the 1921 General Assembly. The memorial, which eventually failed, would have prohibited any Presbyterian minister from marrying a divorced person "save the innocent party where the decree has been granted upon the grounds of adultery."[102] Macartney held devoutly to a belief in a fundamental moral law that undergirded all of life.[103] Divorce violated that law and therefore led inexorably to "national decline and decay."[104] In 1929 he described the grave situation:

> Divorce is now competing with death as a dissolver of marriages in the United States of America. Almost one out of every six marriages ends in the divorce courts. With the home crumbling before our eyes and the very foundations of our social structure being undermined and destroyed, all favorable trade reports, all rejoicing over economic prosperity, and all self-congratulation upon our vast educational system is like the sound of cheerful music as the funeral procession wends its way to the grave.[105]

Macartney was not alone in this concern over the dissolution of the Christian family. As we have seen, liberals like Henry Sloane Coffin, though perhaps not as adamant about the biblical basis of lifelong commitment, also expressed dismay over the increase in divorce. In 1926, in response to an overture from Butler Presbytery, the General Assembly formed a Special Committee on Marriage and Divorce to study the problem. A surprising number of the leading protagonists in the Presbyterian controversy were involved in the workings of this group. Clarence Macartney, Charles Erdman, and Robert Speer sat on it; and J. Gresham Machen wrote two extensive letters to Speer, advising him on the matter of divorce.[106]

In 1926 the Presbyterian Church recognized adultery and desertion as legitimate grounds for divorce. Macartney believed that the biblical witness did not permit divorce for desertion and therefore supported a change in the church constitution sanctioning divorce on the grounds of adultery alone and remarriage solely for the innocent victim of adultery.[107] In a paper entitled "The Teaching of the New Testament on Divorce," Macartney insisted that monogamy was God's will.[108] He buttressed his biblical argument with a natural theology, maintaining, "If either polygamy or polyandry had been the divine plan, the number of men and women of the race would have been proportionately smaller or greater. But the practical numerical equality of the sexes fits in with the plan of monogamy." He concluded, "If Christ sanctioned divorce at all, it was only for *one* cause, infidelity. . . . Our own country and the whole world needs the knowledge of the law as declared by Jesus Christ."[109]

Robert Speer, who served as secretary of the Board of Foreign Missions and who would be elected moderator of the General Assembly in 1927, possessed views similar to Macartney's.[110] In a letter to his close friend Charles Erdman, Speer summarized his beliefs. "The more I think about the matter and study the New Testament carefully," he wrote, "the clearer it seems to me that [its] unmistakable teaching is—(1) That there can be no divorce except for adultery. (2) That where one of the parties is an unbeliever there may be separation but without divorce or remarriage of either party."[111] The "indestructability of the marriage relationship," Speer maintained, was "the greatest social need" of his day.[112]

Speer, who, like Macartney, developed a brief paper on divorce and remarriage for the special committee, solicited Machen's help on the topic in the summer of 1928. Machen lacked the intense concern over this issue manifested by Macartney, Erdman, and Speer and in fact held a much more tentative—some might even say, liberal—view on the biblical grounds for divorce. While Macartney, Erdman, and Speer all believed that adultery was the only biblical basis for divorce, Machen maintained that though he was undecided on the matter, there seemed to be some biblical warrant for allowing divorce in the case of desertion.[113] In a passage reflecting his concern for individual liberty Machen wrote,

> At any rate it is here that the crucial question is to be found: Do the Gospel passages contemplate the case where one party to the marriage has deserted the other; and if not, does such desertion constitute such a destruction of the marriage relationship as that, as in the case of adultery, the remarriage of the innocent party is permitted?
> The question is not settled with perfect clearness, it seems to me, in I Cor. vii.10,11. . . . I do not, with my present light, feel able to answer this question.[114]

The church, like Machen, hesitated to change church law on this issue. Though the assembly committee recommended that the Confession of Faith be altered to state that adultery was the only proper ground for divorce, the presbyteries refused to concur.[115]

The lineup in this episode sheds some further light on the eventual outcome of the Presbyterian controversy. Though in different ways and to different degrees, Macartney, Erdman, and Speer were all heirs to the Northern evangelical concern for the moral welfare of the nation. It was no great surprise, therefore, to find all three addressing the dramatic postwar increase in divorce by advocating reform of the church's law governing divorce. On the other hand, Machen's single-minded emphasis on doctrine above all else meant that family issues such as divorce simply did not appear on his agenda. When pushed to address the question of divorce by Speer, Machen's Southern libertarianism seemed to play as great a part in his response as any strict reading of the Scriptures. He did not want to constrict the personal freedom of church members if there was any question at all about the Scripture's allowance of desertion as a legitimate ground for divorce. In his avoidance of questions of moral reform, his pursuit of pure doctrine alone as a means of influencing culture, and his Southern emphasis on personal liberty, Machen was odd man out. Similarly, Machen's uncompromising defense of doctrine and his Southern passion for individual liberty and principle would place him practically alone at the end of the Presbyterian conflict.

The 1929 assembly, in response to the church's refusal to alter divorce regulations, formed a commission to study marriage, divorce, and remarriage which brought yet another concern of Macartney to the fore: birth control.[116] In an article responding to a report of the 1929 commission Macartney lambasted those who condoned contraception, claiming that birth control violated "the laws of natural morality." To Macartney the use of contraceptives was a pagan practice that had no place in the Christian home. "There is no law requiring people to have a large family, or any family at all," he wrote. "But when Protestant ministers step in and begin to recommend the ill-favored doctrines of Birth Control, things have come to a sorry pass." In a passage reflecting his blend of Old School devotion to doctrine and evangelical commitment to moral reform, Macartney linked lax theology and lax ethics, claiming, "Presbyterians will not fail to note that of the ministerial members of this commission, two, the chairman and the secretary, or editor, signed the iniquitous Auburn Affirmation of 1924. . . . Where loose doctrine prevails, dangerous ethical teaching is sure to follow."[117]

Macartney's ethical concerns were not focused simply on family life. In the 1920s he also expressed alarm over the increasing secularization of higher education. He thought the state universities, which completely ignored Christianity, less harmful than church-related schools that adapted the Christian faith to the spirit of the age.[118] Recognizing the import of the colleges as nurseries of ecclesiastical leadership, Macartney warned, "If our Christian colleges are permitted to sink into the morass of secularism and materialism, then woe to the Church."[119]

Macartney's alarm over the secularization of Christian colleges was mirrored in his concern about the un-Christian mores exhibited in modern books and movies. He contended, "The immersing of the minds of the new generation in sex problems and erotic scenes, which mark a great part of the popular literature of the day and almost all the theatre and moving pictures, can have but one effect upon the life of the people, and that is the lowering of moral standards and the weakening of moral fiber."[120] He condemned motion pictures as "one of the most dangerous and powerful attacks on the Christian way of life" and supported his charges with figures from a study of criminals and delinquents which claimed that "25 percent of 117 delinquent girls in the State Training Schools said that the moving pictures were the direct cause of their downfall." The influence of lewd books and movies, if left unchecked, would only undo the advances of civilization. Just as the downfall of home religion boded no good, so, Macartney warned, "there is no good reason for believing that the unchecked spread of anti-Christian principles and the abandonment of Christian morals will do anything else than plunge the world back again into that abyss out of which Christianity once lifted it."[121]

Another social issue that occupied Macartney's time was Prohibition; and here, as on the question of divorce, Macartney found himself in closer agreement with Speer and Erdman than with Machen. Throughout his career Macartney was a vocal supporter of temperance legislation. Alcohol, he contended, was a major cause of crime, a menace to public health, and a drain on the economy.[122] The liquor traffic was "Public Enemy No. 1."[123] Abstinence, therefore, was the only proper Christian response.[124] The passion of Macartney on this issue was revealed in his response to an invitation to an antiProhibition rally in 1921. He declared, "I would as soon attend a meeting the purpose of which was to support an organization for the corruption of youth, the spoliation of womanhood, the debauching of manhood and the robbing of widows and orphans[?]." In marked contrast to Machen, who opposed Prohibition on the grounds of individual freedom, Macartney sneered to the anti-Prohibitionists, "The object of your association is bad enough, but that it should be carried out under the guise of defending human liberty is unspeakable. What is the 'personal liberty' of dress suit cynics and club loungers compared with the peace and happiness of the great number of the people?" He concluded,

> I have seen too much of the ravages of strong drink and sought to help too many men who had been cursed by it and heal too many hearts that had been broken by it and buried too many who had been slain by it to be misled by this childish talk of personal liberty infringed and drinking increased during the regime of prohibition. You must ask some other, someone besides me, to sit on the stage at your meeting and become a co-conspirator in this odious attempt to bring back the liquor traffic and loose its legion of cruel and defiling devils upon the citizens of our country.[125]

Concern over the decline of the Sabbath filled out Macartney's social agenda. The Sabbath was a gift of God to humanity that was "infixed in the creative order of the universe, inscribed on the heavens and on the earth." It was not simply a ruling for individuals but "God's voice to the Nation," "a chief bulwark and defense of the Republic." He lamented the fact that America, "which owes so much of its moral character to the Christian Sabbath, has invaded its sacred territory with business and pleasure."[126] The Sabbath, he claimed in 1925, "the mainspring of the moral government of God," was "fading and declining, and even in the homes of the ministers themselves." "Here, again," he asserted, "the Church has suffered incalculable loss. This loss is felt in every branch of the life and work of the Church, and nowhere more than in the spiritual influence of the Church."[127]

Ultimately, a decrease in religious zeal lay at the root of all of these difficulties. In 1935 Macartney wrote an open letter to Franklin D. Roosevelt in which he made clear his belief that social reform alone would never solve the increasingly complex problems besetting the nation. Rather, the only true solution to the skyrocketing divorce rate, rampant murder, and despair brought on by strong drink was a rebirth of the "fear of God" in the nation.[128]

Macartney's actions in the Presbyterian controversy were motivated first and foremost by the modernist threat to Reformed orthodoxy. If the theology of Coffin and other liberals in the church was allowed to prevail, he believed, it would destroy the historic witness of the church. But Macartney's fear of the rise of modernism was aggravated by the vast changes that transformed American society after 1920. For Macartney, American civilization was founded on the truths of orthodox Christianity. The concurrent rise of modernistic theology and the decline of morality in America was proof positive of the deleterious effects of liberal religion. The struggle against modernism was, therefore, a battle for both the future of Christianity and a Christian America. In his passion to defend Reformed orthodox doctrine Macartney showed a marked similarity to Machen. He had adopted the Princeton Theology as his own and looked on the Westminster Confession as the greatest of the Protestant statements of faith.[129] But in his concern for the preservation of American Christian civilization through evangelism and social reform—not simply through doctrinal defense—Macartney manifested much greater closeness to those influenced by the culturally dominant tradition of Northern evangelicalism, such as Charles Erdman. In the end, Macartney and Erdman would remain in one church, with Machen on the outside.

One final concern that influenced Macartney's path in the Presbyterian controversy was his deeply held conviction about the optimum use of opportunity. Macartney's most famous sermon, "Come before Winter," dwelt on the importance of using every moment of life for the utmost good.[130] In the course of his ministry Macartney repeatedly told a story about a conversation he had once had with William Jennings Bryan on the topic of opportunity. He related,

> Some years before his death, I was driving across Chicago with the late William Jennings Bryan. On our way we passed near the Coliseum where he delivered the great speech at the Democratic Convention of 1896, the speech which made him three times the candidate of his party for the Presidency. . . . I said to him, "Mr. Bryan, I suppose many times before you had made just as able a speech as that, and it was never heard of?" "Yes," he said, "I suppose that was true. But that Convention was my opportunity and I made the most of it." Then he was silent. . . . After a moment, he broke the silence with these words; "And that's about all we do in this world—lose or use our opportunity."
> Great is your opportunity! May God give you grace to use it, and not lose it, for the welfare of your country, for the good of mankind, and for the glory of God.[131]

Having been raised in a small denomination, Macartney knew firsthand the limited impact smaller churches could have on the culture.[132] When, in 1936, Machen and others opted to leave the Presbyterian Church in the U.S.A., Macartney remained to exploit his opportunities there.

Every bit as dedicated to the preservation of Reformed orthodoxy as Machen, Macartney's concern for the maintenance of Christian civilization through evangelism and moral reform, his dedication to the maximum use of opportunity, and the aversion to schism of his Reformed Presbyterian heritage all would help to inspire his break with Machen in the 1930s. Such divisions lay far in the future, however. In 1924 the fundamentalist forces possessed impressive unity and strength, and the 1924 assembly gave them a prime opportunity to exercise their power. Macartney would not miss his chance to influence the history of the church.

The 1924 General Assembly

Having captured the moderatorship, Macartney and his allies set out to redeem the denomination from liberal influences. Macartney named Bryan to the position of vice-moderator and placed conservative clergy at the head of every committee. As propriety demanded, the defeated moderatorial candidate, Charles Erdman, was offered the chair of a noncontroversial committee, which happened to be Home Missions.[133] The assembly was tense throughout. Coffin, in the thick of the fight, saw little hope for reconciliation. He wrote to his wife, "Personally, I now think that the church will be split.—It may not; but only a miracle can save it."[134]

Though the assembly clearly leaned to the Right, its decisions on controversial matters were overwhelmingly moderate. As it turned out, Coffin's prediction was far too extreme. Despite the fact that the Auburn Affirmation had been denounced by fundamentalists since its publication and despite the fact that an overture from the Presbytery of Cincinnati brought the Affirmation to the attention of the assembly, no action was taken in response to its content or signers. The particular reasons for this silence are elusive. The Bills and Overtures Committee, which handled this issue, appears to have had a number of liberal members; but two conservative stalwarts, Maitland Alexander and William Jennings Bryan, also sat on it.[135] Significantly, Bryan, who a year earlier had tried to engineer a compromise on the Fosdick affair, supported the committee's recommendation of *no action* on the Auburn Affirmation.[136] Perhaps many conservatives were wary of taking action against the large number of clergy who signed the Affirmation; perhaps many believed that retaliatory actions would only hurt the fundamentalist cause. In a letter home Coffin allowed, "I believe[?] the conservatives are frightened and that they shrink from extreme measures, but they have the Assembly in their power."[137] Whatever the reason, an assembly with Machen, Macartney, and Bryan in attendance failed to address the liberals' clearest and most aggressive declaration of faith. This failure would later come back to haunt the fundamentalist forces.

On other matters the assembly decided that rather than fight about the New York Presbytery's licensing of Van Dusen and Lehman, it would refer the issue to the Synod of New York for "appropriate action." The body also rejected a proposal that "all who represent the Church on the Boards, General Council, Theological Seminaries and every other agency of the Church," be required to affirm the five points.[138] Indeed, the only clear-cut fundamentalist victory was the ouster of a liberal from the Board of Foreign Missions.[139]

On the question of Harry Fosdick, which was again before the assembly on appeal, the assembly shifted the entire controversy away from questions of theology to matters of polity. The report adopted by the assembly stated that central to the problem at hand was the unusual nature of Fosdick's relationship to First Church, New York. As such, it argued,

> If he desires to occupy a Presbyterian pulpit for an extended time he should enter our Church through the regular method and become subject to the jurisdiction and authority of the Church. . . .
> We therefore recommend that the Presbytery of New York be instructed, through its committee or through the session of the First Presbyterian Church, to take up with Dr. Fosdick this question to the end that he may determine whether it is his pleasure to enter the Presbyterian Church and thus be in a regular relationship with the First Presbyterian Church of New York as one of its pastors.[140]

The conservative giant Mark Matthews moved that Fosdick be immediately removed from the pulpit of First Church, but the assembly preferred to move with more reserve. They would let Fosdick decide his own fate.[141]

The assembly received mixed reviews. Bryan announced, "We have won at every point"; but Machen and Macartney were less than enthusiastic.[142] Coffin, having anticipated the worst, was nearly beside himself with glee. He wrote to his congregation, "The General Assembly not only did not condemn Dr. Fosdick for any of his teaching but with a full account of his work before it, graciously invited him to enter the Presbyterian ministry. I do not see how a more happy and orderly decision could have been reached."[143]

Despite the pleadings of Coffin and numerous other liberals, Fosdick would not join the Presbyterian Church. He wrote to Coffin, "I simply could not make the sort of even formal assent required of all candidates for your denomination's ministry. I would choke—for, rightly or wrongly, I should feel as if I were lying like a rogue."[144] On 22 October 1924 First Presbyterian Church accepted Fosdick's resignation and on

1 March 1925 he preached his farewell sermon.[145] Though pushed out of the church, Fosdick did not give an inch. He declared,

> These are the things we have stood for: tolerance, an inclusive Church, the right to think religion through in modern terms, the social applications of the principles of Jesus, the abiding verities and experiences of the gospel. And these are right. . . . We have stated an issue that no man nor denomination is strong enough to brush aside. . . .
> We say farewell to each other, but let no man say farewell to the things we have been standing for![146]

Fosdick knew, perhaps better than most, that his preaching had occasioned, but not caused, the Presbyterian conflict. Though his departure may have satisfied a few, it did not bring an end to the controversy. Rather, the intellectual and cultural issues that fueled the conflict continued to demand a response from the church. As the year progressed, polarization in the church increased. Those who had desired a course of compromise found themselves gradually pushed to one side or the other. All of the participants realized that the 1925 assembly would prove to be a decisive battleground.

6

Charles R. Erdman
and the 1925 General Assembly

In the wake of the 1924 assembly, Machen warned his conservative allies that they could not let down their guard. He wrote to a friend, "We did suffer a great defeat at the end of the Assembly; and I think that if we represent it as a victory, or if we give the impression that we regard the battle as over, we are traitors to our cause."[1] In the following months Machen acted on these sentiments. In print and pulpit he strove valiantly to advance the fundamentalist cause. Indeed, from this point on Machen emerged more and more as a leader of militant conservatives within the church.

In July 1924 Machen published an essay entitled, "Does Fundamentalism Obstruct Social Progress?" which not only revealed his dedication to logic, principle, and freedom but clearly demonstrated the connection he perceived between the decline of orthodox Christianity and the increasing secularization of the culture. Conservative Christianity, Machen observed, had been charged with obstructing social progress because it held a static view of historical facts, a "pessimistic view of human nature," an individualistic view of salvation, and a doctrinal view of Christianity. He responded to each charge in turn. Machen argued first, that fundamentalism's static view of historical facts encouraged progress, for all true advance required a factual foundation. Moreover, though realizing the sinful nature of humanity, fundamentalists also emphasized the renewing force of God's Spirit, which was the only genuine power for progress. He denied that conservative Christianity separated the individual and social aspects of the faith but argued that in an age of "soul-killing collectivism" Christians were called to focus on individual salvation. Finally, he asserted that though the church had to attend to both doctrinal and practical matters, its most important task in the 1920s lay in the intellectual and spiritual, not the physical, realms. True progress, progress that resulted not just in the abolition of poverty and disease but gave birth to increased liberty and spirituality, required a foundation of spiritual truth. Fundamentalism, the intellectual defense of orthodoxy, therefore provided the only real basis of progress. Reiterating his dream of a new Reformation, Machen concluded,

> We are looking for a mighty revival of the Christian religion which like the Reformation of the sixteenth century will bring light and liberty to mankind. When such a revival comes, it will destroy no fine or unselfish or noble thing; it will hasten and not hinder the relief of the physical distress of men and the improvement of conditions in this world. But it will do far more than all that. It will also descend into the depths—those depths into which utilitarianism can never enter—and will again bring mankind into the glorious liberty of communion with the living God.[2]

In early 1925 Machen and seven other conservatives sent a letter to over a thousand supporters, claiming that the church was in the midst of a grave crisis that needed immediate attention. Worried that many traditionalists might think that the church had been rescued from modernism by the 1924 assembly, the authors encouraged their readers to hold mass meetings to arouse conservative sentiment and to elect fundamentalist commissioners to the 1925 assembly.[3]

While Machen opposed the liberal foe from the confines of Princeton Seminary, Macartney used his moderatorial office to condemn modernism from pulpits across the nation.[4] "The eyes of the whole Christian world are on the Presbyterian Church," he warned his listeners. "We are not contending for Presbyterian peculiarities, but for the great facts of the Everlasting Gospel."[5] True to the Princeton tradition, he insisted that the "historicity of Christian facts must be reaffirmed."[6] But doctrine was not the only item on Macartney's agenda. Issues such as the decline of the Sabbath, the breakup of the family, and the secularization of education found a prominent place in the moderator's speeches.[7] Notably, though Macartney did not hesitate to speak out against modernist theology, he apparently did not think it appropriate to use his office to organize support for the fundamentalist cause.[8]

Liberals, though pleased with the results of the 1924 assembly, also pressed their position. Early in 1925 they issued three pamphlets in defense of their cause: "Freedom in the Presbyterian Pulpit" by Henry S. Coffin, "Fundamentalism in the Presbyterian Church" by Robert H. Nichols, and "Evolution and Christianity" by John M. Coulter.[9] In the most important of these, Coffin's sermon, the New York preacher repeated the claims that liberals were simply asking for freedoms long established in the church, that liberalism was really the only option for "thoughtful" Christians in the twentieth century, and that the "usefulness" of the church would be destroyed by the separation of its parts.[10]

The ongoing battle in the church was soon reflected in the church's most conservative seminary, Princeton. By 1924 long-simmering tensions at Princeton began to boil over in heated debate. Clearly, the controversy was not about to abate.

Struggles at Princeton

To an outside observer Princeton hardly seemed a likely place for internecine war. The faculty were all men of outstanding conservative credentials with long records of service to the church. Nevertheless, within the cozy confines of the seminary community differences between faculty members were magnified and, by the mid-1920s, threatened to impair the mission of the school. Congruent with its Old School heritage, the faculty of Princeton had, for the most part, always been advocates of a high view of doctrine and strict confessional ordination requirements. On matters of curriculum, this meant that the faculty stressed the theological and biblical disciplines far more than matters of practical ministry.[11] While Princeton students thereby received a solid grounding in the Calvinistic tradition, they were frequently unprepared to address the more pragmatic aspects of the ministry.[12]

In the early part of the twentieth century, the board of directors of the seminary attempted to redress this imbalance by creating a chair of practical theology, slightly modifying the curriculum, and, perhaps most importantly, electing J. Ross Stevenson, a well-known pastor, as president of the school.[13] The strategy of the directors failed to produce the desired results. Gradually, two factions evolved in the seminary faculty: a majority who held tightly to Old School theology and a scholastic view of theological education and a minority concerned less with the maintenance of precise doctrine than with the training of effective evangelical pastors.[14]

The alternate styles and theologies of these two groups resulted in squabbles over course scheduling and degree requirements in the decade preceding the Presbyterian controversy.[15] Not until 1920, however, were these differences revealed to the church at large. In 1920 Stevenson and Erdman supported a proposal that would have united the evangelical churches in the United States, but six other Princeton faculty, led by Machen, publicly condemned the plan for its doctrinal laxity.[16] In the coming years friction between faculty members continued to increase until the situation finally exploded in the winter of 1924/1925. The pulpit of the First Presbyterian Church of Princeton provided the setting for the outbreak of hostilities. In October 1923 Machen accepted an appointment to serve as stated supply preacher at First Church, Princeton. Much to the chagrin of Dr. Henry van Dyke, a professor in Princeton University and noted liberal Presbyterian, Machen used this platform to attack modernist inroads in the church and defend conservative Christianity. As noted above, van Dyke, angered by Machen's pronouncements, gave up his pew at First Church in protest.[17] In December of 1924 Erdman replaced Machen as preacher in First Church and van Dyke returned to his pew. The editor of the conservative periodical *The Presbyterian* could not help but comment on this turn of events. He wrote,

> Does the return of such a pronounced and avowed modernist as Dr. van Dyke to the old church, under the new pastor, mean that he is anticipating more liberal preaching under the new regime? But Dr. Machen and Dr. Erdman are both professors in the same seminary and [share] the Standards of the Presbyterian Church to which it belongs. Does this action of Dr. van Dyke signify that two parties are developing in the faculty of Princeton Seminary, or does it simply show a confusion outside?[18]

Erdman shot off a response to this editorial both to *The Presbyterian* itself and to *The Presbyterian Advance,* defending his orthodoxy and claiming that the only division in the seminary was not in the realm of doctrine but concerned "spirit, methods, or policies." Perhaps the controversy would have died here had not Erdman added, "This division would be of no consequence were it not for the unkindness, suspicion, bitterness and intolerance of those members of the faculty, who are also editors of The Presbyterian."[19] Though Erdman later denied that he had Machen in mind when he penned these words, Machen was the only member of the seminary faculty who was also an editor of *The Presbyterian.*[20]

Machen responded to this attack on his character with an open letter in *The Presbyterian.* First, he allowed that he held Erdman in "high personal esteem" and had never said anything to merit such a desciption of himself. More importantly, contrary to Erdman's claim that there were no serious doctrinal differences among the Princeton faculty, Machen argued that

> There is between Dr. Erdman and myself a very serious doctrinal difference indeed. It concerns the question not of this doctrine or that, but of the importance which is to be attributed to doctrine as such. . . .

Dr. Erdman differs radically from me; and it is a great mistake to call the difference merely one of method or of spirit. On the contrary, it is a difference of principle of the most thoroughgoing kind. Dr. Erdman does not indeed reject the doctrinal system of our church, but he is perfectly willing to make common cause with those who do reject it, and he is perfectly willing on many occasions to keep it in the background. I on the other hand can never consent to keep it in the background. Christian doctrine, I hold, is not merely connected with the gospel, but it is identical with the gospel, and if I did not preach it at all times, and especially in those places where it subjects me to personal abuse, I should regard myself as guilty of sheer unfaithfulness to Christ.[21]

Indeed, Machen and Erdman did differ profoundly on matters of principle. But contrary to Machen's assertion about holding Erdman in "high personal esteem," he had developed a deep distrust, even dislike, for Erdman. In a 1924 letter to his mother Machen described Erdman as "the enemy," and added, "I believe I dislike Erdman even more than Stevenson."[22] The feeling apparently was mutual; for in late 1924 Machen reported in a letter that "I understand that Dr. Erdman, in opposing our ecclesiastical position, has even mentioned Dassy [Machen] adversely in his class. So the warfare is becoming more and more open."[23] Personal feelings were, however, tangential to the debate; the chief cause of the conflict, as Machen realized, lay in the two men's different attitudes toward doctrine. Put simply, the maintenance of precise doctrine was not as important to Erdman as to Machen. The reasons for this disagreement, though perhaps amplified by personality traits, were rooted in the different histories of these two professors. Ultimately, Erdman's position would come to prevail not only at Princeton but in the church. Erdman represented the broad segment of the church that was conservative in theology, tolerant in spirit, and evangelistic in purpose; that is to say, Erdman, perhaps more than any other member of the Princeton faculty, epitomized the values and beliefs of late-nineteenth-century Protestant evangelicalism.

The Theological Heritage of Charles R. Erdman

Charles Rosenbury Erdman, son of William J. and Henrietta R. Erdman, was born in Fayetteville, New York on 20 July 1866.[24] William J. Erdman had been raised in the Dutch Reformed Church but was ordained in the New School Presbyterian Church in 1860 after attending Hamilton College and Union Theological Seminary in New York.[25] He was a man, Charles would recall, of "saintly personality," who manifested a "sunny disposition," good humor, and humility.[26] Though Charles would eventually receive his seminary education at Princeton, William's New School Theology and temper had a deep and lasting impact on his son.

The New School Presbyterian Church had been born in 1837 when differences within the Presbyterian Church resulted in a division in their ranks. Chief among the causes of this schism was the theology of Nathaniel Taylor, professor at Yale Divinity School, which gained popularity among Presbyterians during the Second Great Awakening. In contradistinction to Old School clergy who embraced the Calvinistic doctrine of total depravity, Taylor and his New School disciples argued that sinners could act to escape damnation. Though Taylor's theology was well fashioned for the revivals then sweeping the country, strict Calvinists could see nothing in it but the image of Pelagius. Scripture plainly taught, the Princetonians argued, the inability of mankind to effect its own salvation; any teaching to the contrary was flatly heretical. Underneath this difference between the two parties lay a fundamental disagreement concerning the importance of doctrine itself. While the Old School was convinced that false doctrine produced the greatest possible threat to a lost world, New School clergy, insistent on the priority of evangelism over strict confessionalism, had no difficulty with doctrinal innovations that increased the revivalistic harvest. The Old School did not disapprove of revivalism per se but demanded that the proclamation of Calvinistic orthodoxy take precedence over any concern for evangelistic success.[27]

Taylor's theology had infiltrated the church primarily by means of a Plan of Union between Congregationalists and Presbyterians consummated in 1801. In an effort to christianize the opening frontier, these two Reformed bodies had joined forces in the planting of new churches. Many of the congregations founded under this plan were supplied by pastors trained in New England and sympathetic to the more Pelagian theology of Taylor. Though Old School clergy stood aghast at these theological innovations, they could do little or nothing to discipline the more liberal clergy in presbyteries controlled by the New School.[28]

Tensions over theological differences between the Old and New Schools were aggravated by differences over other issues, such as confessional subscription and ecclesiology. More concerned with saving souls and right living than details of doctrine, New School Presbyterians tended to wear the mantle of Westminster lightly. As seen in the earlier discussion of the Cumberland Church, confessional subscription had long been a point of controversy within the Presbyterian fold. New School clergy maintained that the church had always intended a broad interpretation of confessional subscription, while spokesmen for the Old School insisted that adherence to the Confession implied adherence to all essential doctrines of the system.[29] This argument over confessional subscription would, of course, become a major source of tension in the 1920s, albeit under much different circumstances.

The New School manifested its theological tolerance in its strong backing of the extraecclesiastical agencies that constituted the "evangelical united front." In the early nineteenth century an array of voluntary agencies, such as the American Home Missionary Society, the American Board of Commissioners for Foreign Missions, and the American Education Society, sprang up to further the Christian cause. These institutes were supported by a wide range of evangelicals of various doctrinal positions. But Old School clergy, who adhered to a higher ecclesiology than their New School associates, argued that the missionary activity of the church should be controlled by the church, not by nondenominational societies. In 1837, when the Old School party excised the majority of the New School synods from the church, it also severed the relationship with these independent societies and reestablished denominational control over church missions.[30]

The New School Church, formed as a result of the 1837 excision, was thus less concerned about fine points of doctrinal orthodoxy, and more concerned with revivalism and social reform, than its Old School sister. When William Erdman entered the New School Union Theological Seminary in 1856, these traits were still prominent. New School Theology, however, had begun to take a new form. While the thought of Nathaniel Taylor had dominated in the 1830s, by the 1850s a new professor at Union, Henry Boynton Smith, had become the New School's chief theological spokesman. Smith, who had studied at Bowdoin, Andover, and Bangor Theological Seminary and in Germany, sought to act as a reconciler between the divided parties of American Presbyterianism.[31] Upon his inauguration into the chair of systematic theology at Union he declared the central principle of his theology. "To mediate between our extremes is our vital need," he said, "and such mediation can only be found in Christ. . . . As the central idea of the whole Christian system is in mediation, so should this be the spirit of our theology, the spirit of our lives."[32] Rather than choose between the alternatives of the Old School, Hopkinsian, or Taylorite versions of Calvinism, Smith suggested a theology centered on Christ.[33] "Let us come to Jesus," Smith argued. "The best and the fullest inward experience is that which centres in

Christ; and the centre of the experience is then identical with the centre of divine revelation."[34] By focusing on the reconciling work of Christ, Presbyterians could avoid both the extreme emphasis on the divine sovereignty of the Old School and the extreme ethical emphasis of the New School.[35]

The irenic, activistic, evangelical theology William learned at Union was reinforced by the close relationship he soon developed with Dwight L. Moody, the foremost evangelist of the late nineteenth century. Though Erdman served pastorates in New York, Michigan, Indiana, Massachusetts, and North Carolina, perhaps no position gave him greater honor than his three years of service, from 1875 to 1878, at Dwight L. Moody's Chicago Avenue Church in Chicago.[36] There, his son remembered, he was "highly esteemed as a harmonizer in a congregation where he discovered rather determined 'Congregationalists, Presbyterians, Methodists, Baptists, and Plymouth Brethren.' He was a studious and faithful teacher, and sympathetic with all forms of evangelistic and Gospel work."[37]

In addition to serving the Moody church, William Erdman was a prime mover in the founding of what became the Moody Bible Institute, a frequent visitor at Moody's Northfield summer conferences, and for more than twenty years secretary and leader of the Niagara Bible Conference.[38] Within these circles he was deeply influenced by, and a champion of, Holiness Theology and, until about 1900, dispensational premillennialism.[39] Erdman was renowned among his peers for his outstanding knowledge of the Scriptures. He was reputed to possess "the best knowledge of theology and the Bible among all the ministers who taught at Niagara" and was praised by Moody as "better acquainted with the Bible than any other man he had met."[40]

Moody had an impact on Charles Erdman second only to that of William Erdman. Indeed, it might not be too much to claim that as Thornwell set the tone of ministry for Machen, Moody provided a model for Charles Erdman. An ex–shoe salesman who understood the importance of marketing technique, Moody downplayed the traditional revivalistic emphasis on the wrath of God in favor of a focus on the overwhelming power of divine love. His theology, such as it was, centered on the redeeming power of Christ and regeneration by the Holy Spirit.[41] Though never able to subscribe to many of the intricacies of dispensationalism, Moody did adopt a premillennial eschatology, which undergirded his evangelistic thrust.[42] "I look upon this world as a wrecked vessel," he proclaimed. "God has given me a lifeboat and said to me, 'Moody, save all you can.'"[43] Evangelism was his forte, and bringing lost sinners to Christ took precedence over all other concerns. A rotund, genial man who deplored doctrinal controversy, Moody joined hands with liberals and conservatives in order to advance the cause of Christ.[44]

Not content to spread the gospel through revivals alone, Moody established a variety of educational institutions to train lay Christian men and women. In 1879 he founded the Northfield School for Girls, in 1881 the Mount Hermon School for Boys, and in 1886 the precursor of the Moody Bible Institute in Chicago. In 1880 Moody hosted the first Northfield Summer Conference for students, which gave birth to the Student Volunteer Movement in 1886.[45]

Charles Erdman came to know Moody not only through William Erdman's close association with the evangelist but also by frequent participation at the Northfield conferences. "He was a dynamic and forceful speaker," Erdman later reminisced, "and I availed myself of every opportunity to hear him preach."[46] Writing in the midst of the Presbyterian controversy, Erdman remarked of his mentor, "Mr. Moody's preaching was not only Biblical, but it was positive. With negations he had little to do. He avoided religious controversy, and believed it did more harm than good. . . . Mr. Moody was seeking to save souls, and he knew that controversialists do not usually win followers for Christ or encourage others to study the Bible."[47] In addition to Moody's irenic nature, Erdman made special note of his humor, love, and tendency to emphasize the Christian life more than doctrine. Most important to Erdman was Moody's fervent evangelistic concern. "The life of Mr. Moody," Erdman declared in 1928, "has no more important message for the present day than is found in his insistence that it is the privilege and duty of every professing Christian to exert definite personal influence toward bringing others into a vital relationship with Christ and into membership with his church."[48]

Despite the peripatetic nature of Charles Erdman's early life, he claimed to have had a "happy and thoroughly normal boyhood."[49] He passed the majority of his formative years in Jamestown, New York, where he attended Jamestown Collegiate Institute and enjoyed his leisure time swimming, skating, and playing baseball.[50] At age fourteen Erdman made a public profession of faith and joined the Presbyterian church that his father pastored.[51] Two years later, in 1882, he packed his bags and followed his older brother to the College of New Jersey in Princeton.[52]

In the fifteen years before Erdman's matriculation at Princeton, the college, like many, had been evolving into a university. Under the leadership of President James McCosh, electives for upperclassmen had been introduced, new facilities were constructed, faculty were added, and the population of graduate students swelled.[53] But in 1882 the College of New Jersey was still a far cry from a secular university, and William Erdman believed Princeton's influences safe enough for his sons.

Charles had no particular vocational plans on entering college. "The only thing I was sure of," he later reported, "was that I wished to acquire a good education." By his senior year he had felt the call to the ministry and, seemingly unperplexed by debates over higher criticism and the New Theology, chose to follow in his father's footsteps.[54] After taking a year off for travel and teaching, he matriculated at Princeton Theological Seminary.[55] Even at this early stage in his career, differences between Princeton's scholastic ways and Erdman's New School and premillennial concerns came to the fore. Convinced that he needed a better command of the Scriptures and sure that he could not acquire it at Princeton, he interrupted his studies to spend a year under his father's tutelage. Erdman later explained, "Seminary authorities in those days felt that extensive Bible study was unnecessary. They took the position that all who enrolled to study for the ministry were thoroughly schooled already in the Bible. This was fallacious. I, for one, wasn't, at least not to the extent necessary, even though my father was a clergyman. The emphasis back in my seminary days was given to Latin, Greek, and Hebrew."[56] Erdman graduated from the seminary in 1891 and accepted a call to organize a Presbyterian church in Overbrook, Pennsylvania.[57]

Preaching the gospel was, apparently, not Charles's only interest in Overbrook. While teaching in the area after graduation from college, Erdman had likely made the acquaintance of Mary Estelle Pardee, daughter of Pennsylvania coal magnate Calvin Pardee.[58] At any rate, shortly after Charles moved from Princeton he and Mary became engaged and on 1 June 1892 the two began a partnership that would span nearly sixty-eight years.[59]

After six years of preaching at Overbrook, Erdman accepted a call to the First Presbyterian Church of Germantown, Pennsylvania.[60] Though offered the chair of homiletics at Princeton Seminary in 1902, he opted to remain in the pastorate until 1906, when the seminary again requested his services.[61] In that year the board of directors called Erdman to the newly created chair of practical theology to supplement the more academic offerings in the curriculum.[62] Erdman understood his task to include the teaching of homiletics, polity, pastoral care, Christian education, and evangelism; but his most important responsibility was the teaching of "English Bible"—that is, he was to aim "at such a special, practical, spiritual, and evangelistic interpretation of the Bible as will directly equip the 'preacher for his pulpit and the pastor for all his personal work.'"[63] Machen, who held no brief for "practical" courses, returned from Germany to Princeton the same year, to teach courses in the New Testament department.

Erdman jumped into his new position with enthusiasm and diligence. In addition to his teaching responsibilities, he became advisor to the student association at the seminary. In the coming years he contributed two articles to *The Fundamentals*, was elected as a member and then president of the Board of Foreign Missions of the Presbyterian Church, and attended the 1910 International Missionary Conference in Edinburgh.[64] Though Erdman loosened his earlier ties with the millenarian movement after assuming the chair of practical theology at Princeton, he served as an editorial consultant to the *Scofield Reference Bible* in 1908.[65] While he invested great energy and time in his work at Princeton, Erdman's professional life clearly did not revolve around the seminary alone. Rather, his connections to Presbyterian denominational agencies, to the interdenominational network of conservatives manifested in *The Fundamentals*, and to the nascent ecumenical movement gave him a perspective on ecclesiastical life unavailable to his more narrowly academic peers. Erdman's responsibilities inside and outside the seminary all tended to reinforce his predilection to subordinate theoretical to practical concerns.

The Practical Theology of Charles Erdman

Erdman was a congenial-looking man of moderate height.[66] His acquaintances repeatedly described him as winsome, friendly, sincere, and witty.[67] Indeed, friendliness and a sense of humor seem to have been the two personal traits Erdman esteemed most in others.[68] As professor of practical theology he insisted that though intellectual acuity was an asset to the minister, an "attractive personality" was the most important condition for ministerial success. Time and again Erdman warned against a belligerent spirit. "A Christian minister," he wrote, "must be 'gentle,' sweetly reasonable, eager to show forbearance and kindly consideration; he must not be 'contentious' or quarrelsome, even as to matters of doctrine."[69] Love, joy, and good humor were especially requisite in theological discussions. "In debating Christian doctrines, more than in any other form of effort," he claimed, "one needs a vein of humor, common sense, and brotherly love."[70] Erdman's emphasis on living with a "Christian" temper did not derive merely from his affinity for the sunny side of the street. Rather, he rooted his concern for right living in his theology, particularly in his doctrine of the Holy Spirit. In this he reflected his indebtedness to his two most influential teachers, William Erdman and Dwight L. Moody.

Both the elder Erdman and Moody had been influenced by the Keswick Holiness movement.[71] Keswick Holiness, a brand of Calvinistic perfectionism developed in Great Britain in the 1870s, emphasized the importance of empowerment by the Holy Spirit in order to live a life of Christian service. In contradistinction to more Wesleyan Holiness teachings, Keswick doctrine taught the continuing power of sin in the believer's life and the need for repeated consecrations and "fillings" by the Holy Spirit. Spread by Moody's conferences at Northfield, special conferences on the doctrine of the Holy Spirit, numerous books and pamphlets, and the *Scofield Reference Bible*, Keswick teachings (or variations thereof) gained wide acceptance in American Protestantism by the early twentieth century. William Erdman appears to have adopted the Keswick theology in its entirety; and Moody, though not always using Keswick terminology, subscribed to similar ideas.[72]

Charles Erdman's theology likewise reflected a deep concern with the Holy Spirit and the Spirit's power in the Christian life. He was an enthusiastic advocate of the Keswick theology, claiming in 1912 that the church needed, and should promote, this movement (or one like it) and its message.[73] In his most thorough exposition of his pneumatology, a brief work entitled *The Spirit of Christ: Devotional Studies in the Doctrine of the Holy Spirit* published in 1926, Erdman insisted that Christian ministers at home and abroad needed "a new enduement of the Spirit."[74]

In agreement with Keswick teaching, Erdman believed that the holy life must be renewed by repeated "fillings" with the Spirit.[75] Against Pentecostals who looked for "gifts of tongues" as proof of baptism in the Spirit, he held that spiritual courage, faithfulness, and meekness were far better indicators of God's presence. "In speaking of the work of the Comforter," he demanded, "we should emphasize the power he gives for public service in preaching the Gospel." Above all, the "one supreme condition of spiritual power" lay in "maintaining a right relation to Christ." "If one is to be controlled by the Spirit of Christ," he wrote, "there must be dependence upon Christ, submission to Christ, love for Christ."[76]

Erdman addressed the doctrine of Scripture under the locus of the Holy Spirit. "The inspiration of the Scriptures," he argued, "is the final explanation of their unique character and supreme authority." With the

Westminster divines, Erdman insisted that the ultimate ground of belief in the divine nature of the Bible was the "inner witness borne to the heart of the believer by the Spirit of Christ." In addition, the Scripture's testimony to itself and to Christ, and the "testimony of Christ" to the Scripture's inspiration demonstrated the Bible's supernatural origin. Finally, the Scripture's accuracy, sublimity, splendor, truthfulness, and unity all pointed to its divine nature.[77]

Notably, though Erdman described himself as a fundamentalist and accepted such doctrines as the virgin birth, bodily resurrection, and physical return of Christ, at least by the mid-1920s he held only a limited view of the inerrancy of the Scriptures.[78] In the midst of the Presbyterian controversy he wrote, "The theme and substance of [the apostolic writers'] witness was not to be universal truth; it was definitely limited; it was the truth concerning the Person and work of Christ. In their testimony for him their words and their writings would be free from error, would be trustworthy, would be authoritative, because of the guidance of his Spirit."[79] Though theologically conservative, Erdman carefully circumscribed the area in which the Scriptures were "free from error."

In discussing the Bible, Erdman seems to have been more comfortable with the language of the Westminster Confession than the rhetoric of inerrancy. For example, on accepting the moderatorship of the Presbytery of New Brunswick in 1925 he declared, "I accept this high office with profound gratitude and a deep sense of the honor conferred. In doing so, I, in the first place, again pledge my allegiance to all the doctrinal standards of the Presbyterian Church, including the Westminster Confession of Faith. I accept the Bible as the word of God, the only infallible rule of faith and practice, and in the interpretation of the Bible I have always been a conservative of the conservatives."[80] Erdman followed the Westminster Confession not only in his insistence that God's Spirit inspired the writers of Scripture and testified to their truth in the hearts of believers, but also in his conviction that the Spirit guided in the Bible's right interpretation. Finally, for Erdman, the Spirit applied the Scripture's truth to the lives of the faithful. "If . . . we make diligent use of our Bibles," he concluded, "the Spirit will . . . assuredly use the divine truth to make us more fruitful in service, more holy in character, more patient in suffering."[81]

Erdman also developed his doctrine of the church under the rubric of the Spirit. The Scriptures remind us, he wrote, "that the church is not an organization but an organism, not a society formed by men but a Body created and indwelt by the Spirit of God and composed of living souls united by faith to a living Lord." This being the case, organization, sacraments, and liturgy were all subordinated to that life "created and sustained by the Spirit of Christ, in those who together form the Body of Christ." He continued, "Nothing, therefore, can be of such vital consequence to the church as the nurture of its spiritual life and the proper expression of this life through the activities of its members."[82] Erdman's ecclesiology, which stressed Christian living and "witnessing for Christ," conflicted with Machen's belief that the church was a voluntary society of believers agreed in doctrine and committed to the preservation and propagation of that doctrine.[83] Erdman explicitly denied that complete creedal uniformity had ever existed in the church and doubted its possibility in his day.[84] "However," he stated, "where there is life, produced by the Spirit of Christ, there cannot fail to be consent as to certain great cardinal principles of faith, and these will center in the divine Person and saving work of Christ."[85] The mission of the church was precisely the proclamation of God's love in Christ. In 1926 he declared, "What we need in the church today is cooperation of members, unity of purpose, and strong leadership and more preaching of Christ, the light of the world, for ours is a task of taking the Gospel to the world."[86] Above all else, the church was to be engaged in bringing sinners to Christ.[87]

Erdman worked valiantly to hold right doctrine and right living together. "When creeds are living, when belief is sincere, when doctrine is truly accepted, then character and right conduct and the performance of duty are sure to result," he averred.[88] He insisted that orthodoxy must be maintained but always in the spirit of love.[89] Nonetheless, life, not doctrine, provided the most genuine evidence of true Christian faith. "A man may recite an orthodox creed and believe it," he wrote, "and yet be self-deceived as to his relation to Christ. . . . On the other hand, a real believer follows Christ, obeys Christ and reflects the character of Christ."[90] The critical role of Christian living was nowhere more important than in apologetics. Here Erdman and Machen came into sharpest conflict. While Machen argued that the defense of doctrine, of Christian ideas, had to anchor Christian apologetics, Erdman asserted, "The best defense of the truth is found in the influence of a holy life. Of course the Christian beliefs must be carefully studied and clearly stated, misrepresentations must be denied, and false charges must be answered, but the way 'to contend earnestly for the faith' is not that of physical force or bitter denunciation or social ostracism, but that of consistent living."[91] Indeed, the overwhelming sense of Erdman's writings was that Christian living took precedence over matters of precise doctrine. "To us any man good enough to go to heaven," he once said, "is good enough to be a member of our church, regardless of interpretation of the points of doctrine."[92]

Erdman's persistent emphasis on evangelism was undergirded by the premillennial eschatology he inherited from his father and Moody.[93] He addressed the doctrine of the end times most fully in an essay he wrote for *The Fundamentals* entitled "The Coming of Christ" and in a 1922 volume, *The Return of Christ*. The second coming of Christ, he held, would be a personal return; that is, it would be "visible, bodily, local."[94] Erdman rejected the doctrines of the "secret rapture of the church" and the any-moment return of Christ propounded by dispensationalists. These beliefs, he argued, "led many Premillennialists to take a very despondent view of the future and a very narrow view of their task."[95] He lamented,

> Because "wheat and tares" are to "grow together until the harvest," some teachers fix their thoughts wholly upon the "tares" and forget the "wheat," and the probable proportion of each at "the end of the age." Because Satan is properly called the Prince of this Age, they forget how Jesus declared that all power ("all authority") had been given to himself in heaven and on earth, and that he expected his followers to go forth and to "make disciples of all nations."
>
> Because the supreme task of the Church is to preach the Gospel just as far and just as fast as it can, and among all nations, and because there is no hope of a better world and of a brighter age without the regeneration of human hearts, some forget it is the unquestioned duty of every follower of Christ to show his spirit and to imitate his example in every sphere of social and civil and industrial and political life.[96]

In short, Erdman insisted, "there is no need that one should be a pessimist because he is a Premillennialist."[97] He stood as living proof of the truth of his statement.

The "one great precedent condition" of Christ's return was the proclamation of the gospel to all the world. Here Erdman's eschatology led him to fervent missionary concern. Premillennialism, which in many cases resulted in division between Christians, inspired Erdman to support ecumenical evangelism. In *The Fundamentals* he wrote,

> This is therefore a time, not for unkindly criticism of fellow Christians, but for friendly conference; not for disputing over divergent views, but for united action; not for dogmatic assertion of prophetic programs, but for the humble acknowledgment that "we know in part"; not for idle dreaming, but for the immediate task of evangelizing a lost world.
>
> For such effort, no one truth is more inspiring, than that of the return of Christ. None other can make us sit more lightly by the things of time,

none other is more familiar as a Scriptural motive to purity, holiness, patience, vigilance, love.[98]

Though Erdman, with his premillennial and Holiness heritage, manifested emphases distinctly different from those of conservatives like Machen and Macartney, his conflict with his more militant colleagues was, just as Machen had stated, rooted not so much in disagreement over particular doctrines as over the import of doctrine itself to Christianity. Erdman, in fact, shared many of the epistemological and theological beliefs of Machen and Macartney, but he was not driven by these convictions to the conclusions held by the militant conservatives. He insisted, for example, that the Christian faith was founded on historic facts; but unlike Machen, he was willing to work with those who had different interpretations of these facts.[99] Moreover, he subscribed to the doctrines of the virgin birth, the bodily resurrection, and the miracles of Jesus but, in a way Machen could never understand, emphasized the need for evangelism over the defense of Christian teachings.[100] The ideological similarities between Erdman and Machen led to their persistent disagreement; they were close enough to fight but too far apart ever to reach accord.

Erdman's revivalistic heritage, Holiness theology, and optimistic premillennialism inspired a deep concern for moral reform. In his commentary on the book of Acts he expounded on his understanding of the relationship of Christianity and social responsibility, writing, "Ethics and social reform are absolutely essential parts of the gospel message, but they must not supplant and can only follow the proclamation of a living and divine Christ, through faith in whom alone men receive in all fullness the gift of his Spirit."[101] Erdman was therefore opposed to "the adoption of a so-called 'social gospel' which discards the fundamental doctrines of Christianity and substitutes a religion of good works." "But," he insisted, "a true Gospel of grace is inseparable from a Gospel of good works. Christian doctrines and Christian duties cannot be divorced."[102] Erdman's faith and his social vision for America were closely linked.

Preserving the Moral Order: The Social Concerns of Charles Erdman

Erdman's social concerns bore a striking resemblance to those of Bryan and Macartney. Like his more militant peers, Erdman believed that

Christianity and American culture walked hand in hand. "Patriotism is not a substitute for religion," he wrote, "but it finds in religion its truest support and its highest sanctions."[103] Quoting authorities as diverse as Washington, Teddy Roosevelt, and Moses, Erdman argued that the "welfare of the nation [was] . . . inseparably connected with the knowledge of God and with obedience to his laws."[104] In 1921 he warned his readers, "When moral corruption, impurity, selfishness, dishonesty, greed and cruelty pervade the life of a people, there inevitably follow weakness, deterioration, and ruin. This truth finds its further illustration in the life of all the great empires of the past. Disobedience to divine law is the sole explanation of their decline and fall."[105] The preservation of the Sabbath was therefore a central agenda item for Erdman, as it had been for his mentor, Dwight Moody. The requirement of a weekly day of rest, Erdman wrote, "embodied a divine law which is traced back to the creation."[106] "Sabbath desecration," was, "the forerunner of declension and doom" for a nation. Though he allowed that "Sabbath laws should not be unreasonable or burdensome," he insisted that the state had a responsibility to enforce this day of rest for all citizens.[107] "One who desecrates the Sabbath," Erdman declared, "is an enemy of the human race."[108]

Erdman was also concerned about the decline of home religion. But Erdman's tone in discussing family religion was more upbeat than that of his ecclesiastical rival, Clarence Macartney. Though he recognized the dire need for Christian education among the young and deplored the increasing secularization of the family, he stressed not the decline but the importance of careful Christian nurture in the family and Bible training in the home. Family religion had critical ramifications not only for the individual's salvation but for the future of the nation. "The hope of America today," he said in 1926, "rests on Christian education, beginning with ideals established in the Christian home."[109]

Similarly, Erdman stressed the need for increased educational efforts in the church. Religious education was the "greatest need of the world," he proclaimed in 1926. Never in the history of the nation was education in "things concerning God" more necessary. But the form of religious education Erdman had in mind was not primarily a matter of the exposition of creeds and doctrines. Rather, Erdman emphasized Bible study, Christian life-style, and the "wisdom" that comes with submission to God's will. Characteristically, he believed the church was rising to the occasion. "Our great churches," he said, "are beginning to show their new interest in religious education and they are using superb structures for this work."[110]

Like almost all Presbyterians at the time, Erdman supported Prohibition. Shortly after Congress approved the Eighteenth Amendment he wrote, "This World's Temperance Sunday is for us, in large measure, a day of national thanksgiving, because we believe the destroying demon of drink has received his death blow; but we must still be vigilant; and we must remember the curse that is sapping the life of nations that we love."[111] Erdman's opposition to alcohol was based on biblical precepts regarding "personal hygiene." "The Bible," he said, "is, in fact, the first great book of hygiene, and should be read, at times, with this feature in view." Since the Scriptures taught "physical, moral, and spiritual cleanness," Christians were obliged to abstain from all "voluntary poisoning of the body by injurious habits and indulgences." This necessarily prohibited the use of alcohol, not to mention tobacco and "stronger narcotics, such as opium and cocaine."[112] In a passage that underscored the close connection between evangelism and moral reform, Erdman declared, "World-wide prohibition would make for the world-wide proclamation of the Gospel of Christ."[113]

Erdman's writings seemed to lack the urgency, the sense of crisis, that permeated the speeches of his more militant peers in the 1920s. For example, in discussing the increasing secularization of family life, Erdman declared, "It is true that youth today has more liberties, is exposed to more temptations and is lacking the full influence of family life, which is disintegrating to some degree. Youth is however self-reliant and essentially is no different now from any other generation. Things are not so bad with them as is often sensationally painted." Or again, "The state of the church is good. . . . Life is getting more complex, and many persons do not now devote to church work the time they did formerly. But the situation is not disastrous. It is not even such as calls for pessimism."[114] To be sure, the upbeat nature of Erdman's analyses may be attributed in part to his optimistic outlook on life in general. But the sanguine aspects of Erdman's statements should not blind one to the anxious undercurrents running throughout his words and work. His concern with Sabbatarianism, Prohibition, divorce, and family worship; his insistence that religious education was more necessary in the twenties than ever before; and his warnings that "spiritual illiteracy is the forerunner . . . of national decay"—all point to the presence of an underlying fear that society may, in fact, be up against insuperable problems.[115] In holding that "things were not so bad," Erdman appears to have been reassuring himself as much as his audiences.

This analysis is supported by the concern for order in Erdman's speeches. In defense of the Sabbath he appealed not simply to biblical

precept but to national security: "Without the Sabbath, worship becomes difficult; without worship, the church loses its power; without the
church, morality loses its sanction; without morality, there is no security
for society or the state."[116] Similarly, he pressed for an increase in home
religion as a means of "instilling principals which would hold the man
and woman to the principals [sic] of law abiding citizenship" and was
concerned lest Prohibition increase "lawlessness" among the citizens of
the nation.[117]

   Erdman had good reason to be concerned with questions of law and
order in the twenties. In the wake of World War I the United States
witnessed a dramatic increase in the violence and brazenness of crime.
"No topic," reported historian Preston Slosson, "was more common in
news and editorial columns than the 'crime wave.'" Aided by the au-
tomobile, sawed-off shotguns, and machine guns, professional robbers
and assassins did not hesitate to hold up banks or mow down targets in
broad daylight. Extortion rings and bootleggers thrived. Just as troubling
to American evangelicals, the open flouting of Prohibition and lax enforcement of the Volstead Act manifested complete disregard for the
law and the Constitution.[118] To many, America seemed to be coming
unhinged. Senator William E. Borah, addressing the 1926 General Assembly of the Presbyterian Church, well summarized the concerns of
most Protestant Americans. "I believe the liquor traffic to be a curse
to the human family," he declared. But, he continued,

> Even a greater question than the liquor question is the capacity of the
> American people for constitutional government. . . .
>   The supreme test of good citizenship is to obey the Constitution and
> the laws when written. To disregard our Constitution, to evade it, to
> nullify it, while still refusing to change it, is to plant the seeds of destruction
> in the heart of the nation—it is to confess before the world that we have
> neither the moral courage, nor the intellectual sturdiness for self-
> government.[119]

   The only solution to the disorder and moral decay Erdman perceived
in the society was, of course, the gospel of Jesus Christ. For Erdman,
the church provided the moral ballast of society; without the proclamation of the gospel and religious education the nation was doomed.
"There can be no abiding morality aside from the influences and sanctions of the church," he insisted. "And without morality, neither society
or state can continue to exist."[120] But a church in chaos, a church disordered by its own lawlessness and abandonment of constitutional procedure, could never provide order for society. The turmoil in the church,

therefore, threatened not only to destroy the mission of the church, but to destroy America as well. Above all, Presbyterians needed to cease their bickering and return to their calling.

It was thus no coincidence that Erdman's platform for order in the church echoed the cry of Prohibitionists demanding order in the society. "Constitutionalism and law enforcement," was the overwhelming concern of the day for American evangelicals.[121] In his bid for moderator in 1925 Erdman staked his claim on the question of order itself, stating, "I belong to no particular group or clique, but stand for the constitution of the Church. That means loyalty to our Church doctrine as well as to our form of government. . . . We must guard the doctrine of the Church, but we must do so by constitutional methods and by the law of the Church. I believe all differences will be settled if the parties abide by the law."[122] To be sure, Erdman's primary motivation in seeking ecclesiastical peace was his desire for the gospel to be effectively preached to individual sinners. But tied closely to this was his concern for the church's mission to society. Inasmuch as Christianity provided the moral adhesive of the nation, the future of the civilization depended on the successful mission of the church. In the face of the cultural upheaval of the 1920s, this aspect of the church's mission took on critical import; the order of society depended on order in the church.

Erdman's sanguine analyses of the cultural situation in the 1920s concealed a more deep-seated anxiety about the future of the church and American society. His passion for the orderly prosecution of the mission of the church and the maintenance of American Christian civilization led Erdman to work feverishly for reconciliation between militant conservatives and increasingly aggressive liberals. The 1925 assembly offered Erdman one more chance to bring order out of the increasingly chaotic situation in the church and thereby strengthen the moral underpinnings of the society.

The 1925 Assembly

As the 1925 assembly approached, the conflicts in the seminary and church intensified. In October 1924 a number of Princeton students, disturbed about the liberal leanings of the interseminary student organization to which Princeton belonged, decided to form the League of Evangelical Students.[123] Though Erdman did not oppose the formation of the league, he did, by his own account, "question its advisability."[124] Erdman's reservations concerning this venture, aggravated no doubt by the continuing differences between Erdman and many of the more Old School faculty, led to his replacement by Robert D. Wilson as student advisor in the spring of 1925.[125] A number of papers picked up this story and portrayed Erdman's ouster as simply one more incident in his running feud with Macartney and Machen.[126] Though such reports, especially those implicating Macartney, were at best misleading, the fracas furthered the perception that Erdman was being unfairly persecuted by his obsessed militant peers.[127] In the course of events such perceptions did nothing to help the cause of the fundamentalist faction.

Shortly after this incident Erdman was endorsed as a candidate for the moderator of the 1925 General Assembly by the Presbytery of New Brunswick.[128] On 28 March in anticipation of Erdman's candidacy, a circle of eight conservatives, including Machen, operating under the name Presbyterian Press Association, distributed a "news release" that described Erdman as a candidate of the modernists.[129] Erdman's defenders condemned this letter as a "deliberate misrepresentation of his position by the extreme Fundamentalist faction of the Presbyterian Church headed by William J. Bryan, Dr. Clarence Macartney of Philadelphia . . . and Professor J. Gresham Machen."[130] Erdman himself, however, declared that he did not hold Bryan or Macartney responsible for the adverse publicity.[131] Machen was notably absent from this exoneration.

As winter turned to spring, Machen's declarations concerning the controversy grew more intense. On 8 March he preached a sermon on "The Separateness of the Church" that he later published and distributed at his own expense.[132] The church, he argued, had throughout history been threatened by the pagan ideas of the world; but time and again true Christians had refused to compromise their faith. Now, he declared, orthodoxy was challenged once more; and the future of the Presbyterian church hung in the balance. If the church resorted to paganism, Machen averred, true Christians would have no choice but to withdraw. "Once in the course of history," he reminded his listeners, "at the beginning of the sixteenth century, that method of withdrawl was God's method of preserving the precious salt." But secession was not necessary yet; the church could still be saved if believers would stand up and be counted.[133]

In May Machen applied these ideals to the upcoming General Assembly in an article entitled "The Present Situation in the Presbyterian Church." "The greatest need of the hour," he insisted, "is that the central administration of the church should be placed increasingly in the hands of evangelical men who understand the great issue of the day and have decided with regard to that issue to stand for Christ." Believing that the time had come to play hardball, Machen openly condemned Erdman's policies. Machen allowed that Erdman's personal beliefs were orthodox; but he charged that in 1925, as in 1924, he would be the candidate of the "Modernist and indifferentist party in the church."[134] Conservative opposition to Erdman, Machen claimed, had nothing to do with personalities; it was based on the imminent threat of modernism in the church. The situation, to Machen, was clear: "There are many evangelical men who in this great crisis have not the appreciation of the danger in which the church stands to make them safe occupants of the moderator's chair. So it is with Dr. Erdman. . . . A policy of palliation and of compromise will in a few years lead to the control of our church as has already happened in the case of many churches, by agnostic Modernism."[135]

Erdman responded to Machen's claims by standing on his platform of "purity and peace and progress."[136] Erdman repeatedly defended his orthodoxy. "I have always been a Fundamentalist in my beliefs," he declared. "I refuse to be labeled as a Modernist or as a liberal, but if any men of liberal theological views desire to vote for me this year it is, of course, their privilege to do so."[137] Erdman's protests failed to address Machen's concerns: Erdman's willingness to cooperate with liberals for the sake of evangelism—not his personal orthodoxy—was at the heart of Machen's opposition. The conflict was rooted in a different understanding of the essence of Christianity and of the mission of the church. For Machen the truth of Christianity was primarily doctrinal; for Erdman, existential. For Machen the church's mission was the preservation and propagation of true belief; for Erdman its task was to bring men and women into right relation with God. For Machen the church influenced culture by furthering right dogma; for Erdman, the faith ordered society through the lives of redeemed men and women. Though neither would deny the validity of the points the other stressed, differing emphases caused sharp divisions.

The conflict between Erdman and Machen pointed to issues that would, in time, separate even Bryan and Macartney from Machen. Prior to 1925 Machen, Macartney, and Bryan were almost inevitably mentioned in the same breath as the ruling triumvirate of Presbyterian fundamentalism. But both Macartney and Bryan eventually moved away from the dogmatic separatism of Machen. These changes in the shape of the fundamentalist party revealed significantly different understandings of the nature of Christianity and its mission to the world. Though Macartney and Machen would not part ways for a number of years, Bryan, in 1925, was already showing signs of disenchantment with the militant game plan. Of course, Bryan, who had been raised in a tradition much closer to Erdman's than to Machen's, had always maintained a rather curious relationship to the Old School Presbyterians. His concern for doctrine was generated less by a passion for creedal purity than by a belief that fundamental Christian doctrines provided the foundation for American Christian civilization; that is, he was primarily concerned with social, not theological or ecclesiastical, questions. Perhaps just as important, Bryan was a seasoned politician who understood the value of compromise. These differences had resulted in Bryan's attempt to arrange a compromise in the Fosdick case in 1923 and his approval of the motion for *no action* against the Auburn Affirmation in 1924. In 1925 the break became open when Bryan refused to endorse the militants' standard-bearer, Lapsley McAffee, in favor of William O. Thompson.[138] With this move, Bryan placed himself squarely in the camp of the tolerant conservatives so scorned by Machen.[139] By all accounts, Thompson and Erdman were in agreement on all major questions of theology and ecclesiology.[140] In a curious twist, then, Bryan, who only a few weeks after this assembly would establish himself as the high priest of fundamentalism at the Scopes Monkey Trial, was breaking his fundamentalist alliances in the ecclesiastical realm. Had he not died shortly after the trial, it seems clear that Bryan would have moved into the camp of the tolerant evangelical conservatives.

Even as the militant party was encountering defections, liberals worked to build closer relationships with inclusivist traditionalists. On 6 April and 2 May 1925 Coffin wrote letters to Erdman, encouraging him in the face of attacks from the Right.[141] In reply Erdman wrote, "At least one very great compensation for passing through the experiences of this present year is that I have come to know you so much better and that my affection for you has deepened." Erdman confessed to his newfound friend that if elected, he would "do everything in my power to see that the affairs of the Church were carried on in accordance with constitutional processes," so that the mission of the church might once again be prosecuted with vigor "at home and abroad."[142]

At the Columbus assembly Herbert B. Smith nominated Erdman for moderator, describing his candidate as "the best loved man in the Presbyterian Church today." He reiterated Erdman's platform of "constitutionalism, a united church, and a forward movement for the Church, especially along the lines of evangelism and foreign missions."[143] Garnering support from people as diverse as Coffin and the fundamentalist evangelist Billy Sunday, Erdman captured the second ballot by a margin of fifty votes over his closest competitor.[144] The mood of the assembly seemed to be one of peace. Erdman opened his administration with a plea for goodwill. "We want to feel that we are one great court of the Lord," he declared. "I plead with you to be patient and to support me with your prayers. I shall allow you to exercise Christian charity, but I want us to believe that there is not one man here who is not absolutely loyal to the Divine Lord and Master whose presence we wish to acknowledge."[145] In an effort to build consensus, the new moderator handed out committee chairs to representatives of every faction.[146] Though Erdman's election boded well for those desiring peace, the issues before the assembly—as all well knew—carried a strong potential for schism.

Key among the items before the assembly were a memorial and a complaint addressing licensing procedures in the New York Presbytery. The presbytery, motivated by repeated challenges to its decisions, had asked the assembly "to determine by its Judicial Commission, the proper status of a Presbytery in its Constitutional powers in the matter of the licensing of candidates." Additionally, New York Presbytery's licensing of Henry P. Van Dusen and Cedric A. Lehman, who could not affirm the virgin birth, came before the assembly again.[147] In a preemptive move, Coffin met with Erdman before any decisions were made to warn him that an attack on the Presbytery of New York would "cause a split in the church."[148] Erdman, determined to do all in his power to prevent such a result, agreed to let Coffin present a formal protest if the commission ruled against the presbytery.[149]

The judicial commission reported on Tuesday afternoon, 26 May. In response to the complaint against New York's licensure of Van Dusen and Lehman, the commission recognized two central issues: "the right of the General Assembly to review the action of a Presbytery in licensing candidates for the ministry; and the necessary requirements for licensure." On the first question the commission ruled that "the General Assembly has supervisory power to review and control the action of the Presbyteries in issuing and continuing licenses to preach." Having thus established its prerogative to address the case of Van Dusen and Lehman, the commission declared that inasmuch as these two could not affirm their belief in the virgin birth, a doctrine repeatedly affirmed by previous assemblies, the presbytery should have deferred their licensing. As such, it returned the matter to the presbytery for appropriate action.[150]

To Coffin's mind, the dreaded worst had happened; but he and his allies were not unprepared. Modernists, long on the defensive, took the offense. Coffin quickly left his seat, mounted the dais, and read a prepared statement. "The sixteen commissioners of the Presbytery of New York," he stated, "on behalf of the said Presbytery, respectfully declare that the Presbytery of New York will stand firmly upon the constitution of the Church, reaffirmed in the reunions of 1870 and 1906, which forbids the Assembly to change or add to the conditions for entrance upon or continuance in the holy ministry, without submitting such amendment to the Presbyteries for concurrent action."[151] The atmosphere, one observer noted, was "charged with the danger of revolt and schism."[152] The split that Coffin had threatened and Erdman had feared looked imminent.

The moderator, determined to do his best to prevent such an outcome, proposed one further peace initiative. Surrendering his chair, Erdman moved "that a Commission of Fifteen members be appointed to study the present spiritual condition of our Church and the causes making for unrest, and to report to the next General Assembly, to the end that the purity, peace, unity and progress of the Church may be assured."[153] The motion, which had been first suggested by the conservative Mark Matthews, was seconded by both Bryan and Coffin[154] and passed unanimously.[155]

At a meeting of liberals that evening, many expressed a strong desire to walk out of the assembly. Coffin and Erdman counseled restraint. According to church historian Lefferts Loetscher, Erdman told the group that "there was no need for them to leave the Church on the constitutional issue, because their interpretation of the constitutional question was the correct one."[156] Tempers were calmed and a possible schism was averted. But in one swift move the tables had been dramatically turned. Though the liberal threat to bolt the church was apparently sincere, it also served the strategic purpose of demanding a choice from the moderate conservatives. Strict doctrinal orthodoxy and a united church were no longer an option; one or the other, the liberals implied, would have to go. In a letter to Morgan Noyes written shortly after the assembly, Coffin outlined the modernist game plan:

> I agree entirely with your diagnosis of the situation and I can assure you that I talk up very boldly to the Moderator and to all the Moderate group. We must put the fear of God upon them. Just now I am trying to organize some of our wealthy men so that if a crash should come there will be money for men in economic straits. A strong organization of vigorous laymen will do much to strengthen our own position and force the Conservatives to yield. I think a very small change in the form of government, giving Presbyteries final authority in licensure is all we need ask just now.[157]

Reactions to the assembly revealed more than ever the split that was developing within the fundamentalist ranks. While Macartney claimed that the fundamentalist program had been upheld in its entirety, Machen feared that "the evangelical movement has been stopped and the Modernists are in even more complete control than . . . before."[158] Machen was disturbed by the fact that conservatives like McAffee and McEwan had supported aspects of Erdman's administration.[159] Nevertheless, he admitted that the decision regarding Van Dusen and Lehman was "one of the most important decisions that has ever been made in the entire history of the Presbyterian Church or of any great Church in recent years."[160]

Having anticipated the worst, Coffin was well pleased with the results. The 1925 assembly, he declared, had "been one of the finest assemblies in the history of the Church." In a paean to Erdman he claimed that the moderator had acted with "admirable tact, tenderness, good judgment and manifest fairness."[161] His satisfaction with the spirit of the assembly notwithstanding, Coffin deplored the decision of the judicial commission regarding Van Dusen and Lehman. In a comment revealing Coffin's blindness to the differences appearing in the fundamentalist ranks, Coffin argued that the commission's decision flung "wide the door for the complete Bryanizing of the Presbyterian Church." He continued,

It is possible for Mr. Bryan as an elder to ask a candidate for the ministry whether he believes the world was created in six days. If the young man replies in the negative, Mr. Bryan has only to take a complaint through the Synod to the General Assembly, and by the same logic which governs this decision, the Permanent Judicial Commission will have no option but to propose to the Assembly a verdict making that an essential to ordination, and evolution is impossible to any man seeking ordination in our Church.[162]

Despite this concern, the bold New Yorker encouraged his congregation to take heart. True, separation might be forced on the liberals, but the time was not yet. "Intellectual integrity" was still an option in the Presbyterian Church. But freedom of belief was not the only issue. "We are contending," he concluded, "for a great principle—for the principle that nothing shall be made essential which Jesus Christ does not make essential, in order that with as much as in us is we may freely proclaim Him with His emphases and His present power to save the world."[163] As with Erdman, evangelism provided the final reason for unity. The similarities would not be lost on the church.

William Jennings Bryan and the Scopes Trial

Coffin's allusions to Bryan's antievolution crusade were especially apposite in the late spring of 1925. In early May, Bryan had agreed to serve as prosecution counsel in the trial of John T. Scopes in Dayton, Tennessee.[164] Scopes, a young science teacher, had been charged with violating a recently adopted statute prohibiting the teaching of biological evolution in Tennessee's public schools. As quickly as Bryan signed on with the prosecution, the American Civil Liberties Union and the famous agnostic attorney Clarence Darrow came to Scopes's defense.[165] The trial, billed by Bryan as a "duel to the death" between Christianity and atheism, was set for 10 July 1925.[166]

As the trial approached, Bryan asked Machen and Macartney to come and assist him at Dayton, but both demurred. Machen deftly avoided accepting Bryan's invitation, writing,

> I am deeply interested in the contention in which you are engaged against the naturalistic doctrine of evolution, and I am morally certain as to the debasing chracter [sic] of much of the teaching with regard to this subject that has been going on in the public schools. At the same time, I have never myself engaged in any such study of the subject as[?] would make me competent to give expert testimony; and with regard specifically to the teaching in the Public schools my information is merely of a somewhat vague and hearsay kind, which, though sufficient to convince me, would not be admitted in a court of law. It is with the very greatest regret, therefore, that I confess my incompetence to help you in the approaching trial.[167]

Macartney was unable to assist Bryan because of previous plans to travel overseas. Even if he had been available, however, Macartney might not have traveled to Dayton. Remembering the event he wrote,

> The last word I had from Mr. Bryan was a letter inviting me to come and assist him in the famous, and somewhat notorious, Scopes trial at Dayton, Tenn. Scopes was on trial for teaching the hypothesis of Evolution in violation of the laws of Kentucky [sic]. I was just as glad that it was not possible for me to take part in that trial, as I was no expert in the field of biology. But I could have testified, with great earnestness and enthusiasm, as to the sad and evil effect of the hypothesis of Evolution in the field of morals and religion.[168]

As it was, Bryan had to fight his battle without the aid of his former ecclesiastical allies.

Dayton, Tennessee, a rural hamlet of about seventeen hundred, became the news capital of the nation for the duration of the trial. Almost 150 reporters sent nearly 150,000 words a day by telephone and telegraph to eager readers.[169] The town itself took on the atmosphere of a carnival, with "hot dog venders, lemonade merchants, preachers" and interested parties of every sort crowding the streets.[170] Dayton was suddenly on the map.

The outcome of the trial was a foregone conclusion. Despite efforts of the defense to have the charges dismissed on legal grounds, Scopes was convicted of teaching evolution and fined a hundred dollars.[171] More important than Scopes's conviction, however, was a verbal battle between Bryan and Darrow that discredited the fundamentalist movement across America. At the climax of the trial, Scopes's attorneys, who had been denied the right to bring testimony of expert scientific witnesses, called Bryan to the stand as witness for the defense.[172] Bryan, who had been opposing evolution for years on the stump, could hardly refuse the offer.

For Bryan and his allies the move was an unmitigated disaster. Bryan floundered under Darrow's relentless examination, revealing his shallow thinking and ill preparation in the realm of religion. Though he maintained that he accepted the biblical accounts of Jonah and the big fish and the creation of Eve from Adam's rib, he could not speculate on such a simple question as where Cain might have found a wife. More important, he admitted that he had no knowledge of geology, comparative religions, or ancient civilizations.[173] In short, Bryan's performance confirmed all of the worst stereotypes of fundamentalists as uneducated, unthinking, and reactionary. Though the debate would later be expunged from the records, Bryan's words had already been wired across the nation.[174] The damage was done.

Bryan's plan to examine Darrow the following day was thwarted by Attorney General Stewart and Judge Rawlston, who had decided that they had seen enough forensic pyrotechnics. Moreover, when the defense declined the right to closing argument, they prevented Bryan from delivering a long-planned speech denouncing the evils of evolution.[175] Bryan was thus left unable to redress the damage he had done on the witness stand. His testimony, combined with Dayton's Southern country setting, left the indelible impression that fundamentalism was a rural phenomenon, a function of social backwardness, that would pass with the advances of an educated, urban culture.[176]

With Bryan's death five days after the trial, fundamentalism lost its most conspicuous leader. On his return from Europe, Clarence Macartney eulogized his former companion as the "incarnation of genial good nature and kindness." Notably, Macartney used this sermon to recall, once again, Bryan's example of the use of opportunity. Of his friend he said, "What he was most grateful to God for was that through the name and the fame given him through his political activities he had been granted an unusual opportunity to do good to his fellow men, and that he had made use of that opportunity meant far more to him than the high office of the Presidency."[177]

Though no one could fill Bryan's shoes as a leader of interdenominational fundamentalism, many of his allies sought to perpetuate his legacy through organizations such as Bryan University and the Bryan Bible League.[178] The backers of Bryan University, seemingly oblivious to the vast theological and cultural differences between Machen and Bryan, twice sought Machen's support for their institution. In December 1925 Machen turned down an offer to serve on the Bryan University National Campaign Committee, citing "the great pressure of duties" he was under.[179] Then in 1927 Machen was invited to assume the position of president of the new school. Again he declined to connect himself with the project, this time citing his desire to remain at Princeton and his lack of training in administration. Nevertheless, in closing his letter of decline he wrote,

> I sympathize fully with your desire to promote an education that shall be genuinely Christian. And I pray that those who, like you, wherever they may be, cherish such a desire may not be discouraged by the opposition of the world. You represent a cause which cannot ultimately fail. And even now, despite all the forces of unbelief, despite hostile actions even of the organized church, the gospel of Jesus Christ still shines out from the Word of God and is still enshrined in Christian hearts.[180]

In the not-too-distant future Machen would be founding his own institute for the preservation of "genuinely Christian" education.

The Special Commission of 1925

Erdman announced the members of the Special Commission of 1925 in June. Henry C. Swearingen, one-time pastor of Bryan, was named chair of the committee.[181] Though two well-known conservatives, Mark Matthews and Lapsley McAffee, were appointed, the moderating tendencies of most of the members led Machen to declare that the "partisan character" of the commission was even stronger than he had feared.[182] Among the moderates, perhaps none would play a more important role in the final shape of the commission's report than Robert E. Speer, a close friend of Erdman and senior secretary of the Presbyterian Board of Foreign Missions.[183]

The commission held four meetings between the 1925 and 1926 assemblies, soliciting testimony from representatives of various factions, among whom were Machen, Macartney, and Coffin.[184] The statements of Machen and Macartney were, of course, similar. The causes of the controversy, Machen asserted, were "reducible to one great underlying cause," namely, the presence of modernism in the church.[185] Likewise, Macartney charged that the conflict had been precipitated by "the presence in the Church of those who hold views which others in the Church regard as hostile to the purpose of the Church and contrary to the Scriptures." Perhaps the most notable difference in the testimonies of these two crusaders was Macartney's claim that the teaching of evolution in church-related schools and colleges had contributed to the furor.[186] Machen, as noted earlier, insisted on a supernatural understanding of the creation of humanity but never opposed biological evolution as vociferously as did Macartney and Bryan. For Machen, doctrine was always the paramount concern.

Coffin, naturally, had a completely different analysis of the situation. "The differences," he claimed, "are due to misapprehension."[187] Instead of dwelling on these imagined disagreements, then, he warned about the dangers of division and the importance of a united evangelical witness. Coffin declared,

> I for one, and I think I speak for all of the liberal party, have no desire to see the Church split. But that is not true of our laymen. In the church I serve, a number of men have said, "The time has come when the split is inevitable, and it is nonsense for you to delay." . . . And they wanted to get out. "If law cases are involved we will fight it to the bitter end," they said. But that would plunge the Church into calamitous litigation and hinder us from doing our work and building up the kingdom of God. When you face the perfectly dreadful condition of the world today, the moral breakdown in all cities, the people who are disaffected from the Church, it is ruinous to divide existing forces. We ought to work harmoniously together and emphasize those things in which we agree.[188]

Coffin's implied threat of schism and appeal for pragmatic tolerance was taken to heart by the commission, which sought to steer a course that would offend neither liberals nor conservatives. In practice this meant finding a way to eliminate the fundamentals as requirements for ordination without denying their truth or import. Despite "sharp differences" on the commission, the group arrived at a consensus and presented a unanimous report to the 1926 assembly.[189]

At the opening of the 1926 General Assembly on 27 May Erdman preached on a characteristic theme, "The Power of the Holy Spirit." Though he did not directly address the controversy in the church, neither did he avoid the topic. "A man who is factious and causes separations among Christians shows that he is out of fellowship with Christ and is not controlled by his Spirit," Erdman declared, "and a divided church is always spiritually weak and impotent." Theological debate was fine, he allowed, but only in spirit of love. Above all, Erdman contended, the church needed to yield to the power of the Spirit. Only then could the church successfully prosecute its evangelistic mission to the world.[190]

With Erdman's backing, W. O. Thompson decisively defeated Lapsley McAffee as moderator of the 1926 assembly. In turning over the gavel to Thompson, Erdman noted that the peace and progress of the church were safe in Thompson's hands.[191] Coffin, who was again a delegate to the assembly, wrote home, "Here everything has begun most favorably and I think we are in for better days. It seems to be everyone's wish to keep the peace."[192]

The commission reported to the assembly on Friday, 28 May.[193] In its preliminary statement the commission revealed its allegiance to the program advanced by Erdman the preceding year. "If there be any constitutional way of stilling unrest and of adjusting differences," the report stated, "the Commission believes itself obligated to find that way." The report listed five major causes of unrest in the church: general intellectual movements, historical differences in the church, diverse attitudes toward questions of polity, theological changes, and misunderstanding. Under the first category the commission noted the "so-called conflict between science and religion," naturalistic worldviews, different understandings of the nature of God, changes in language, and the decline of religion in school and home. Divisions deriving from former Old School–New School differences, variant interpretations of the authority of the General Assembly, disagreement over recent changes in the structure of the church, and the "lack of representation of women in the Church" all added to the ecclesiastical unrest. In response to the fundamentalist claims that liberalism was an entirely different religion than Christianity, the commission stated that as far as it could discern, there was no radically liberal party within the church and that "the Assembly believed in its own evangelical unity and in the evangelical unity of our Church at large." Finally, the report admonished the church to desist from all "unfair and untrue statements which have been made in speech and in printed publications." "If we are to have peace and purity in the Church," the fifteen members demanded, "all slander and misrepresentation must be brought to an end."[194]

An analysis of the historical precedents for doctrinal toleration in the church provided the heart of the report. After examining four controversies in the church's history the commission stated, "From the events of our own history we cull the remedy for many of our present ills. Two controlling facts emerge. One is, that the Presbyterian system admits of diversity of view where the core of truth is identical. Another is, that the Church has flourished best and showed most clearly the good hand of God upon it, when it laid aside its tendencies to stress these differences, and put the emphasis on its unity of spirit."[195] Contrary to the claims of Machen that doctrine was paramount, the commission went on to argue that "Presbyterianism is a great body of belief, but it is more than a belief; it is also a tradition, a controlling sentiment. The ties which bind us to it are not of the mind only; they are ties of the heart as well." Inasmuch as this was the case, Presbyterians needed to manifest a spirit of toleration toward their fellow believers.[196]

Of course, the commission did not want to imply that toleration meant doctrine was unimportant. "Toleration does not involve any lowering of the Standards," they insisted. "It does not weaken the testimony of the Church as to its assured convictions." But the limits of doctrine had to be established "either *generally*, by amendment to the Constitution, or *particularly*, by Presbyterial authority, subject to the constitutional right of appeal."[197] According to this reading of history, toleration of diverse doctrinal views for the sake of evangelical unity—not concern for precise orthodoxy—had been the dominant, and successful, tendency in the church. Echoes of the Auburn Affirmation were clearly audible in this interpretation of American Presbyterianism.

These echoes resounded even more distinctly in the section of the report that addressed the constitutional power of the assembly. As a legislative and administrative body, the assembly could make deliverances that, though "entitled to great respect and deference," were liable to repeal by any subsequent assembly. As a judicial body, the assembly could render final decisions for a particular case; but such a ruling, the commission argued, did not set unalterable precedent for all similar future cases. In none of these capacities, however, could the assembly alter the Constitution. Rather, only the General Assembly acting in concert with the presbyteries could change constitutional provisions.[198] Though the commission did not draw out the ramifications of these principles for the Presbyterian controversy at this time, the meaning was clear to all: the five essentials had no binding authority. The arguments of the Auburn Affirmation had, essentially, been accepted in toto.[199]

In closing, the commission recommended that the report be accepted, that the term of the commission be extended for another year for further study, that clergy and members be enjoined to "patience and forbearance," and that the assembly reaffirm its loyalty to "the whole body of evangelical truth" and to the Constitution of the church.[200] At the conclusion of the report, *Time* magazine reported, the assembly rose in applause for three minutes.[201]

When the time to debate the commission's report arrived, it looked, at first, as if objection would be nil. Macartney could not allow such a travesty. Though the seasoned politician lauded many aspects of the document, he objected to the section that maintained the right of an assembly to ignore the judicial precedents of previous assemblies. Such, he maintained, encouraged the Presbytery of New York, which would now look to reject the virgin birth as an essential tenet of the church. He therefore moved the excision of various sections addressing this point, asked that the commission be dismissed, and retired to his seat to see what might develop.[202]

Unfortunately for the fundamentalists, the next commissioner recognized by the moderator was Albert J. McCartney, Clarence's elder and more liberal brother. Arriving at the platform, McCartney opened, "Mr. Moderator, fathers and brethren, and brother Clarence."[203] After the laughter subsided, he continued,

> Clarence is all right friends. The only trouble is he isn't married. If that old bachelor would marry he would have less time to worry over other people's theology. I'm for this report from cover to cover—not so much for what it says as the spirit that pervades it. We were brought up together, Clarence and I, and our mother sang the same hymns to us—"Rock of Ages" for me and "There Is a Fountain Filled with Blood" for him. We didn't know what those words meant then, but it was the same Christianity we both profest.
>
> I know that if mother could come back there would be room for him and for me to say our prayers in the same words on her knee at that old home of ours in western Pennsylvania. I believe there is room for him, and for you and me, to say our prayers in identical language in the Presbyterian Church.[204]

Albert returned to his seat to thunderous applause. The die was cast. Clarence Macartney's motion was defeated and the report was carried with only one opposing vote.[205]

The following year the commission presented its final report. While noting that the General Assembly had "an undoubted right to interpret the Constitution in declaratory deliverances," it suggested that "most of the ministers and members of our church will agree that the risk of such action is great, and that the General Assembly may well refrain from taking such a course, especially as it may be misconstrued as a virtual amending of our organic law by another method than that prescribed by the Constitution." More importantly, the commission contended that the judicial decisions of the General Assembly "cannot be made to rest properly upon a merely declaratory deliverance of a former Assembly." Rather, the report continued,

> it seems quite clear . . . that, granting for the moment the authority of the General Assembly, acting in any capacity, to declare broadly that an article is essential and necessary, it would be required to quote the exact language of the article as it appears in the Confession of Faith. It could not paraphrase the language nor use other terms than those employed within the Constitution, much less could it erect into essential and necessary articles doctrines which are only derived as inferences from the statements of the Confession.[206]

In short, the "five fundamentals" enumerated by the assemblies of 1910, 1916, and 1923 were now officially declared to be nonbinding.[207] Erdman's efforts to bring order out of the chaos of the church had, apparently, succeeded. With the adoption of the report of the special commission, tolerance for "liberal evangelicals" was almost guaranteed. Now, in the eyes of Erdman, the church could return to its task of proclaiming the gospel. The mission of the church—to individuals and thus to America and the world—was safe.

Despite the wave of toleration that swept in the reports of 1926 and 1927, goodwill did not extend to all corners of the church's life. The 1926 assembly tabled the appointment of J. Gresham Machen to the chair of apologetics and Christian ethics at Princeton and established a special committee to investigate the increasing conflicts at Princeton. Having lost the church to the forces of tolerant evangelicalism, militant conservatives found themselves making their last great stand at Princeton. Machen, of course, stood center stage in the controversy.

7

The Reorganization of Princeton and the Birth of Westminster

The appointment of a special committee to study the "conditions affecting the welfare of Princeton Seminary" and the concurrent suspension of a decision on Machen's appointment to the chair of apologetics and Christian ethics was but the culmination of the tensions growing at the seminary since 1920. Differences within the faculty, manifested in disagreements over the 1920 Plan of Union, the van Dyke incident, the League of Evangelical Students, and the controversy in the church at large, threatened to undo the institution.[1] Despite efforts to reconcile the parties, internal strife had, by 1926, reached such a pitch that many of the trustees and directors of Princeton had requested the 1926 assembly to appoint a committee to address the situation.[2]

The faculty majority at Princeton—composed of Machen, Robert Wilson, Geerhardus Vos, Caspar Hodge, William Greene, and Oswald Allis—were convinced that Princeton, by its charter, was committed to defending and propagating Old School Calvinism alone.[3] The faculty minority, composed of President J. Ross Stevenson, Charles Erdman, Frederick Loetscher, John Davis, and J. Ritchie Smith exhibited a willingness to accept more liberal views and a desire to make Princeton's teaching more nearly approximate the evangelical mainstream of the church.[4]

By the spring of 1925 the impending retirement of Professor Greene from the chair of apologetics threatened the possible undoing of the Old School majority. Everyone in the faculty was well aware that a shift in one vote between the factions could dramatically affect the character of the faculty's decisions. Thus, when on 10 November 1925 Macartney was elected to succeed Greene, Machen was delighted.[5] Machen pleaded with Macartney to accept the position, writing, "The whole future of

Princeton Seminary, I am almost tempted to say, depends upon your decision. I am bound to say that if you decline I fear the battle so far as Princeton is concerned is practically lost."[6]

Despite Machen's entreaties, Macartney was not at all sure he wanted to accept the post. Numerous alumni opposed his election.[7] More importantly, Macartney viewed himself primarily as a preacher, not an academic.[8] In this moment of indecision, Macartney turned to Frederick Loetscher for advice. Loetscher, who knew Macartney's talents and was also well aware of the balance of faculty at the school, recommended that Macartney remain in the pastorate.[9] Ultimately, Macartney followed Loetscher's advice. In May he turned the appointment down, only to accept a lucrative call to First Presbyterian Church, Pittsburgh nine months later.[10]

In response to Macartney's decision, the board of directors elected Machen to the position of professor of apologetics and Christian ethics; but he, too, hesitated to accept. His training was in the field of New Testament, not apologetics. More important, his acceptance of the chair would not strengthen the conservative voting block, as would the addition of a new exclusivist faculty member. Though perhaps loathe to admit it, a third factor also played on Machen's mind. He knew that his appointment required the approval of the General Assembly and that his reputation among many was tarnished. His fear surfaced in a letter home when he wrote, "My election has to be confirmed by the General Assembly; but hated though I am, I hardly think that the unprecedented step will be taken of contesting the confirmation of a professor's election by a Seminary Board of Directors."[11] Machen accepted the election, but his deepest fears would be realized. In full view of the church and the world, after twenty years of teaching at Princeton, his appointment would not only be challenged but, for all intents and purposes, rejected.

On the last day of the 1926 assembly, the Standing Committee on Theological Seminaries, responding to the request of members of the board of trustees and board of directors of Princeton, moved that the assembly appoint a committee to study and attempt to reconcile the differences at Princeton and that no action be taken on Machen's appointment until the following year.[12] Both Stevenson and Erdman supported this request on the floor of the assembly. The controversy at Princeton, Stevenson declared, stemmed not from doctrinal disagreement but rather from conflicting attitudes toward Princeton's mission. What was at stake was whether Princeton would teach Old School scholasticism alone or tolerate divergent theological views. "We are the agency of the combined old school and new school," he argued, "and my ambition as President of the seminary is to have it represent the whole Presbyterian Church and not any particular faction of it."[13]

Erdman expressed similar views. "I love the institution I have served for twenty years," he professed, "but I love still more peace and the progress of the Presbyterian Church." He encouraged the assembly to examine the seminary's life, and, just as importantly, recommended that Machen's promotion be tabled pending results from the investigation. The battle scars left from years of fighting were evident in Erdman's evaluation of his colleague, "What is questioned is whether Dr. Machen's temper and methods of defense are such as to qualify him for a chair in which his whole time will be devoted to defending the faith. . . . We want a kindly commission to investigate. Shall we calmly await its report or shall we prejudice the case and confirm the election."[14]

An important, though unmentioned, issue in the discussion of Machen's qualifications for the chair was his view of Prohibition. As discussed in the preceding chapter, the enforcement of the Eighteenth Amendment was a vital concern among American evangelicals in the 1920s.[15] Though rooted in biblical and theological convictions, the crusade against beverage alcohol also reflected deep concerns about the direction of American civilization. As sociologist Joseph R. Gusfield has argued, Prohibition became a symbol of the hegemony of Anglo-Saxon, Protestant culture. "The Eighteenth Amendment was," Gusfield claims, "the high point of the struggle to assert the public dominance of old middle-class values. It established the victory of Protestant over Catholic, rural over urban, tradition over modernity, the middle class over both the lower and upper strata."[16] Though Gusfield may overstate his case, for most Presbyterians—as for almost all evangelicals—Prohibition stood as a bulwark against the social movements threatening American Christian civilization. In the minds of many, opposition to Prohibition, in any form, was tantamount to religious and cultural apostasy.

Prohibition became a live issue in the controversy surrounding Machen when, in April 1926, the New Brunswick Presbytery considered a resolution endorsing the Eighteenth Amendment and the Volstead Act.[17] Machen opposed the resolution, not so much because of his libertarian opposition to Prohibition but because of his convictions about the "spirituality of the church." In a letter to Macartney he explained, "My vote was directed against a policy which places the Church in a corporate capacity as distinguished from the activities of its members, on record with regard to such political questions."[18] Wide publicity was given to this vote; and Macartney, for one, feared that Machen's conviction would seriously erode his support. "Many of our friends are exceedingly anxious about the press reports of your attitude towards the Eighteenth Amendment," Macartney wrote Machen before the assembly. "Our enemies are making use of this report of your action, and some are afraid that it will be introduced at the General Assembly in connection with your confirmation."[19]

Though Machen's attitude toward Prohibition was never raised on the floor of the assembly, it appears that the issue played a role in the eventual outcome. Prohibition was a central concern at the 1926 assembly, which adopted a resolution "opposing any modification of the Volstead Act" and urging all Presbyterians to redouble their efforts in support of the Eighteenth Amendment.[20] Given this support for Prohibition, it is inconceivable that Machen's views on this matter would have been dismissed as inconsequential by the assembly's commissioners. Even apart from all the other issues surrounding Machen's appointment, it is questionable whether the assembly would have elected a man to the chair of apologetics and Christian ethics who could not support the denomination's stance on the most important ethical question of the day. That the issue did, in fact, play a role in the assembly's decision was confirmed by a supporter of Machen who reported, "The fact that Professor Machen could not support a resolution in his presbytery approving the Eighteenth Amendment was the chief thing used by his enemies in working up sentiment in Baltimore against him."[21] For whatever reason—theological, ethical, administrative, or personal—the assembly saw fit to table Machen's appointment until the following year.

Understandably, Machen was irate over his rejection. Though he refused to make any official public response to the assembly's action, he bared his soul in a letter to his mentor Francis Patton, claiming, "It was a very bitter experience to me; and even the many expressions of sympathy which I have received can not serve to remove its bitterness."[22] Macartney, in a valiant effort to see a silver lining amidst the clouds, declared the assembly "a blessing in disguise." He continued, "The extraordinary events of this General Assembly will awaken the great number in our Church who think all is well with the Presbyterian Church, and will unite in solid ranks all those who are determined to stand for our precious blood-bought inheritance."[23] He would soon learn that such was not to be the case.

The Princeton Committee

The assembly committee to study Princeton held its first meeting at Princeton in November 1926. The seminary alumni, faculty, students, and administrative boards were all interviewed in hopes of gaining a clearer perspective on the history of the conflict.[24] All of these groups manifested a deep division in their analyses of the nature and mission of the seminary. Though opinions varied as to who was chiefly at fault in initiating and maintaining the controversy, most alumni, according to the committee's report, believed "that much of the difficulty in Princeton could be found in the Faculty; that the situation which had developed was greatly to be deplored . . . [and] that the contention in the Faculty must be ended."[25]

The testimony of the faculty revealed, the committee reported, a division on "matters of administration" and "Church polity."[26] The faculty majority, in a report to the committee, reviewed the various points of controversy since the 1920 Plan of Union and concluded that the hard-line conservatives had consistently pursued the proper course of action.[27] At the heart of their statement was the claim that Princeton was by tradition and character an Old School seminary. As such, it could not represent the "whole Church doctrinally . . . without departing from its historical position." The "future usefulness" of the seminary to the church, they claimed, depended on Princeton's maintaining its distinctive doctrinal identity. As Hodge analyzed the situation, "two entirely opposite attitudes toward truth or doctrine" existed at Princeton and in the church, "so that no peace between them is either possible or desirable."[28]

Stevenson's diagnosis of the conflict painted a radically different picture. "There has been in the faculty," he argued, "suspicion, distrust, dissension and division, and as I stated before the Assembly, in this Dr. Machen is involved." A censorious spirit among the faculty had given birth to a "divisive spirit among the students and . . . a departure from the historic position of the institution."[29] In a statement Machen later contested, Stevenson condemned the League of Evangelical Students because it connected Princeton with "small institutions and sects which are committed to separation and secession."[30] The solution to the controversy engulfing the seminary, he concluded, would be the triumph of a spirit of inclusivism, which, while not tolerating modernism, would make the seminary representative of the theology of the entire Presbyterian Church.[31]

Machen's testimony before the committee was largely a defense of his actions and positions over the preceding years.[32] He charged that Erdman had "impaired my good name in the community and throughout the Church at large" and without apology.[33] But the controversy was not, at root, a matter of personalities. Rather, as ever, Machen maintained that the real issue was doctrinal. "It concerns," he insisted, "the maintenance of the historic position of Princeton Seminary in the defense of faith."[34]

The different theological positions in the faculty were aggravated by the method in which Stevenson exercised the powers of his office. The position of president was a relatively new one at Princeton, initiated only in 1902 with the inauguration of Francis Patton. Though the president was, by right, the administrative head of the seminary, Patton limited the use of his authority and operated merely as the senior member of the faculty. Stevenson, who succeeded Patton in 1914, not only possessed a different view of Princeton's mission but assumed a more assertive posture as president. He believed the president should play a major role in developing seminary policy, recruiting faculty, and interpreting Princeton's mission to the church. The faculty majority, much more familiar with, and desirous of, a weak president, balked at this strong leadership, especially when used to counteract their program.[35]

The furor among the seminary faculty was echoed in differences between the administrative boards of the school. From its inception in 1811, the seminary had been governed by a board of directors subject to the authority of the assembly. The seminary's property, though initially held by the trustees of the General Assembly, was transferred in 1822 to the care of a distinct board of trustees of the seminary.[36] Although this bicameral structure provided the opportunity for conflicts, not until 1926, with the election first of Macartney and then of Machen to the chair of apologetics, was the full potential for controversy realized. The trustees, who tended to support Stevenson and his agenda, disapproved of the election of Macartney and Machen; while the board of directors, which sympathized with the faculty majority, felt that both Macartney and Machen were admirable candidates for the chair of apologetics.[37] Thus, while the trustees stood, "almost to a man . . . behind the President," the majority of the directors blamed Stevenson for Princeton's troubles and desired his resignation. Despite the wishes of the president, the directors held, Princeton had a mission to represent "the conservative wing of the Church."[38]

In its report to the 1927 assembly, the committee subscribed to the analysis of the controversy held by Stevenson and the faculty minority. All of the professors, the committee reported, were "loyal to the Standards of the Church" and no faculty advanced policies that supported "departure from the historic position of Princeton Seminary." Nevertheless, the report maintained, "Under present conditions the drift of Seminary control seems to be away from the proper service of the Church and toward an aggressive defense of the policy of a group." Given this situation, the committee believed that strife within the seminary would be eliminated not by addressing questions of doctrine but by administrative reconstruction. "The root and source of the serious difficulties at Princeton," the committee concluded, "and the greatest obstacle to the removal of these difficulties, seem to be in the plan of government by two Boards." Therefore, the committee recommended that the assembly expand the investigative committee to nine and that the new body be given the authority to establish a "single Board of Control" for the seminary. Moreover, the committee recommended that the appointments of Machen and any other faculty be deferred until the realization of the proposed reorganization.[39]

The mood of the 1927 assembly was demonstrated by the uncontested election of Robert E. Speer, secretary of the Board of Foreign Missions, as moderator. Speer, a Christocentric evangelical in the tradition of Horace Bushnell, possessed a comprehensive theology concerned primarily for the furtherance of the church's mission to preach the gospel of Christ.[40]

Despite the harmonious tone struck in Speer's unanimous election, the Princeton report was not to pass uncontested. Macartney characterized the report as "merely a throwing of dust to becloud the real issue."[41] Debate on the report was long and heated. The assembly finally approved the committee's report but not without making significant changes. In an effort to move cautiously, the assembly expanded the committee to eleven members and instructed the new committee to report proposed changes to the following Assembly.[42] Additionally, the promotions of Machen and, now, Oswald T. Allis, were held in abeyance.[43] After the final vote, J. Ross Stevenson with tears in his eyes thanked the assembly for its endorsement of his policies. Princeton would, he pledged, "carry forward the teachings of God."[44]

Reorganization Confirmed

The 1927 assembly was, Machen declared, "probably the most disastrous meeting, from the point of view of evangelical Christianity, that has been held in the whole history of our Church."[45] If reorganization succeeded, he held, Princeton would "be destroyed" and a "new institution of an entirely different type" would replace it.[46] By December, Machen had composed and printed a forty-eight-page document, entitled "The Attack Upon Princeton Seminary: A Plea for Fair Play." Princeton

Seminary, he argued, had for over a century "stood firmly for the full truthfulness of the Bible as the Word of God and for the vigorous defence and propagation of the Reformed or Calvinistic system of doctrine . . . that the Bible teaches." But with Stevenson's election to the presidency, Princeton's heritage had come under attack. In time, the differences between Stevenson's faction and the faculty majority led to confrontation and dissension. The solution to the conflict proposed by the investigative Committee, far from remedying the situation, would ruin Princeton and imperil the maintenance of scholarly Reformed evangelicalism.[47]

Princeton, Machen argued, had become a lighthouse of orthodoxy in an increasingly secular world. It stood "practically alone" as a defender of orthodoxy among the older theological institutions in the English-speaking world. "Despite the drift of the times," he declared, "our institution still defends the full truthfulness of the Bible as the Word of God, and still propagates, with all its rebuke to human pride, with all its proclamation of God's wondrous love, the gospel of the crucified and risen Lord."[48]

Princeton's almost singular position in the theological world raised the stakes in the battle for the seminary. "The end of Princeton Seminary," Machen contended, "will, in some sort, mark the end of an epoch in the history of the modern Church and the beginning of a new era in which new evangelical agencies must be formed." In the past, he noted, great universities and theological colleges had maintained the scholarly evangelical tradition. But secularizing tendencies had overcome these institutions one by one. Machen knew that many read the isolation of Princeton as a sign of its anachronistic thought, but he proffered a different analysis. "Instead of holding that we have been left behind in the march of progress," he argued, "one might also conceivably hold that in a time of general intellectual as well as moral decadence we are striving to hold aloft the banner of truth until the dawn of a better day."[49]

Machen's view of the unique position of Princeton in the theological world drove him to the conclusion that if Princeton were reorganized, a "truly evangelical seminary" would have to be founded to take its place. Thus, more than two years before Machen led in the founding of Westminster Seminary, he had determined his options. But in 1927 Machen still held out hope. Though ecclesiastical leaders were "running rough-shod over the principles of liberty in the church," the seminary could still be saved by the "evangelical people" in the church.[50]

Other documents addressing the situation at Princeton followed in rapid succession. Stevenson offered a paper of his own, maintaining that his position reflected the true Princeton heritage of Alexander, Miller, and Hodge. In addition, a majority of the board of directors distributed a letter blaming Stevenson for Princeton's turmoil; and two individual directors, W. Courtland Robinson and Frank H. Stevenson, offered personal evaluations in printed pamphlets.[51] Clarence Macartney, now settled in his new position as pastor of First Presbyterian Church, Pittsburgh, addressed the church in an article in *The Presbyterian Banner* in January asking, "Shall Princeton Pass?" The issue before the church was clear enough to the former moderator. "Should the next two General Assemblies adopt the plan recommended by the General Assembly of 1927," Macartney maintained, "it will mean nothing less than the passing of Princeton." Raising the specter of the Auburn Affirmation, Macartney charged that the plan to eliminate the board of directors "meets with the hearty and unanimous support of all those in the Presbyterian Church who are on record as subscribing, for instance, to the thoroughly un-Presbyterian and unevangelical statements of the Affirmation of 1924." As such, it was subject to serious questioning. But the struggle at Princeton had ramifications that exceeded even the boundaries of the Presbyterian Church. Inasmuch as Princeton was a major armory of orthodoxy in the struggle against modernism, its demise would have worldwide consequences. "In this crisis," Macartney concluded, "for the Presbyterian Church to dismiss and dissolve the Board of Directors which has kept its greatest Seminary so true to these doctrines, would discourage loyal men in the Church and dishearten evangelical Christians throughout the world."[52]

Erdman contributed his part to the discussion by circulating a public letter in late March to correct "misrepresentations" prevalent in the church. "No person is endeavoring to change the doctrinal teachings of Princeton Seminary nor are any influences working to that end," he asserted. The issues separating the trustees and directors were not doctrinal but grounded in personal and administrative differences. Given this situation and "in view of [the church's] great task and the world's infinite need," he pleaded for peace and evangelism. "This is no hour for strife but for united action in proclaiming the gospel message which Princeton has ever taught and which Presbyterians ardently love."[53]

Erdman's contention that no influences were at work to alter the doctrinal position of Princeton points to yet one more important difference between Erdman and Machen. As was argued earlier, Machen's Southern upbringing and experience in Germany allowed him to see more clearly than most the changes that secular ideas were producing in American culture and the church. This perspective, combined with Machen's insistence on pressing all ideas to their logical conclusion, drove him to the conviction that any concession to modernism at all would lead ineluctably to the apostasy of the church. But Erdman, raised in a tradition of Northern revivalism that allowed doctrinal variance for the sake of positive evangelism, could never see the dangers that Machen insisted lay down the path of toleration. In one aspect Erdman was right. No one at Princeton, it appears, was self-consciously attempting to "change the doctrinal teachings of Princeton Seminary." But Erdman was mistaken in asserting that no influences were "working to that end." For better or for worse, tolerance of doctrinal variation would, as Machen saw, eventually move Princeton away from its Old School Calvinistic roots.[54]

As the 1928 assembly approached, supporters of the board of directors circulated a petition, asking the assembly "to reject the reorganization of the Seminary recommended to the General Assembly of 1927 by the Special Committee to visit Princeton, and thus to leave the control of this great institution where it now resides."[55] In a massive show of traditionalist strength, about ten thousand ministers and elders signed this request.[56] Though the assembly took no specific action in response to this petition, it likely had a major impact on the commissioners' deliberations concerning Princeton.[57]

The General Assembly of 1928, meeting in Tulsa, Oklahoma, received two reports from the Committee of Eleven. The majority report recommended alterations in the seminary's charter and plan that would create a single controlling board at Princeton and broaden the powers of the president of the seminary. The minority report, submitted solely by Ethelbert D. Warfield, criticized the expansion of the president's powers and the method of choosing board members proposed by the majority. Over the objection of many conservatives, the assembly directed the Committee of Eleven to "nominate the members of the new Board of Trustees, and report the names for approval to the Assembly."[58] Sensing imminent defeat, conservatives took a page from the liberal playbook. Much as Coffin had threatened schism in order to put pressure on inclusivist traditionalists, Macartney now warned, in the words of the *New York Times*, "If the report is adopted the matter will be transferred from the ecclesiastical court to the civil courts at once and 'a long legal battle will ensue.'"[59] Much to Macartney's relief, the assembly, on the motion of Mark Matthews, decided to postpone any further consideration of the Princeton matter and directed the board of directors "to proceed immediately to compose the differences at the

Seminary" and to report to the next assembly.[60] Though Machen's elevation had been tabled once again, the opponents of reorganization had bought another year of time.

In response to the decisions of the assembly, Machen considered withdrawing from the Princeton faculty but opted simply to retract his acceptance of the chair of apologetics. The board of directors of the seminary made one more effort to reconcile their differences with the trustees and among the faculty, but to no avail.[61]

With all other avenues exhausted and the 1929 assembly on the horizon, various members of the board of directors forged new alliances in a final effort to avert total reorganization. A new majority proposed a new board composed of all the members of the former boards of directors and trustees. The compromise pleased few. Machen charged the directors with "selling out," and the trustees maintained that the proposed remedy was no solution at all.[62]

The 1929 assembly received six different reports addressing the Princeton situation.[63] In order to facilitate debate on the matter, speeches were restricted to ten minutes each.[64] Machen, a commissioner from New Brunswick Presbytery, used his limited time to set the issue squarely before his peers. As he rose before the assembly, Machen must have realized that his cause was undone. Since 1925 the General Assemblies had eschewed controversy for the sake of a unified evangelical mission, and this assembly seemed no different. Nonetheless, the battle had to be fought; principle had to prevail. Looking out across a sea of faces, he girded himself to plead his cause one more time:

> We at Princeton Seminary have been proclaiming an unpopular gospel, which runs counter to the whole current of the age; yet it is a gospel of which we are not ashamed. . . .
>
> We have derived our authority to preach this unpopular gospel not from any wisdom of our own, but from the blessed pages of God's Word. But from this gospel that the Scriptures contain the . . . world has gradually been drifting away. Countless colleges and universities and theological seminaries throughout the world, formerly evangelical, have become hostile or indifferent to that which formerly they maintained. They have done so often with many protestations of orthodoxy, and often with true evangelical intentions too, on the part of those who were unwitting instruments in the change. So it is with Princeton Seminary. We impugn no man's motives today; many of those who are lending themselves to this reorganization movement no doubt themselves believe in the Bible and are unaware of what is really being done. But no one who has the example of other institutions in mind, who knows the trend of the times, and who knows the facts about the present movement, can doubt but that we have

here only a typical example of the same old story, so often repeated, of an institution formerly evangelical that is being made to drift away by insensible degrees from the gospel that it was founded by godly donors to maintain. . . .

I cannot reach your minds, for the time does not suffice for that; and God has granted me no gift of eloquence that I might reach your hearts. I can only hope that a greater and more mysterious persuasion may prevent you from doing unwittingly that which is so irrevocable and so wrong. One thing at least is clear—there are many Christians in many lands who will feel that if the old Princeton goes, a light will have gone out of their lives.[65]

For those with ears to hear, Machen's Common Sense philosophy rang clear: the assembly would agree with him if only it "knew the facts." Machen's view of reality, as George Marsden has noted, "virtually eliminates any legitimate place whatsoever for perspective or point of view. All points of view other than the correct one are simply failures to see the facts as they actually are."[66] Machen did not understand that his own upbringing, his Southern heritage, his struggles with liberalism, and his inherited philosophy provided him with a perspective virtually unavailable to most of his listeners. Perhaps better than anyone else in the assembly hall he perceived the vast intellectual changes that were transforming America and its institutions of higher learning. But perhaps less than anyone present could he fathom why others, seeing the same data he saw, arrived at conclusions different from his own. He left no room for varying interpretations based on different perspectives, histories, philosophies, or values. As such, his appeal fell on deaf ears. The majority report of the committee passed.[67] The seminary would be reorganized.

The Founding of Westminster Theological Seminary

The unified board elected by the 1929 assembly consisted of eleven members from each of the two former boards and eleven members from the church at large.[68] Two of the thirty-three men, W. Beatty Jennings of the former board of trustees and Asa J. Ferry, an at-large addition, had signed the Auburn Affirmation five years earlier. Herein lay Machen's major difficulty with the new board of trustees. Though two "Affirmationists" hardly threatened to destroy Princeton in a day, Machen contended that this was a certain sign of Princeton's inevitable decline.[69] He therefore quickly came to the conclusion that he could not serve under the new administration. To remain at the seminary, he believed, would only "conceal what has been done" by the church.[70]

Though Machen considered pressing a battle for Princeton in the civil courts, he seemed to be most taken with the idea of founding a new seminary that would self-consciously carry on the Princeton tradition.[71] As early as July 1927 some members of the board of directors had mentioned the possibility of a new school, and after the 1929 assembly these discussions rapidly accelerated.[72] In his musings about a new seminary, Machen disclosed that the thought of a new church had also crossed his mind. In a letter to his mother he wrote, "Allis is all for the founding of a new Seminary at once, and so is Frank Stevenson. It is not beyond the bounds of possibility. . . . Who can say? It might be the beginning of some genuine evangelical effort. . . . A really evangelical Seminary might be the beginning of a really evangelical Presbyterian Church."[73] Though wary of the enormous task of founding a new school, the idea appealed to Machen.

On 17 June a group of ministers, laymen, Princeton faculty, and former directors of the seminary met in New York to discuss the possibility of founding a new school to continue the legacy of the "old Princeton."[74] The gathering resolved to support the former board of directors in any action they might pursue "toward preventing by legal means the misuse of the seminary's funds" or "toward the formation of a new seminary if they decide that it is necessary."[75] From this point on plans developed quickly, for on 8 July Rev. Charles Schall of Wayne, Pennsylvania convened a meeting of Machen, Allis, Wilson, and several Presbyterian businessmen to lay the groundwork for a new school.[76] Finally, on 18 July a meeting of over seventy persons, including former directors, faculty, and students of Princeton, resolved to launch a new school to "continue the policy of unswerving loyalty to the Word of God and to the Westminster Standards for which Princeton Seminary has been so long and so honorably known."[77] Westminster Theological Seminary had been born.

The creation of a new institution was not without friction. Chief among the conservative opponents of this endeavor was Clarence Macartney. Macartney had been elected to the new board of trustees of Princeton but hesitated to accept or decline this invitation.[78] Though he had fought beside Machen to this point, schism was not in his blood; and he strove to reconcile the disputing parties. Machen, in a 14 July letter to his brother, reported, "Macartney is still writing silly letters to Frank Stevenson expressing the hope that Allis and I will stay at Princeton."[79]

As plans for Westminster developed and Macartney still had not declined his election to the Princeton board, Machen's temper flared. He wrote of Macartney, "He is now talking very much as Erdman did in 1924— almost about dividing conservatives if we go forward with our move. *We* followed him, and now *he* deserts us. It's really quite base. My only hope is that he will not actually do it. I am not sure that he has given his final answer to the new Board."[80] Though Macartney eventually refused to serve on the Princeton board and became a director of Westminster, this developing division signaled the beginning of the end of the fundamentalist coalition.[81]

A number of reasons for Macartney's differences with Machen may be teased from the records. First, Macartney's concern for the maximum use of opportunity contributed to his desire to maintain a presence on the Princeton board. By all measures—wealth, status, size, tradition— Princeton was the paramount Presbyterian school in the nation and the leading conservative seminary in the country. In abandoning Princeton, Macartney must have realized, militant conservatives would not only split the conservative witness in the church but would leave the immense resources of the school in the hands of moderates and liberals. In the midst of his deliberations Macartney surely wondered whether, by maintaining a staunch orthodox presence at Princeton, traditionalists might still influence the direction of the seminary and thereby the direction of the church. Given Princeton's resources, it was not at all clear to Macartney that abandoning Princeton was the most responsible tack for conservatives to take.

A second factor contributing to Macartney's growing disagreement with Machen can be found in Machen's belief, first articulated in 1912, that the chief battleground of Christianity and secular culture lay in institutions of higher learning, not in the pulpit.[82] Machen's conviction that the academy held the preeminent position in the defense of Christianity essentially demanded that he organize a separate school upon Princeton's "apostasy." While Macartney certainly agreed with Machen that the defense of Christian ideas was imperative, he apparently did not assess the relative importance of pulpit and academy in the same way as Machen. If Macartney, like Machen, had viewed the seminary as the single most important bulwark of Christianity against secularism, he surely would have surrendered his pulpit for the professor's chair in 1925. But Macartney, following his Reformed Presbyterian heritage, believed the church had to further the cause of Christianity on a number of fronts: academy, pulpit, and society. Though he realized a great loss at Princeton's reorganization, it represented but one major battle in the effort to preserve the influence of orthodoxy. To Machen, the reorganization was almost the entire war.

Torn by his concern for the defense of true doctrine and for the witness of the church in the culture, Macartney hesitated to divide the fundamentalist party. On the question of Westminster Seminary Macartney finally came to follow Machen's lead; he could not serve on the board of a reorganized Princeton. But in 1933, when Machen organized an Independent Board for Presbyterian Foreign Missions, the results would be different. A final division was not far off.[83]

Of the Princeton faculty, Machen, Oswald Allis, Robert Wilson, and Cornelius Van Til opted not to remain under the new Princeton administration. These four were joined at Westminster by Ned Stonehouse, Allan Macrae, Paul Wooley, and R. B. Kuiper.[84] Significant donations to the cause—not the least of which came from Machen, his mother, and Allis—guaranteed financial solvency for the fledgling institution; and fifty students provided a constituency.[85] On 25 September Westminster Seminary held its opening exercises in Witherspoon Hall, Philadelphia.[86]

The Meaning of Westminster Theological Seminary

In 1927 Machen had claimed that "among the older institutions of theological learning in the English-speaking world" Princeton stood almost alone in its devotion to "the full truthfulness of the Bible as the Word of God."[87] But with the reorganization, Princeton had succumbed to the intellectual currents of the day. He wrote,

Fifty years ago many colleges and universities and theological seminaries were devoted to the truth of God's Word. But one by one they have drifted away, often with all sorts of professions of orthodoxy on the part of those who were responsible for the change. Until May, 1929, one great theological seminary, the Seminary at Princeton, resisted bravely the current of the age. But now that seminary has been made to conform to the general drift. . . . Princeton Seminary is lost to the evangelical cause.[88]

Though colored by Machen's insistence on pressing all ideas and movements to their logical conclusion, his exposition of the history of theological education in the United States was, on the whole, accurate.

Since the Civil War, America's seminaries and divinity schools had been profoundly influenced by the massive social and intellectual changes transforming the nation. The specialization of knowledge; developments in the study of history, sociology, and psychology; the advent of the research university; the New Theology; and changing conceptions of the role of the pastor—all affected the method and content of teaching at most of the leading seminaries and divinity schools across the nation. While in 1870 all schools focused on exegetical and systematic theology, by the 1920s many seminaries had expanded their curricular offerings to include courses such as the history of religions, religious education, psychology of religion, sociology, philosophy of religion, city missions, and social science. Often these curricular changes coincided with a liberalizing of the theological position of the schools. Indeed, by the end of World War I most of the largest, wealthiest, and most influential seminaries in the nation had responded to the rise of modernism by migrating toward the liberal end of the theological spectrum. Of the handful of schools that dominated the Northern theological landscape in 1920, only Princeton remained staunchly conservative.[89]

In a 1924 study entitled *Theological Education in America*, Robert L. Kelly acknowledged Princeton's stature in the theological world. Princeton, he observed, not only set the standard for Presbyterian schools but had "a wide influence among other denominations as well." In fact, with Union Seminary in New York, Princeton was probably one of the two leading theological schools in the nation.[90]

Though Machen may have overstated his case in arguing for Princeton's near-singular position as a defender of "the full truthfulness of the Bible" his allegations were clearly not unfounded. Other schools in the United States maintained a conservative witness in the theological world, but none approached Princeton's stature.[91] While most leading seminaries had altered their curriculum and theological stance to address the trends of the age, Princeton's faculty had resisted such cultural currents almost every step of the way. When, in Machen's eyes, Princeton also gave way to the secularizing tendencies of modernity, the only alternative was to found a new school based on traditional principles.

In founding Westminster Seminary, Machen and his supporters were making a number of statements to the church. First, and most obviously, they were declaring in the strongest possible way that with the reorganization of 1929, Princeton Seminary had abandoned its heritage. Westminster Seminary was to be Princeton reincarnate, founded to "carry on and perpetuate the policies and traditions of Princeton Theological Seminary, as it existed prior to the reorganization thereof in the year 1929."[92] In his address at the opening of the school, Machen expanded on this theme, declaring, "Though Princeton Seminary is dead, the noble tradition of Princeton Seminary is alive. Westminster Seminary will endeavor by God's grace to continue that tradition unimpaired."[93] Westminster stood as a visible, institutional protest against the reorganization of 1929.

More positively, Westminster, in maintaining Princeton's tradition, was to set the pace for conservative theological education in the nation and the world; the founding of Westminster Seminary was a statement about the importance of scholarly evangelicalism. Machen and his allies had a vision of Westminster as a world-class theological academy with global influence. In a speech before supporters of the seminary on 16 September 1929 Robert Dick Wilson claimed, "Westminster must take rank with the best schools in Scotland and Germany. It must be respected by powerful schools of theology like Union Theological Seminary and the theological departments of the University of Chicago and Harvard."[94] Indeed, "Unless Westminster attained an international reputation," Wilson believed, "it would fail."[95]

Machen subscribed completely to this vision for the infant seminary.[96] "We believe," he announced at the opening of Westminster, "that a theological seminary is an institution of higher learning whose standards should not be inferior to the highest academic standards that anywhere prevail."[97] Westminster would teach the Reformed faith, one advertisement declared, "upon a basis of scholarship second to none."[98] Machen was certain that, founded on such a high intellectual plane, Westminster's impact would be worldwide. "In many lands and in many communions," he declared, "there are those who will give thanks to God if the true Princeton tradition is made to live again."[99]

Westminster's commitment to academic excellence would be married to a particular vision of theological education that demanded biblical expertise and militant defense of the Reformed faith. In marked opposition to the tendency of many theological schools to offer an increasing number of courses rooted in the social sciences, Westminster, Machen insisted, would focus solely on the Bible. In order to become "specialists in the Bible," students at Westminster would study Hebrew and Greek, biblical exegesis, biblical theology, and, most important, systematic theology.[100] But Westminster graduates were not to be simply experts on the Scriptures. Maintenance of the Princeton tradition demanded not only scholarly training in the Bible but also a willingness to fight for the faith.[101]

Westminster Seminary was to be, in a very important way, a theological military academy. In large part its task was to train soldiers of orthodoxy ready and eager to do battle against the secular trends of the day. At the opening of Westminster, Machen warned his listeners that the school's students would be pariahs in modern culture. "Westminster Theological Seminary," he claimed, "will hardly be attended by those who seek the plaudits of the world or the plaudits of a worldly church." This was so because the seminary stood in self-conscious opposition to the secular intellectual tendencies coming to dominate American culture. Against the apostasy of church and culture, Machen held out hope for a brighter future, for a rebirth of orthodox Christianity to reform church and culture.[102] But such a revival, Machen insisted, would come not through the activities of "theological pacifists." No; what the church needed—and what Westminster would endeavor to provide—were "real men," "earnest contenders for the faith" who would, like Princeton's men of old, "hold aloft the banner of truth until the dawn of a better day."[103]

All of these emphases of Westminster Seminary pointed to Machen's deep-seated belief in the immense power of ideas. In 1924 Machen had declared, "The really great moments of history are the moments which mark the first enunciation of great ideas. Ideas, after all, are the great conquerers; they cross the best-dug trenches; they cut the most intricate barbed wire; they move armies like puppets; they build empires and pull them down."[104] Here is why Westminster had to be founded, why it had to provide an education second to none, why its graduates had to be determined gladiators on the intellectual battlefield of the modern world. Christianity was, at root, based on ideas. It was "a life founded upon a doctrine."[105] As such, "false ideas" were "the greatest obstacles to the reception of the gospel." If the intellectual foundation of the faith were destroyed by the secularization of the church, Christianity would be lost.[106]

Better than any other leader in the Presbyterian controversy Machen realized that the cultural and religious upheaval of the 1920s was the result of the ideological changes that had been working their way in America since the Civil War. Against the rise of secular ideas, Princeton had maintained and defended orthodox Calvinist doctrine. When Princeton was "lost to the evangelical cause," therefore, a new font of scholarly Calvinism had to be initiated to propagate true doctrine. Westminster stood as an institutional symbol of the essential place of doctrine in Christianity. Machen, feeling more and more the outsider, declared that in the midst of a hostile culture, Westminster would work to maintain "an intellectual atmosphere in which the acceptance of the Gospel will seem to be something other than an offence against truth." In so doing, Machen hoped, it would prepare for that day when the world would witness "a mighty revival of the Christian religion" that would restore the influence of Christianity in modern civilization.[107]

In the decade after reorganization Princeton, though hardly becoming a modernist institution, did experience a change in theological emphasis. Of the faculty at Princeton before 1929, only Armstrong and Loetscher continued on after 1937. Retirements, resignations, and death resulted in dramatic changes in faculty, giving a new tone to the school by the late 1930s.[108] Most important was the increasing influence of neo-orthodoxy on the Princeton campus, signaled by the inauguration of President John A. Mackay in 1937 and the appointment of neo-orthodox faculty such as Otto Piper and Elmer G. Homrighausen.[109] Noting this trend, Clifton Olmstead claimed that "during the late 1930's Princeton Theological Seminary . . . became the chief center of theological existentialism in the United States."[110] As such, Princeton abandoned the theology of Alexander, Hodge, and Warfield that had determined its course for so long.

Despite the grand visions held for Westminster by its founders, the seminary would, in the 1930s, experience serious controversy and division. In 1933 Machen, convinced that the Presbyterian Church tolerated liberals in the mission field, organized an Independent Board for Presbyterian Foreign Missions in competition with the denominational board. The General Assembly responded to this maneuver by instructing all clergy and laity of the Presbyterian Church to sever their relations with the independent board or face disciplinary action.[111] By 1936 disagreement over the wisdom of the independent board led thirteen trustees (including Clarence Macartney) and one faculty member of Westminster to resign.[112] In the course of this struggle over missions, Machen took on one of the most eminent and beloved servants of the church: Robert E. Speer. The results of this contest were all but a foregone conclusion. In challenging Speer and the Board of Foreign Missions, Machen would pick his last fight in the Presbyterian Church in the U.S.A.

Harry Emerson Fosdick, liberal Baptist preacher who, by preaching the sermon "Shall the Fundamentalists Win?", ignited the Presbyterian controversy. Courtesy of the First Presbyterian Church in the City of New York.

J. Gresham Machen, a leader of the militant conservatives, who, in *Christianity and Liberalism*, declared that liberalism was a different religion than Christianity. Courtesy of Westminster Theological Seminary, Philadelphia, Pennsylvania.

Clarence E. Macartney, prominent conservative preacher who led the fundamentalist response to Fosdick's "Shall the Fundamentalists Win?" by preaching "Shall Unbelief Win?" Courtesy of the Department of History, Presbyterian Church (U.S.A.), Philadelphia, Pennsylvania.

William Jennings Bryan, staunch opponent of Darwinism and "the most widely influential layman in the church." Photo by Bushnell. Courtesy of the Nebraska State Historical Society, Lincoln, Nebraska.

Henry Sloane Coffin, New York minister, educator, and leader of liberal Presbyterians. Courtesy of the Department of History, Presbyterian Church (U.S.A.), Philadelphia, Pennsylvania.

Charles R. Erdman, professor of practical theology at Princeton Seminary, known as "the best loved man in the Presbyterian Church." Photo by Underwood & Underwood. Courtesy of Mrs. Charles R. Erdman, Jr.

The faculty of Westminster Theological Seminary in the early 1930s, dedicated to preserving the tradition of the "old Princeton." Machen is in center. Courtesy of Westminster Theological Seminary, Philadelphia, Pennsylvania.

Charles R. Erdman with President Calvin Coolidge after a worship service at which Erdman preached. Coolidge is center, hat in hand. Erdman is to his left. Courtesy of Mrs. Charles R. Erdman, Jr.

Robert E. Speer, long-time
Secretary of the Presbyterian Board
of Foreign Missions and "Apostle
of Christian Unity." Courtesy of
the Department of History,
Presbyterian Church (U.S.A.),
Philadelphia, Pennsylvania.

Robert E. Speer speaking at the
1927 General Assembly of the
Presbyterian Church. Courtesy of
the Department of History,
Presbyterian Church (U.S.A.),
Philadelphia, Pennsylvania.

"All Calvinists." Left to Right: Clarence Macartney (Moderator of the 1924 General Assembly), President Calvin Coolidge, Lewis Mudge (Stated Clerk), and William Jennings Bryan (Vice Moderator) meet in 1925. From *North Church News* (Pittsburgh), 7 June 1925. Courtesy of McCartney Library, Geneva College, Beaver Falls, Pennsylvania. By permission of Pittsburgh Presbytery, Presbyterian Church (U.S.A.).

The Princeton Seminary faculty and Class of 1929. Charles R. Erdman is second row, far left. President J. Ross Stevenson is second row, center. J. Gresham Machen is third row, sixth from left. Courtesy of Princeton Theological Seminary, Princeton, New Jersey.

Henry Sloane Coffin (center), president of Union Theological Seminary in New York, with some of the faculty of Union in the 1930s. Courtesy of David D. Coffin.

8

Robert E. Speer and the Board of Foreign Missions

Even as Machen was fighting desperately to preserve the "old Princeton" in the spring of 1929, he was gearing up for combat with Robert E. Speer, senior secretary of the Board of Foreign Missions, over the orthodoxy of the board. Machen had long held suspicions about the faithfulness of many missionaries sent out by the board but, at least until the middle of the 1920s, had been able to support this enterprise. In a 1925 letter he allowed, "It is not now contrary to my conscience to give to our Foreign Board, though I cannot say that I give with much enthusiasm."[1] By 1929 his distrust of the board and of Speer had intensified to such a degree that he composed an essay entitled, "Can Evangelical Christians Support Our Foreign Board?" and sent it to Speer for his examination and comment.[2]

Speer and Machen were, of course, no strangers to each other and had found themselves on opposite sides of the ecclesiastical fence before. Speer had served on the Special Commission of 1925 and, as moderator of the 1927 General Assembly, presided over the approval of the commission's final report. Additionally, as a trustee of Princeton Seminary, he supported reorganization of the school.[3] None of these activities endeared Speer to his militant foe. By one account, Machen believed Speer to be "the most dangerous and injurious man in the Presbyterian Church."[4] Though Speer never said as much, the feeling was, most probably, mutual.

Given such differences in other arenas, it was no great surprise to find Machen up in arms about Speer's administration of the church's mission program. In the paper Machen sent to Speer he criticized the application procedure of the board for its tendency to discriminate against militantly conservative applicants and pointed out that four of the fifteen clerical members of the board and the candidate secretary had all signed the Auburn Affirmation.[5]

181

Just as disturbing was Speer's latest book, *Are Foreign Missions Done For?*—which Machen found fraught with difficulties. Speer had introduced this short work as "an attempt to meet fairly and honestly some of the present day questions which are raised with regard to the foreign missionary enterprise."[6] Machen, who had hoped that such a endeavor would address the specific doctrinal positions on which evangelical missions rested, was sorely disappointed. Citing in particular Speer's failure to insist that such doctrines as the inerrancy of Scripture and the virgin birth, bodily resurrection, and substitutionary atonement of Christ were essential to any true mission work, Machen condemned the book as "dishearteningly evasive and vague."[7] He reserved for special criticism Speer's praise of a Board of Foreign Missions statement declaring that the primary goal of missions work was to make Jesus Christ known among all people as their Divine Savior and to gather new disciples into indigenous churches.[8] The statement was, in Machen's eyes, "couched in just the vague, ambiguous language that Modernism loves."[9]

Despite this strong criticism of Speer and the board, Machen did not advise withdrawing support from the overseas missions of the church. Rather, he maintained that because many faithful missionaries were still supported by the church, evangelical Christians should support the board at least until a "truly evangelical agency" was created to sponsor foreign missions. Here, at the conclusion of his attack, Machen tipped his hand. He asked, "But has the time not come for the establishment of a truly evangelical missionary agency in the Presbyterian Church—an agency to which evangelical Christians can contribute, not with hesitation and distrust, but with all confidence and joy, an agency which shall keep clear of entangling alliances and shall proclaim the full glories of the Reformed Faith as they are found in the Word of God?"[10] While he therefore urged support for the board, he also threatened Speer with the creation of a rival missions board.[11] Four years later, with the organization of the Independent Board for Presbyterian Foreign Missions, Machen would make good on his threat.

Speer responded to Machen's twelve-page essay with a twenty-page letter in which he defended himself and the board against Machen's charges. "I believe that my own Christian convictions are not less evangelical than yours," he opened, "and I believe that our foreign missionary work and workers are also truly evangelical." Speer took Machen to task for failing to realize that "the Gospel is to be preached not by word only but also and not less or less fundamentally by deeds of love and mercy" and defended the trustworthiness of the board and the missionary application process. Moreover, he pointed out that the statement of missionary purpose condemned by Machen had been composed with the aid of J. Walter Lowrie, later secretary of the conservative Bible Union of China.[12]

Toward the end of the letter, Speer summarized what he perceived to be the similarities and differences between himself and Machen.

> I find myself in deep and thankful accord with almost all of your great convictions. I am full of admiration and gratitude for "The Origin of Paul's Religion" and agree with you in your emphasis on the historicity and supernaturalness of the facts of Christianity's beginning and the necessity of the great Christian doctrines undetachable from these facts, on the need of reasoned doctrinal statement and defense, on the great doctrines of sin and faith, on the Person of Christ, on miracles, on Christianity as a message as well as an experience and a life, and I might go on with the long list of all the evangelical convictions. Where I differ from you is at the points where, it seems to me, you differ from the Scriptures. Some great Scripture truths you ignore or qualify. You twist or interpret some passages out of their plain and obvious statement.[13]

Criticizing Machen's use of such nonscriptural terminology as "the Gospel of the Cross," Speer contended that the Bible "teaches not that the Cross saves us or that we are saved by the Cross. It teaches that Christ saves us, and that He saves us by Himself, by His death and by His life." Moreover, the full gospel of Christ—including his life, death and resurrection—needed to be proclaimed in a positive manner. "The Cross is indeed to many a stumbling block," Speer allowed; but "there is clearly in Paul's view a vast difference between the preaching of the offence of the Cross and the offensive preaching of the Cross."[14] Both Machen's message and method, Speer argued, strayed from the straight and narrow of biblical Christianity.

The sixty-two-year-old ecclesiastical veteran closed with an appeal for peace and goodwill. "Can we not," he wrote, "be spared the shame and waste of such a baseless controversy as a controversy like this between you and me would be and give ourselves and all our strength to better and truer things."[15] Speer's desire for ecclesiastical unity, his passion for evangelism, and his Christocentric emphasis had roots that stretched back to his college days and beyond. It was in his boyhood home in central Pennsylvania that Speer first heard the good news of God's grace revealed in Christ Jesus.[16]

Robert E. Speer: The Formation of a "Missionary Statesman"

Robert E. Speer grew up in Huntingdon, Pennsylvania, a small town nestled in the Allegheny Mountains. The second son of Robert Milton

Speer and Martha McMurtrie Speer, Rob was born on 10 September 1867, only two years after the close of the Civil War. Like the fathers of Machen and Coffin, Robert M. Speer was a successful attorney. Descended from a long line of prosperous and prominent citizens, he was for thirty years a leader in the Democratic party in Pennsylvania and twice won election to Congress.[17]

Martha Speer's death in 1876 thrust Robert into the position of sole religious leader of the household. A Presbyterian of Scotch–Irish descent, the elder Speer was "a constant reader of the Bible," taught a Bible class at the local church, and gathered his clan around the family altar every morning and evening to pray. He passed on his Reformed heritage by requiring his offspring to memorize not simply the Shorter Westminster Catechism but the Larger as well.[18]

Speer was educated at local schools, where he studied such basics as reading, writing, and mathematics. The unspoiled Pennsylvania countryside surrounding Huntingdon encouraged the boy's enthusiasm for fishing, hunting, canoeing, and swimming. The quiet hills of central Pennsylvania provided an atmosphere that was in many respects worlds away from the urban bustle of Coffin's New York or even the Southern aura of Machen's Baltimore.[19]

Speer's horizons were not to be limited to the surroundings of central Pennsylvania, however. As a child of one of the first families of Huntingdon, he was, at age sixteen, sent east to Phillips Academy in Andover, Massachusetts to procure a college preparatory education. The academy, which offered a mix of "work, athletics, good fellowship, and religion," provided a fertile environment for the cultivation of Speer's talents. Possessed of a quick mind, a reserved but appealing personality, and impressive physical stature, he soon excelled not only in the classroom but on the athletic field and at the debating podium as well. Though elected president of the class of 1886, Speer decided to graduate early and matriculated at the College of New Jersey in the fall of 1885, one year before Erdman received his Princeton degree.[20]

As at preparatory school, Speer soon rose to the top of his class in the academic, athletic, and social arenas. He held numerous elected class offices, served as president of the student YMCA, edited *The Princetonian*, played on the Princeton football team, and developed his speaking skills as a thespian and debater. In 1889 he received the Bachelor of Arts magna cum laude and delivered the class valedictory address.[21]

Though Speer matured intellectually and socially at Princeton, his most important development was in the spiritual realm.[22] While at Phil-

lips Academy Speer had become acquainted with the "liberal evangelicalism" that was coming to dominate Andover Seminary. By Speer's
own account, the seminary had a profound influence on the academy;
and Speer apparently took a special liking to William J. Tucker, George
Harris, and George F. Moore, three liberal members of the Andover
faculty.[23] Early in his career at Princeton, Speer lamented the difference
between the religious life of Princeton and that which he had known at
Andover, writing, "I just returned from prayer meeting. The spirit of
such meetings here, especially those conducted by the fellows, is so very
different from that of those I saw and felt in New England. These seem
almost hypocritical. Perhaps it is only diffidence."[24] About a week later
he complained, "The sermons here, though perhaps more orthodox in
an old Presbyterian's eyes, are not so good as the ones we heard at
Andover."[25] While these emotions could perhaps be partially attributed
to a longing for the familiar, they are also an early indication of Speer's
later tendency to prefer the pious liberal evangelicalism of the mid–
nineteenth century to the scholastic orthodoxy of Princeton Seminary.

In time, Speer became more comfortable with the conservative tenor
of the Princeton campus. Despite the devout character of Speer's home
life and of Phillips Academy, he had not, by the time of his matriculation
at Princeton, made a public affirmation of faith. Indeed, he was the only
member of his entering class who was not a church member.[26] Such was
not the case for long. In January of his freshman year, Speer, moved
by the preaching of the premillennialist Arthur T. Pierson, acknowledged Christ as his Savior and joined the First Presbyterian Church of
Princeton.[27] From this point on Speer's life and thought centered more
and more on the things of religion.

In the same year as Speer's conversion, Dwight Moody's summer
conference at Northfield gave birth to the Student Volunteer Movement
(SVM), an event that would profoundly influence Speer's life. The SVM,
which was essentially the missionary agency of the YMCA, would, over
the next thirty years, recruit literally thousands of college students for
overseas mission work. Speer was among the first to hear the call. In
early 1887 Robert Wilder and John Forman, two workers for the infant
movement, inspired Speer to commit his life to foreign missions. Though
he had long planned to follow his father into the legal profession, the
prospect of untold numbers of heathens dying daily without knowledge
of Christ convinced him of a higher calling.[28] Adopting the language of
the SVM he wrote to his father, "Ever since a boy I have drifted toward
the profession of law as my life work because I thought it was what you
wanted me to do especially after Will entered Journalism, but I have

come to a new conclusion today. I am going to be a foreign missionary. ...I should feel ashamed of myself if I stayed in this country while millions of heathen perish daily, and 'their blood is on my head.'"[29] Speer, like so many other young men of the era, thereby came within Moody's sphere of influence.

Speer met Moody for the first time at Northfield in the summer of 1887 and was impressed by the evangelist's honesty and openness. One historian has noted that Speer "deeply admired Moody's activism, modesty, speaking ability, and aversion to speculative thought."[30] He was clearly sympathetic to Moody's evangelistic emphasis and came to share Moody's concern for holy living and, at least early on, his premillennial eschatology.[31] Speer acknowledged the evangelist's stature in 1931 when, in an address at Northfield School, he called Moody "one of the half dozen greatest and most influential personalities our country has produced."[32]

Over the next few years Speer, inspired by the watchword of the SVM, *The evangelization of the world in this generation*, pursued his calling with a vengeance. In his final two years at Princeton he actively promoted the foreign missions movement in churches, colleges, preparatory schools and on campus.[33] On graduation, he accepted a one-year position with the Student Volunteer Movement as a recruiter and traveled to 110 colleges enlisting eleven hundred undergraduates for the missionary enterprise.[34] In 1890 Speer matriculated at Princeton Seminary in preparation for his foreign service; but before he could complete his course of study, his career plans took one final, and critical, turn. The Board of Foreign Missions of the Presbyterian Church, having recognized Speer's talents in "arousing the missionary Spirit among the young," offered him a position as a secretary of the board in 1891.[35] Though not keen on abandoning his commitment to overseas work, he decided to try the position for a while and then reevaluate his professional options.[36] The "trial" appointment lasted forty-six years.

Speer worked in various capacities with the Board of Foreign Missions from 1891 until his retirement in 1937. In the course of these years he became one of the two leading "missionary statesmen" in the world, the Methodist layman John R. Mott being his only peer. Speer's position with the board entailed not only massive amounts of administrative work, correspondence, and fund-raising, but also included extensive travel at home and abroad. In the course of his tenure with the board, Speer traveled to Great Britain, Persia, South America, Mexico, China, Japan, India, Korea, the Philippines, and Siam.[37] Under his leadership the Presbyterian Church came to support over sixteen hundred missionaries in foreign lands and became, by at least one account, "the most powerful single denominational Board in the whole world."[38]

Though Speer exercised his talents within the Presbyterian Church, he was devoted, above all, to the unified mission of the worldwide fellowship. True to his roots in the interdenominational Student Volunteer Movement, Speer was a devout ecumenist.[39] "I am a member of the Presbyterian Church," he once wrote, "but I have not the slightest zeal to have the Presbyterian Church extended throughout the length and breadth of the world."[40] Speer played a major role in both the 1910 World Missionary Conference in Edinburgh and the 1928 International Missionary Conference in Jerusalem.[41] He chaired the Wartime Commission of the Churches from 1916 to 1918, chaired the Committee on Co-operation in Latin America from 1916 to 1936, and stood at the helm of the Federal Council of Churches from 1920 to 1924.[42] In fact, despite all his other responsibilities, Speer never relinquished his concern for the Student Volunteer Movement and spoke at every national student volunteer gathering from 1890 to 1935.[43]

In 1894, at one of the early conventions of the Student Volunteer Movement, Speer expounded on some of the theological convictions that undergirded his lifelong commitment to the unity and mission of the church. In a speech praising "Paul, the Great Missionary Example," he lauded the "simplicity" of Paul's message:

"This is a faithful saying and worthy of all acceptation, that Christ Jesus came into the world to save sinners; of whom I am chief." Fellow students, that is our Gospel. Don't preach a system of truth. What good is a system of truth anyhow? Don't preach salvation; don't preach redemption. Preach the Saviour. Preach the Redeemer. What is wanted the world round is not more truth; it is a Divine Person. What is wanted is not a larger doctrine; it is the advent of the Divine Life. And however much we shall fail, as we surely shall fail, if we go preaching a large, and concrete and well-connected system, we shall never fail if we go preaching the simple, the omnipotent, the irresistible Christ.[44]

He went on, chastising denominations for insisting on peculiar doctrines and organizations in the face of a needy world:

We Presbyterians and Methodists have no business being apart on questions of doctrine and polity. These things on which we differ are not things connected with the great vital purpose of the Church of God in the world . . . and when we have once decided what the purpose of the Church is, namely to do the work Christ sent us here to do, which is to preach and live His simple Gospel and leave the result to Him, we have no business to let the differences on unessential points delay the full accomplishment of that purpose.[45]

Speer's emphasis on a simple Christocentric gospel, conducive to Christian unity and missionary success, his disparagement of systematic theology, and his understanding of the church as a missionary body persisted throughout his career.

The unsystematic and eclectic character of Speer's theology makes him a difficult character to label.[46] Historian Ernest Sandeen called Speer a "conservative Calvinist," James Patterson classified him as a "nineteenth century evangelical," and Lefferts Loetscher described him as "a culminating product of nineteenth-century evangelicalism at a time of transition to evangelical liberalism, although he himself did not make that transition."[47] William Hutchison, on the other hand, paints Speer as a moderate who strove to "walk the tightrope of the theological center"; and Robert Handy apparently agrees, seeing him as a theological centrist.[48]

Perhaps part of the difficulty in classifying Speer stems from the fact that his theological position apparently changed in the course of his life. Having been drawn into the Christian fold by the likes of Arthur T. Pierson and Dwight L. Moody, Speer early manifested premillennial tendencies and was active in the Keswick movement. He published a pamphlet, "The Second Coming of Christ," in 1903 and in 1916 delivered a speech at the first American Keswick Conference.[49] Through at least the earliest years of the century Speer appears to have been a comfortable member of the Moody camp and was perceived to be conservative enough to pen two articles for *The Fundamentals*.[50]

Nevertheless, by the 1910s Speer seems to have been drifting out of the orbit of Pierson and Moody. Though this move is difficult to trace, and though many of Speer's key emphases remained constant throughout his career, Speer appears to have abandoned the more conservative aspects of the Moody heritage as the years passed. As Hutchison has noted, even Speer's contribution to the last volume of *The Fundamentals*, "Foreign Missions or World-Wide Evangelism," was a decidedly moderate document, containing (unattributed) quotes from the liberal theologian William Newton Clarke.[51] The numerous works Speer published after World War I manifest a similar moderation. Moreover, Speer's social vision, as shall be seen, showed marked similarities to that of his good friend, Henry Sloane Coffin.[52] This is not to say that Speer ever became a liberal; he subscribed to the doctrine of the virgin birth and accepted the "whole of Christianity as set forth in the New Testament."[53] But Speer's personal study and experiences in ecumenical and missionary circles appear to have resulted in a broadening of his theological outlook over the years. Certainly, by the time of the Presbyterian controversy, Speer can be fairly classified as a theological centrist.

Speer's mature theology might, in fact, be best described as "Bushnellian." His writings reveal that he was an avid student and admirer of the the nineteenth-century liberal evangelical, Horace Bushnell. While Speer drew his theology from a variety of thinkers and his direct dependence on Bushnell is in many cases difficult to document, his Christological emphasis, understanding of religious language, "comprehensive" theology, and passion for Christian unity all show striking similarities to the thought of Horace Bushnell.[54]

The Legacy of Horace Bushnell

Horace Bushnell was, in the words of Sydney Ahlstrom, "the most creative and interesting theologian to emerge from the New England Puritan tradition during the nineteenth century."[55] Born in 1802 in New Preston, Connecticut, Bushnell was educated at Yale College and Yale Divinity School.[56] During Bushnell's tenure as a divinity school student, Connecticut Congregationalism was torn by theological controversy between advocates of the Pelagian theology of Yale professor Nathaniel Taylor and adherents of the conservative Calvinist thought of Bennet Tyler. When Bushnell accepted a call to North (Congregational) Church of Hartford in 1833 he found himself thrust into the middle of this controversy by virtue of the composition of his congregation, which was split almost evenly between the disciples of Taylor and Tyler.[57] Bushnell, who saw truth in both positions, attempted to act as a reconciler and succeeded quite admirably in bringing peace to the saints in Hartford.[58]

Bushnell blamed unnecessary and unessential theological speculation for the controversies that had perennially rocked the church. Influenced by the romanticism of Samuel Taylor Coleridge and by the native tradition of transcendentalism, Bushnell insisted that Christianity was not so much a matter of doctrine or speculative theology, as it was "spirit and life."[59] "It is no judgment of the flesh," he declared in *God in Christ*, "it is no wisdom of this world, it is not the letter, but it is spirit and life—Christ dwelling in us."[60] But in the course of history, Bushnell argued, the "living words that Jesus spoke to the world's heart" hardened into the dogmas that precipitated conflict and schism.[61]

In lieu of the systematic divinity that led to church conflicts, the Hartford divine proposed a theological program of "Christian comprehensiveness." Just as Christ proved his "superhuman quality" in "the comprehensiveness of his spirit and his doctrine," so, Bushnell held, the churches should strive to incorporate all truths into the one truth of Christ.[62] Bushnell declared, "Let Calvinism take in Arminianism, Arminianism Calvinism; let decrees take in contingency, contingency decrees; . . . not doubting that we shall be as much wiser as we are more comprehensive, as much closer to unity as we have more of the truth." Under such a program, Bushnell looked for the day when all sects would "either dissolve each other and lodge their contents at last in a grand comprehensive unity, or else wear themselves into similar shapes by their mutual attrition." In the one truth of Christ, he hoped, "the church, in all lands and under whatever diversities, will know itself as one, in common works, a common faith, and an accordant worship."[63]

Bushnell's program for Christian comprehensiveness was founded on an analysis of the nature of language that discounted doctrinal disagreements as matters of "forms of truth," not truth itself.[64] In *God in Christ*, Bushnell argued that all religious language was necessarily figurative and that this poetic nature of the discourse of faith precluded the possibility of absolute doctrinal statements.[65] Religious dogmatism was, therefore, difficult if not impossible to maintain; and sectarian division was based on nothing more than imagined disagreement.[66] The realization of ecclesiastical unity waited for the day when theologians would come to an understanding of the true poetic nature of religious language.[67]

For Bushnell, the form in which the earliest Christians "summed up the Christian truth," the Apostles' Creed, provided the ultimate rallying point for Christian unity. This simplest of creeds offered a perfect example of the undogmatic gospel Bushnell so admired. "It is," he wrote, "purely historic, a simple compendium of Christian fact, without a trace of what we sometimes call doctrine; that is, nothing is drawn out into speculative propositions, or propounded as a dogma, in terms of science." Here, in the faith of the earliest believers, the faithful the world around could find liberation from the bondage of their doctrines, and join together, "sect to sect, and people to people," singing their creed "as a hymn of love and brotherhood."[68]

Robert Speer: "Apostle of Christian Unity"

Speer's published works reveal that he was a diligent student of Bushnell. He not only quoted Bushnell repeatedly in his works, but lifted him up as a model of Christian discipleship and praised him for having penned the noblest essay ever written, and "one of our greatest sermons."[69] Though Speer referred to a number of theologians in his books, his mature thought exhibits a remarkable similarity to the theology of Horace Bushnell.

Like that of Bushnell, Speer's theology was centered solidly on the revelation of God in Christ. A brief statement of faith that Speer composed in 1923 clearly manifested his Christocentric emphasis:

He accepts the whole of Christianity as set forth in the New Testament. He believes unqualifiedly every article of the Apostles' Creed. No language is adequate to state his conception of Christ. He believes that He is more and greater than any words can ever express, "the Word made flesh," God incarnate, reconciling the world to Himself, the only Saviour, our Lord and our God. He believes in the truthfulness of the record of Christ's life, including His miracles, and rejoices with great joy in the miracles of the Virgin Birth and of the real Resurrection of Christ and of His future, personal advent. He believes that it is God alone who through Christ saves men, not by their characters, nor by any works of righteousness which they can do, but by His own grace through the death and life of His dear Son. As to the Bible, he accepts the doctrine of the Westminster Confession and regards its authority as supreme, not in faith only but also in the practice, conduct and relations of men.[70]

Echoing Bushnell's claim that Christianity was "Christ dwelling in us," Speer argued that Christianity was "Christ, the divine Lord moving in history and human hearts."[71]

In a lecture published in 1935 Speer gave his fullest account of the essence of Christianity. In language that sounded much like Machen's, he claimed that "Christianity is a body of facts in history, but it is also a set of convictions with regard to the meaning, the significance, and the value of those facts." Moreover, he contended, "there must be a life springing out of these facts, directed and purposed by these great understandings; a life of love and purity and self-control, of unselfishness and sacrifice." But Speer refused to stop at this understanding of Christianity as life founded upon doctrine. Rather, for Speer, Christianity was, above all else, "the Lord Jesus Christ." It is "Christ for men and in men. It is the saving power of Christ and the possibility and reality of the mystical presence of God in Human life."[72] Though Speer thereby maintained the necessity of a doctrinal basis of Christianity, its true essence was Christological and existential.[73] The gospel was "the simple, the omnipotent, the irresistible Christ."[74]

Speer's Christocentric theology led him, like Bushnell, to derogate speculative theology. "The New Testament," he insisted, "does not lay its emphasis on metaphysical theory, it lays it on supernatural life."[75] In his Stone Lectures at Princeton in 1932 Speer summarized,

> The contention of these lectures is not only that the whole essential content of the Gospel was in the elementary faith of the first disciples and of the primitive Church that Jesus Christ, the Son of God, who died for our sins and rose again, is the only Lord and Saviour for all mankind, but also that in this elementary faith and not in the translation of Christianity into the categories of Hellenistic or other thought, or in the development of a comprehensive system of dogmatic theology, or in the elaboration of a compact ecclesiastical organization, whatever the place of these may be in God's providence, lay the power of the survival and extension of Christianity. Categories of thought, systems of theology, ecclesiastical organization—all these were appurtenances and instrumentalities of Christianity.[76]

Speer turned to no less an authority than St. Paul to support his view of Christian doctrine. He wrote, "The core of Christian things in Paul's view was not Christian doctrine. . . . Neither was it the body of facts with which Christian doctrine deals. . . . In Christianity, according to Paul, the fundamental thing . . . is God in the soul, the soul in God— not independent of the facts and truth of the Gospel, but through them and in them."[77] As such, the gospel was best spread through Christian living and preaching a simple message of God's revelation in Christ.[78]

Speer's low opinion of speculative theology resulted in a vision of theological comprehensiveness that mirrored Bushnell's. He approvingly noted that Bushnell's attitude was "one of taking in all there was."[79] In *Some Living Issues* Speer expounded on his comprehensive view of doctrine, particularly as related to missions:

> The conviction of the writer of this volume is that in our co-operative missionary undertakings and associations identity of opinion on the whole body of Christian doctrine is not requisite; that in many matters a diversity of view which assures a fuller apprehension and presentation of the truth than any one individual or group of individuals can achieve is desirable, is indeed the very *raison d'être* both of our individualism and of our fellowships, but that one thing only is essential, and that is that we should hold a fundamentally unitary faith in and about our Lord Jesus Christ as

He is set forth in the New Testament. . . . St. Paul knew no fundamental
issue but the issue of Christ. He is the one and only foundation, the
sufficient and indispensable condition. . . . And the possession of Christian
spirit is the essential and sufficient credential. . . . One may hold earnestly
his own convictions on these issues which exist among us, and may desire
to see his convictions prevail, and yet as long as other men hold with him
the New Testament view of Christ, he ought to be willing to allow, within
the associations which he supports, the presentation of convictions which
in all probability are as defective as his own are likely to be, in the patient
hope of some larger and richer comprehension of the truth.[80]

Speer hoped that Calvinism and Arminianism would complement each
other, allowing for a more unified and complete theology.[81] Until that
occurred, however, "the possession of the Christian spirit," faith in the
Lord Jesus Christ, provided sufficient basis for Christian cooperation.
Ultimately, like Bushnell, Speer looked to the Apostles' Creed as a basis
of Christian unity. This "common possession" of all Christians represented "the great central body of . . . Christian conviction" sufficient for
the preaching of the gospel.[82]

Speer rested his commitment to Christian comprehensiveness at least
partially on a belief in "the inadequacy of language in the sphere of
truth which is beyond language";[83] that is, Speer, like Bushnell, felt that
ultimately words were incapable of carrying the full supernatural message of Christianity. "No language is adequate to state [my] conception
of Christ," Speer claimed. Likewise, he argued that "No human thought
or speech can fathom all that the Cross meant in God."[84] In *The Gospel
and the New World* Speer addressed the malleable and ambiguous nature
of language. Though the Bible was written in "forms of words that never
lose their grip," he argued, even the best creedal statements become
outdated and need new interpretations. The gospel had to be restated
in terms of "our living experience of God to-day, in a new understanding
of what revelation means, of eternal truth made available for men."
The problem of language was only amplified by Speer's missionary experience. He noted, "There is not a missionary who has not already
restated the Gospel by virtue of the necessity under which he was of
phrasing that Gospel in a different vernacular from that in which he
received it and in which all of his previous religious experience had been
described. And whether abroad or here, the very necessities of language
oblige us constantly to vary the words in which the old message shall
be expressed."[85]

Here, perhaps more than anywhere else, Speer found himself in closest agreement with theological liberals like Coffin and Fosdick. Though

Speer himself held fast to the doctrines of the virgin birth and "real Resurrection" of Christ, his beliefs about the nature of language, when pressed, would allow liberals to "rephrase" such doctrines in terms that for all intents and purposes, denied their historicity.[86] It was this similarity with modernist thought that enabled Speer to view his more liberal colleagues as within the Christian fold. Speer contended that inasmuch as the signers of the Auburn Affirmation affirmed their belief in the inspiration of the Bible, and the incarnation, atonement, resurrection, and supernatural power of Christ, they were "entitled to be trusted and believed."[87] If missionaries had to reformulate the "old message," surely theologians at home, within the bounds of a broad evangelicalism, had the same right.[88]

In considering the necessity of reformulation of Christian doctrine, Speer insisted that "this message must be restated in terms of unity, not in terms of our differentials."[89] Here, reflecting his concern for Christian harmony as well as his pragmatic desire for efficient missionary work, Speer emphasized an ideal that permeated his mature life and thought: the quest for ecclesiastical and global unity. In 1921 Speer proclaimed, "The one great need of the world to-day is Unity. The central principle of Christianity is Unity. The fundamental element of all life is Unity."[90] This passion for oneness, rooted in the One Lord Jesus Christ and undergirded by a Bushnellian approach to language and doctrine, directed Speer's thoughts and actions in the course of the Presbyterian controversy. He abhorred ecclesiastical controversy for the harm it did to the church and for the damage it inflicted on Christ's mission: "All rivalry is disloyalty to Christ and all waste is disloyalty to the world. Rivalry and friction are disloyalty to Christ because they argue a different spirit, inferior to his spirit of brotherhood and trust and love. And all waste is disloyalty to the world because it diminishes the extent to which the gospel could be spread, if it were not for waste and duplication and over-lapping."[91] Speer was, in the words of Samuel McCrae Cavert, "an Apostle of Christian Unity."[92]

Early in his career Speer acknowledged that in the past the church had had to fight to preserve right doctrine. But the time for conflict, he believed, had long since passed. Now the church needed a different method of opposing heresy. "A Church wholly surrendered to Christ's personal leadership," he suggested, "utterly bent upon the largest human service, filled with the passion of a great and divine love, will escape heresy by subduing unbelief."[93] Under the umbrella of a comprehensive theology, Speer thereby proposed a pragmatic solution to doctrinal dif-

ferences. Rather than "playing with details while men die," he challenged, "let the Church rise and move and we shall know what elements
in her are true and which are false by the place they will press to fill in
her advancing assault upon all evil, in her self-forgetful realisation of
the unity of love, in the exaltation of Christ, His Cross and His
Throne."[94] This aversion to doctrinal controversy and concern for a
unified evangelical witness above all else remained unchanged throughout Speer's career.[95]

Unity was necessary not only because it reflected the spirit and desire
of the One Lord Jesus Christ but also because it was an essential prerequisite to the full evangelization of the world.[96] "On no divisions of
the Christian world or the Christian Church," he maintained, "shall we
convince the world of the truth of our message."[97] Though Speer tended
to accentuate the need for interdenominational cooperation more than
church union, he did not shy away from suggesting the need for organic
unity as a prerequisite to missionary success.[98] Missions—the proclamation of the gospel of Christ in word and deed—were fundamental to
the church's life, and Christian unity was essential to the success of
missions.[99]

Speer, who had been dedicated to Christian cooperation since his
days with the Student Volunteer Movement, was given a renewed
sense of the power and possibilities of ecumenism during his service
as chairman of the General War-Time Commission of the Churches.
Spurred by the crisis of World War I, Christians across the land had
ignored theological and organizational differences to pursue wartime
ministry at home and abroad. As John Piper has pointed out, Speer
believed that "Christian unity was the great lesson of the war."[100] At
the close of the hostilities Speer observed that the churches "have actually found themselves working together in great common tasks in a
way which they had not realized to be possible before. But the tasks
that now confront the Church are no less challenging than those that
faced it during the war. The Church cannot hope to deal with them
adequately unless it approaches them in a spirit of common purpose
and united endeavor."[101] Speer, ever the ecumenist, thus approached
the Presbyterian controversy with a new commitment to the cause of
Christian unity.

Speer's quest for unity did not—indeed to his mind could not—stop
at the borders of the church. As the central principle of the faith and
the fundamental element of all of life, the ideal of unity provided the
heart of Speer's social vision and the basis of his hope for a new world
order.

Saving the World: The Social Vision of Robert E. Speer

World War I not only demonstrated the need and possibility of Christian oneness but (as Speer noted in 1919) showed "with an amazing and convincing suddenness that the world is a unity."[102] Though Speer had long emphasized the unity of mankind in Christ, this theme came to dominate his social vision in the years after the war.[103] At times it almost seemed as if Speer equated the gospel with the message of the oneness of humanity. "Nobody can live in the Gospels," he wrote, "without realizing that the fundamental message of Christianity must be a united message of a united humanity." For Speer, the gospel could not even be apprehended "except in the implication of human unity."[104]

This vision of human unity had enormous implications for the missionary movement. Inasmuch as "the Gospel was sent to the end that the family life of humanity in God might be restored in Christ," the church had to strive mightily for harmony among and between all peoples.[105] The church was to be both "the norm of brotherhood and unity" and "the agency . . . of the unity of mankind"; missionaries, as ambassadors of Christ, were "to advance the cause of human unity . . . [and] bind all men together in Christ."[106]

Speer's passionate dedication to the unity of all peoples in Christ led to three distinctive emphases in his work, the most notable of which was, perhaps, his view of race. The issue of race relations held a key position in Speer's thought.[107] In marked opposition to commonly held assumptions about the superiority of the Anglo-Saxon race, Speer insisted that Christianity taught the equality of all peoples the world around.[108] In 1898, shortly after returning from a world tour, Speer commented, "When one pierces beneath the superficial, differentiating characteristics, one understands how closely akin all peoples of this world are; how that though our reasoned intellectual judgments may differ from one another, our fundamental moral instincts are pretty much the same; how true it is that God has made of one blood all the races of men, and looks down upon them as the Father of them all, His children!"[109] Speer only strengthened these convictions in the course of his career. In 1918, having witnessed the horror of World War I, he insisted, "Humanity is a unity. It is one flock. The sheep may be of different strains. The hues of their wool may vary. But there is one Shepherd, and all the sheep are His sheep and one flock as they follow Him."[110] Christ was the answer, and the only answer, to the racial animosities that fueled international controversy.[111]

Speer rooted his views of race in the Scriptures, particularly in Acts

17:26, "God hath made of one blood all nations of men for to dwell on all the face of the earth."[112] He used this passage in a college essay on race relations and titled one of his studies of the race problem, *Of One Blood*, after it.[113] In the latter, Speer explained the import of the passage claiming, "The thesis of this book is simply the Christian view of [racial] questions. It holds that God made of one blood all races of men and that all races are but parts of one human race."[114] True adherence to the biblical message meant realizing the essential unity of all peoples under the one God revealed in Christ.[115]

Speer's insistence on the equality of the races was mirrored by a passionate concern for the equality of the sexes. In this, Speer was encouraged by his wife, Emma Bailey Speer, who accompanied her husband on many of his overseas ventures and was for years president of the national board of the Young Women's Christian Association.[116] Christ himself, Speer held, was the bearer of words of liberation to the women of the world. "Christ comes into the lives of the women of the world," he wrote, "teaching them new dignity, giving them real human interests, assuring them that they are to walk side by side with men and that they are the daughters of the Father on high."[117]

The Scriptures, Speer argued, contained absolutely nothing "to warrant a discrimination against women as women or their exclusion as a sex from any work of God in His Church." Against those who pointed to St. Paul's injunctions that women were to keep silent in the church and were not to teach, Speer contended that within a proper hermeneutic such passages could be understood as allowing women full equality. Galatians 3:28 provided Speer with all the support he needed to argue for women's rights: "There is neither Jew nor Greek, there is neither bond nor free, there is neither male nor female; for ye are all one in Christ Jesus." Speer declared, "Here is the great charter of human equality. Here we are, beyond all question of documents and precedents, at the very foundation of spiritual principle, deep in the purpose of God in Christ. Here is ultimate authority. And here is no warrant for discrimination on any ground whatever but capacity for service, regardless of sex."[118] Therefore, expressing a view far ahead of his time, Speer declared that the church would be wise to engage the service of women as elders, evangelists, and ordained ministers.[119]

Christ, as the revealer of the equality and unity of all people, bore the solution to international difficulties. Like the church, all humanity was one body under the one Lord. Inasmuch as a truly just international order could be based only on the ideas of one God and one law, the "moral and biological unity of humanity," universal human goodwill, and righteousness (ideas that Christianity alone could provide), the Christian faith offered the only basis of a "just and secure international order."[120]

Speer's proposal to organize all international relations under the rule and principles of Christ points to the strong social emphasis in his thought. Though Speer always insisted on the primacy of the gospel message to the individual, he also maintained that Christianity had important social consequences.[121] "There will be no saving of the world without the saving of sinners," he argued but then added, "and the saving of sinners is to the end of the saving of the world."[122]

In the final analysis, Speer believed, the distinction between a social and personal gospel was a false dichotomy. The foreign missionary movement had settled the "controversy over the social gospel" by realizing that "the oral statement and the personal and institutional expression of the Gospel" were necessarily bound together.[123] All of life was to be brought under Christ's dominion.[124] Surveying the destruction of World War I, Speer lifted up a vision of a new world lived under Christian principles:

> It will be a new world in which the principle of competition shall have given way to the principle of association and fellowship. It will be a new world in which the principle of unity shall have replaced the principle of division, or in which at least the principle of division will see itself only as the servant of the principle of a larger synthesis. It will be a new world in which the sacredness of property will find its sanction only in the greater sanctity and dignities of personality and human life. It will be a new world in which the social and individual ideals and services will be reciprocal and complementary. It will be a new world in which brotherliness and friendship will have displaced all antagonisms except the war against evil. It will be a new world in which obedience to truth and duty will find its ground in the Will of a transcendent, sovereign God. It will be a new world in which Jesus Christ will be the head of humanity and His life and spirit will do for men what no injunctions or ordinances can ever avail to do.[125]

Christian missionaries, of course, would play a crucial role in bringing about the advent of this commonwealth of unity and brotherhood. Speer continued,

> The only thing that is going to save the world from a bitter strife, vaster and more terrible than anything the world has known for ages past, is the unity of men in one Lord, one faith, one God and Father of all, who is in all, over and through all. And it is because the missionary represents that, and because he is embodying this saving principle in the life of the

world that we stand in debt to him as to no other man. . . . because at last there shall have come through him, more than through any other, that Kingdom of God on earth which will be like the Kingdom of God on high.[126]

The missionary movement, in proclaiming the gospel of Christ, declared the way of salvation not just for individuals but for the world.[127]

Speer, of course, was not oblivious to the more conventional social issues plaguing his peers. He believed the church was called to christianize America, asserting that the country "has been strong and great as it has been Christian, and weak and evil as it has forgotten God."[128] As such he supported Prohibition, was a strict Sabbatarian, and, as shown above, worried about the declining influence of religion in the home.[129] Aside from the question of divorce, however, no issue claimed Speer's attention as did his vision of a world united in Christ by the proclamation of the gospel. A global citizen, Speer focused on worldwide social issues. Speer's evangelicalism, though rooted in a preliminary concern for the proclamation of the gospel to individuals, included a distinctly social component centered in the sure hope of a world redeemed by and united in the One Lord Jesus Christ.[130]

Re-Thinking Missions: The Crisis of Foreign Missions

In the course of the controversy of the 1920s Speer's work for Christian unity had been amply rewarded. The commission òf 1925, of which he was a member, had calmed the troubled waters of the church; and the reorganization of Princeton, though inspiring a splinter movement, had restored peace to the seminary campus. If Speer thought that calm might return to his life after the settlement of these two conflicts, however, he was sorely mistaken. The Presbyterian conflict was far from over, and this time the battle would revolve around the cause nearest to Speer's heart: foreign missions.

In 1930 a group of Baptist laymen, called together by John D. Rockefeller, Jr., concluded that the time had come for a serious reevaluation of the foreign missions enterprise. Securing the moral support of seven major denominations, including the Presbyterians, and with the financial support of Rockefeller, this gathering gave birth to the Laymen's Foreign Missions Inquiry. The "Laymen's Inquiry" commissioned the Institute for Social and Religious Research to study missionary activity in India, Burma, China, and Japan. In conjunction with this investigation a fifteen-member Board of Appraisal, chaired by Harvard professor William Ernest Hocking, conducted its own fact-finding tour of these nations and returned home to compile its data and propose future directions for the American missionary movement. A one-volume summary of the enterprise, entitled *Re-Thinking Missions: A Laymen's Inquiry after One Hundred Years*, authored by the board and based on modernist theological principles, precipitated the final stage of the Presbyterian controversy.[131]

The theological sections of the report were composed by Hocking, a prominent philosopher and liberal Congregationalist.[132] As William Hutchison has noted, "the integrating vision" of the report "was that of Christianity's active participation in an emerging world religion."[133] Christianity's uniqueness, the study claimed, lay not in any particular historical or doctrinal claims but rather in its selection of truths available in all religions and in the simplicity of its central teachings. As such, the Christian faith, in the face of modern secularism, should make common cause with other world religions in the search for unified religious truth.[134]

The permanent function of the missionary, Hocking held, should be that of "promoting world understanding on the spiritual level." Deprecating the importance of preaching and the value of doctrinal formulations in evangelism, he suggested that evangelization proceed "by living and by human service." Missionaries were not to be evangelists seeking to conquer the world for Christ but rather ambassadors, "representing the Christian way of thought and life . . . and trying to minimize the strains of an abrupt breach with tradition."[135]

The report's syncretistic program, while receiving considerable commendation from liberal Christians, met almost immediate condemnation from more conservative believers.[136] Almost all of the mainline missions boards, which had given tentative support to the inquiry at the outset, rapidly distanced themselves from the more radical aspects of its theology, especially its failure to assert the uniqueness of Christianity.[137] The Board of Foreign Missions of the Presbyterian Church, for example, responded by issuing a statement that reaffirmed the board's commitment to "the evangelical basis of the missionary enterprise" and to "Jesus Christ as the only Lord and Saviour."[138] In the Presbyterian church *Re-Thinking Missions* led eventually to open conflict, involving, most notably, the Presbyterian missionary and renowned novelist Pearl S. Buck, Robert E. Speer, and J. Gresham Machen.

Soon after the publication of the report, Buck, an unabashed theological liberal, dropped two theological bombshells that sent shockwaves rumbling through the church.[139] In a review of *Re-Thinking Missions* in the *Christian Century*, she lavished praise on the report calling it "a unique book, a great book." Gushing with enthusiasm, she continued, "I think this is the only book I have ever read which seems to me literally true in its every observation and right in its every conclusion." *Re-Thinking Missions*, she believed, should be read by every American Christian, "translated into every language," and adopted by every missions board.[140]

Having thus aroused the suspicions of her conservative brothers and sisters, Buck, in a January speech to Presbyterian women and members of the Board of Foreign Missions, went on to confirm conservatives' worst fears. Before a large audience at the Astor Hotel in New York, Buck rejected the doctrine of original sin, the finality of Christianity, and the need for missionaries to found churches. Perhaps most important, she seemed to deny the divinity of Christ or even the importance of his historical reality.[141] Her questions about traditional orthodoxy notwithstanding, Buck believed that missions should continue, if only to share the image of Christ as "the essence of men's dreams of simplest and most beautiful goodness."[142] The speech, published in *Harper's* magazine and in pamphlet form, in conjunction with her review of *Re-Thinking Missions*, would lead eventually to Buck's resignation as a Presbyterian missionary.[143]

Speer's response to *Re-Thinking Missions* appeared in a lengthy article in the *Missionary Review of the World* in January of 1933. Though privately disturbed over the conclusions and consequences of the report, he made every effort to offer a balanced and courteous evaluation.[144] He expressed thanks for the high motives and generosity of the authors of the project, noting that some connected with the inquiry were among his "best and dearest friends." Speer spent considerable time applauding a number of the practical recommendations in the report, such as its call for self-supporting indigenous churches, for cooperation on the mission field, and for improved Christian literature. But Speer also pointed out serious problems with the appraisal. The time alloted for the study was vastly inadequate, the investigators were sorely untutored in the history of missions, and the report was pervaded by a spirit of exclusivity and partisanship. Most importantly, the theological foundations of the report were flatly unacceptable.[145]

Speer characterized the theology of the report as "the old Protestant liberalism which has been already superseded in Europe by a deep evangelical wave." It viewed Jesus, he charged, not as the unique and final revelation of God, but as a great religious teacher and moral example. Speer, whose life and thought were grounded in a Christocentric theology, could not tolerate such a foundation for Christian missions. In the most impassioned section of the essay he wrote, "For us, Christ is still *the* Way, not *a* way, and there is no goal beyond Him or apart from Him, nor any search for truth that is to be found outside of Him, nor any final truth to be sought by a universal religious quest, except it be sought in Him who is the Way, the Truth and the Life."[146]

Speer closed with a warning about the dangers of division and the report's pernicious effects on Christian unity. It had, he noted, already inspired discord on the mission fields and among the denominations and threatened the carefully cultivated relationships between American and European missions boards. Perhaps even more disturbing, the report intimated that if the established missions boards did not respond to the report's suggestions, a new missionary agency might have to be organized. In the face of such dangers of division, Speer declared, Christians must "work together in faith and trust to get all the good and as little as possible of evil out of this situation." "Every missionary board," he concluded, "should settle itself anew on the Rock that is Christ, the one and only basis and foundation, never to be altered, the true motive and message and aim" and from this vantage point evaluate themselves in light of the report's criticisms.[147]

Machen, who was none too keen on the Board of Foreign Missions before the publication of *Re-Thinking Missions*, took hold of this occasion to launch a full-scale critique of the orthodoxy of the board in general and Speer in particular. His attack took the form of an overture to the 1933 General Assembly encouraging the assembly to elect only staunchly conservative board members and to warn the board of the great danger of union movements. In conjuction with this memorial Machen printed a 110-page booklet articulating his charges against the board, not the least of which were its tolerance of Pearl Buck and its failure to repudiate the theology of *Re-Thinking Missions* sufficiently.[148]

In the course of the argument Machen took special issue with Speer's theology, which he characterized as "middle-of-the-road." Though he lavished praise on Speer as "one of the most eloquent men of our time" and one of "the most distinguished religious leaders in the world," Machen did not hesitate to point out Speer's errant ways. In refusing to adopt a militant attitude against modernism, Speer was unwittingly doing at least as much harm to the church as the most aggressive liberals. "It is this palliative or reassuring attitude," Machen declared, "which, we are almost inclined to think, constitutes the most serious menace to the life of the Church today."[149]

In a cursory review of Speer's *Finality of Jesus Christ*, Machen argued that Speer had nowhere presented a clear statement about "the super-natural authority of the Bible." "There is an authority of 'Christ,'" Machen observed, "but no real justice is done to that tremendous view of Scripture upon which our Lord based His own life as a man and which He also inculcated in His followers."[150] Though Machen perhaps overstated the case, he here recognized an important difference between himself and Speer. Speer staunchly maintained the historicity of such events as the virgin birth and the resurrection and held that "the sacred book of Christianity is of a class wholly above the books of the ethnic religions" but apparently never subscribed to the Princeton view of Scripture.[151] Rather, Speer's declarations about scriptural authority stuck closely to the traditional language of the church, attesting to the Bible's supreme authority in faith and life, not to its "inerrancy."[152] For Speer, absolute authority rested with Christ as made known in the Scriptures, not in the Scriptures themselves.[153]

Machen also noted that Speer's theology tended to be "anti-creedal" and "anti-intellectualistic."[154] Within Machen's strict definitions of these terms Speer was certainly guilty of the former and probably guilty of the latter. Apart from the Apostles' Creed, which Speer praised because of its simplicity and avoidance of speculative thought, Speer discounted the value of creeds. He always tried to use only the language of the Scriptures and, as previously seen, criticized Machen for not doing the same. Christ was the central and sufficient theology for Speer. But this type of talk, to Machen, was nothing short of incipient modernism and therefore tantamount to "anti-intellectualism." Christianity was centered on doctrine, or it was not Christianity.

The thrust of Machen's essay was that the Board of Foreign Missions, under Speer's leadership, was operating in a deliberately dishonest manner. In order to receive support from both liberals and conservatives in the church, Machen charged, the board was concealing the "real state of affairs," which was that the board tolerated and even supported modernism. By defending the board's orthodoxy Speer, far from helping the cause of Christianity, was in actuality hurting the evangelical purpose by diverting conservative dollars to modernist propaganda.[155]

The Presbytery of New Brunswick, of which Machen was a member, received Machen's overture in January 1933 and voted to consider the matter at its April meeting. The body, in order to make a more informed decision, invited Speer to this meeting to present the position of the board.[156]

Speer, Machen, and Buck were not, however, the only players in this controversy. On 8 January 1933 Clarence Macartney let loose against

Re-Thinking Missions in a sermon at his Pittsburgh church. He denounced its syncretistic proposals as a "complete repudiation of historic and evangelical Christianity." Nevertheless, the project was not a complete waste. For, Macartney observed, it was galvanizing conservative sentiment across the church.[157] By March, the session of First Presbyterian Church of Pittsburgh had forwarded a letter to the Board of Foreign Missions, expressing its concern about the failure of the board to condemn and repudiate the doctrinal statements of *Re-Thinking Missions* directly and inquiring whether Pearl Buck, in light of her unorthodox public statements, was still associated with the board. Reflecting Macartney's perennial diplomacy, the letter did not question the orthodoxy of the board and concluded by affirming the session's "loyalty to the Presbyterian Church, to the work of our Board of Foreign Missions, and to that Gospel to which our church has made so glorious a witness."[158]

Charles Erdman, as president of the Board of Foreign Missions, responded to this letter.[159] Erdman reviewed the board's response to *Re-Thinking Missions*, noting that the body had reaffirmed its "unbroken allegiance to the evangelical standards of the Church" and explicitly declared "its loyalty to the standards of the Presbyterian Church and its maintenance of the absolute finality, sufficiency, and universality of the Gospel of Christ." In relation to the status of Buck, Erdman allowed that the matter was "exceedingly difficult and perplexing" but expressed hope that Buck might be won back to the missionary cause. After mentioning various issues that impinged on the board's final decision on this issue, Erdman reassured the session that the matter was constantly in the thought of the board and that it was seeking to resolve the problem in the most Christian way possible.[160]

The final installment of this epistolary dialogue, sent by First Church to the board, demonstrated the posture that Macartney had chosen to assume against modernism. The session was not satisfied with Erdman's reply concerning either *Re-Thinking Missions* or Pearl Buck. On both matters, they felt, strong and forthright action, true to the church's evangelical heritage, was necessary. This disagreement, however, did not prevent the congregation from supporting what it deemed to be the essential mission of the church. Reminding the board that First Church had already sent $1,200 in support of missionaries in China, it enclosed another $450 for Korean missions and $100 for work in Africa. Macartney and his church stood as a vocal conservative witness in the church but did not think that their differences with others in the fold required separation or withholding support. Rather, they intended to use their position in the church to influence its direction. Whenever the church sends out faithful missionaries, they closed, "it will have the loyal support of the First Presbyterian Church." But "wherever and whenever the Board maintains missionaries who are disloyal to Christ and the Gospel, the First Church will enter its earnest and prayful [*sic*] protest."[161] Though earnest and prayerful protest might content Macartney and his congregation, it would soon prove to be an insufficient response in the eyes of Machen.

The Bittersweet Victory of Robert Speer

As scheduled, Machen's overture was considered at the April meeting of the New Brunswick Presbytery, and Speer was on hand to address the motion. Machen reiterated the charges against the board contained in his booklet, insisting that the Scriptures alone, not "changed lives" or "the mind of Christ" or "the teachings of Jesus," must be the criterion by which to judge the orthodoxy of the Board of Missions.[162]

Speer, declaring that he had not come to engage in controversy or debate, read a prepared statement that criticized the proposed overture's ambiguous, unconstitutional, and misinformed proposals and defended the board's policies in light of the rulings of past General Assemblies.[163] In response to Machen's concerns about the dangers lurking in "union enterprises," Speer appealed to the familial devotion and patriotism of his listeners:

> There *are* dangers in union enterprises, whether matrimonial, political or religious. But there are dangers outside of them as well. And there are times when the safety of union is greater than its dangers. None of us who know the joy of the perfect love which casts out fear give any reckoning to its dangers. In our national life no doubt there are dangers in the union of these states but there are vastly greater dangers in their disunion. I rejoice that my great-great-grandfather voted in the Pennsylvania Convention for the adoption of the Constitution of the United States and the creation of our nation in the face of the opposition of his constituents who feared the great dangers that lurked in the American union.[164]

Speer admitted that out of the nearly fifteen hundred missionaries supported by the board two had given the board cause for concern but that in both instances he hoped for resolution that would "glorify Christ by the winning and not the losing of lives." In closing, the veteran administrator made still one more appeal for peace and unity: "Not by suspicion and strife but by confidence and concord is the great work of our Redeemer to be done in the world by us who love Him. . . . What we need today is not conflict and division among us who hold this common faith but a united front against all that is opposed to Christ and His Gospel."[165]

Though Machen's motion failed in the New Brunswick Presbytery, it passed in the Presbytery of Philadelphia, ensuring its presentation to the 1933 General Assembly.[166] The Board of Foreign Mission's acceptance with "deep regret" of Pearl Buck's resignation on 1 May far from calming conservatives' fears, only deepened their resolve to push for reform of the denomination's foreign missions enterprise.[167]

The Standing Committee of Foreign Missions of the 1933 assembly responded to the Machen overture and other similar memorials with majority and minority reports. The majority report reaffirmed the church's adherence to its standards, expressed its confidence in the orthodoxy of Speer and the Board of Missions, and repudiated all theological statements in *Re-Thinking Missions* that conflicted with the theological positions of the church. The minority report, maintaining that Machen's charges against the board were true, reaffirmed the church's devotion to the pure gospel of Christ rooted in Christ's substitutionary atonement, pledged the Board of Foreign Missions to preach this gospel alone, and nominated a slate of conservative candidates to serve on the board for the following three years. The majority report passed by an overwhelming margin; and Speer, as he came forward to present the report of the Board of Foreign Missions, was greeted by a standing ovation.[168] His cause and his orthodoxy had been vindicated. But true victory for Speer would have required reconciliation with Machen, and such was not to be the case. Though the support of the church was no doubt welcome, the unity of the church would be broken.

In response to the defeat of the minority report, H. McAllister Griffiths, in conjuction with Machen, announced the formation of an Independent Board for Presbyterian Foreign Missions "to promote truly Biblical and truly Presbyterian mission work."[169] Machen had anticipated this course of events and had, he admitted to Macartney, set out on this quest with the expressed intent of forming a new board.[170] But with the formation of a rival board of foreign missions Machen had exceeded Macartney's limits of protest. It is significant that Machen's decision to separate from the board over matters of principle was consistent with his Southern heritage. At the same time, Macartney's devotion to the Northern evangelical tradition and his concern for the maximum use of opportunity led him to see division as a grave theological and tactical error. Despite Machen's entreaties, Macartney refused to join in a move so blatantly schismatic.[171] On 27 June 1933 the independent board was organized without the blessings of Clarence Macartney, and on 17 October Machen was elected its first president.[172] Speer, who only six months earlier was openly worrying about the formation of a competing liberal missions board, now had to face the reality of a competitor on his conservative flank.[173]

Speer's actions in the Presbyterian controversy were motivated by his vision of the mission of the church, which entailed, first and foremost, the proclamation of the gospel of Christ.[174] His tolerant Christocentric theology, in the tradition of Horace Bushnell, led him to eschew all controversy that would injure that mission. As a member of the Special Commission of 1925, as moderator of the 1927 General Assembly, as a director of Princeton Seminary, and as senior secretary of the Board of Foreign Missions, Speer strove to reconcile differences in the name and for the sake of Christ. Doctrinal conflict, to Speer's mind, was nothing but "playing with details while men die."[175] What was most essential for the prosecution of the church's mission was Christian unity. Only when the church was bound together under the One Lord Jesus Christ could the evangelization of the world become a reality. Time and again, therefore, throughout the 1920s and 1930s Speer directed his energies toward the peaceful resolution of conflicts that threatened to tear the church apart and destroy its witness.

Yet in his efforts to further the unity and mission of the church, Speer was concerned not simply with the conversion of individuals. The gospel was, Speer insisted, directed to individual men and women. Nevertheless, it had critical social and cultural consequences. All of life was to be "brought under Christ's Lordship." "Industry and legislation, economics and politics, . . . art, and literature, and education" all needed to be consecrated to Christ.[176] Most important, international relations had to be brought under the sway of the One Lord. The Christian faith alone, with its message of the unity of humanity, could provide a solid basis for a just and stable global order.[177]

Speer's passionate concern for human unity provided the integrating factor for his mature social thought. "Mankind is all one family, or ought to be," he argued in 1919, "and the Gospel was sent to the end that the family life of humanity in God might be restored in Christ."[178] In preaching Christ, the church was planting the seed of a world commonwealth.[179] If the people and nations of the world would only submit to Christ and Christ's principles, the Kingdom of God on earth could become a reality.[180] But divisions within the fellowship of faith, divisions that injured the mission of the church, threatened Speer's grand plans for a world redeemed and united by Christ. A divided church could never unite a divided world.[181] In struggling to preserve the church's unity and thereby the church's mission, Speer endeavored to ensure not only the conversion of individuals but the conversion of America and the world to Christ as well.[182] Though a hesitant soldier, Speer fought his battles in the Presbyterian controversy in the fervent hope that one day all peoples—men and women of every race and nation—would be united in the One Savior of the world, Jesus Christ.

9

The Close of the Controversy: The Entanglement of Religion and Culture

The 1934 General Assembly declared the Independent Board for Presbyterian Foreign Missions unconstitutional. This decision was based largely on a lengthy study of the Constitution of the Presbyterian Church, prepared for the assembly, which asserted that church members were obligated to "promote the officially authorized missionary program" of the church and that the operation of any missionary board independent of the General Assembly within the church was illegal. The assembly thus ordered the independent board to cease its solicitation of funds within the church and directed all Presbyterian clergy and laity to sever their connections with the board or face disciplinary action.[1]

Both Clarence Macartney and Henry Coffin issued public statements opposing the action of the assembly. Macartney charged that the assembly had "erred grievously, deeply, and dangerously" in its actions against members of the independent board. Not only was this action unconstitutional but, Macartney charged, it was "in spirit and tone harsh, severe, unscriptural, and un-Presbyterian."[2] Coffin, while completely unsympathetic with the motives of Machen, nevertheless believed that the assembly had "acted unwisely" in its decision.[3]

Less than a month after the assembly adjourned, the Presbytery of New Brunswick, under whose jurisdiction Machen remained despite an abortive attempt to transfer to Philadelphia Presbytery, sought Machen's response to the assembly's statement. Machen informed the presbytery that he had no intention of resigning and that the mandate of the General Assembly was unconstitutional. In December he sent a statement to the presbytery committee handling the matter explaining his position in detail. Obeying the order of the General Assembly, he argued, would involve him in the support of un-Christian propaganda, the substitution of human authority for the Word of God, and "acquiescence in the principle that support of benevolence of the church is not a matter of free-will but the payment of a tax." All three of these actions would be contrary to the teaching of Scripture. Though disobeying the assembly, Machen concluded, he had every right to remain in the church for he was in full accord with the church's Constitution.[4]

The Presbytery of New Brunswick consequently brought charges against Machen on numerous offenses including violation of his ordination vows and renunciation of the rules and authority of the church. On 29 March 1935 he was convicted by a special commission of the Presbytery and suspended from the ministry. The sentence was held in abeyance pending appeal to the higher judicatories.[5]

Following the 1935 General Assembly, which reaffirmed the action of the preceding assembly in regard to members of the independent board, Macartney penned a letter to Machen in the name of many "strong Conservative men," encouraging Machen to moderate his stance. While granting that Machen and others would make "a noble witness to conscience and Christian liberty" in their suspension from the ministry, Macartney expressed concern about the future influence of Westminster graduates and the independent board. He wrote:

> If these trials are pushed, it will be impossible in most Presbyteries to have men from Westminster licensed or ordained. They might be licensed or ordained elsewhere, in other denominations, and the suspended members of the Independent Board might continue it, but not as ministers of the Presbyterian Church, U.S.A. This is not what you had in mind when you led in the establishment of the Seminary and of the Independent Board.

As tactfully as possible, Macartney suggested that for the sake of continued conservative influence in the church, Machen might dissolve the independent board and reestablish it in a less controversial form.[6] Perhaps, Macartney thought, he could nudge Machen into a slightly more moderate position and strengthen the conservative witness in the church.

The strategy did not work. In his response to Macartney, Machen completely rejected any possibility of compromise:

> If I voted for the reorganization of The Independent Board for Presbyterian Foreign Missions in some way that would enable its members to avoid the ecclesiastical displeasure which the enemies of the Gospel of Christ are now venting upon them, I should regard myself as having denied my Saviour and Lord. If I did that, the rest of my life upon this earth would seem to me to have no meaning whatever. It would be simply a living death.[7]

Far from worrying about the influence of Westminster graduates or the independent board within the church, Machen was hoping desperately for a schism. "I pray God with all my heart that there may come of [the turmoil] a real Presbyterian Church, no matter whether it be large or small," he wrote to Macartney. "I believe that God has hardened the hearts of these men who are opposing the gospel in order that at last the liberation of God's people might be accomplished."[8]

The day before Machen responded to Macartney, he had taken steps to ensure the realization of his hope. On 27 June 1935 Machen had assisted in the formation of the Presbyterian Constitutional Covenant Union, a group dedicated to "perpetuate the true Presbyterian Church in the U.S.A., regardless of cost."[9] Given Machen's devotion to doctrine and principle, as well as his Southern heritage, separation was the only possible path to follow.

In October the differences between Macartney and Machen over the independent board spread to Westminster Seminary. The faculty, at a meeting of the board of trustees, issued an ultimatum to the trustees, claiming, in essence, that if the trustees did not support the independent board and the covenant union, the faculty would have no choice but to resign.[10] In this case, also, Macartney attempted to act as a reconciler but to no avail.[11] At the meeting of the trustees of Westminster on 7 January 1936 thirteen trustees, including Macartney and one faculty member, resigned due to their inability to support the independent board and covenant union.[12] In an article in *Christianity Today*, Samuel D. Craig, one of the resigning trustees, attempted to summarize the motives of his party. "As far as we know," he wrote, "there was not a single member of the Board that did not (and that does not) favor a militant and aggressive opposition to Modernism in the councils of the Church." But this did not necessarily mean, Craig claimed, that board members would agree with every possible antimodernistic scheme. Wisdom as well as militancy were necessary and, he believed, the formation of the Presbyterian Constitutional Covenant Union and the independent board were not in the best interest of conservatism.[13] Macartney largely agreed with these sentiments.[14]

Eight ministers, including Machen, were tried by the 1936 General Assembly.[15] Prior to the assembly Macartney made one final attempt to prevent schism by offering to defend Machen before the assembly's Permanent Judicial Commission. Machen, however, gratefully refused the offer because he and Macartney differed on the issue at hand. Machen summarized,

You desire our continuation for the present in the present organization of the Presbyterian Church in the U.S.A., hoping that there will be reform of that Church or hoping that evangelicalism may prosper by such continuation; whereas I, on the other hand, am longing for a division, and hoping and praying with all my soul that the division may come soon. I am perfectly convinced that the Presbyterian Church in the U.S.A. is an apostate Church at its[?] very heart. I do not think there is any blessing of God for us so long as we continue in such an apostate organization.[16]

Inasmuch as anything Macartney might say might be attributed to Machen, Machen could not risk securing counsel who disagreed with him on such a fundamental matter. Though Machen argued that he did "not desire to do evil that good may come," he concluded by insisting that if acquitted, he would "adopt every means of forcing the issue immediately in some other way."[17] Machen was committed to the cause of separation.

As expected, the 1936 General Assembly suspended Machen and other clerical members of the independent board from the ministry and, as expected, soon thereafter Machen led the Constitutional Covenant Union in the formation of a new church, the Presbyterian Church of America.[18] At the opening General Assembly of the new church Machen declared the joy he found in the schism:

On Thursday, June 11, 1936, the hopes of many years were realized. We became members, at last, of a true Presbyterian Church; we recovered, at last, the blessing of a true Christian fellowship. What a joyous moment it was! How the long years of struggle seemed to sink into nothingness compared with the peace and joy that filled our hearts!.. With that lively hope does our gaze turn now to the future! At last true evangelism can go forward without the shackle of compromising associations.[19]

This joy would not be his for long; within six months Machen had been ousted as president of the Independent Board for Presbyterian Foreign Missions, and his infant church was torn by dissent over premillennialism and the use of alcoholic beverages.[20] Worn down by such battles, in December of 1936 he traveled to North Dakota to encourage a small band of his followers. There he contracted pneumonia and on 1 January 1937 died in Bismarck.[21] Pearl Buck, who had experienced her share of trouble at Machen's hand, reflected on the death of her former opponent, writing, "We have lost a man whom our times can ill spare, a man who had convictions which were real to him and who fought for them through every change in time and human thought."[22]

After the Conflict: Alternate Responses

For all intents and purposes the Presbyterian conflict came to a close with Machen's supension from the ministry and the formation of the Presbyterian Church of America in 1936. In other ways as well, the mid-1930s proved to be a watershed. In 1936 Charles Erdman, after thirty years as professor of practical theology at Princeton Seminary, retired.[23] The following year Robert E. Speer, having completed forty-six years with the Board of Foreign Missions, also reached mandatory retirement and stepped down.[24] Although both of these septuagenarians maintained active lives in retirement, their sway over the life of the church necessarily declined as the years passed.[25]

Henry Sloane Coffin and Clarence Macartney, on the other hand, both had a number of years of professional ministry before them. Coffin had been elected president of Union Theological Seminary in 1926 and presided over the appointments of Reinhold Niebuhr and Paul Tillich, among others, to the seminary faculty.[26] Influenced by the course of world events and the advent of neo-orthodoxy, Coffin's theology took on a different tenor in the 1930s and 1940s. Though never making the turn to neo-orthodoxy, Coffin's liberalism was undeniably chastened.[27] In 1947 he declared,

Unquestionably the popular ideas of the last generation—evolution, progress, the immanence of God, the inherent divinity and limitless possibilities of man—became, when used by Christian thinkers, means of obscuring the historic Gospel. Man's religious experience, not God's Self-revelation, was the main subject of investigation. The contemporary reaction, stressing decisive crises in history, the unbridgeable difference between God and man, the necessity for His redemptive Self-revelation to close the chasm, His—rather than man's—part in their fellowship, is salutary.[28]

By the 1940s Coffin had moderated his earlier stress on divine immanence and his high view of humanity.[29] Echoing the neo-orthodox message of divine transcendence and human sinfulness, Coffin began to emphasize God's holiness and humanity's limitations.[30] "A sense of human insufficiency is now for us indispensable to any experience we call Christian," Coffin wrote. "Our hope is placed not in powers within ourselves, but in forces of truth and love outside and above us in which we can participate." Nevertheless, Coffin refused to abandon the liberal doctrine of divine immanence. This teaching, he insisted, gave insight into God's "presence as the cohesive factor in nature and man," rightly asserted a "divine element in man," and "broke down the false division between the sacred and the secular." Though liberals had perhaps over-emphasized the closeness of God, Coffin maintained that it was "devoutly to be desired that the preaching of the transcendence of God" not be pushed to the extremes of Barthian theology.[31] Coffin also took the earlier liberalism to task for overemphasizing the normative nature of religious feeling. "This exclusive concern with religious experience," he claimed, "fitted in with the 'Humanism' of the post-War decade, and the practical abandonment of the attempt to identify the God of personal religion with the God of nature and of history." Taking a page from Machen's criticism of modernism, Coffin condemned the "anti-intellectualism" of a theology that stressed feeling to the detriment of reason. Belief and experience, he observed, had to be held together in the Christian faith.[32]

By the 1940s Coffin was also criticizing the liberal naïveté that led modernists to adjust all theology to the dominant ideas of the age. "It did not occur to these earnest Christians," he said, "that there might be something faulty in the spirit of their day and in their own ideals, that the ethical and intellectual tendencies of the age might not be a divine standard to which the Christian Church should be adjusted." Admitting his indebtedness to neo-orthodox thought, Coffin claimed that modernism too readily baptized cultural movements. "Men rightly despise a chameleon Church taking the color of current thought and adjusting to the standards of contemporary society," he wrote.[33] Nonetheless, he could not completely abandon the modernist belief in "cultural immanentism."[34] "It is never easy to be both stalwart in fidelity to the distinctive Christian heritage and hospitable to the message of the living God through contemporary culture," he argued. "If we are reacting from Modernism which was too open to current influences, we must be careful not to become slaves of tradition." The solution was for Christians to be in, but not of, the world. Christianity "must have a *foothold* in its world, presenting its message to its mind, rendering its principles relevant to the circumstances in which men live, laying hold in its worship on their aspirations and lifting them Godward, [but] it dare not have *roothold* in it."[35]

Though World War I had led Coffin to concede that "the world moves in no steadily advancing evolution," in 1918 he still anticipated the formation of the Kingdom of God on earth.[36] By 1952 he had abandoned the progressivism of his early theology altogether. "The climax of history," he wrote, "is the arrival of the city of God. It does not emerge as the development of the trends and happenings in history. . . . Christians think of His coming in Jesus. History will conclude in another such coming."[37] Though no premillennialist, Coffin's understanding of the course of history had changed considerably since his early days.

One final note that came more and more into Coffin's writings in the 1930s and 1940s was concern over the secularization of American culture. In 1940 he declared,

> Today the Christian task is neither to combat science nor to reconcile the findings of theologians with those of the scientists; but to deal with secularism, which now lacks a convincing intellectual basis, and which thousands are finding incapable of affording them a satisfactory explanation of the world or inspiration to live in. The void in which naturalism left men, without meaning in existence and without anything to claim their loyalty and devotion, has been filled for many by substitute religions— nationalism, racialism, allegiance to class.... As these ideologies prove themselves both intellectually and practically inadequate, religion has, and will have increasingly, its chance as the one hope for the human race in a desperate age.[38]

The "secularism" of American society, he wrote after World War II, gave cause for American Christians to "hang [their] heads in shame."[39] Like some of his conservative counterparts years earlier, Coffin was growing increasingly concerned with the mounting influence of purely naturalistic thought. But unlike Machen, Coffin did not blame the rise of secularism on liberal theology or see its solution in a "new Reformation." What was needed to combat the secular tide was not opposition to modern ideas but a redoubling of the church's efforts in spreading the Christian faith. Only by recovering the "Gospel of Christ," which proclaimed God's love for all people, was there hope for the justice, brotherhood, and peace so needed in the world.[40]

While Coffin adjusted to new theological and cultural currents in the years after the Presbyterian controversy, Macartney by and large held fast to the gospel he had been preaching since his ordination in 1905. In 1939 Macartney contributed an article to a series in the *Christian Century* entitled "How My Mind Has Changed in This Decade," in which he noted that his convictions regarding the "grand particularities" of the faith had not changed at all. He acknowledged his distrust of church union movements and his difficulty with the Social Gospel but found hope in the church's apparent "swing back from the extreme modernistic position toward what may be described as the conservative or evangelical position."[41] Macartney realized that many liberals, like Coffin, were taking noticeable steps toward the center of the theological spectrum. The orthodoxy of the church was improving.

Macartney did concede an important shift of emphasis in his ecclesiology. "Events of the last ten years," he wrote, "have somewhat shaken my old-time confidence in the effectiveness of a denominational witness. A creedal church is a great institution, but its only strength is in its witness to its creed." With the suspension of Machen from the ministry, he lamented, the Presbyterian Church "seemed to witness against its creed rather than for it." Because of such events, Macartney claimed,

> More and more, I despair of getting a united witness from churches which embrace in their point of view and preaching almost any and every religious opinion. Therefore, I value less the whole ecclesiastical structure, and feel that more and more for the true witness to the gospel and the Kingdom of God we must depend upon the particular local church, the individual minister and the individual Christian. Between such believers and such Christians there is indeed a real church unity.[42]

On this point Macartney demonstrated a key difference between himself and his former ally, Machen. While Machen had separated from the church because of its alleged unfaithfulness, Macartney had decided to tolerate diversity within the larger church structure in order to carry on his effective evangelical ministry to church and world.

The remainder of Macartney's career, which lasted until 1953, reflected his disenchantment with the larger structure of the church.[43] Though he did not completely abandon service to the national church (he served on a General Assembly Committee in 1937 and was a commissioner to the assembly in 1947) his attendance at meetings of the presbytery was infrequent and perfunctory.[44] A puritan of the highest order, Macartney attempted to influence the direction of the church and culture in other ways.

One effort in which Macartney invested his energies was the League of Faith, a group formed in 1931 to maintain a conservative witness in the church.[45] Macartney, elected president of the league in June 1936 presided over the adoption of constitutional changes designed to make the body "broadly representative of the Church as a whole."[46] As reorganized, its purpose was "to promote loyalty to the Scriptures and to the Standards of the Presbyterian Church in the U.S.A." through books and articles, to promote fellowship among those sympathetic to the purpose of the league, and "to work within the Church for the eradication of such tendencies as are destructive of her life and witness."[47] In the next few years this group opposed proposed changes in the Westminster Confession's sanctioning of "just and necessary" wars, and questioned the appointments of the neo-orthodox thinkers E. G. Homrighausen and Emil Brunner to the faculty of Princeton Seminary.[48]

The chief means Macartney used to further the conservative cause was preaching. For twenty-six years, from 1927 until 1953, Macartney carried on a popular and vibrant ministry in his Pittsburgh church. The congregation at Sunday morning worship consistently numbered from twelve hundred to sixteen hundred and the Sunday evening service drew about nine hundred.[49] In 1930 Macartney founded the Tuesday Noon Club for Businessmen, an interdenominational group that met once a week for lunch, singing, and a brief inspirational message. Beginning with a core of twelve men, the membership grew to over two thousand with an average attendance of over eight hundred.[50] Finally, Macartney directed a Wednesday evening service for which he wrote many of the sermons later published in such volumes as *Things Most Surely Believed* and *What Jesus Really Taught.*[51]

Macartney's influence was not limited to his listeners in Pittsburgh alone. His sermons, disseminated in pamphlets and in over forty books, were read worldwide.[52] He was a frequent preacher on college campuses and in the course of his ministry delivered numerous lectures, including the Stone Foundation Lectures at Princeton, the Smythe Lectures at Columbia Theological Seminary, and the Payton Lectures at Fuller Theological Seminary.[53]

Finally, Macartney advanced conservative Christianity both in the Presbyterian Church and the broader Christian community by nurturing over a dozen assistant pastors, including Harold J. Ockenga, founder of the National Association of Evangelicals, during his ministry at Pittsburgh.[54] Macartney wielded enormous influence over these young men during their tenure under him and maintained relationships with them even after they left Pittsburgh.[55] By serving as a teacher of pastors Macartney extended his legacy into the next generation.

Issues in the Presbyterian Controversy: Theology, Philosophy, and Ecclesiology

On the surface the major protagonists in the Presbyterian controversy— J. Gresham Machen, William Jennings Bryan, Henry Sloane Coffin, Clarence E. Macartney, Charles R. Erdman, and Robert E. Speer—all look surprisingly similar. All were economically secure, well-educated, patrician-minded gentlemen of the late Victorian era. All were members of the dominant cultural tradition in America. Within the larger Anglo-Saxon, Protestant tradition from which they all hailed, however, these men had distinctly different histories that provided them with variant theological, philosophical, and cultural assumptions. These differences significantly influenced their understandings of the relationship of Christianity and culture and the roles each would play in the conflict. All of these factors—theological, ecclesiological, philosophical, and cultural—contributed to the advent and final outcome of the Presbyterian conflict.

In reviewing the lives of the half-dozen ecclesiastical leaders examined here, some differences and similarities become immediately apparent. The two subjects on the furthest ends of the theological spectrum under examination—Machen and Coffin—hailed from the two cities most representative of each of their respective cultures, Baltimore and New York. In the late nineteenth century Baltimore was the leading city of the South. Unmatched in wealth and intellectual influence, Baltimore earned its reputation as the "metropolis of the South."[56] A devoted son of a devout Southern Presbyterian who was also a Daughter of the Confederacy, Machen inherited an appreciation for orthodox doctrine and the values of Southern culture.

Machen's Southern upbringing gave him a distinct perspective on the intellectual and social movements that were transforming America in the early twentieth century. He lamented the spiritual decline of the nation in the face of increasing secularization and looked back to a former age, a time when Christianity ruled the ideas and the goals of society. Then poetry, art, music, and literature reflected the spiritual values of the faith. Then liberty still reigned in society. But all this had been lost in the modern world, a world dragged down by the naturalistic materialism that had come to dominate the intellectual arena. Throughout the controversy Machen harbored a dream of a "new Reformation," a rebirth of orthodox Christianity, that would restore the "glories of the past," and the treasure of liberty.[57]

At the other extreme, Coffin lived almost his entire life in New York City, the epitome of the secular, urban, industrial society that was coming to dominate the Northern United States. From his childhood Coffin had witnessed the wonders of modern technology: the elevated trains, high-rise buildings, and the Brooklyn Bridge. Far from disparaging modern intellectual trends, Coffin gloried in the movements of the age and sought to adjust the theology of the church to the intellectual currents of the modern world. Inspired by evolutionary thought and the material advance of the period, Coffin looked for the day when those accepting the "purpose of Jesus" would transform the world into the Kingdom of God.[58] A true child of New York, the modern capital of the nation, Coffin held dearly to the value of modern thought and the promise of modern civilization throughout the conflict.

Of the remaining characters—Macartney, Bryan, Erdman, and Speer—two were raised in Pennsylvania, one in Western New York, and one in Illinois. It is probably more than coincidence that the four individuals in the center of the theological spectrum all hailed from small towns in the Northern United States. Indeed Speer, Macartney, and Erdman grew up within one hundred and fifty miles of each other. Though the emphases in each of these individual's households were different (especially for Macartney who grew up in a Reformed Presbyterian home), all of these men matured in a traditional theological and cultural environment.

Significantly, none of these more centrist leaders escaped the influence of the faith of the "Middle Border" that so shaped the ideals of Bryan. Bryan's father, as an evangelical Christian who held public office, instilled a love of Christ and country in his son.[59] Likewise, Erdman insisted that "the hope of America" rested in the propagation of the Christian faith; and Speer enthusiastically supported the christianization of America.[60] Macartney, his heritage of "political dissent" notwithstanding, declared that America, the greatest nation in the world, had an important mission to the world.[61] "The American Republic," Macartney proclaimed in 1932, "is still to have a part, and an important part, in that great plan which Omnipotence is working out through the ages for the good of mankind and the glory of God."[62] Though in different ways and to different degrees, faith in Christ, in the mission of America, and in the salutary effect of Christianity on American civilization influenced the homes of the centrist leaders of the Presbyterian controversy.

The battles the church fought between 1922 and 1936 revolved primarily around questions of theology and ecclesiology. The theological variations within the Presbyterian Church in the 1920s are amply manifested by the varying positions of the leaders of the conflict on the "five fundamentals." Machen, Macartney, and Bryan, though for various reasons, all endorsed the five fundamentals declared by the General Assemblies of 1910, 1916, and 1923. Erdman and Speer were a bit more selective on these points: while both accepted the virgin birth, bodily resurrection, and miracles of Christ, Erdman held to a limited notion of inerrancy and Speer avoided the rhetoric of inerrancy altogether. Both, in fact, seemed much more comfortable with the language of the Westminster Confession: the Scriptures were the supreme authority in matters of faith and life. Coffin, insisting that theology had to accommodate itself to the thought of the modern world, accepted none of the "fundamentals." What is most striking is that despite this doctrinal diversity, the church leadership—and, we may therefore assume, the church—was overwhelmingly evangelical. Aside from Coffin, all of these characters accepted the historical accuracy of the Gospel narratives and the normative authority of the Scriptures. Modernists were a decided minority.

The theological positions of Erdman—and to a lesser extent, Speer—raise serious questions about Ernest Sandeen's thesis that fundamentalism was essentially the result of a marriage between millenarianism and the Princeton Theology.[63] Sandeen lifts up Charles Erdman as the incarnation of this union; Erdman was, he says, "a living symbol of the alliance between the two movements."[64] Unfortunately, Erdman fails to fit Sandeen's model at two critical points. First, Erdman seems not to have been heavily influenced by the Princeton tradition. Second, and more significant, Erdman failed the fundamentalist test on the most important point—militancy. Like his mentor Dwight L. Moody, Erdman was constitutionally averse to conflict.[65] In fact, the two church leaders who did demonstrate sympathy with premillennialism (Erdman and, early on, Speer) worked for peace throughout the conflict; while the directors of the fundamentalists (Machen, Macartney, and Bryan) all had nothing whatever to do with the millenarian heritage. Though millenarianism had a profound impact on the wider fundamentalist movement in America, and eventually contributed to a split in Machen's infant church, it did not hold a prominent place in the conflict within the Presbyterian Church.

Even more important than questions about specific doctrines was the question of the importance of doctrine itself. Macartney, in accord with his Reformed Presbyterian and Princetonian roots, insisted that doctrine was of paramount importance and took Fosdick to task for his liberal theology. Likewise, Machen, true to the Old School tradition he learned in Baltimore and at Princeton, roundly scored modernism for its understanding of creeds as the "changing expression of unitary Christian experience."[66] Coffin provided a stunning example of just the modernist attitude toward doctrine that Machen abhorred. Convinced that creeds were only "man's attempt in the best thought and language at his command to express his religious experience" and that Christians had to adapt their creeds to modern times, Coffin ascribed no normative value to doctrines as such.[67] To the likes of Machen and Macartney, this severing of doctrines from historical events was nothing less than the abandonment of the Christian faith.

Bryan, Erdman, and Speer all fell between these two extremes. Bryan and Erdman, both raised in homes committed to the Northern evangelical heritage, were conservative theologically but placed more value on the moral and practical aspects of the faith and less stress on doctrine than their Old School peers. The best defense of Christianity, Bryan held, was to be found not in reasoned argument but in Christian living.[68] Erdman echoed this sentiment in his claim that "A man may recite an orthodox creed and believe it, and yet be self-deceived as to his relation to Christ.... A real believer follows Christ, obeys Christ and reflects the character of Christ."[69] Speer, influenced by Dwight L. Moody and the tradition of Horace Bushnell, maintained that "the New Testament does not lay its emphasis on metaphysical theory, it lays it on supernatural life."[70] At rock bottom, Christianity was "Christ for men and in men. It is the saving power of Christ and the possibility and reality of the mystical presence of God in human life."[71] Though these three, raised in small town America, were theologically more conservative than Coffin, their tendency to emphasize Christian life more than doctrine helps to explain the alliance between Erdman, Speer, and Coffin and sheds light on Bryan's move in the direction of inclusivism in the months before his death.

Doctrinal differences within the church, particularly between the extremes of Machen and Coffin, were at least partially attributable to the differing intellectual underpinnings of the fundamentalist and liberal positions. The fundamentalist–modernist controversy in general has, of course, frequently been painted as a battle between intellectually sophisticated liberals and intellectually stunted conservatives. H. Richard Niebuhr attributed fundamentalist beliefs in part to the "inadequate development of educational institutions for both clergy and laity" and to the "fundamentalist distrust of reason and the emphasis upon emotion."[72] Norman Furniss argued that fundamentalists wore the badge of ignorance proudly, Robert Handy painted the battle as "another round in the long struggle between faith and reason," and Richard Hofstadter condemned the fundamentalists to the domain of the antiintellectuals.[73]

That there were fundamentalists who derogated the import of the intellect cannot be doubted. Bryan, for one, did no credit to the intellectual aspects of conservative Christianity when he condemned Darwinism as encouraging "mind-worship."[74] But the examples of Machen and Macartney, both well-educated and articulate defenders of orthodoxy, make it impossible to paint the controversy in the Presbyterian Church as essentially one of ignorance versus intelligence. Rather, fundamentalists and modernists operated with incompatible views of history and science.

While conservatives like Machen held to an understanding of history based on Scottish Common Sense Realism and Baconianism, modernists like Coffin subscribed to the views of historicism, which had come to prominence in the late nineteenth and early twentieth centuries. As George Marsden has suggested, the conflict between these two understandings of history played a major part in the fundamentalist–modernist controversy in general and the Presbyterian conflict in particular. For those rooted in a Common Sense view of history, the past was immediately available to current thinkers. Individuals did not merely remember an idea of the past but remembered something of the past itself. Moreover, the "facts" of the past were not merely interpretations but events that had actually happened. Liberals, on the other hand, believed that the past, as such, was gone and that what contemporaries had were only memories of the past. History was necessarily a matter of interpretation.[75]

These two views were obviously incompatible. Machen claimed that "the facts of the Christian religion remain facts no matter whether we cherish them or not; they are facts for God; they are facts both for angels and for demons; they are facts now, and they will remain facts beyond the end of time."[76] Variant interpretations of the virgin birth (like those implied in the Auburn Affirmation) were absurd. But Coffin argued just as adamantly that the description of events in the biblical narrative, historically conditioned as they were, were open to interpretation within the bounds of "evangelical Christianity." Thus, while he affirmed his belief in the incarnation, atonement, and resurrection, he insisted that this did not necessarily imply belief in the virgin birth, substitutionary atonement, or bodily resurrection. Operating with such different paradigms, the two simply talked past each other.[77]

Likewise, fundamentalists did not reject science per se, but operated with a different model of science than their modernist opponents. For fundamentalists, operating on Newtonian and Baconian presuppositions, the task of science was to gather and classify facts, including the facts of the Bible. But modernists had accepted an alternate paradigm for scientific thought. Marsden summarizes,

> Fundamentalists had committed themselves totally to a "normal science." That is they took one model of perception as normal for all persons. This was a "Baconian" model based on common sense. Almost all their apologetic and interpretation of Scripture rested on this foundation. Their opponents, however, belonged to a philosophical tradition that, especially since Kant, was willing to see perception as an interpretative process.

Hence they were more open to speculative theories. They nevertheless considered these theories to be reliable inferences from the facts, and felt that no modern scientific person could seriously doubt them.[78]

Granted that there was much antiintellectualism within fundamentalism at large, fundamentalists and modernists within the Presbyterian community were divided not so much because they valued the intellect differently but because they subscribed to variant philosophical presuppositions. While fundamentalists had adopted the dominant philosophical model of nineteenth-century America, modernists embraced the new views of science and history that would come to control twentieth-century intellectual life.

In addition to doctrinal and philosophical differences, diverse ecclesiologies, as numerous scholars have pointed out, also fueled the conflict.[79] Again, Machen and Coffin provide the clearest evidence of the different views within the church. Since doctrine was at the very center of Christianity for Machen, he viewed the church as a body of like-minded individuals devoted above all to the propagation of right doctrine.[80] For Coffin, on the other hand, the church was a community united by "oneness of purpose with Christ"; it was "the company of those who share the purpose of Jesus and possess His Father's Spirit for its accomplishment."[81] Quite predictably, the two were at loggerheads. Machen could not tolerate those who would dismiss the doctrinal basis of the church, and Coffin could not tolerate those who insisted on a doctrinal grounding for the church. Inasmuch as both were willing to fight for their positions, battle necessarily ensued.

Much to Machen's chagrin, those in the middle of the church, such as Speer—who viewed the church more as a "missionary society" to preach Christ than an agency for the defense and propagation of doctrine—saw conflict as a greater threat to the church than loose theology.[82] Concerned with maintaining the united witness of the church to Christ, and convinced, with good reason, that the church was essentially orthodox, Speer and his party sought ecclesiastical peace.

In the face of dramatic intellectual changes that overtook church and culture in the late nineteenth and early twentieth centuries, the church had to determine the essence of the faith and decide how much doctrinal diversity it would tolerate in its ranks. But the battle was not concerned with theological and ecclesiological issues alone. Focus on these concerns, while imperative, has tended to obscure other factors that contributed to the timing, intensity, and duration of the conflict.

Most notably, different views of the relationship of Christianity and culture dramatically affected the alliances within, and the final outcome of, the conflict.

Issues in the Controversy: Christianity and Culture

As members of the dominant cultural tradition in America, all of the major protagonists in the Presbyterian controversy strove mightily not simply to defend their particular theological and ecclesiological views but also to maintain the influence of Christianity in the dramatically changed and rapidly changing culture of post–World War I America. But differing theological and cultural roots within the wider Protestant, Anglo-Saxon tradition led to different understandings not only of the essence of Christianity but also of the role of Christianity in culture. How the church was to influence the culture and what that influence was to entail were crucial questions underlying the battles fought over ordination requirements, Princeton Seminary, and foreign missions.

Machen's response to the changes of post–World War I America was unique among the characters here examined. True to the Old School beliefs of his native church and of Princeton Seminary, Machen held that the primary means by which the church influenced culture was through ideas. Warfield had taught Machen that Christianity was "to *reason* its way to dominion."[83] False ideas were not only "the greatest obstacles to the reception of the gospel" but were "responsible even for the physical evils in the world."[84] The role of ideas in transforming culture only gained in importance when combined with Machen's adherence to the Southern Presbyterian doctrine of the spirituality of the church. Unlike any of the other five protagonists in the story, Machen alone insisted that the church had no business addressing specifically social and political issues, and he alone stressed the unequaled power of ideas to transform the culture.

These convictions help to explain Machen's dogged insistence that the church, then Princeton Seminary, then the Board of Missions had to hold unswervingly to the faith of orthodox Christianity. Doctrine was important first because Christianity, particularly as formulated by the Westminster divines and expounded by the Princeton theologians, was true. But beyond this, doctrine was important because only correct ideas held by individual Christians had the power to instigate a mighty Reformation that would restore civilization to its former glory. In this way, then, Machen sought to address the social issues of the day. By defending

Reformed orthodoxy Machen sought not simply to preserve the Christian truth but to redeem the real and imagined values of a culture that was fast passing away.[85]

Finally, Machen's Southern upbringing provided him with a response to the Presbyterian controversy that was largely unavailable to his Northern peers. In the late 1920s and early 1930s, as Machen marched inexorably toward secession, his Northern counterpart, Clarence Macartney, tried repeatedly to keep him in the fold. But Machen would have none of it. Separation was an honorable solution to irreconcilable differences of principle. Once Machen had decided that the church was apostate, he believed he had no choice but to work for a new church to preserve the Christian tradition for the sake of church and culture.

Macartney, Machen's closest ally for the first half of the conflict, grew up in a Reformed Presbyterian home in Western Pennsylvania. On most theological points the Reformed Presbyterians were one with Southern Presbyterians. Both churches were dedicated to the theology of the Westminster Confession and a high view of Scripture. But the Reformed Presbyterians were fully committed to making America a Christian nation not by the power of reason alone but also through their evangelical witness and social reform. The Covenanters had ardently opposed slavery, the liquor traffic, Sabbath desecration, and lax divorce laws. Macartney's understanding of the church's role in the culture was therefore significantly different than Machen's. While both held to the Calvinistic belief that the church was called to transform the culture, Macartney's forebears were determined to redeem America through social reform and legislative action. As Galbraith Todd said of Macartney, "With his background in the Covenanter Church, where a passionate concern for social righteousness was joined to orthodox theology, it would have been surprising had he not enunciated the social and moral teachings of the Bible and Christianity."[86] Macartney married an unshakable commitment to the preservation of orthodox doctrine with a more evangelical emphasis on the preservation of a Christian America.

Though Macartney's theological position was closer to Machen's than to that of any of the other leaders, his views of America and of the church's role in American culture showed far more affinity with Bryan, Erdman, and even Speer. Against all who would secularize the church, Macartney insisted on sound doctrine. But defense of doctrine alone would not save the culture from apostasy. He also spoke out emphatically and repeatedly against the moral evils of the day. The issues he addressed—divorce, Prohibition, the decline of the Sabbath, religion in the schools—were issues that Bryan and Erdman also addressed. While

Bryan and Macartney echoed each other on the moral and social perils of Darwinism, Machen worried about doctrine and civil liberty. While Macartney, Erdman, and Speer agreed on the need for the church to tighten up on divorce, Machen could see no mandate for change. While Macartney and virtually the entire Presbyterian Church supported Prohibition, Machen opposed the Eighteenth Amendment and denied the church's right to address such issues at all. Throughout the 1920s a significant pattern emerged. Macartney's agreement with other leaders in the church on the church's role in culture placed him much closer than Machen to the evangelical mainstream of the church. At stake in the Presbyterian controversy was not just the preservation of right doctrine but the moral order of American civilization. The church had a duty both to preach orthodoxy and to maintain a moral sway over the nation. This, combined with Macartney's concern for the maximum use of opportunity and the Covenanter antipathy to schism go a long way toward explaining why Macartney remained in the church while Machen left.[87]

Bryan, a Presbyterian more in name than in doctrine, entered the fray in the Presbyterian Church in an attempt to save American Christian civilization from the evils of Darwinism. It was his last great moral crusade. Born and raised on the Middle Border, Bryan merged his faith in America with his faith in Christ. Bryan wrote, "[My father] saw no necessary conflict—and I have never been able to see any—between the principles of our government and the principles of Christian faith."[88] He was committed less to a rigorous defense of doctrine than to the propagation of Christian life and living. In this Bryan showed tendencies much closer to Erdman than to Machen and Macartney. Indeed, on some matters of social reform Bryan began to sound like Speer and Coffin. Bryan served on the temperance committee of the Federal Council of Churches and praised the ecumenical body as "the greatest religious organization in our nation."[89] A theologically conservative proponent of the Social Gospel, Bryan argued that taxation, labor reform, the economic system, international relations, and women's suffrage were all within the purview of the church.[90] But Bryan's primary concern in the Presbyterian conflict was his fight against Darwinist thought; and here, as in the culture at large, he was striving to preserve the influence of Christianity in American civilization. Doctrine was important mostly because it served as a chief defense against the spread of a materialist Darwinian might-makes-right philosophy.

The motivations of the ruling triumvirate of Presbyterian fundamentalism—Machen, Macartney, and Bryan—were, therefore, to say the least, diverse. While all three, for various reasons, argued for the maintenance of traditional Christian orthodoxy within the church, their concerns were not solely—or in the case of Bryan, even primarily—doctrinal. All, for theological and cultural reasons, were also concerned with the influence of Christianity in the culture. For Machen, however, the preeminent means of addressing the secularization of the culture was through the realm of ideas, while for Macartney and Bryan evangelism and social reform also played a key part in the maintenance of the church's influence on the civilization.

Given the eventual outcome of the controversy, it is important to realize that Machen was not the most representative example of the fundamentalist faction of the church. It was Bryan who nearly won election as the moderator of the 1923 assembly, and it was Macartney who did win that post in 1924. Though unquestionably a keen thinker and perceptive analyst of the intellectual trends in America, Machen's unflagging devotion to the pursuit of pure doctrine alone, his lack of concern for the social issues plaguing most of his conservative allies, and his predilection for separation as a means of solving disputes of principle placed him out of the mainstream evangelical tradition. He was a lone Southern Presbyterian in a Yankee church.

Macartney serves as a much better representative of the ideas and ideals that motivated Presbyterian fundamentalism in the 1920s than does his Southern colleague. His Reformed Presbyterian upbringing and the influence of the Northern evangelical tradition in general inspired a concern for the preservation of orthodoxy and the advance of Christian civilization through evangelism and moral reform. Having followed Machen in the founding of Westminster Seminary in order to preserve a source of orthodox ministers for the church, he could see no benefit in abandoning the church—and therefore the church's evangelical potential—to those less concerned with doctrinal matters. Rather, in the face of a steadily secularizing society, he was determined to hold his position, preach the "grand particularities of the faith," point out the evils of a faithless life and culture, and defend orthodoxy against its foes.

Erdman, Speer, and Coffin—all inclusivists—were no less concerned with the church's relationship to culture than their exclusivist brethren; but the inclusivists, for theological and cultural reasons, analyzed the problems of the culture differently and therefore arrived at different conclusions. Erdman, raised in a New School, premillennial home in Western New York, manifested a deep interest in the spiritual health of America. The welfare of the nation, he held, was "inescapably connected with the knowledge of God and with obedience to his laws."[91] Erdman mirrored many of Macartney's social concerns—Prohibition, divorce, family religion, Sabbath decline—but his chief worry in the 1920s was not the secularization of society. In the midst of the cultural turmoil of the 1920s, Erdman was concerned above all with the vast disorder of society itself. For Erdman the church, through its evangelism, provided the moral adhesive of the nation. "There can be no abiding morality aside from the influences and sanctions of the church," he wrote, "and without morality, neither society or state can continue to exist."[92] But a disordered church could never bring order to a nation in chaos. Erdman's concern for the welfare of the nation, combined with his New School derogation of fine points of doctrine, led him to work for peace in the church in order to preserve its influence on individuals and society. Though no doubt motivated primarily by theological and ecclesiological concerns, Erdman's actions in the controversy also depended on his understanding of the church's role as the moral custodian of the nation.

Finally, Speer and Coffin, though not of one mind on specifically theological issues, possessed remarkably similar views on the church's calling in the modern world. Both of these men, like Bryan, were deeply shocked by the shattering of Christendom and Western civilization in World War I. In the aftermath of the Great War, Speer and Coffin became convinced that Christianity's role in the world was the building up of a human commonwealth—the Kingdom of God—through the proclamation of the gospel. Agreeing that possession of the Christian spirit was sufficient basis for Christian fellowship, both worked indefatigably for a united Christian church to unite the world.[93] Speer, raised in a more traditional environment than Coffin and influenced by Moody and Bushnell, had a more Christocentric ecclesiology than did Coffin.[94] Nevertheless, these differences could not obscure the virtual agreement of these two leaders concerning the role of the church in the world. Disagreement on matters of doctrine, over which Machen battled to the death, took a back seat to their desire that in a world torn apart by economic and international strife, the church serve as the agent of global reconciliation.

The leaders of the Presbyterian controversy, while all members of the dominant cultural tradition in America, had adopted varying theological, philosophical, ecclesiological, and cultural attitudes, which led to extended church conflict in the 1920s and 1930s. The Presbyterian controversy was waged primarily over questions of doctrine and ecclesiology. Faced with increasingly assertive liberalism in the church, Machen, Macartney, and (at least for a while) Bryan worked to ensure that the clergy would accept the supernatural elements of the New Testament narratives and the doctrines of the substitutionary atonement and inerrancy of Scripture. When Princeton was reorganized, Machen and (eventually) Macartney supported the founding of Westminster to preserve the Old School tradition. Finally, Machen, convinced that the Board of Foreign Missions was apostate, founded his own competing agency to support missionaries willing to pursue a militant defense of the faith. Throughout, Machen desired a church anchored in the Westminster Confession and willing to fight for its doctrine.

On purely theological grounds it is curious that Machen ended up outside of the church, while Coffin remained inside. Machen's Old School faith was, after all, in most matters, much closer to the dominant evangelical theology in the church than was Coffin's liberalism. But Machen's ecclesiology prohibited him from maintaining fellowship with a church that tolerated modernism. Inasmuch as Speer, Erdman, and their constituency refused to pursue a course of militant conservatism in a church they perceived to be essentially orthodox, Machen believed he had no recourse but to withdraw.

Added to these theological and ecclesiological factors were issues of culture and the church's role in culture. Machen's understanding of the church's relationship to culture segregated him from the rest of the group. While all the other players were influenced in one way or another by the Northern evangelical tradition of evangelism and social reform, Machen stood fast in his belief that the church must avoid addressing social issues and that propagation of right doctrine was the primary means by which the church should influence the culture. These convictions, buttressed by his Southern predilection for secession as a solution to disagreements of principle, encouraged him to withdraw from the church, thus putting an end to the Presbyterian controversy.

Though Machen's opponents were no doubt relieved to see him exit the church, his departure was a loss to the fellowship. Early on, Machen saw the pervasive power of secular ideas and ideals and the need to present a scholarly defense of Christianity in the face of secularism. By the 1930s even Coffin was worried about the rising secularism of the culture, though he never charged liberal theology with complicity in the trend. Clearly, Machen was correct in insisting that the church could not truly prosper if it abandoned the intellectual realm to the exponents of a naturalistic worldview. But by leaving the Presbyterian Church and separating himself from the vast majority of Presbyterians who accepted a supernatural gospel, Machen severely limited his opportunities to influence church and culture.

While the players in the Presbyterian controversy fought among themselves, in a very important way they were really fighting to preserve the influence of Christianity in a world moving steadily away from distinctively Christian influences. Each of the participants in the struggle possessed definite views of what that influence should be and how it should be exercised, but none doubted that Christianity had a role to play in the future of America and the world.

Ironically, the path the church finally took in an effort to maintain its witness to the world probably only served to undermine that witness. Having loosened its doctrinal standards, the church, always affected by the cultural trends surrounding it, opened its doors even wider to the influences of a secularizing society. Without clear theological boundaries, the church, in the years ahead, would find it more and more difficult to maintain an identity separate from the culture and offer a unique message and vision to the world it sought to serve.[95]

Epilogue

The current decline of mainstream Protestantism in America in general, and the Presbyterian Church (U.S.A.) in particular, has attracted widespread attention and comment in the past decade.[1] Studies addressing the current plight of the mainstream denominations have spawned a number of interpretations that incorporate historical, sociological, and theological factors. The increasing social activism of the churches in the 1960s, low birth rates among those affiliated with mainline denominations, broad value shifts in the culture stressing individualism, tolerance, and personal freedom, and a decrease in switching from conservative to liberal denominations have all been noted as possible reasons for this drop in membership.[2] Yet another cause of mainstream decline, enunciated by Dean Kelley in his key work *Why Conservative Churches Are Growing*, is the failure of the mainline bodies to require distinct commitments and articulate a clear belief system. Churches that stress pluralism and relativism, rather than distinctive beliefs and lifestyles, Kelley shows, are those that have experienced the greatest membership losses.[3]

There is, of course, no single reason for the current decline in vigor of mainstream Protestantism and no single "solution" will address the problems besetting the churches. Nevertheless, one apparent contributor to the current malaise in the Presbyterian Church is its unfocused theological identity.

In 1976, Dean R. Hoge described the United Presbyterian Church as "pluralistic and Culture-affirming" and continued:

> this policy [of pluralism] has effectively been in force since the 1920s. Ecclesiastical and creedal statements have been written abstractly enough, or with enough internal pluralism, to include all shades of theology in the denomination. The concept of "mission" has been defined so broadly that its usefulness as a meaningful word is threatened. One problem with this policy in any denomination is lack of identity. The question Who are we?

or What do we believe? is not satisfactorily answered by a recitation of diverse viewpoints current in the church. Evangelism is barely possible when the identity of the church and its gospel are difficult to state clearly.[4]

As Hoge astutely notes, the current identity crisis of the Presbyterian Church has its roots in the conflicts of the 1920s when the church opted for institutional above strict doctrinal unity. The Presbyterian Church, of course, is not alone in this. Most mainstream churches, having embraced doctrinal pluralism to some degree, have difficulty in clearly articulating the essence of their faith.

This confusion has manifested itself in diverse areas of the church's life such as preaching, piety, theological education, and church polity. For example, John McClure, in a recent study of Presbyterian preaching in the twentieth century, concluded that "there seems to be no coherent and consistent theological message system at work in much of Presbyterian preaching today."[5] Benton Johnson, in a study of Presbyterians and Sabbath practice in the twentieth century, asserts that "there is uncertainty in the churches on the matter of teaching, and there is a serious neglect of spirituality. The church's mission, whatever it is, cannot continue without the energy generated by its teachings and its spiritual practice."[6] Similarly John M. Mulder and Lee S. Wyatt have discovered that the diverse curricula at the church's theological seminaries have imparted a "blurred and inchoate identity . . . to the church's leadership and to its members."[7] Finally, James Moorhead and David McCarthy have pointed out that theological pluralism has led the church to address most controversial issues as questions of polity rather than matters of theology.[8]

This nebulous identity has contributed to the exodus of many young adults from the churches into apparently secular lifestyles, one factor in the decline of mainstream churches.[9] Leonard Sweet, an astute observer of contemporary mainstream Protestantism, recently made the connection, declaring, "Spurred on by pluralism, and by the Spockean focus on the individual child's power of self-realization, modernist church members sent their children on individual quests for meaning— and their children kept going, not into conservative churches but into 'secularized' life-styles."[10] When churches have difficulty enunciating a clear statement of faith distinct from the vision and world-view of the culture, they cannot, it appears, hold their children. As such, many young adults have left the communions of their parents to live as unchurched Americans.

Viewing these difficulties in light of the events of the 1920s and 1930s provides a perspective that can perhaps assist in understanding better the current predicament of the mainstream churches. The leaders in the Presbyterian conflict were all concerned with maintaining the church's witness in the world. Machen, Macartney, and to a certain degree, Bryan insisted that that witness, if it was to survive in the midst of a secular culture, had to be grounded in precise doctrine. Erdman, Speer, and Coffin, to different degrees and for very different reasons, placed less stress on doctrine and more on the united work of the church. In the midst of the controversy reconciliation between the various parties became impossible and the church opted to widen its doctrinal boundaries to preserve its united mission.

Other options, of course, were at least theoretically if not practically possible for the church in the 1920s. The church could have chosen to maintain the standards affirmed by the assemblies of 1910, 1916, and 1923. Most members of the church, however, apparently had concluded with Erdman and Speer that insisting on the fundamentals did more damage than good to the church's evangelical witness. Had the church opted to keep such strict requirements, controversy may well have continued and the church's mission suffered. Indeed, the continued small size of the communion founded by Machen, now called the Orthodox Presbyterian Church, seems to indicate that an overriding concern for precise doctrine does not provide an adequate foundation for a vital and appealing communion.[11]

Another possibility would have been for the church to move away from the idea of the fundamentals but to affirm a broad evangelical theology, similar to that adhered to by Erdman or Speer, but which did not incorporate a thoroughly inclusivist or pluralistic ecclesiology. Such a strategy might have avoided the ecclesiastical difficulties that accompanied the theological precisionism of Machen while maintaining clearer doctrinal boundaries for the church. But in the heat of the controversy, affirming such a middle position apparently did not appear to be a viable option. Instead, theological centrists like Erdman and Speer found themselves thrust into an alliance with liberals like Coffin in an effort to put an end to the fighting and preserve the unity and mission of the church.

Of course, one reason that Speer and Erdman so willingly supported a theologically broadening church in the 1920s was the church's overwhelmingly conservative, evangelical tenor. Given the orthodoxy of the vast majority of the church's clergy and laity, moderate conservatives could see little danger in widening the church's doctrinal boundaries. This, combined with the detrimental effects of continued infighting on the church's mission, convinced centrists that a more inclusive doctrinal stance provided the best available solution to the conflict.

In retrospect, however, it appears that Machen's fears about the secularization of the church without distinct doctrinal boundaries were well founded. One certainly need not agree with Machen's strategies, theology, or ecclesiology to concede that without a focused theological identity the church and the church's mission to the world have suffered. Lefferts Loetscher, writing in the 1950s, recognized the potential for doctrinal confusion left in the wake of the Presbyterian controversy. Analyzing the church's decision to eliminate the "fundamentals" as ordination requirements Loetscher wrote:

> But in sweeping away by a stroke of interpretation much of the previously exercised power of the General Assembly to define and thus to preserve the Church's doctrine, the commission established a principle which has much broader implications than the Church has yet had occasion to draw from it. If the Church now has no means of authoritatively defining its faith short of the amending process . . . ecclesiastical power is seriously hindered for the future from preventing more radical theological innovations than those discussed in the "five points."[12]

Of course, in abandoning the idea of the fundamentals the church did not eliminate all theological standards. The Westminster Confession—interpreted in diverse ways—remained the single confession of the church until 1967, and this, combined with the theological movement known as neo-orthodoxy, helped to maintain some sort of theological consensus in the church until the 1960s.[13] The decades since, however, have witnessed the theological fragmentation allowed by the church's earlier decisions, so that a report adopted by the 1988 General Assembly of the Presbyterian Church could conclude, "our unity is merely formal and our diversity is divisive."[14] This is hardly the outcome Speer and Erdman envisioned in the 1920s.

If the Presbyterian Church is any indication, the mainstream churches decided to eschew theological discussion and accept doctrinal pluralism, at least in part, to further their mission. As Lefferts Loetscher summarized this view, " 'The less theology the better' seems to be the lurking implication—at least so far as the Church's statistical growth is concerned."[15] This strategy made sense to many wise and devout Presbyterians in the 1920s when there seemed to be little danger that the Presbyterian Church would ever suffer from an unfocused theological identity. Moreover, the church's solution did work for a time in encouraging the unity and vitality of the church. In the long run, however, this course has contributed to the current identity crisis of the church and helped to undermine the foundation of the church's mission to the world.

Perhaps the contemporary mainstream churches can, in some manner, do what the Presbyterian Church torn by controversy in the 1920s would not or could not do, and affirm a normative middle theological position with clear boundaries. If so, the churches may well recover from their current theological confusion and thereby successfully address one of the many factors contributing to their current decline. Clearly, if the mainstream churches are to resolve their identity crises, they will have to do so on the basis of a biblical and creedal faith that is distinct from the values and norms of the surrounding culture.

Notes

Introduction

1. George Gallup, Jr. and David Poling commented in 1980, "The Presbyterian, Episcopalian and United Church of Christ communions cannot long exist as viable church organizations nationally if the declines of the 1970s persist in the 1980s" (*The Search for America's Faith* [Nashville: Abingdon, 1980], 83), quoted in William McKinney and Wade Clark Roof, "Liberal Protestantism: A Sociodemographic Perspective," in *Liberal Protestantism: Realities and Possibilities*, ed. Robert S. Michaelsen and Wade Clark Roof (New York: Pilgrim, 1986), 38.

2. For membership figures see Lauris B. Whitman, ed., *Yearbook of American Churches: Information on All Faiths in the U.S.A., Edition for 1968* (New York: National Council of Churches of Christ, 1968), 199–200; Constant H. Jacquet, Jr., ed., *Yearbook of American Churches, 1972* (Nashville: Abingdon, 1972), 228; Constant H. Jacquet, Jr., ed., *Yearbook of American and Canadian Churches, 1989* (Nashville: Abingdon, 1989), 243–44.

3. Wade Clark Roof and William McKinney, *American Mainline Religion: Its Changing Shape and Future* (New Brunswick: Rutgers University Press, 1987), 241.

4. In a recent dissertation William Weston, though from a different perspective, also sees the 1920s as an important period for the development of "religious pluralism" in the Presbyterian Church ("The Emergence of the Idea of Religious Pluralism within the Presbyterian Church in the U.S.A., 1890–1940" [Ph.D. diss., Yale University, 1988]).

5. McKinney and Roof, "Liberal Protestantism," in *Liberal Protestantism*, ed. Michaelsen and Roof, 40.

6. In 1939 the Presbyterian Church of America became the Orthodox Presbyterian Church. See Edwin H. Rian, *The Presbyterian Conflict* (Grand Rapids: William B. Eerdmans, 1940), 231–34.

7. For a helpful account of this period, see William Leuchtenburg, *The Perils of Prosperity: 1914–1932* (Chicago: University of Chicago Press, 1958).

8. In this work, reflecting use in the period under study, I use the terms *liberal* and *modernist* interchangeably. Though some scholars have attempted to draw a distinction between modernists and evangelical liberals, this effort is finally

not very helpful in understanding this theological movement, as William Hutchison has argued, (*The Modernist Impulse in American Protestantism* [Cambridge: Harvard University Press, 1976; reprint, New York: Oxford University Press, 1980], 7–9).

9. Stewart G. Cole, *The History of Fundamentalism* (New York: Richard R. Smith, 1931), 321.

10. Though Machen became a leading spokesman of the militant conservative or fundamentalist party in the church, he was somewhat reluctant to adopt the label *fundamentalist*. See C. Allyn Russell, *Voices of American Fundamentalism: Seven Biographical Studies* (Philadelphia: Westminster, 1976), 142–44.

11. The term *traditionalist inclusivist* is Delwin Nykamp's. In his very helpful dissertation Nykamp distinguishes between three groups in the Presbyterian conflict. "*Traditionalist exclusivists* were traditional Calvinists who intended to ensure that only clergy with that theology were allowed in the ministry. *Modifier inclusivists* endorsed change from Calvinism and intended to ensure that such modifications were acceptable for the Church's ministry. The 'swing' group that determined the outcome on most issues were *traditionalist inclusivists*. Traditional in their own theology, they were amenable to other views within the ministry" ("A Presbyterian Power Struggle: A Critical History of Communication Strategies Employed in the Struggle for Control of the Presbyterian Church, U.S.A., 1922–1926" [Ph.D. diss., Northwestern University, 1974], 4). These terms roughly correspond to my *fundamentalists, modernists*, and *moderates*, respectively.

Chapter 1

1. Robert M. Miller, *Harry Emerson Fosdick: Preacher, Pastor, Prophet* (New York: Oxford University Press, 1985), 115.

2. Harry E. Fosdick, *The Living of These Days: An Autobiography* (New York: Harper & Brothers, 1956), 145.

3. See William J. Bryan, "God and Evolution," in *Evolution and Religion: The Conflict between Science and Religion in Modern America*, ed. Gail Kennedy (Boston: D. C. Heath, 1957), 23–29; Cole, *History of Fundamentalism*, 101–2; Harry E. Fosdick, "A Reply to Mr. Bryan in the Name of Religion," in *Evolution and Religion*, ed. Kennedy, 30–34; Fosdick, *Living of These Days*, 135–36; Lefferts A. Loetscher, *The Broadening Church: A Study of Theological Issues in the Presbyterian Church since 1869* (Philadelphia: University of Pennsylvania Press, 1954), 104–8; Miller, *Harry Emerson Fosdick*, 113–15.

4. Harry E. Fosdick, "Shall the Fundamentalists Win?" in *American Protestant Thought in the Liberal Era*, ed. William R. Hutchison (Lanham: University Press of America, 1968), 170–82.

5. Ibid., 174–75.

6. Ibid., 175–78.

7. Ibid., 178–81.

8. Modified by a public relations man, Mr. Ivy Lee, it was published in *Christian Century*, 8 June 1922; *Baptist*, 10 June 1922; and *Christian Work*, 10 June 1922. In addition, John D. Rockefeller, Jr. paid for the publication of 130 thousand copies of the sermon for distribution (Miller, *Harry Emerson Fosdick*, 115–17).

9. Letter of J. Gresham Machen, 14 March 1916, quoted in Ned B. Stonehouse, *J. Gresham Machen: A Biographical Memoir* (Grand Rapids: William B. Eerdmans, 1954), 230.

10. Miller, *Harry Emerson Fosdick*, 68–72, 115.

11. Clarence E. Macartney, *The Making of a Minister: The Autobiography of Clarence E. Macartney*, ed. J. Clyde Henry (Great Neck, NY: Channel, 1961), 183–84.

12. Clarence E. Macartney, "Shall Unbelief Win? An Answer to Dr. Fosdick," pt. 1, *Presbyterian*, 13 July 1922, p. 8.

13. Ibid., 9, 26; Clarence E. Macartney, "Shall Unbelief Win? An Answer to Dr. Fosdick," pt. 2, *Presbyterian*, 20 July 1922, p. 8.

14. Macartney, "Shall Unbelief Win?" pt. 2, p. 10.

15. Quoted in Miller, *Harry Emerson Fosdick*, 119; Dorothy G. Fowler, *A City Church: The First Presbyterian Church in the City of New York, 1716–1976* (New York: First Presbyterian Church, 1981), 165–66. See also Loetscher, *Broadening Church*, 109–10; and *Minutes of the General Assembly of the Presbyterian Church in the U.S.A.* (hereafter *Minutes of GA*) 1923, 2 vols., (Philadelphia: Office of the General Assembly, 1923), 1:252–53.

16. Henry Adams, *The Education of Henry Adams: An Autobiography* (Cambridge: Riverside, 1918; reprint, Boston: Houghton Mifflin, 1946), 53.

17. Sydney E. Ahlstrom, *A Religious History of the American People* (New Haven: Yale University Press, 1972), 766–67.

18. Bert J. Loewenberg, "Darwinism Comes to America: 1859–1900," *Mississippi Valley Historical Review* 28 (December 1941): 339.

19. "Professor Agassiz on the *Origin of Species*," *American Journal of Science and the Arts* 30 (July 1860): 142–54, quoted in Bert J. Loewenberg, "The Reaction of American Scientists to Darwinism," *American Historical Review* 38 (July 1933): 689, 691.

20. Loewenberg, "Reaction of American Scientists," 692–93.

21. Ibid., 696–97; Asa Gray, "Darwin and His Reviewers," *Atlantic Monthly* 6 (October 1860): 406, quoted by Loewenberg, "Reaction of American Scientists," 697.

22. Charles Hodge, *What Is Darwinism?* (New York: Scribner, Armstrong, 1874), 177. Bert Loewenberg notes, "Yet even Hodge in 1873 expressed the possibility of a theistic interpretation of evolution" ("The Controversy over Evolution in New England," *New England Quarterly* 8 (June 1935): 287).

23. James McCosh, *Christianity and Positivism* (New York, 1871), 42, 63–64, quoted in Richard Hofstadter, *Social Darwinism in American Thought* (Philadelphia: University of Pennsylvania Press, 1944; reprint, Boston: Beacon Press, 1955), 27. On Reformed responses to Darwinism, see also Dennis R. Davis,

"Presbyterian Attitudes toward Science and the Coming of Darwinism in America, 1859 to 1929" (Ph.D. diss., University of Illinois at Urbana-Champaign, 1980); Deryl F. Johnson, "The Attitudes of the Princeton Theologians toward Darwinism and Evolution from 1859–1929" (Ph.D. diss., University of Iowa, 1968); David N. Livingstone, *Darwin's Forgotten Defenders: The Encounter between Evangelical Theology and Evolutionary Thought* (Grand Rapids: William B. Eerdmans, 1987); Gary S. Smith, "Calvinists and Evolution, 1870–1920," *Journal of Presbyterian History* 61 (Fall 1983): 335–52; idem, *The Seeds of Secularization: Calvinism, Culture, and Pluralism in America: 1870–1915* (Grand Rapids: Christian University Press, 1985), 95–111.

24. Quoted in Loewenberg, "Darwinism Comes to America," 357. See also Henry Ward Beecher, "The Two Revelations," in *Evolution and Religion*, ed. Kennedy, 19.

25. Ferenc M. Szasz, *The Divided Mind of Protestant America: 1880–1930* (University, AL: University of Alabama Press, 1982), 2–10.

26. Mark A. Noll, ed., *The Princeton Theology, 1812–1921: Scripture, Science, and Theological Method from Archibald Alexander to Benjamin Warfield* (Grand Rapids: Baker Book House, 1983), 27.

27. Szasz, *Divided Mind*, 17–19, 26–29, 33–41.

28. Francis P. Weisenburger, *Ordeal of Faith: The Crisis of Church-Going America, 1865–1900* (New York: Philosophical Library, 1959), 84–85; Szasz, *Divided Mind*, 68–83.

29. Szasz, *Divided Mind*, 12, 13.

30. Ahlstrom, *Religious History*, 772–74. See also Henry F. May, *The End of American Innocence: A Study of the First Years of Our Own Time, 1912–1917* (New York: Alfred A. Knopf, 1959; reprint, New York: Oxford University Press, 1979); and Morton White, *Social Thought in America: The Revolt against Formalism* (New York: Viking Press, 1949; reprint, New York: Oxford University Press, 1976).

31. Grant Wacker, "The Demise of Biblical Civilization," in *The Bible in America: Essays in Cultural History*, ed. Nathan O. Hatch and Mark A. Noll (New York: Oxford University Press, 1982), 125–27.

32. Carl N. Degler, *The Age of the Economic Revolution: 1876–1900*, 2d ed. (Glenview: Scott, Foresman, 1977), 17–18, 28, 30, 32.

33. Degler, *Economic Revolution*, 34–35; James T. Patterson, *America in the Twentieth Century: A History* (New York: Harcourt Brace Jovanovich, 1976), 21, 24.

34. Degler, *Economic Revolution*, 35–36.

35. Ibid., 36–37; Patterson, *America in the Twentieth Century*, 25.

36. Robert H. Wiebe, *The Search for Order, 1877–1920* (New York: Hill & Wang, 1967), 8; Patterson, *America in the Twentieth Century*, 26.

37. Patterson, *America in the Twentieth Century*, 26, 28.

38. Ibid., 6–8.

39. George M. Marsden, "The Era of Crisis: From Christendom to Pluralism," in *Eerdmans' Handbook to Christianity in America*, ed. Mark Noll et al.

(Grand Rapids: William B. Eerdmans, 1983), 285. See also Blake McKelvey, *The Urbanization of America, 1860–1915* (New Brunswick: Rutgers University Press, 1963), 67–69; and Arthur M. Schlesinger, *The Rise of the City, 1878–1898* (New York: Macmillan, 1933), 53–64.

40. McKelvey, *Urbanization of America*, 63; Schlesinger, *Rise of City*, 64. See also Oscar Handlin, *The Uprooted*, 2d ed. (Boston: Little, Brown, 1973).

41. Ahlstrom, *Religious History*, 735; Degler, *Economic Revolution*, 8; Patterson, *America in the Twentieth Century*, 15–16, 19–20.

42. Patterson, *America in the Twentieth Century*, 16, 19; Robert T. Handy, *A Christian America: Protestant Hopes and Historical Realities*, rev. ed. (New York: Oxford University Press, 1981), 74; Marsden, "Era of Crisis," in *Eerdmans' Handbook*, ed. Noll, 286; Weisenburger, *Ordeal of Faith*, 46.

43. Marsden, "Era of Crisis," in *Eerdmans' Handbook*, ed. Noll, 285–86. See also Stow Persons, "Religion and Modernity, 1865–1910," in *Religion in American Life*, vol. 1. *The Shaping of American Religion*, ed. James W. Smith and Leland Jameson (Princeton: Princeton University Press, 1961), 372.

44. Marsden, "Era of Crisis," in *Eerdmans' Handbook*, ed. Noll, 286. See also George Marsden, "The Collapse of American Evangelical Academia," in *Faith and Rationality: Reason and Belief in God*, ed. Alvin Plantinga and Nicholas Wolterstorff (Notre Dame: University of Notre Dame Press, 1983), 219–64; Richard Hofstadter, "The Revolution in Higher Education," in *Paths of American Thought*, ed. Arthur M. Schlesinger, Jr. and Morton White (Boston: Houghton Mifflin, 1963), 269–90; Frederick Rudolph, *The American College and University: A History* (New York: Random House, 1962); and Laurence R. Veysey, *The Emergence of the American University* (Chicago: University of Chicago Press, 1965).

45. Ralph Henry Gabriel, *The Course of American Democratic Thought*, 2d ed. (New York: John Wiley & Sons, 1956), 230.

46. C. Wright Mills, *Sociology and Pragmatism: The Higher Learning in America* (New York: Paine Whitman, 1964), 44, 58. Tax money spent on public colleges increased from seventy million dollars in 1871 to two hundred million dollars in 1900 (p. 40).

47. Rudolph, *American College and University*, 432, 433.

48. Hofstadter, "Revolution in Higher Education," 279.

49. Weisenberger, *Ordeal of Faith*, 46–48.

50. Marsden, "Era of Crisis," in *Eerdmans' Handbook*, ed. Noll, 287; quote from Gabriel, *Course of American Democratic Thought*, 158.

51. See Max Lerner, "The Triumph of Laissez-faire," in *Paths of American Thought*, ed., Schlesinger and White, 147–66; Gabriel, *Course of American Democratic Thought*, 151–69.

52. Weisenburger, *Ordeal of Faith*, 121–25.

53. See James F. Findlay, Jr., *Dwight L. Moody, American Evangelist: 1837–1899* (Chicago: University of Chicago Press, 1969), esp. 301.

54. W. H. Daniels, ed., *Moody: His Words, Work, and Workers* (New York: Nelson & Phillips, 1877), 256, quoted in George M. Marsden, *Fundamentalism*

and American Culture: The Shaping of Twentieth-Century Evangelicalism, 1870–1925 (New York: Oxford University Press, 1980), 35.

55. Quoted in Szasz, *Divided Mind*, 39.

56. Marsden, *Fundamentalism and American Culture*, 33, 38.

57. Findlay, *Moody*, 339–41, 350, 354–55. See also C. Howard Hopkins, *John R. Mott, 1865–1955: A Biography* (Grand Rapids: William B. Eerdmans, 1979); Clifton J. Phillips, "The Student Volunteer Movement and Its Role in China Missions, 1886–1920," in *The Missionary Enterprise in China and America*, ed. John K. Fairbank (Cambridge: Harvard University Press, 1974), 91–109; and Ernest R. Sandeen, *The Roots of Fundamentalism: British and American Millenarianism, 1800–1930* (Chicago: University of Chicago Press, 1970), 183.

58. Donald Tinder, "Foreign Missions, 1865–1930," in *Eerdmans' Handbook*, ed. Noll, 299–302.

59. Marsden, "Era of Crisis," in *Eerdmans' Handbook*, ed. Noll, 296; Winthrop S. Hudson, *Religion in America: An Historical Account of the Development of American Religious Life*, 3d ed. (New York: Charles Scribner's Sons, 1981), 236–38.

60. Marsden, "Era of Crisis," in *Eerdmans' Handbook*, ed. Noll, 298, 303–4; Handy, *Christian America*, 73–80, 99; Clifton E. Olmstead, *History of Religion in the United States* (Englewood Cliffs: Prentice-Hall, 1960), 462–64.

61. Ahlstrom, *Religious History*, 783.

62. Hutchison, *Modernist Impulse*, 95–99, 113–22.

63. Ibid., 2.

64. Sydney E. Ahlstrom, ed., *Theology in America: The Major Protestant Voices from Puritanism to Neo-Orthodoxy* (Indianapolis: Bobbs-Merrill, 1967), 64–77; William E. Hordern, *A Layman's Guide to Protestant Theology*, rev. ed. (New York: Macmillan, 1968), 73–110; Marsden, "Era of Crisis," in *Eerdmans' Handbook*, ed. Noll, 321–24; H. Shelton Smith, Robert T. Handy, and Lefferts A. Loetscher, *American Christianity: An Historical Interpretation with Representative Documents*, 2 vols. (New York: Charles Scribner's Sons, 1960–1963), 2: 255–308.

65. Hutchison, *Modernist Impulse*, 164–74.

66. See Robert T. Handy, ed., *The Social Gospel in America, 1870–1920: Gladden, Ely, Rauschenbusch* (New York: Oxford University Press, 1954), 9; C. Howard Hopkins, *The Rise of the Social Gospel in American Protestantism, 1865–1915* (New Haven: Yale University Press, 1940), 35; Hutchison, *Modernist Impulse*, 169; Henry May, *Protestant Churches and Industrial America* (New York: Harper & Brothers, 1949), 91–124.

67. Hopkins, *Rise of the Social Gospel*, 25–27, 30–32.

68. Handy, *Social Gospel in America*, 9–13.

69. Hutchison, *Modernist Impulse*, 165.

70. Smith, *American Christianity*, 2:394–97; Handy, *Social Gospel in America*, 12–13; Paul A. Carter, *The Decline and Revival of the Social Gospel: Social and Political Liberalism in American Protestant Churches, 1920–1940* (Ithaca: Cornell University Press, 1954), 15.

71. Carter, *Decline and Revival of the Social Gospel*, 16.
72. Marsden, "Era of Crisis," in *Eerdmans' Handbook*, ed. Noll, 331–36. This account of conservative developments largely follows Marsden, *Fundamentalism and American Culture*. On dispensationalism, see Marsden, 48–62; Sandeen, *Roots of Fundamentalism*, 59–80, 132–61, 222–24; and Timothy P. Weber, *Living in the Shadow of the Second Coming: American Premillennialism, 1875–1982*, enl. ed. (Grand Rapids: Zondervan, 1983).
73. Marsden, *Fundamentalism and American Culture*, 52–54.
74. Sandeen, *Roots of Fundamentalism*, 71, 182–83, 223–24.
75. Marsden, *Fundamentalism and American Culture*, 72.
76. Robert M. Anderson, *Vision of the Disinherited: The Making of American Pentecostalism* (New York: Oxford University Press, 1979), 28.
77. Marsden, *Fundamentalism and American Culture*, 74–75, 78, 83.
78. On *The Fundamentals* see Paul Carter, "The Fundamentalist Defense of the Faith," in *Change and Continuity in Twentieth-Century America: The 1920's*, ed. John Braeman et al. (Columbus: Ohio State University Press, 1965), 179–214; Hutchison, *Modernist Impulse*, 196–99; Marsden, *Fundamentalism and American Culture*, 118–23; Sandeen, *Roots of Fundamentalism*, 188–207; idem, "The Fundamentals: The Last Flowering of the Millenarian-Conservative Alliance," *Journal of Presbyterian History* 47 (March 1969): 55–73.
79. Amzi C. Dixon, Louis Meyer, and Reuben A. Torrey, eds., *The Fundamentals: A Testimony to the Truth*, 12 vols. (Chicago: Testimony, 1910–1915), 12:4.
80. Marsden, *Fundamentalism and American Culture*, 119.
81. Ibid., 122.
82. Archibald A. Hodge and Benjamin B. Warfield, "Inspiration," *Presbyterian Review* 2 (April 1886): 239, quoted in Marsden, *Fundamentalism and American Culture*, 113; Marsden, *Fundamentalism and American Culture*, 109–18. For more on the Princeton Theology see also W. Andrew Hoffecker, *Piety and the Princeton Theologians: Archibald Alexander, Charles Hodge, and Benjamin Warfield* (Grand Rapids: Baker Book House, 1981); Noll, *Princeton Theology*; Jack B. Rogers and Donald K. McKim, *The Authority and Interpretation of the Bible: An Historical Approach* (San Francisco: Harper & Row, 1979), 263–379; Ernest Sandeen, *Roots of Fundamentalism*, 103–31; Ernest Sandeen, "The Princeton Theology: One Source of Biblical Literalism in American Protestantism," *Church History* 31 (September 1962): 307–21; John C. Vander Stelt, *Philosophy and Scripture: A Study in Old Princeton and Westminster Theology* (Marlton, NJ: Mack, 1978); and David Wells, ed., *Reformed Theology in America: A History of Its Modern Development* (Grand Rapids: William B. Eerdmans, 1985). Dissertations on the subject include William D. Livingstone, "The Princeton Apologetic As Exemplified by the Work of Benjamin B. Warfield and J. Gresham Machen' (Ph.D. diss., Yale University, 1948); and John Nelson, "The Rise of the Princeton Theology" (Ph.D. diss., Yale University, 1935).
83. Max G. Rogers, "Charles Augustus Briggs: Heresy at Union," in *American Religious Heretics: Formal and Informal Trials*, ed. George H. Shriver

(Nashville: Abingdon, 1966), 89–91. See also Robert T. Handy, *A History of Union Theological Seminary in New York* (New York: Columbia University Press, 1986), 53–63.

84. Ibid., 91–95. See also Handy, *Union*, 63–67.

85. Handy, *Union*, 64–67; Rogers, "Charles Augustus Briggs," 95.

86. Rogers, "Charles Augustus Briggs," 95–96.

87. Handy, *Union*, 131–32.

88. C. A. Briggs, "The Inaugural Address," in *The Edward Robinson Chair of Biblical Theology* (New York, 1891), 35, quoted in Loetscher, *Broadening Church*, 50. For more on the Briggs case, see Carl E. Hatch, *The Charles A. Briggs Heresy Trial: Prologue to Twentieth-Century Liberal Protestantism* (New York: Exposition, 1969); and Channing R. Jeschke, "The Briggs Case: The Focus of a Study in Nineteenth-Century Presbyterian History" (Ph.D. diss., University of Chicago, 1966).

89. Loetscher, *Broadening Church*, 50–53.

90. *Minutes of GA*, 1892, 1:179–80. See also Loetscher, *Broadening Church*, 56.

91. Rogers, "Charles Augustus Briggs," 111.

92. Loetscher, *Broadening Church*, 54–60.

93. *Minutes of GA*, 1893, 1:165.

94. Ibid., 161, 163.

95. Loetscher, *Broadening Church*, 63–68.

96. Ibid., 39–47, 87, 89.

97. John T. Ames, "Cumberland Liberals and the Union of 1906," *Journal of Presbyterian History* 52 (Spring 1974): 5. Benjamin Warfield, for one, insisted that the doctrinal revisions did not alter the Calvinism of the Confession at all (ibid., 12).

98. Ibid., 5, 9. Other issues, such as the educational requirements for ordination, also contributed to the initial break. For more on the development of the Cumberland Presbyterian Church see chap. 3.

99. Ibid., 5.

100. Loetscher, *Broadening Church*, 96.

101. Ames, "Cumberland Liberals," 8–9.

102. *Minutes of GA*, 1905, 1:67; Loetscher, *Broadening Church*, 96.

103. Ames, "Cumberland Liberals," 18.

104. Ibid., 12–15.

105. Loetscher, *Broadening Church*, 97–99.

106. May, *End of American Innocence*, xi.

107. Quoted in Leuchtenburg, *Perils of Prosperity*, 30.

108. Ibid., 39–40.

109. Quoted in ibid., 46.

110. Leuchtenburg, *Perils of Prosperity*, 57–64.

111. William A. Brown, *The Church in America* (New York: Macmillan, 1922), 119, quoted in Ahlstrom, *Religious History*, 897.

112. Ahlstrom, *Religious History*, 897–98; Hudson, *Religion in America*, 360–61.

113. Leuchtenburg, *Perils of Prosperity*, 66–83. See also Frederick Lewis Allen, *Only Yesterday: An Informal History of the Nineteen-Twenties* (New York: Harper & Brothers, 1931).
114. Ibid., 158–77.
115. Macartney, "Shall Unbelief Win?" pt. 2, p. 10.

Chapter 2

1. J. Gresham Machen, "Liberalism or Christianity," *Princeton Theological Review* 20 (January 1922): 93–117.
2. Stonehouse, *Machen*, 339–41.
3. J. Gresham Machen, *Christianity and Liberalism* (New York: Macmillan, 1923; reprint, Grand Rapids: William B. Eerdmans, 1946), 2, 10, 14–15.
4. Ibid., 2, 7, 15.
5. Ibid., 5–6, 15–16, 7.
6. Ibid., 18.
7. Harry E. Fosdick, *As I See Religion* (New York: Harper & Brothers, 1932), 5.
8. Machen, *Christianity and Liberalism*, 19, 29, 47.
9. Ibid., 62, 65–66.
10. Ibid., 78, 72, 75–76, 79.
11. Ibid., 74, 75.
12. Ibid., 107–12, 117–19, 95–96.
13. Ibid., 172–73.
14. Ibid., 160, 166–67, 173–74.
15. Stonehouse, *Machen*, 17–25.
16. Mary Gresham Machen, Review of *J. Gresham Machen, A Biographical Memoir* by Ned B. Stonehouse, J. Gresham Machen Papers, Montgomery Library, Westminster Theological Seminary, Philadelphia (hereafter "Machen Papers").
17. Ernest T. Thompson, *Presbyterians in the South*, 3 vols. (Richmond: John Knox, 1963–1973), 2:182–84; Arthur W. Machen, Jr., ed., *Letters of Arthur W. Machen with Biographical Sketch* (Baltimore: Author, 1917), 33.
18. Mary Gresham Machen, Review of *J. Gresham Machen*.
19. Quoted in Stonehouse, *Machen*, 27.
20. Stonehouse, *Machen*, 27–28.
21. Ibid., 28–29. See also Machen, *Letters of Arthur W. Machen*, 334.
22. Ibid., 29, 30.
23. J. Gresham Machen, English composition dated 21 March 1899, quoted in Stonehouse, *Machen*, 44. The description reveals as much about J. Gresham Machen's feelings toward the Lost Cause of the South as it does about his mother's roots. Machen's allegiance to the cult of the Lost Cause will be addressed below.
24. Stonehouse, *Machen*, 33; John T. Boufeuillet, "Three Notable Georgia

Women—Mary Day, Minnie Gresham, Clare de Graffenreid," *Atlanta Journal*, quoted in Stonehouse, *Machen*, 34.

25. See Stonehouse, *Machen*, 38, 144; J. Gresham Machen, "Christianity in Conflict," in *Contemporary American Theology: Theological Autobiographies*, 2 vols., ed. Vergilius Ferm (New York: Round Table, 1932), 1:248–50; Mary Gresham Machen, Review of *J. Gresham Machen*.

26. Machen, "Christianity in Conflict," 247–49; Machen, *Letters of Arthur W. Machen*, 340.

27. Machen, "Christianity in Conflict," 249. See also Stonehouse, *Machen*, 40–42.

28. Stonehouse, *Machen*, 58.

29. George M. Marsden, *The Evangelical Mind and the New School Presbyterian Experience: A Case Study of Thought and Theology in Nineteenth-Century America* (New Haven: Yale University Press, 1970), 67.

30. Morton Smith, "The Southern Tradition," in *Reformed Theology*, ed. Wells, 196.

31. Quoted in Theodore D. Bozeman, "Science, Nature, and Society: A New Approach to James Henley Thornwell," *Journal of Presbyterian History* 50 (Winter 1972): 307.

32. Joseph M. Wilson, ed. *The Presbyterian Almanac*, 1863, 211–12, quoted in James O. Farmer, *The Metaphysical Confederacy: James Henley Thornwell and the Synthesis of Southern Values* (Macon: Mercer University Press, 1986), 63.

33. Farmer, *Metaphysical Confederacy*, 52–59.

34. Paul L. Garber, "James Henley Thornwell: Presbyterian Defender of the Old South," *Union Seminary Review* 54 (February 1943): 99. The American church historian, H. Shelton Smith, claimed that Thornwell's theology "dominated most of the history of Southern Presbyterianism" ("The Church and the Social Order in the Old South As Interpreted by James H. Thornwell," *Church History* 7 [June 1938]: 116).

35. "Thornwell's Inaugural Address," *Southern Presbyterian*, 1857, quoted in E. Brooks Holifield, *The Gentlemen Theologians: American Theology in Southern Culture, 1795–1860* (Durham: Duke University Press, 1978), 111.

36. "Thornwell's Inaugural Address," *Southern Presbyterian*, 1857, quoted in Holifield, *Gentlemen Theologians*, 111.

37. On Common Sense philosophy I have followed Sydney E. Ahlstrom, "The Scottish Philosophy and American Theology," *Church History* 24 (September 1955): 257–72; Theodore D. Bozeman, *Protestants in an Age of Science: The Baconian Ideal and Antebellum American Religious Thought* (Chapel Hill: University of North Carolina Press, 1977); Elizabeth Flower and Murray G. Murphey, *A History of Philosophy in America* (New York: G. P. Putnam's Sons, 1977); S. A. Grave, *The Scottish Philosophy of Common Sense* (Oxford: Clarendon, 1960); Darryl G. Hart, "The Princeton Mind in the Modern World and the Common Sense of J. Gresham Machen," *Westminster Theological Journal* 46 (1984): 1–25; Holifield, *Gentlemen Theologians*; Herbert Hovenkamp, *Science and Religion in America: 1800–1860* (Philadelphia: University of Penn-

sylvania Press, 1978); Marsden, *Fundamentalism and American Culture*; Henry May, *The Enlightenment in America* (New York: Oxford University Press, 1976); and Noll, *Princeton Theology*.

38. Holifield, *Gentlemen Theologians*, 115.

39. Marsden, *Fundamentalism and American Culture*, 15. See also Hart, "Princeton Mind," 5.

40. Marsden, *Fundamentalism and American Culture*, 14–16.

41. Noll, *Princeton Theology*, 31, 22.

42. Marsden, *Fundamentalism and American Culture*, 14; Holifield, *Gentlemen Theologians*, 119.

43. Farmer, *Metaphysical Confederacy*, 46.

44. Bozeman, "Science, Nature, and Society," 309; quote from p. 313.

45. John B. Adger, ed., *The Collected Writings of James Henley Thornwell*, 4 vols. (Richmond, 1871), 3:51, quoted in Paul L. Garber, "A Centennial Appraisal of James Henley Thornwell," in *A Miscellany of American Christianity*, ed. Stuart C. Henry (Durham: Duke University Press, 1963), 114.

46. Garber, "Centennial Appraisal," 125. See also Bozeman, "Science, Nature, and Society," 321.

47. Thornwell, *Works*, 4:386–87, quoted in Smith, "Church and the Social Order," 119.

48. Thornwell, *Works*, 4:383, quoted in Smith, "Church and the Social Order," 117. Jack P. Maddex has challenged the claim that Thornwell made the doctrine of the spirituality of the church one of his principal emphases, arguing instead that this doctrine found its strongest support in the border states during the war and was then ascribed to Thornwell. While Maddex may overstate his case, he does show the enduring influence of Thornwell's name and demonstrates that the doctrine of the spirituality of the church and J. Gresham Machen matured in the same neighborhood ("From Theocracy to Spirituality: The Southern Presbyterian Reversal on Church and State," *Journal of Presbyterian History* 54 (Winter 1976): 438–57; and Farmer, *Metaphysical Confederacy*, 256–60).

49. Smith, "Church and the Social Order," 117. The Machens' pastor, Dr. J. J. Bullock, especially reflected this aspect of Thornwell's heritage. In 1863 he protested his synod's support of the Union, claiming "While we express no opinion on the policy of the civil government, we emphatically deny the right of the church—the Lamb's wife—to usurp the throne of Caesar, to gird the bloody sword and counsel subjection to any earthly or heavenly power." Disagreement over the nature and mission of the church finally led Bullock to spearhead a schism in 1866 whereby the Franklin Street Church and two other congregations withdrew from the Northern denomination to unite with the Presbyterian Church in the United States. Bullock later became moderator of the Southern Church (Thompson, *Presbyterians in the South*, 2:182–84). See also Maddex, "From Theocracy to Spirituality," 451.

50. Thornwell, *Collected Writings*, 4:531, quoted in Thompson, *Presbyterians in the South*, 1:555. See also Farmer, *Metaphysical Confederacy*, 266–70.

51. Farmer, *Metaphysical Confederacy*, 278.

52. Thompson, *Presbyterians in the South*, 2:91–92, 365, 371.

53. Ibid., 2:446; see also pp. 228, 257.

54. See Stonehouse, *Machen*, 135.

55. Thomas D. Clark and Albert D. Kirwan, *The South since Appomattox: A Century of Regional Change* (New York: Oxford University Press, 1967), 20–22.

56. Charles R. Wilson, *Baptized in Blood: The Religion of the Lost Cause, 1865–1920* (Athens: University of Georgia Press, 1980), 3. See also Rollin G. Osterweis, *Romanticism and Nationalism in the Old South* (New Haven: Yale University Press, 1949); idem, *The Myth of the Lost Cause, 1865–1900* (Hamden: Archon Books, 1973); William R. Taylor, *Cavalier and Yankee: The Old South and American National Character* (New York: George Braziller, 1961).

57. Wilson, *Baptized in Blood*, 3; Taylor, *Cavalier and Yankee*, 15.

58. Osterweis, *Myth of the Lost Cause*, ix–x.

59. *Augusta Weekly Constitutionalist*, 21 March 1866, quoted in E. Merton Coulter, *The South during Reconstruction, 1865–1877* (Baton Rouge: Louisiana State University Press, 1947), 178.

60. Ibid., 179.

61. Osterweis, *Myth of the Lost Cause*, 10, 26, 51–52.

62. Ibid., 92–93.

63. Mary B. Pappenheim et al., *The History of the United Daughters of the Confederacy* (Richmond: Garrett & Massie, 1938), 49–50, quoted in Osterweis, *Myth of the Lost Cause*, 94.

64. Ibid., 94–99.

65. See Mary Gresham Machen, "To the Officers and Members of the United Daughters of the Confederacy, Maryland Division, Baltimore Chapter," United Daughters of the Confederacy Reference Department, Richmond. Mary Machen was admitted on 25 January 1898.

66. Daniel J. Singal, *The War Within: From Victorian to Modernist Thought in the South, 1919–1945* (Chapel Hill: University of North Carolina Press, 1982), 8–9. See Paul M. Gaston, *The New South Creed: A Study in Southern Myth-making* (New York: Alfred A. Knopf, 1970).

67. David D. Hall, "The Victorian Connection," in *Victorian America*, ed. Daniel W. Howe (Philadelphia: University of Pennsylvania Press, 1976), 83. Singal quotes Hall and makes this connection in *War Within*, 23–24.

68. See, e.g., Albert T. Bledsoe, "Chivalrous Southrons," *Southern Review* 6 (July 1869): 109.

69. Coulter, *The South during Reconstruction*, x. See also Gaston, *New South Creed*, 160–67.

70. See, e.g., Basil Gildersleeve, "The Creed of the Old South," *Atlantic Monthly*, 1892, quoted in Stonehouse, *Machen*, 50. See also Bledsoe, "Chivalrous Southrons," 108.

71. C. Vann Woodward, *Origins of the New South, 1877–1913* (Baton Rouge: Louisiana State University Press, 1951), 162.

Notes 249

72. Hamilton Owens, *Baltimore on the Chesapeake* (Garden City: Doubleday, Doran, 1941), 302.

73. Woodward, *Origins of the New South*, 162, 440.

74. Charles Hirschfeld, *Baltimore, 1870–1900: Studies in Social History*, Johns Hopkins University Studies in Historical and Political Science, series 59 no. 2 (Baltimore: Johns Hopkins University Press, 1941), 32–33.

75. *Manufacturers' Record. A Weekly Southern Industrial Railroad and Financial Newspaper* 7, p. 743, and 32, p. 75, quoted in Hirschfeld, *Baltimore*, 33.

76. Hirschfeld, *Baltimore*, 32–83.

77. See Stonehouse, *Machen*, 135, 444–45, 465–68.

78. For example, in 1925 J. Gresham Machen praised as a "masterpiece" an inscription his brother Arthur wrote for a United Daughters of the Confederacy monument lauding the Southern defense of the "Fundamental American Principle that Local Autonomy is an Essential Safeguard of Liberty" (Mary Gresham Machen to J. Gresham Machen, 23 January and J. Gresham Machen to Mary Gresham Machen, 27 January 1925, Machen Papers). A year earlier Machen had written to Rev. G. H. Hospers that "the truth is that far from thinking that the Southern states in 1861 were guilty of treason or rebellion, I am convinced that they were acting in the plainest possible exercise of constitutional rights, and that the real revolution was entered into by those who endeavored to prevent such plainly guaranteed rights" (J. Gresham Machen to G. H. Hospers, 27 December 1924, Machen Papers). See also J. Gresham Machen to Mary Gresham Machen, 11 December 1924; J. Gresham Machen to J. O. Caldwell, 14 March 1925; and J. Gresham Machen to Clarence Macartney, 2 October 1925—Machen Papers.

79. Stonehouse, *Machen*, 44, 46.

80. Ibid., 48–49, 53–54, 58; W. Reginald Wheeler, *A Man Sent From God: A Biography of Robert E. Speer* (Westwood, NJ: Fleming H. Revell, 1956), 54.

81. Russell, *Voices*, 136; Stonehouse, *Machen*, 55.

82. Stonehouse, *Machen*, 49, 59–60. See also Machen, "Christianity in Conflict," 250.

83. Noll, *Princeton Theology*, 13–18.

84. Morton Smith notes that after the war "relatively few scholars arose from the South" ("Southern Tradition," 201).

85. Noll, *Princeton Theology*, 13, 15; Stonehouse, *Machen*, 60. See also Smith, "Southern Tradition," 194.

86. Stonehouse, *Machen*, 60, 71.

87. See Smith, "Southern Tradition," 194.

88. Charles Hodge, *Systematic Theology* (New York, 1874), 1:18, quoted in Marsden, *Fundamentalism and American Culture*, 112.

89. Ibid., 112–13.

90. Smith, *Seeds of Secularization*, 47.

91. Ibid., 63, 69–71.

92. Thompson, *Presbyterians in the South*, 1:515–16.

93. Stonehouse, *Machen*, 85–86.

94. J. Gresham Machen to Mary Gresham Machen, 24 October 1905, quoted in Stonehouse, *Machen*, 106. See also pp. 95, 105–8, 123.

95. J. Gresham Machen to Arthur W. Machen, 28 October 1905, quoted in Stonehouse, *Machen*, 106.

96. J. Gresham Machen to Arthur W. Machen, Jr., 2 November 1905, quoted in Stonehouse, *Machen*, 107. In 1932 Machen was to write, "If Herrmann was a Christian, he was a Christian not because of but despite those things which were most distinctive of his teachings" ("Christianity in Conflict," 257).

97. Claude Welch, *Protestant Thought in the Nineteenth Century*, 2 vols. (New Haven: Yale University Press, 1972–1985), 2:44. This section follows Welch's account of Herrmann.

98. Wilhelm Herrmann, *The Communion of the Christian With God*, ed. Robert T. Voelkel, trans. J. Sandys Stanyon (New York: G. P. Putnam's Sons, 1906; reprint, Philadelphia: Fortress, 1971), 47–48, quoted in Welch, *Protestant Thought*, 2:46. See also Herrmann, *Communion*, xxii.

99. Welch, *Protestant Thought*, 2:51–52.

100. Welch, *Protestant Thought*, 2:48.

101. Welch, *Protestant Thought*, 2:49–54. Quotes are from Herrmann, *Communion*, 9, 95.

102. Stonehouse, *Machen*, 108–9. Quote is from J. Gresham Machen to Arthur W. Machen, Jr., 31 January 1906, in Stonehouse, *Machen*, 115.

103. Stonehouse, *Machen*, 127–28. About religious belief Machen claimed, "Nor am I by any means certain where the truth lies" (quoted in Stonehouse, *Machen*, 128).

104. J. Gresham Machen to Mary Gresham Machen, 14 September 1906, quoted in Stonehouse, *Machen*, 140.

105. See J. Gresham Machen, "Christianity and Liberty," in *What Is Christianity?* ed. Ned B. Stonehouse (Grand Rapids: William B. Eerdmans, 1951), 262. See also Stonehouse, *Machen*, 241–42.

106. Dallas Roark also emphasizes the critical aspect of Machen's experience in Germany, but he addresses theological issues alone ("J. Gresham Machen and His Desire To Maintain a Doctrinally True Presbyterian Church" [Ph.D. diss., State University of Iowa, 1963], 67–97).

107. Stonehouse, *Machen*, 145–69.

108. Stonehouse and Roark note the importance of these three. See Stonehouse, *Machen*, 64–70; Roark, "J. Gresham Machen," 26–54.

109. Machen, "Christianity in Conflict," 252. Machen revealed the personal and scholastic debt he owed to Armstrong by dedicating *The Origin of Paul's Religion* to him (Stonehouse, Machen, 327).

110. Stonehouse, *Machen*, 64–65, 209. See also Roark, "J. Gresham Machen," 26–41; and Nykamp, "Power Struggle," 538, n. 166.

111. Ibid., 310.

112. Rogers and McKim, *Authority and Interpretation*, 323.

113. Ibid., 325.
114. Benjamin B. Warfield, *Studies in Theology* (New York: Oxford University Press, 1932), 4, quoted in Rogers and McKim, *Authority and Interpretation*, 328.
115. David F. Wells, "Charles Hodge," in *Reformed Theology*, ed. Wells, 41.
116. Rogers and McKim, *Authority and Interpretation*, 328.
117. Benjamin B. Warfield, *Selected Shorter Works of Benjamin B. Warfield—II*, ed. John E. Meeter (Nutley, NJ: Presbyterian and Reformed Publishing, 1973), 99–100, quoted in Rogers and McKim, *Authority and Interpretation*, 329.
118. Archibald A. Hodge and Benjamin B. Warfield, "Inspiration," in *Princeton Theology*, ed. Noll, 229.
119. Noll, *Princeton Theology*, 15.
120. W. Andrew Hoffecker, "Benjamin B. Warfield," in *Reformed Theology*, ed. Wells, 71.
121. Smith, *Seeds of Secularization*, 51; Benjamin B. Warfield, *Princeton Theological Review* 1 (Jan. 1903): 140, quoted in Smith, *Seeds of Secularization*, 48.
122. Smith, *Seeds of Secularization*, 48–49; Hoffecker, "Benjamin B. Warfield," 67.
123. See J. Gresham Machen, *God Transcendent and Other Selected Sermons*, ed. Ned B. Stonehouse (Grand Rapids: William B. Eerdmans, 1949), 128.
124. Stonehouse, *Machen*, 219, 310. In 1913 Machen and Warfield had a two-hour argument over a "colored man" being assigned a dormitory room on the seminary campus. Machen vigorously opposed any such arrangement and wrote to his mother that Warfield "is himself, despite some very good qualities, a very heartless, selfish, domineering sort of man" (J. Gresham Machen to Mary Gresham Machen, 5 and 12 October 1913, Machen Papers). My thanks to George Marsden, Duke University, for bringing these letters to my attention.
125. J. Gresham Machen, "Christianity and Culture," *Princeton Theological Review* 11 (1913): 10–11, 7. Also republished in Machen, *What Is Christianity?* 156–69.
126. Machen, "Christianity and Culture, 7.
127. Marsden, *Fundamentalism and American Culture*, 136.
128. Machen, "Christianity and Culture," 12, 13.
129. Stonehouse, *Machen*, 190, 193–95, 197, 205.
130. Herrmann, *Communion*, 74–79.
131. J. Gresham Machen, "History and Faith," *Princeton Theological Review* 5 (July 1915): 337–38, republished in Machen, *What Is Christianity?* 170–84.
132. George M. Marsden, "J. Gresham Machen, History, and Truth," *Westminster Theological Journal* 42 (Fall 1979): 157–75.
133. Machen, "History and Faith," 349, 351. As George Marsden and Grant Wacker have shown, Machen's understanding of historical truth was, in the early twentieth century, something of an anachronism. While most of America had come to believe that "human thought was best understood in terms of the

changing patterns of cultural development," Machen clung tightly to the historical views of Victorian orthodoxy. Historical facts, he had concluded, were not conditioned by history and were not open to various interpretations (Marsden, "J. Gresham Machen, History, and Truth," 158; Grant A. Wacker, *Augustus H. Strong and the Dilemma of Historical Consciousness* (Macon: Mercer University Press, 1985), 21–42; and J. Gresham Machen, *What Is Faith?* (New York: Macmillan, 1925), 249.

134. Stonehouse, *Machen*, 240, 250, 254, 257–97.

135. Loetscher, *Broadening Church*, 100–101.

136. Stonehouse, *Machen*, 304–9, 311–14; quote from p. 306.

137. Loetscher, *Broadening Church*, 101.

138. It should be noted that Warfield shunned ecclesiastical activity. Nevertheless, his scholarly stature and position in the seminary had made him the clear leader of the most conservative faction in Princeton Seminary. With his death in February 1921, the mantle of leadership seemed to fall, somewhat ironically, on Assistant Professor Machen.

139. Machen, *Christianity and Liberalism*, 2.

140. Machen, *What Is Christianity?* 263. See also pp. 273–76.

141. Patterson, *America in the Twentieth Century*, 173–74.

142. As noted above, a central tenet of the cult of the Lost Cause was that the South had fought to protect her constitutionally guaranteed liberties. See, e.g., Basil Gildersleeve, "The Creed of the Old South," *Atlantic Monthly* (1892), quoted in Stonehouse, *Machen*, 50.

143. Russell, *Voices*, 146.

144. Russell, *Voices*, 148–149. In opposing the Child Labor Amendment Machen joined a lobbying group called the Sentinels of the Republic, which he identified as "followers of R. E. Lee rather than Abraham Lincoln" (J. Gresham Machen to Mary Gresham Machen, 11 December 1924, Machen Papers).

145. Russell, *Voices*, 147; J. Gresham Machen to Simon Walker, 18 January 1934; J. Gresham Machen to the editor of the *Public Ledger* (Philadelphia), 3 December 1931(?), Machen Papers.

146. Machen, *God Transcendent*, 112.

147. Machen, *What Is Christianity?* 248.

148. Machen, *What Is Christianity?* 267, 269. See also Machen, *What Is Faith?* 181; idem, *God Transcendent*, 87, 96, 115, 152–53; idem, *The Christian Faith in the Modern World* (New York: Macmillan, 1936), 97.

149. Ibid., 270.

150. Machen, *What Is Christianity?* 251–52. See also Machen, *God Transcendent*, 24.

151. Thompson, *Presbyterians in the South*, 1:538. See also Farmer, *Metaphysical Confederacy*, 267.

152. Thompson, *Presbyterians in the South*, 2:29–31, 182–84.

153. "Transcript of the Hearings by the General Assembly's Special Committee To Visit Princeton Theological Seminary: 5–6 Jan. 1927," 192, Machen Papers.

154. Stonehouse, *Machen*, 166.
155. Stonehouse, *Machen*, 324–28, 339–41.
156. J. Gresham Machen, "Apology and Polemic in the New Testament," *Presbyterian*, 13 September 1923, p. 11.

Chapter 3

1. *Christian Century*, 31 May 1923, p. 696.
2. William J. and Mary B. Bryan, *The Memoirs of William Jennings Bryan* (Philadelphia: Winston, 1925), 284–95; Robert W. Cherny, *A Righteous Cause: The Life of William Jennings Bryan* (Boston: Little, Brown, 1985), 166; Russell, *Voices*, 164–66; Ferenc M. Szasz, "Three Fundamentalist Leaders: The Roles of William Bell Riley, John Roach Straton, and William Jennings Bryan in the Fundamentalist–Modernist Controversy" (Ph.D. diss., University of Rochester, 1969), 182.
3. Paolo Coletta, *William Jennings Bryan*, 3 vols. (Lincoln: University of Nebraska Press, 1969), 3:201; Lawrence Levine, *Defender of the Faith: William Jennings Bryan, The Last Decade, 1915–1925* (New York: Oxford University Press, 1965), 268; and Bryan and Bryan, *Memoirs*, 479.
4. William J. Bryan, *The Bible and Its Enemies: An Address Delivered at the Moody Bible Institute of Chicago* (Chicago: Bible Institute Colportage Association, 1921), 43.
5. Coletta, *William Jennings Bryan*, 3:211; Szasz, "Three Fundamentalist Leaders," 150.
6. William J. Bryan, *In His Image* (New York: Fleming H. Revell, 1922), 89.
7. Ibid., 86–87, 110, 117–18, 112. Darwinism, Bryan held, also lay at the root of higher criticism ("The Menace of Darwinism," *Commoner* 21 [April 1921]: 7).
8. Ibid., 123–26.
9. Ibid., 126.
10. William J. Bryan, "The Fundamentals," *Forum* 70 (July 1923): 1674.
11. Bryan, *In His Image*, 107.
12. Bryan was not denying truth if proven in his "commonsense" manner but saying that given Darwinism's lack of "scientific" support, one had to consider its effects. See Bryan, "God and Evolution," 27.
13. Bryan, *In His Image*, 91, 94, 119.
14. See Bryan, *In His Image*, 67; and Richard Hofstadter, *Anti-Intellectualism in American Life* (New York: Random House, 1962), 127.
15. William J. Bryan, "The Modern Arena," *Commoner* 21 (June 1921): 3.
16. William J. Bryan, "The Menace of Darwinism," 7.
17. Bryan, *In His Image*, 131, 202.
18. Ibid., 133–35.

19. Quoted in Szasz, *Divided Mind*, 110; idem "Three Fundamentalist Leaders," 150.

20. Szasz, "Three Fundamentalist Leaders," 158.

21. Bryan, "God and Evolution," 24, 26, 28.

22. Coletta, *William Jennings Bryan*, 3:220; Levine, *Defender of the Faith*, 282.

23. Bryan, "God and Evolution," 28–29.

24. George Zucker to William J. Bryan, 15 December 1922, William Jennings Bryan Manuscripts, Library of Congress, Box 36; quoted in Szasz, "Three Fundamentalist Leaders," 181.

25. Levine, *Defender of the Faith*, 282; Coletta, *William Jennings Bryan*, 3:221–22; Szasz, "Three Fundamentalist Leaders," 181.

26. Levine, *Defender of the Faith*, 282; Coletta, *William Jennings Bryan*, 3:222. Bryan had been elected an elder by the Westminster Presbyterian Church, Lincoln, Nebraska, early in the century and had attended General Assemblies in 1913, 1916, 1917, 1919, and 1920. Additionally, he attended the 1910 World Missionary Conference in Edinburgh as a delegate of the Presbyterian Church and was a popular Sunday school teacher at First Presbyterian Church of Miami. See Bryan and Bryan, *Memoirs*, 50, 257, 438, 455; Szasz, "Three Fundamentalist Leaders," 102–3; idem, *Divided Mind*, 99; Levine, *Defender of the Faith*, 106.

27. *New York Times*, 10 May 1923, p. 29 and 17 May 1923, p. 21. See also Levine, *Defender of the Faith*, 282–83; and Coletta, *William Jennings Bryan*, 3: 222.

28. L. Gordon Tait, "Evolution: Wishart, Wooster, and William Jennings Bryan," *Journal of Presbyterian History* 62 (Winter 1984): 308.

29. *New York Times*, 17 May 1923, p. 21.

30. Russell, *Voices*, 166–69.

31. Russell, *Voices*, 162; Paul W. Glad, *The Trumpet Soundeth: William Jennings Bryan and His Democracy, 1896–1912* (Lincoln: University of Nebraska Press, 1960), 21. The following discussion of the formative influences on Bryan's life is largely indebted to Glad. See also Henry Steele Commager, *The American Mind: An Interpretation of American Thought and Character since the 1880's* (New Haven: Yale University Press, 1950), 182. Other works that have proven especially helpful for this study are Cherny, *Righteous Cause*; Kendrick A. Clements, *William Jennings Bryan: Missionary Isolationist* (Knoxville: University of Tennessee Press, 1982); Coletta, *William Jennings Bryan*; Paul Glad, ed., *William Jennings Bryan: A Profile* (New York: Hill & Wang, 1968); Louis W. Koenig, *Bryan: A Political Biography of William Jennings Bryan* (New York: G. P. Putnam's Sons, 1971); and Willard H. Smith, *The Social and Religious Thought of William Jennings Bryan* (Lawrence, KS: Coronado, 1975).

32. Cherny, *Righteous Cause*, 1, 4–5.

33. Koenig, *Bryan*, 18; Coletta, *William Jennings Bryan*, 1:1.

34. Coletta, *William Jennings Bryan*, 1:1–3.

35. Coletta, *William Jennings Bryan*, 1:1–2; Paolo Coletta, "The Youth of

William Jennings Bryan—Beginnings of a Christian Statesman," *Nebraska History* 31 (March 1950): 1–2; Cherny, *Righteous Cause*, 1.

36. Coletta, *William Jennings Bryan*, 1:2–3.

37. Ibid., 1:3; Coletta, "Youth of William Jennings Bryan," 1–2, 10.

38. Coletta, "Youth of William Jennings Bryan," 3.

39. Bryan and Bryan, *Memoirs*, 32, 34.

40. Coletta, "Youth of William Jennings Bryan," 5.

41. Bryan and Bryan, *Memoirs*, 35; Koenig, *Bryan*, 20.

42. Coletta, *William Jennings Bryan*, 1:4–5. See also Cherny, *Righteous Cause*, 5; Bryan and Bryan, *Memoirs*, 32–35.

43. Coletta, "Youth of William Jennings Bryan," 5.

44. Coletta, *William Jennings Bryan*, 1:6; Clements, *Bryan*, 4.

45. Bryan and Bryan, *Memoirs*, 27.

46. Bryan and Bryan, *Memoirs*, 28, 48; Szasz, "Three Fundamentalist Leaders," 103–4.

47. Bryan and Bryan, *Memoirs*, 23–24; Szasz, "Three Fundamentalist Leaders," 102; Clements, *Bryan*, 3; Coletta, *William Jennings Bryan*, 1:5; Coletta, "Youth of William Jennings Bryan," 6; Glad, *Trumpet Soundeth*, 22.

48. Bryan and Bryan, *Memoirs*, 43; Clements, *Bryan*, 4; Coletta, "Youth of William Jennings Bryan," 4, 7.

49. Cherny, *Righteous Cause*, 4, 8. The churches included three Methodist, two Baptist, two Presbyterian, and a Church of Christ (p. 8).

50. Bryan and Bryan, *Memoirs*, 47–49, 44.

51. William J. Bryan, *Heart to Heart Appeals* (New York: Fleming H. Revell, 1917), 153.

52. The other Presbyterian Church in town was a former Old School congregation (Cherny, *Righteous Cause*, 8). The Old School–New School division of 1837 was repaired in 1869. See Marsden, *Evangelical Mind*; and chap. 6 below.

53. Ben M. Barrus, "Unresolved Differences: A New Church" and "Old Issues Revisited: An Interpretation," in *A People Called Cumberland Presbyterians*, ed. Ben M. Barrus, Milton L. Baughn, and Thomas H. Campbell (Memphis: Frontier, 1972), 76, 88, 95.

54. See Leonard J. Trinterud, *The Forming of an American Tradition: A Reexamination of Colonial Presbyterianism* (Philadelphia: Westminster, 1949).

55. Barrus, "Old Issues Revisited," 88; Loetscher, *Broadening Church*, 3–4.

56. Ahlstrom, *Religious History*, 444.

57. Barrus, "Old Issues Revisited," 88–90.

58. Ibid., 89–92; Olmstead, *History of Religion*, 304–6.

59. Barrus, "Old Issues Revisited," 94.

60. Quoted in Olmstead, *History of Religion*, 305.

61. Barrus, "Old Issues Revisited," 88, 95.

62. *Minutes of the General Assembly of the Cumberland Presbyterian Church*, 1887, p. 44, quoted in Milton L. Baughn, "Extending the Missionary Frontier, 1861–1900," in Barrus, Baughn and Campbell, *Cumberland Presbyterians*, 177.

63. Milton L. Baughn, "The Church and the 'World'," in Barrus, Baughn, and Campbell, *Cumberland Presbyterians*, 253–58.

64. *Minutes of the General Assembly of the Cumberland Presbyterian Church*, 1890, pp. 49–50, quoted in Baughn, "Extending the Missionary Frontier," 184.

65. Robert Donnell, *Thoughts on Various Subjects* (Louisville: Cumberland Presbyterian Church, 1856), 173, quoted in Hubert W. Morrow, "Progressive Theology," in Barrus, Baughn, and Campbell, *Cumberland Presbyterians*, 289.

66. Glad, *Trumpet Soundeth*, 27.

67. Marsden, *Fundamentalism and American Culture*, 134. See also Bryan and Bryan, *Memoirs*, 456.

68. Bryan, *Heart to Heart Appeals*, 128.

69. Bryan and Bryan, *Memoirs*, 40–41; Glad, *Trumpet Soundeth*, 183, n. 5.

70. This section largely follows Glad, *Trumpet Soundeth*. In addition see Lewis E. Atherton, *Main Street on the Middle Border* (Bloomington: Indiana University Press, 1954); Richard D. Mosier, *Making the American Mind: Social and Moral Ideas in the McGuffey Readers* (New York: Russell & Russell, 1965); John H. Westerhoff III, *McGuffey and His Readers: Piety, Morality, and Education in Nineteenth-Century America* (Nashville: Abingdon, 1978).

71. Westerhoff, *McGuffey*, 13–14, 21, 30. McGuffey was born in Western Pennsylvania on 23 September 1800 and grew up in Ohio (Westerhoff, *McGuffey*, 13, 30).

72. Ibid., 14, 34–35, 40.

73. Atherton, *Main Street*, 65.

74. Glad, *Trumpet Soundeth*, 10–12, 14; Atherton, *Main Street*, 65–72; and Westerhoff, *McGuffey*, 91–104.

75. Atherton, *Main Street*, 68–72; Glad, *Trumpet Soundeth*, 12.

76. Westerhoff, *McGuffey*, 76–82, 86–90; Glad, *Trumpet Soundeth*, 12.

77. *McGuffey's New Sixth Eclectic Reader: Exercises in Rhetorical Reading, with Introductory Rules and Examples* (Cincinnati, 1857), 421–23, quoted in Atherton, *Main Street*, 69.

78. *McGuffey's Fourth Eclectic Reader* (Cincinnati, 1879), 152–53, quoted in Glad, *Trumpet Soundeth*, 12.

79. Glad, *Trumpet Soundeth*, 13; Westerhoff, *McGuffey*, 76–83.

80. Westerhoff, *McGuffey*, 98.

81. Bryan and Bryan, *Memoirs*, 34. Bryan stated, "My father taught me to believe in Democracy as well as in Christianity" ("Applied Christianity," *Commoner* 19 (May 1919): 12).

82. William J. Bryan, "But Where Are the Nine?" *Commoner* 20 (September 1920): 7.

83. Bryan, *Heart to Heart Appeals*, 106–7.

84. Coletta, *William Jennings Bryan*, 1:7–8; Cherny, *Righteous Cause*, 18–19.

85. Richard Hofstadter, *The American Political Tradition and the Men Who Made It* (New York: Random House, 1948), 194.

86. Coletta, *William Jennings Bryan*, 1:293, 3:198. For a brief account of

Bryan's life see Allen Johnson et al., ed. *Dictionary of American Biography* (New York: Charles Scribner's Sons, 1927), s.v. "Bryan, William Jennings."
    87. Coletta, *William Jennings Bryan*, 1:293–94. See also Bryan and Bryan, *Memoirs*, 287; and Szasz, "Three Fundamentalist Leaders," 251.
    88. See Gay MacLaren, *Morally We Roll Along* (Boston: Little, Brown, 1938), 169. Bryan started lecturing at Chautauquas in 1894 (Harry P. Harrison and Karl Detzer, *Culture under Canvas: The Story of Tent Chautauqua* [New York: Hastings House, 1958], 158). On the Chautauqua see also Joseph E. Gould, *The Chautauqua Movement: An Episode in the Continuing American Revolution* (New York: State University of New York, 1961); Charles Horner, *Strike the Tents: The Story of the Chautauqua* (Philadelphia: Dorrance, 1954); and John H. Vincent, *The Chautauqua Movement (Boston: Chautauqua, 1886)*. For figures on Chautauqua attendance see Horner, *Strike the Tents*, 97–98. On Bryan's popularity see Horner, *Strike the Tents*, 105–31 and MacLaren, *Morally We Roll Along*, 204–11.
    89. Vincent, *Chautauqua Movement*, 16, 18.
    90. Harrison and Detzer, *Culture under Canvas*, 41.
    91. Ibid., 41–43.
    92. Ibid., 50.
    93. Glad, *Trumpet Soundeth*, 16.
    94. MacLaren, *Morally We Roll Along*, 133, 134, 136, 138, 145, 147–48.
    95. Bryan reflected this attitude perfectly. Lawrence Levine states, "To Bryan the function of all culture was didactic and inspirational. The value of a painting or a poem or a piece of music was in direct proportion to its resemblance to a sermon" (*Defender of the Faith*, 230). In this, both Bryan and the Chautauqua mirrored the Victorian stress on didacticism. Daniel Howe contended, "'Art for art's sake' was not a principle widely accepted among American Victorians; literature and the other arts were expected to benefit society by elevating or instructing their audience" (Daniel D. Howe, "Victorian Culture in America," in *Victorian America*, ed. Howe [Philadelphia: University of Pennsylvania Press, 1976], 23).
    96. Glad, *Trumpet Soundeth*, 17; MacLaren, *Morally We Roll Along*, 166–94.
    97. Sometimes the lectures addressed the political questions of the day, but the majority of speeches steered away from blatantly partisan politics. See Harrison and Detzer, *Culture under Canvas*, 116–55.
    98. Glad, *Trumpet Soundeth*, 18–19.
    99. Harrison and Detzer, *Culture under Canvas*, 20–22, 158–68, 183–84.
    100. Bryan and Bryan, *Memoirs*, 287.
    101. William J. Bryan, *Speeches of William Jennings Bryan*, 2 vols. (New York: Funk & Wagnalls, 1909), 2:261–62.
    102. Ibid., 2:264, 268–69, 284.
    103. William J. Bryan, *The Prince of Peace* (New York: Barse & Hopkins, n.d.), 43–46.
    104. Ibid., 40.

105. Bryan, *Speeches*, 2:247–48.
106. *Commoner*, 20 August 1909, p. 1, quoted in Willard H. Smith, "William Jennings Bryan and the Social Gospel," *Journal of American History* 53 (June 1966): 53. See also Coletta, *William Jennings Bryan*, 3:198.
107. Smith, "Bryan and the Social Gospel," 44, 53.
108. Quoted in Smith, "Bryan and the Social Gospel," 53.
109. Szasz, "Three Fundamentalist Leaders," 182.
110. Bryan, "Applied Christianity," 11.
111. Szasz, "Three Fundamentalist Leaders," 182; Levine, *Defender of the Faith*, 253.
112. Bryan and Bryan, *Memoirs*, 10.
113. Smith, "Bryan and the Social Gospel," 58.
114. *Commoner*, 21 April 1911, pp. 1ff., quoted in Smith, "Bryan and the Social Gospel," 58.
115. Levine, *Defender of the Faith*, 262.
116. Bryan, *Speeches*, 2:269.
117. See Levine, *Defender of the Faith*, 262; Ferenc M. Szasz, "William Jennings Bryan, Evolution, and the Fundamentalist–Modernist Controversy," *Nebraska History* 56 (Summer 1975): 264.
118. Levine, *Defender of the Faith*, 262–63.
119. *Commoner* 19 (Febuary 1919): 14. See also Szasz, *Divided Mind*, 110.
120. William J. Bryan, "Brother or Brute?" *Commoner* 20 (November 1920): 11.
121. Levine, *Defender of the Faith*, 263.
122. Ibid., 264, 268.
123. See, e.g., *Presbyterian*, 14 May 1925, p. 12; Henry S. Coffin, *Some Christian Convictions: A Practical Restatement of Present Day Thinking* (New Haven: Yale University Press, 1915), 4–5; idem, *What To Preach* (New York: Harper & Brothers, 1926), 59; idem, "The Portrait in the Revelation of John," in *The Portraits of Jesus Christ in the New Testament* (New York: Macmillan, 1926), 82.
124. "Jews in Crisis Erdman Claims," unidentified newspaper clipping, Charles R. Erdman Papers, Speer Library, Princeton Theological Seminary, Princeton (hereafter, "Erdman Papers"). Robert E. Speer, another important moderate, apparently subscribed to a similar notion. See Robert E. Speer, *Seeking the Mind of Christ* (New York: Fleming H. Revell, 1926), 26.
125. J. Gresham Machen to Ralph H. Goodwin, 30 June 1925, Machen Papers.
126. Stonehouse, *Machen*, 401.
127. J. Gresham Machen to George S. Duncan, 18 February 1926, Machen Papers.
128. See J. Gresham Machen to William Kerr, 9 January 1923; J. Gresham Machen to Ralph H. Goodwin, 30 June 1925; J. Gresham Machen to George S. Duncan, 18 Febuary 1926—Machen Papers. See also J. Gresham Machen, *The Christian View of Man* (New York: Macmillan, 1937), 132–42.

129. J. Gresham Machen to George S. Duncan, 18 Febuary 1926, Machen Papers.

130. J. Gresham Machen to George S. Duncan, 18 Febuary 1926, Machen Papers. See also J. Gresham Machen to Ralph H. Goodwin, 30 June 1925, Machen Papers.

131. Though Bryan publicly rejected theistic evolution, it appears that privately he allowed for views like Machen's. In a letter written shortly before the Scopes trial in 1925 Bryan maintained that one need not necessarily object to "evolution before man." Bryan explained his differing public and private attitudes, writing, "A concession as to the truth of evolution up to man furnishes our opponents with an argument which they are quick to use, namely, if evolution accounts for all the species up to man, does it not raise a presumption in behalf of evolution to include man?" In his battles in the church, as elsewhere, Bryan certainly conceded nothing to those who would advocate a mediating position. (Quoted in George M. Marsden, "A Case of the Excluded Middle: Creation Versus Evolution in America," in *Uncivil Religion: Interreligious Hostility in America*, ed. Robert N. Bellah and Frederick E. Greenspahn (New York: Crossroad, 1987), 145–46.)

132. See Stonehouse, *Machen*, 402–5.

133. "Evolution and Religion" unidentified newspaper clipping dated 15 January 1926, Clarence E. Macartney Papers, McCartney Library, Geneva College, Beaver Falls, PA (hereafter, "Macartney Papers"); Clarence Macartney, "A Christian's Difficulty with Evolution," *Presbyterian*, pt. 1, 3 June 1937, pp. 8–9; pt. 2, 10 June 1937, 5–6; and pt. 3, 17 June 1937, 6–7.

134. Wilhemina Guerard, "Biographical Notes," Macartney Papers; Macartney, "Difficulty with Evolution," pt. 1, 8.

135. Macartney, "Difficulty with Evolution," pt. 1, 8.

136. Ibid., pt. 1, 9; pt. 2, 5–6; pt. 3, 6.

137. Ibid., pt. 3, 7.

138. Tait, "Evolution," 307–11, 314.

139. Levine, *Defender of the Faith*, 282.

140. Tait, "Evolution," 315.

141. *New York Times*, 18 May 1923, p. 1.

142. Tait, "Evolution," 314.

143. *Presbyterian Advance*, 24 May 1923, 9.

144. Tait, "Evolution," 315.

145. *New York Times*, 19 May 1923, p. 5. See also Tait, "Evolution," 315; Nykamp, "Power Struggle," 139.

146. *New York Times*, 23 May 1923, p. 1. See also Coletta, *Bryan*, 3:223; *Minutes of GA*, 1923, 2:203.

147. Ibid., 1.

148. *Presbyterian Advance*, 31 May 1923, 8; Coletta, *William Jennings Bryan*, 3:223; *New York Times*, 23 May 1923, pp. 1, 4 and 28 May 1923, p. 2.

149. *New York Times*, 23 May 1923, p. 1.
150. *Presbyterian Advance*, 31 May 1923, 8–9.
151. *New York Times*, 23 May 1923, p. 4.
152. *Minutes of GA*, 1923, 2:212.
153. *New York Times*, 23 May 1923, p. 1. See also Tait, "Evolution," 315–16.
154. *Presbyterian Advance*, 31 May 1923, 9.
155. *Minutes of GA*, 1923, 2:253; *New York Times*, 24 May 1923, pp. 1, 6; *Presbyterian Advance*, 31 May 1923, 13.
156. Nykamp, "Power Struggle," 141, 147–49.
157. See Bryan, "God and Evolution" and Fosdick, "A Reply to Mr. Bryan in the Name of Religion," both in *Evolution and Religion*, ed. Kennedy, 23–29 and 30–34.
158. Macartney Scrapbook, Presbyterian Historical Society, Philadelphia, quoted in Nykamp, "Power Struggle," 542, n. 224. Nykamp also quotes an alternate rendering of this speech: "The disturbance of peace and unity is not important. Where in the life of Christ can you find any preference given to peace and unity in place of truth? I am here as a harmonizer. Let us show that we believe in the standards of our faith handed down in 1910. Let us again reiterate them, or let us repeal these essentials if we want to repeal them" (Nykamp, "Power Struggle," 145–46). The version quoted in the text is supported by a report in the *Presbyterian Advance* stating, "Mr. Bryan declared that the real issue before the church was presented in these two reports and proposed that the minority report be embodied in that of the majority" (*Presbyterian Advance*, 31 May 1923, 18).
159. Bryan, "Fundamentals," 1666, 1675, 1679.
160. The *New York Times* credited Bryan with leading the fundamentalist fight in this battle, reporting, "Mr. Bryan made a speech in favor of the minority resolution and was credited with a large share in swinging the vote" (*New York Times*, 24 May 1923, p. 6). While Bryan may well have helped swing the vote against the majority report, the *Times* may have overstated his leadership role in this particular battle.
161. "Excerpts from Dr. Macartney's Closing Argument at the Assembly," *Presbyterian*, 7 June 1923, 8–9, quoted in Nykamp, "Power Struggle," 146.
162. "Excerpts from Dr. Macartney's Closing Argument," 8–9, quoted in Nykamp, "Power Struggle,"149.
163. *New York Times*, 24 May 1923, p. 6.
164. Nykamp, "Power Struggle," 151.
165. William J. Bryan to Grace Bryan Hargreaves, 3 June 1923, Grace Bryan Hargreaves Manuscripts, William Jennings Bryan Papers, Library of Congress, quoted in Levine, *Defender of the Faith*, 285.
166. See Marsden, *Fundamentalism and American Culture*, 132–35.
167. *New York Times*, 25 May 1923, p. 10.
168. Ibid., 10.

Chapter 4

1. Robert H. Nichols, "Leader of Liberal Presbyterianism," in *This Ministry: The Contribution of Henry Sloane Coffin*, ed. Reinhold Niebuhr (New York: Charles Scribner's Sons, 1946), 45–46; Charles E. Quirk, "The Auburn *Affirmation*: A Critical Narrative of the Document Designed to Safeguard the Unity and Liberty of the Presbyterian Church in the United States of America in 1924" (Ph.D. diss., University of Iowa, 1967), 12, 31–39; Robert H. Nichols, *Presbyterianism in New York State: A History of the Synod and Its Predecessors* (Philadelphia: Westminster, 1963), 218.

2. Quirk, "Auburn *Affirmation*," 78–81.

3. Ibid., 87–89.

4. Ibid., 97–106, 389.

5. Auburn Affirmation, quoted in Quirk, "Auburn *Affirmation*," 389–97.

6. Auburn Affirmation, quoted in Quirk, "Auburn *Affirmation*," 397–99. See also Morgan P. Noyes, *Henry Sloane Coffin: The Man and His Ministry* (New York: Charles Scribner's Sons, 1964), 166–67; Nichols, "Leader of Liberal Presbyterianism," 49; and Quirk, "Auburn *Affirmation*," 102.

7. Auburn Affirmation, quoted in Quirk, "Auburn *Affirmation*," 399–400.

8. Quirk,"Auburn *Affirmation*," 107, 109, 144–49. See also *New York Times*, 10 January 1924, p. 4, for Machen's response.

9. See Nichols, "Leader of Liberal Presbyterianism," 43–45, 47, 49–53; Noyes, *Coffin*, 161–79; Henry S. Coffin, *Joy in Believing: Selections from the Spoken and Written Words and the Prayers of Henry Sloane Coffin*, ed. Walter R. Bowie (New York: Charles Scribner's Sons, 1956), vii–viii.

10. Noyes, *Coffin*, 2–3; Morgan P. Noyes, "Parish Minister," in *This Ministry*, ed. Niebuhr, 2.

11. Albert Fein, "Centennial New York, 1876," in *New York: The Centennial Years, 1676–1976*, ed. Milton M. Klein (Port Washington, N.Y.: Kennikat, 1976), 75; Schlesinger, *Rise of the City*, 82–83.

12. Fein, "Centennial New York," 75, 76; Patterson, *America in the Twentieth Century*, 7.

13. Fein, "Centennial New York," 84–85, 101; Schlesinger, *Rise of the City*, 89.

14. Fein, "Centennial New York," 98–100.

15. David M. Ellis et al., *A Short History of New York State* (Ithaca: Cornell University Press, 1957), 605–17.

16. *New York Times*, 26 November 1954, p. 29.

17. Noyes, *Coffin*, 3, 5–7, 9.

18. *Minutes of GA*, 1893, 1:165. See Chapter 1 above for an account of the Briggs trial.

19. Rogers, "Charles Augustus Briggs," 111.

20. Noyes, *Coffin*, 62.

21. Henry S. Coffin, "Why I Am a Presbyterian," in *Twelve Modern Apostles and Their Creeds*, Gilbert K. Chesterton and others (New York: Duffield, 1926;

262 *Notes*

reprint, Freeport, NY: Books for Libraries, 1968), 54; Union Theological Seminary, *One Hundredth Anniversary*, quoted in Handy, *Union*, 194.
22. Noyes, *Coffin*, 4–5, 8.
23. Coffin, "Why I Am a Presbyterian," 53–54.
24. Noyes, *Coffin*, 8–12.
25. Ibid., 2, 8–9, 17; Henry S. Coffin to Euphemina Coffin, n.d.in file "Henry Sloane Coffin: Letters to His Mother: July 28, 1893–June 6, 1894," Henry Sloane Coffin Papers, Burke Library, Union Theological Seminary in the City of New York (hereafter, "Coffin Papers"); quoted with permission.
26. Noyes, *Coffin*, 10–11.
27. George T. Peck, *A Noble Landmark of New York: The Fifth Avenue Presbyterian Church, 1808–1958* (New York: Van Rees, 1960), 41.
28. Ibid., 53, 56; Noyes, *Coffin*, 11.
29. Noyes, *Coffin*, 10–13.
30. Ibid., 14.
31. Brooks M. Kelley, *Yale: A History* (New Haven: Yale University Press, 1974), 274–93.
32. "Henry Sloane Coffin, Class of 1897," 28 November 1958, Coffin Papers.
33. Noyes, *Coffin*, 16, 22–23, 29.
34. Ibid., 24. See also "Dwight L. Moody and College Students," typed manuscript, 27 October 1937, Coffin Papers.
35. Noyes, *Coffin*, 26–28; quote from p. 27.
36. Henry S. Coffin to Euphemina Coffin, 7 November 1893(?), Coffin Papers; Noyes, *Coffin*, 27.
37. "Henry Sloane Coffin, Class of 1897," 28 November 1958, Coffin Papers; Noyes, *Coffin*, 26. Coffin also earned a master of arts degree from Yale in 1900 by writing a thesis comparing the philosophy of Tennyson and Carlyle (Noyes, *Coffin*, 52–53).
38. Edmund Coffin to Henry S. Coffin, n.d. in file "Henry Sloane Coffin, Family Correspondence: 1885–1941," Coffin Papers; Noyes, *Coffin*, 12, 32–33.
39. Noyes, *Coffin*, 32–33, 35.
40. Quoted in Noyes, *Coffin*, 42–43. For more on the attitude of New College faculty toward higher criticism, see Hugh Watt, A. Mitchell Hunter, and W. A. Curtis, *New College, Edinburgh: A Centenary History* (Edinburgh: Oliver & Boyd, 1946), 89–91.
41. Quoted in Noyes, *Coffin*, 43–44.
42. Ibid., 44.
43. See, e.g., *Time*, 15 November 1926, p. 24; Henry S. Coffin, "What Liberal Presbyterians Are Standing for," *Summer Monthly*, 5 June 1925, p. 6 (in Coffin Papers).
44. Noyes, *Coffin*, 54–56.
45. Henry S. Coffin to Euphemina Coffin, n.d. in file "Henry Sloane Coffin: Letters to His Mother, April 13, 1899–June 15, 1899," Coffin Papers.
46. Henry S. Coffin to Euphemina Coffin, 4 June 1899, Coffin Papers.
47. Loetscher, *Broadening Church*, 71.

48. *Minutes of GA*, 1898, 1:108.

49. Loetscher, *Broadening Church*, 72; *Minutes of GA*, 1899, 1:96–98. In response to the assembly's action the New York Presbytery condemned a number of McGiffert's views but did not prosecute him for heresy. A member of the presbytery, George Birch, however, did press charges and, when the presbytery refused to act, appealed to the General Assembly. McGiffert, realizing that he would most probably be convicted by the General Assembly, resigned from the Presbyterian ministry and became a minister in the Congregational Church. See Loetscher, *Broadening Church*, 73–74.

50. Henry S. Coffin to Euphemina Coffin, 5 June 1899, Coffin Papers.

51. Ibid.

52. Noyes, *Coffin*, 60–63.

53. Ibid., 67.

54. Henry S. Coffin, "Freedom in the Presbyterian Church," *Christian Century*, 19 May 1927, 621–22.

55. Coffin, "Why I Am a Presbyterian," 63.

56. Henry S. Coffin, *University Sermons* (New Haven: Yale University Press, 1914), 83.

57. Noyes, *Coffin*, 69–74; quote from p. 66.

58. *New York Journal and American*, 22 December 1901 (in Coffin Papers).

59. Noyes, *Coffin*, 79–80, 82.

60. Ibid., 83, 92, 95–103.

61. Ibid., 111–15, 117–18.

62. In all, Coffin collected eighteen honorary doctorates from schools at home and abroad. On receiving a doctor of divinity from Harvard in 1922, the proud Eli wrote to his wife, "Harvard is stingy in that it does not present a hood to its honorary alumni" (Henry S. Coffin to Dorothy Coffin, 23 June 1922, Coffin Papers; Noyes, *Coffin*, 157–58). See Henry S. Coffin, *The Creed of Jesus and Other Sermons* (New York: Charles Scribner's Sons, 1907); idem, *In a Day of Social Rebuilding: Lectures on the Ministry of the Church* (New Haven: Yale University Press, 1919); idem, *Social Aspects of the Cross* (New York: Hodder & Stoughton, 1911); idem, *Some Christian Convictions*; idem, *The Ten Commandments with a Christian Application to Present Conditions* (New York: Hodder & Stoughton, 1915).

63. Noyes, *Coffin*, 131–35.

64. As early as 1915 the *Presbyterian* had noticed Coffin as a leader of liberal Presbyterians. This prominence increased after the war (Nykamp, "Power Struggle," 162).

65. Henry S. Coffin, "The Practical Aims of a Liberal Evangelicalism," 18 May 1915, p. 1, Coffin Papers.

66. Ibid., 2–4. See also Coffin, *Social Rebuilding*, 20–21, 44.

67. Coffin, *Some Christian Convictions*, 21–22. In contrast see Machen, *Christian Faith*, 94–95.

68. See Marsden, "J. Gresham Machen, History, and Truth," 162.

69. Ibid., 161–64.
70. Noyes, *Coffin*, 64, 79; Arthur C. McGiffert, "The Historical Study of Christianity," in *Protestant Thought*, ed. Hutchison, 75. See also Wacker, *Strong*, 153–55.
71. McGiffert, "Historical Study," in *Protestant Thought*, ed. Hutchison, 77–78.
72. "Dr. Coffin Finds That Faith Endures," *New York Times Magazine*, 28 November 1926, 18. See also Coffin, *Some Christian Convictions*, 97.
73. Coffin, *Some Christian Convictions*, 23, 25–27.
74. Coffin, *Creed of Jesus*, 22.
75. Coffin, *University Sermons*, 234.
76. Marsden, "J. Gresham Machen, History, and Truth," 166–68.
77. Coffin, *Some Christian Convictions*, 46–47.
78. Coffin, *University Sermons*, 208.
79. Coffin, *Some Christian Convictions*, 49, 51.
80. Ibid., 52–55, 65–67.
81. Ibid., 67–72; quote is from pp. 71–72.
82. Ibid., 74–75.
83. Ibid., 84–92.
84. Coffin, *Creed of Jesus*, 255.
85. Coffin, *Some Christian Convictions*, 93–94.
86. Ibid., 113. See also Coffin, *University Sermons*, 165.
87. Coffin, *Some Christian Convictions*, 118–19. See also Coffin, *Social Rebuilding*, 43–44.
88. Coffin, *Some Christian Convictions*, 98–102.
89. Coffin, *Creed of Jesus*, 266; idem, *University Sermons*, 168.
90. Coffin, *University Sermons*, 168.
91. Coffin, *Some Christian Convictions*, 141, 143–47, 151, 153–56.
92. Henry S. Coffin, *A More Christian Industrial Order* (New York: Macmillan, 1920), 81–82.
93. Coffin, *University Sermons*, 44.
94. Coffin, *In a Day of Social Rebuilding*, 36.
95. Coffin, *Some Christian Convictions*, 218.
96. Coffin, *Creed of Jesus*, 122.
97. Coffin, *Some Christian Convictions*, 221–22.
98. Ibid., 121–22.
99. Ibid., 122–24, 129–32.
100. Ibid., 184–85, 186.
101. Coffin, *University Sermons*, 75.
102. Ibid., 82, 84–85.
103. Coffin, *Some Christian Convictions*, 189–90, 193–95.
104. Ibid., 195.
105. See Coffin, "Practical Aims of a Liberal Evangelicalism," 5–6; Noyes, *Coffin*, 238–55.
106. Noyes, *Coffin*, 240–41, 248–53, 227.

107. Henry S. Coffin, "Are Denominations Justified?" *Presbyterian Life*, January 1950, p. 19, quoted in Noyes, *Coffin*, 238–39.
    108. Henry S. Coffin, "The Religious Opportunity of the Present Social Awakening," in *Some Social Aspects of the Gospel: An Address and A Sermon*, by Henry S. Coffin and Francis Brown (New York: Union Theological Seminary, 1912), 13.
    109. Coffin, *Creed of Jesus*, 11.
    110. Coffin, *Some Christian Convictions*, 161. Though the social gospel emphasis seems strongest in the late 1910s and 1920s, he never abandoned this concern. See, e.g., Henry S. Coffin, *God Confronts Man in History* (New York: Charles Scribner's Sons, 1947), 81.
    111. Coffin, *What To Preach*, 162.
    112. Coffin, *Social Rebuilding*, 54–55, 125.
    113. Coffin, *Some Christian Convictions*, 203.
    114. Coffin, *Social Rebuilding*, 72, 55, 26, 30, 39, 36.
    115. Coffin, *What To Preach*, 103.
    116. See *New York Times*, 18 October 1927, p. 17.
    117. Coffin, *Ten Commandments*, 147.
    118. Coffin, *What To Preach*, 105.
    119. Coffin, *Social Rebuilding*, 99.
    120. Coffin, *What To Preach*, 106.
    121. Noyes, *Coffin*, 224–25. For more on the Labor Temple, see Charles Stelzle, "Labor Temple," in *The Presbyterian Enterprise: Sources of American Presbyterian History*, ed. Maurice W. Armstrong, Lefferts A. Loetscher, and Charles A. Anderson (Philadelphia: Westminster, 1956), 270–74.
    122. Coffin, *Industrial Order*, 2–4. See also Coffin, *Ten Commandments*, 165.
    123. Coffin, *Industrial Order*, 22–23; idem, *Social Rebuilding*, 101.
    124. Coffin, *Industrial Order*, 23.
    125. Ibid., 33; Coffin, *Ten Commandments*, 164.
    126. Coffin, *Industrial Order*, 31–32. See also Coffin, *Ten Commandments*, 165.
    127. Coffin, *Industrial Order*, 34–35.
    128. Ibid., 66–67.
    129. Coffin, *Social Rebuilding*, 39–40.
    130. Coffin, *Industrial Order*, 73.
    131. Smith, *Social and Religious Thought*, 24, 8.
    132. Levine, *Defender of the Faith*, 251; *Commoner*, October 1919, p. 2, quoted in Smith, "Bryan and the Social Gospel," *Journal of American History*, 53.
    133. *Commoner*, September 1920, p. 8, quoted in Smith, *Social and Religious Thought*, 31.
    134. Coffin, *Social Rebuilding*, 28, 32, 35, 14, 36. For Coffin's views on American participation in the war see Noyes, *Coffin*, 129–31.

135. Smith, *Social and Religious Thought*, 67.

136. *Commoner*, July 1919, p. 5, quoted in Smith, *Social and Religious Thought*, 146.

137. Smith, *Social and Religious Thought*, 152, 158.

138. April bulletin of the Federal Council of Churches quoted in the *Chattanooga News*, 9 May 1925, quoted in Smith, *Social and Religious Thought*, 158.

139. Coffin, *Social Rebuilding*, 45.

140. Ibid., 47–48.

141. Ibid., 41.

142. Noyes, *Coffin*, 87–89.

143. Coffin, "The Religious Opportunity of the Present Social Awakening," in Coffin and Brown, *Social Aspects*, 17.

144. Coffin, *Social Rebuilding*, 30; See also pp. 70, 156.

145. Ibid., 111–12, 162–63, 159.

146. See Henry S. Coffin, "What Liberal Presbyterians Are Standing for," *Summer Monthly*, 5 June 1925, p. 6 (in Coffin Papers).

147. Coffin, *Social Rebuilding*, 35, 32, 45.

148. Coffin, *What To Preach*, 145; idem, *Social Rebuilding*, 26.

149. Quirk, "Auburn *Affirmation*," 212–13; Miller, *Harry Emerson Fosdick*, 130.

150. Rian, *Presbyterian Conflict*, 36.

151. *Presbyterian*, 10 January 1924, 12.

152. Quirk, "Auburn *Affirmation*," 224–28, 181, 185.

153. Ibid., 239, 228–34, 242–44.

154. *Presbyterian*, 8 November 1923, pp. 8–9.

155. Clarence E. Macartney, "The Irrepressible Conflict," *Presbyterian*, 14 Febuary 1924, p. 6.

156. Ibid., 8–9.

157. Clarence E. Macartney, "Dr. Clarke and the Presbyterian Standards," *Presbyterian*, 13 March 1924, 7.

158. Ibid., 9. See also Machen, "An Earnest Plea for Christian Freedom—and Honesty!" *Lookout*, 2 March 1924, p. 6 (in Machen Papers).

159. J. Gresham Machen, "The Parting of the Ways," *Presbyterian*, 17 April 1924, pp. 7–9 and 24 April 1924, pp. 6–7 (reprint in Machen Papers). See also J. Gresham Machen, "Sermon on the Present Issue in the Church," *Presbyterian*, 24 January 1924, pp. 16–18; idem, "Dr. Merrill in the World's Work," *Presbyterian*, 7 Febuary 1924, pp. 6–7; idem, "An Earnest Plea for Christian Freedom"; idem, "Religion and Fact," *Real Issue*, 15 April 1924, pp. 3–4 (in Machen Papers).

160. *Presbyterian*, 2 December 1923, p. 8.

161. "A Most Important Resolution," *Presbyterian*, 11 October 1923, pp. 4–5, quoted in Nykamp, "Power Struggle," 184.

162. Quirk, "Auburn *Affirmation*," 244–45; Loetscher, *Broadening Church*, 122.

Chapter 5

1. "Proceedings of the One Hundred and Thirty-Sixth General Assembly,"
Presbyterian, 29 May 1924, 12, quoted in Nykamp, "Power Struggle," 293.
    2. *New York Times*, 23 May 1924, p. 7.
    3. Henry S. Coffin to Dorothy Coffin, 22 May 1924, Coffin Papers.
    4. Macartney, *Autobiography*, 27–28, 45; Harry E. Farra, "The Rhetoric of
Reverend Clarence Edward Macartney: A Man under Authority" (Ph.D. diss.,
Pennsylvania State University, 1970), 23; S. Bruce Willson to J. Clyde Henry,
9 October 1959, Macartney Papers; Russell, *Voices*, 265, n. 5.
    5. Farra, "Rhetoric of Macartney," 17–18.
    6. Macartney, *Autobiography*, 35.
    7. Farra, "Rhetoric of Macartney," 21.
    8. Macartney, *Autobiography*, 35, 37; Farra, "Rhetoric of Macartney,"
18–19.
    9. Macartney, *Autobiography*, 41. See also Farra, "Rhetoric of Macart-
ney," 21.
    10. Farra, "Rhetoric of Macartney," 21–22.
    11. Clarence E. Macartney, "Warm Hearts and Steady Faith," *Christian
Century*, 8 March 1939, 315; Clarence Macartney, "A Son's Tribute to His
Mother," (Philadelphia: Wilber Hanf, n.d.), 4, 7 (in Macartney Papers); Macartney, *Autobiography*, 38; Farra, "Rhetoric of Macartney," 28.
    12. Catherine R. McCartney, "A Word to Mothers," (Chicago: Ruby I.
Gilbert, n.d.), 1–6 (in Macartney Papers).
    13. Farra, "Rhetoric of Macartney," 23.
    14. "Dr. Macartney Dies after Long Illness," *Pittsburgh Sun–Telegraph*, 20
Febuary 1957 (in Macartney Papers).
    15. Farra, "Rhetoric of Macartney," 23, 28.
    16. J. C. McFeeters, *The Covenanters in America: The Voice of Their Tes-
timony on Present Moral Issues* (Philadelphia: Spangler & Davis, 1892), 32–35,
38–39; Macartney, *Autobiography*, 32.
    17. Farra, "Rhetoric of Macartney," 19; Robert M. Copeland, *Spare No
Exertions: 175 Years of the Reformed Presbyterian Theological Seminary* (Pittsburgh: Reformed Presbyterian Theological Seminary, 1986), 52.
    18. McFeeters, *Covenanters in America*, 30–31, 121–29; Smith, *Seeds of Sec-
ularization*, 68; Lewis G. Vander Velde, *The Presbyterian Churches and the
Federal Union: 1861–1869* (Cambridge: Harvard University Press, 1932), 10–
11, 398–99.
    19. Joseph M. Wilson, ed., *Presbyterian Historical Almanac and Annual Re-
membrance of the Church* (Philadelphia, 1863), 395–96, quoted in Vander Velde,
Presbyterian Churches, 400.
    20. Vander Velde, *Presbyterian Churches*, 402.
    21. David McAllister, *A Manual for Christian Civil Government* (Allegheny,
PA: Christian Statesman, 1898), 154.
    22. Smith, *Seeds of Secularization*, 59.

23. McAllister, *Civil Government*, 17–18.
24. Smith, *Seeds of Secularization*, 59, 63, 197, n. 41. Though Southern Presbyterians did not support the NRA, J. H. Thornwell had endorsed amending the Constitution of the Confederacy to make it an explicitly Christian document. This lends credence to the claim of Jack Maddex that "it was the overthrow of the Confederacy and slavery which turned Southern Presbyterians to belief in a wholly "non-secular" church." See Eugene D. Genovese, "James Thornwell and Southern Religion," *Southern Partisan* (Summer 1987): 21; and Maddex, "From Theocracy to Spirituality," 448.
25. Farra, "Rhetoric of Macartney," 24; Wilhemina Guerard, "Biographical Notes: Clarence Macartney," typed manuscript, 9–10, 15, Macartney Papers.
26. Macartney, *Autobiography*, 68.
27. Clarence Macartney, "A Christian Home," typed manuscript, 1–2, Macartney Papers.
28. Macartney, *Autobiography*, 56–57, 77.
29. Guerard, "Biographical Notes," 7.
30. Macartney, *Autobiography*, 69–75.
31. Farra, "Rhetoric of Macartney," 27–28.
32. Macartney, *Autobiography*, 78–88; Farra, "Rhetoric of Macartney," 30; Guerard, "Biographical Notes," 20–21.
33. Guerard, "Biographical Notes," 21–22.
34. Macartney, *Autobiography*, 81, 88–90, 83; Guerard, "Biographical Notes," 23–25.
35. Guerard, "Biographical Notes," 25–27.
36. Farra, "Rhetoric of Macartney," 33–34; Guerard, "Biographical Notes," 27.
37. Guerard, "Biographical Notes," 29–30; Farra, "Rhetoric of Macartney," 34; Clarence Macartney, "Wisconsin As I Remember Her," typed manuscript, 12, Macartney Papers.
38. Farra, "Rhetoric of Macartney," 35–36.
39. Macartney, *Autobiography*, 114. Clarence's parents had departed from Madison after one year to travel in Europe for two years. Their peripatetic life finally came to a close in 1901 when they returned to "Fern Cliffe," the family home in Beaver Falls (Guerard, "Biographical Notes," 29).
40. Guerard, "Biographical Notes," 31–32.
41. G. Hall Todd, "The Heritage from Clarence Edward Macartney," in "Tributes to Clarence Edward Noble Macartney, 1879–1957: Minister of the Arch Street Presbyterian Church, Philadelphia, Penn., 1914–1927" (n.p.: 1979[?]), (in Macartney Papers); Guerard, "Biographical Notes," 32.
42. Guerard wrote, "I remonstrated with him on his attitude toward revealed religion. His reply was striking, in the light of his later development: 'It is all very well if you can believe those things: I cannot'" (Guerard, "Biographical Notes," 32). See also Farra, "Rhetoric of Macartney," 36.
43. See Farra, "Rhetoric of Macartney," 37.
44. Macartney, *Autobiography*, 114–18; Farra, "Rhetoric of Macartney," 37–39.

45. Farra, "Rhetoric of Macartney," 39. Macartney wrote to his mother, "It will not be necessary for you to tell anyone that I am in the Divinity School" (Clarence E. Macartney to Catherine R. McCartney, 25 September 1902, Macartney Papers, quoted in Farra, "Rhetoric of Macartney," 40).

46. Macartney, *Autobiography*, 119. See also Guerard, "Biographical Notes," 34.

47. McCartney, *Autobiography*, 120.

48. Guerard, "Biographical Notes," 37–38.

49. Macartney, *Autobiography*, 124–25; quote is from p. 124.

50. Orion C. Hopper, *Biographical Catalogue of Princeton Theological Seminary, 1815–1954* (Princeton: Trustees of the Seminary, 1955), 166; Loetscher, *Broadening Church*, 139.

51. *First Church Life*, 27 April 1952, p. 9 (in Macartney Papers).

52. Macartney, *Autobiography*, 119.

53. Ibid., 131. Examples of his biographical sermons can be found in Clarence E. Macartney, *Great Women of the Bible* (New York: Abingdon-Cokesbury, 1943); idem, *The Greatest Men of the Bible* (New York: Abingdon, 1941).

54. McCartney, *Autobiography*, 162. Examples of his works on the Civil War include Clarence E. Macartney, *Lincoln and His Generals* (Philadelphia: Dorrance, 1925); idem, *Lincoln and the Bible* (New York: Abingdon-Cokesbury, 1949). Macartney's interest in the Civil War was also spurred by a lecture he heard as a child (G. Hall Todd, "He Being Dead Yet Speaketh," in "Tributes to Clarence Edward Noble Macartney" (n.p., 1957), 17 (in Macartney Papers).

55. "Dr. Macartney Dies after Long Illness," *Pittsburgh Sun–Telegraph*, 20 Febuary 1957 (in Macartney Papers).

56. Guerard, "Biographical Notes," 38.

57. Macartney, *Autobiography*, 129–30, 133.

58. Todd, "Heritage," 17.

59. Macartney, *Autobiography*, 145, 136, 138, 149, 150–51, 168.

60. Ibid., 168.

61. Todd, "He Being Dead Yet Speaketh," 13.

62. Macartney, *Autobiography*, 169, 173–81.

63. Todd, "He Being Dead Yet Speaketh," 12.

64. Clarence E. Macartney, "The Fall of Germany and the Vindication of the Moral Order," *Presbyterian*, 4 September 1919, p. 11.

65. Clarence E. Macartney, "A New Kind of Christianity," *Presbyterian Banner*, 3 July 1919, pp. 7–8, Macartney Papers.

66. Harry E. Fosdick, "The Trenches and the Church at Home," *Atlantic Monthly* 123 (January 1919): 22–33.

67. Clarence E. Macartney, "In the House of My Friends," *Presbyterian*, 6 March 1919, p. 31.

68. Clarence E. Macartney, "The Heroism of the Ministry in the Hour of Christianity's Peril," *Princeton Theological Review* 20 (July 1922): 362.

69. Clarence E. Macartney, *Twelve Great Questions about Christ* (New York: Fleming H. Revell, 1923; reprint, Grand Rapids: Baker Book House, 1956), 56.

70. Clarence E. Macartney, *Things Most Surely Believed: A Series of Sermons on the Apostles' Creed* (Nashville: Cokesbury, 1930), 22.

71. Farra, "Rhetoric of Macartney," 72.

72. "The Mightiest Power on Earth," *Presbyterian Banner*, 25 September 1919, p. 8, quoted in Farra, "Rhetoric of Macartney," 72.

73. Macartney, "Irrepressible Conflict," 7.

74. Clarence Macartney, *The Christian Faith and the Spirit of the Age* (New York: American Tract Society, 1940), 31, 24. See also Russell, *Voices*, 198–99.

75. Macartney, *Christian Faith and the Spirit of the Age*, 25–26.

76. Clarence Macartney, "The Authority of the Holy Scriptures," *Princeton Theological Review* 23 (July 1925): 395.

77. "Declaration of Faith," *First Church Life* (October 1950): 16, quoted in Arnold A. Kurtz, "A Rhetorical Analysis of the Preaching of Dr. Clarence Edward Macartney, Twentieth Century Exponent of the Traditional Orthodoxy" (Ph.D. diss, Michigan State University, 1966), 95.

78. Clarence Macartney, "Providence and Predestination" (pamphlet, n.d.) and Macartney, "A Son's Tribute to His Mother," 8, both quoted in Kurtz, "Rhetorical Analysis," 96–97.

79. Clarence E. Macartney, "Another Gospel Which Is Not Another," *Presbyterian*, 23 January 1930, p. 8.

80. Macartney, "Warm Hearts," 318.

81. Clarence E. Macartney, *The Faith Once Delivered* (New York: Abingdon-Cokesbury, 1952), 94. See also Macartney, *Twelve Great Questions about Christ*, 112; and Kurtz, "Rhetorical Analysis," 106.

82. Clarence E. Macartney, "The Great Defection," 6, Macartney Papers.

83. Clarence E. Macartney, *The Greatest Questions of the Bible and of Life* (New York: Abingdon-Cokesbury, 1948), 111. See also Clarence E. Macartney, "The Great Revolt against Rationalism in the Presbyterian Church" (Philadelphia: Wilber Hanf, n.d.), 11 (in Macartney Papers).

84. Macartney, *Greatest Questions of the Bible*, 109.

85. Macartney, *Things Most Surely Believed*, 72–75, 78.

86. Clarence E. Macartney, *Putting on Immortality* (New York: Fleming H. Revell, 1926), 187.

87. Macartney, *Christian Faith and the Spirit of the Age*, 192.

88. Smith, *Seeds of Secularization*, 15, 153.

89. Clarence E. Macartney, "To the Survivors of the Grand Army of the Republic: 1861–1937," typed manuscript, Macartney Papers.

90. Clarence Macartney to John L. and Catherine R. McCartney, 4 November 1900, Macartney Papers, quoted in Kurtz, "Rhetorical Analysis," 21.

91. "Twenty-fifth Anniversary for Dr. Macartney," *Pittsburgh Sun–Telegraph*, 26 April 1952, p. 7, Macartney Papers.

92. Clarence E. Macartney, "Historical Address Delivered at the General Assembly on Last Tuesday, June 1, by Dr. Clarence E. Macartney," *Presbyterian*, 3 June 1926, p. 10.

93. Ibid., 10–11.

94. Of course, for Macartney, concern for the salvation of souls preceded concern for moral reform; and he worried about the liberal stress of a purely social gospel. See Clarence E. Macartney, "Is America on the Road to Ruin?" 28 January 1945, Macartney Papers.

95. Clarence E. Macartney, "The Worship of the Beast; or, The Renaissance of Paganism," *Christian Statesman* 58 (April 1924): 31–32.

96. Clarence E. Macartney, "America, Her Great Leaders, and God," 25 November 1943, Macartney Papers.

97. Clarence Macartney, "Their Name Liveth Forevermore," *Presbyterian*, 14 July 1927, p. 7.

98. Clarence E. Macartney, "The Christian Home," 14 May 1929, p. 4, Macartney Papers.

99. "Sees Nation's Fate in Home Religion," *Philadelphia Evening Bulletin*, 25 October 1926 (in Macartney Papers).

100. Macartney, "Worship of the Beast," 35.

101. Clarence E. Macartney, "The State of the Church," *Princeton Theological Review* 23 (April 1925): 186.

102. Clarence E. Macartney, "The Overture on Divorce," *Presbyterian*, 19 May 1921, p. 7; *Minutes of GA*, 1921, 1:28.

103. Macartney, *Christian Faith and the Spirit of the Age*, 134–35.

104. Macartney, "Overture on Divorce," 7; Macartney, *Christian Faith and the Spirit of the Age*, 133–34.

105. Clarence Macartney, "The Overture on Divorce," *Presbyterian Banner*, 17 January 1929, 12, Robert E. Speer Papers, Speer Library, Princeton Theological Seminary, Princeton (hereafter, "Speer Papers").

106. *Minutes of GA*, 1926, 1:96, 256–57; J. Gresham Machen to Robert E. Speer, 29 June and 23 July 1928, Speer Papers.

107. "Minutes of the General Assembly Special Committee on Marriage and Divorce, 29 November 1927," Speer Papers. See also *Presbyterian*, 12 May 1927, pp. 9, 27.

108. Clarence E. Macartney, "The Teachings of the New Testament on Divorce," typed manuscript, 3, Department of History, Presbyterian Church (U.S.A.), Philadelphia, PA. See also Clarence E. Macartney, *What Jesus Really Taught* (New York: Abingdon, 1958), 91–96.

109. Ibid., 3, 7.

110. See Robert E. Speer to J. Gresham Machen, 22(?) June 1928, Speer Papers. See also Robert E. Speer, "A Brief and Provisional Study of the New Testament Teaching on Marriage, Divorce, and Remarriage," typed manuscript, Speer Papers.

111. Robert E. Speer to Charles Erdman, 16 February 1928, Speer Papers.

112. Robert E. Speer, *Some Living Issues* (London: Morgan & Scott, 1930), 180.

113. Robert E. Speer to J. Gresham Machen, 18 July 1928, Speer Papers.

114. J. Gresham Machen to Robert E. Speer, 23 July 1928, Speer Papers.

115. *Minutes of GA*, 1928, 1:61; *Minutes of GA*, 1929, 1:53–55.
116. *Minutes of GA*, 1929, 1:53–55, 75–76.
117. Clarence E. Macartney, "Birth Control and the Presbyterian Church," *Presbyterian*, 7 May 1931, p. 26.
118. "Dr. Macartney's Lamentations over the Christianity of our Christian Colleges," *Christian Work*, 2 February 1924, p. 158 (in Macartney Papers).
119. Macartney, "State of the Church," 185.
120. "Sees Rationalism As Destroyer of Home," unidentified newspaper clipping, Macartney Papers. See also Clarence Macartney, "The Teaching of Ethics in the Public Schools," unidentified newspaper clipping, Macartney Papers.
121. Macartney, *Christian Faith and the Spirit of the Age*, 125, 128.
122. Clarence E. Macartney, "Two Years of Prohibition in Philadelphia," *Presbyterian*, 16 March 1922, pp. 9–10, 26.
123. Clarence E. Macartney, "Awake, O America!" 30 June 1935, Macartney Papers.
124. Clarence E. Macartney, "The Destroyer of Souls," 16 October 1949, Macartney Papers.
125. "Minister Resents Bid To 'Wet' Rally," *Philadelphia Evening Bulletin*, 16 December 1921 (in Macartney Papers).
126. Clarence E. Macartney, "The Sabbath," 15 May 1952, pp. 4–5, 7–8, Macartney Papers.
127. Macartney, "State of the Church," 186.
128. Clarence E. Macartney, "Dr. Clarence Macartney Answers the President," *Presbyterian*, 24 October 1935, p. 5.
129. Farra, "Rhetoric of Macartney," 65–66.
130. Clarence E. Macartney, "Come before Winter," *Presbyterian Life*, 13 October 1951, pp. 8–11.
131. Clarence E. Macartney, "A Man under Authority," typed manuscript, 10, Macartney Papers.
132. I am indebted to Harry E. Farra of Geneva College, Beaver Falls, Pennsylvania, for suggesting this line of thought (Harry E. Farra, interview by author, 25 March 1987, Beaver Falls, PA).
133. Nykamp, "Power Struggle," 295.
134. Henry S. Coffin to Dorothy Coffin, 26 May 1924, Coffin Papers.
135. Rian, *Presbyterian Conflict*, 53–55.
136. Quirk, "Auburn *Affirmation*," 255.
137. Henry S. Coffin to Dorothy Coffin, 24(?) May 1924, Coffin Papers.
138. *Minutes of GA*, 1924, 1:194, 196–97.
139. Quirk, "Auburn *Affirmation*," 249.
140. *Minutes of GA*, 1924, 1:195–96.
141. Miller, *Harry Emerson Fosdick*, 132.
142. *New York Times*, 30 May 1924, p. 6; Miller, *Harry Emerson Fosdick*, 132, 141–42; Stonehouse, *Machen*, 369.

143. *Summer Monthly*, 6 June 1924, pp. 1–2 (in Coffin Papers).
144. Harry E. Fosdick to Henry S. Coffin, 11 December 1924, quoted in Noyes, *Coffin*, 169.
145. Miller, *Harry Emerson Fosdick*, 139, 144–45.
146. Harry E. Fosdick, "The Farewell Sermon of Harry Emerson Fosdick to the First Presbyterian Church of New York" (n.p., 1925), 23.

Chapter 6

1. J. Gresham Machen to Maitland Alexander, 10 June 1924, quoted in Stonehouse, *Machen*, 369.
2. J. Gresham Machen, *What Is Christianity?* 244–52.
3. Nykamp, "Power Struggle," 331–32.
4. Ibid., 317.
5. Clarence E. Macartney, "The Presbyterian Church at the Cross Roads," *Presbyterian*, 19 Febuary 1925, p. 7.
6. Nykamp, "Power Struggle," 317.
7. Clarence E. Macartney, "The Moderator's Message," *Presbyterian*, 8 January 1925, pp. 10–11.
8. Nykamp, "Power Struggle," 317, 332.
9. Quirk, "Auburn *Affirmation*," 260.
10. Henry S. Coffin, "Freedom in the Presbyterian Pulpit" (Auburn, NY: Jacobs, 1925), 12, 15–16.
11. Francis Patton, "A Theological Seminary," *Princeton Theological Review* 14 (January 1916): 74. See also Ronald T. Clutter, "The Reorganization of Princeton Theological Seminary Reconsidered," *Grace Theological Journal* 7, no. 2 (1986): 181–85.
12. Clutter, "Reorganization," 184.
13. Ibid., 183–85.
14. Loetscher, *Broadening Church*, 138–39.
15. Stonehouse, *Machen*, 218–19; Clutter, "Reorganization," 186–87.
16. Loetscher, *Broadening Church*, 138.
17. Stonehouse, *Machen*, 356–57.
18. *Presbyterian*, 15 January 1925, p. 4, quoted in Nykamp, "Power Struggle," 336.
19. Charles R. Erdman, "Dr. Erdman Speaks in Self-Defense," *Presbyterian Advance*, 22 January 1925, p. 24.
20. Stonehouse, *Machen*, 376–77.
21. J. Gresham Machen, "Dr. Machen Replies to Dr. Erdman," *Presbyterian*, 5 Febuary 1925, pp. 20–21. See also Charles R. Erdman to William P. Armstrong, 27 November 1926, Erdman Papers.
22. J. Gresham Machen to Mary Gresham Machen, 19 October 1924, Machen Papers.

23. J. Gresham Machen to Mary Gresham Machen, 11 November 1924(?), Machen Papers.
24. Elmer G. Homrighausen, Charles T. Fritsch, Bruce M. Metzger, "In Memoriam: Charles Rosenbury Erdman, July 20, 1866–May 10, 1960," *Princeton Seminary Bulletin* 54 (November 1960): 36.
25. Daniels, *Moody*, 505; "Class of 1856: William J. Erdman," Erdman Papers; Willis J. Beecher, *Index of Presbyterian Ministers: 1706–1881* (Philadelphia: Presbyterian Board of Publication, 1883), 171.
26. William J. Erdman, *Notes on the Revelation*, ed. Charles Erdman (New York: Fleming H. Revell, 1930), 7.
27. Marsden, *Evangelical Mind*, 63, 50, 58, 75, 78–79. This account follows Marsden closely.
28. Ibid., 10–11, 69.
29. Ibid., 67–69.
30. Ibid., 71–72, 74–75. To the factors contributing to the division already mentioned Marsden adds the question of slavery; see pp. 67, 88–103.
31. Ibid., 156, 158–60, 177. This account of the theology of Henry B. Smith follows Marsden's chapter on Smith in *Evangelical Mind*.
32. Henry B. Smith, *Faith and Philosophy: Discourses and Essays by Henry B. Smith, D.D., Ll.D.*, ed. George L. Prentiss (New York, 1877), 6, quoted in Marsden, *Evangelical Mind*, 158.
33. Marsden, *Evangelical Mind*, 166–67.
34. Henry B. Smith, *Faith and Philosophy*, 31–46, quoted in Marsden, *Evangelical Mind*, 167.
35. Marsden, *Evangelical Mind*, 175–76.
36. "Class of 1856: William Jacob Erdman," Erdman Papers; "Dr. Erdman's Remarkable Career Covers 67 Years," *Trenton Sunday Times–Advertiser*, 23 Febuary 1958 (in Erdman Papers).
37. Charles Erdman, *D. L. Moody: His Message for To-day* (New York: Fleming H. Revell, 1928), 125.
38. Sandeen, *Roots of Fundamentalism*, 182, 135, 142, 157, 160, 167, 175; Daniels, *Moody*, 506; W. J. Erdman, *Notes on the Revelation*, 7.
39. Marsden, *Fundamentalism and American Culture*, 37. After the turn of the century William Erdman rejected some critical doctrines of dispensational premillennialism (Sandeen, *Roots of Fundamentalism*, 210–24). For William Erdman's views on Holiness, see esp. William J. Erdman, *The Holy Spirit and Christian Experience* (New York: Gospel, 1909); idem, "The Holy Spirit and the Sons of God," *The Fundamentals*, ed. Dixon, Meyer, and Torrey, 10: 64–78.
40. Sandeen, *Roots of Fundamentalism*, 142; Moody, quoted in C. R. Erdman, *D. L. Moody: Message*, 139.
41. Marsden, *Fundamentalism and American Culture*, 35. The standard work on Moody is Findlay, *Moody*. Other works that are helpful are Richard K. Curtis, *They Called Him Mr. Moody* (Garden City, NY: Doubleday, 1962);

Daniels, *Moody*; Stephen N. Gundry, *Love Them In: The Proclamation Theology of D. L. Moody* (Chicago: Moody, 1976); and John C. Pollock, *Moody: A Biographical Portrait of the Pacesetter in Modern Mass Evangelism* (New York: Macmillan, 1963).

42. Marsden, *Fundamentalism and American Culture*, 38.
43. Dwight L. Moody, *The Best of D. L. Moody*, ed. Wilbur M. Smith (Chicago, 1971), 194, quoted in Marsden, *Fundamentalism and American Culture*, 38.
44. Marsden, *Fundamentalism and American Culture*, 33.
45. Gundry, *Love Them In*, 53–56.
46. "Dr. Erdman's Remarkable Career."
47. Erdman, *D. L. Moody: Message*, 84.
48. Ibid., 100, 85–86, 102.
49. "Dr. Erdman's Remarkable Career." During Charles Erdman's childhood his father served churches in Fayetteville, New York; Ann Arbor, Michigan; Fort Wayne, Indiana; Chicago, Illinois; and Jamestown, New York. For a brief chronology of William Erdman's life, see W. J. Erdman, *Notes on the Revelation*, 13.
50. "Dr. Erdman's Remarkable Career"; John A. Garrity, ed., *Dictionary of American Biography*, Suppl. 6 (New York: Charles Scribner's Sons, 1980), s.v. "Erdman, Charles Rosenbury."
51. Homrighausen, "In Memoriam, Charles Erdman," 36.
52. Frederick Evans, ed., *After Twenty-Five Years: Class Record of 1886* (Princeton: Princeton University Press, 1911), 31.
53. Thomas J. Wertenbaker, *Princeton: 1746–1896* (Princeton: Princeton University Press, 1946), 290–343.
54. "Dr. Erdman's Remarkable Career."
55. Homrighausen, "In Memoriam, Charles Erdman," 36; "Dr. Erdman's Remarkable Career."
56. "Dr. Erdman's Remarkable Career." See also Evans, *After Twenty-Five Years: Class Record of 1886*, 31.
57. Homrighausen, "In Memoriam, Charles Erdman," 36.
58. Newspaper clippings in "Diaries and Day Books," vol. 4, Erdman Papers. One clipping announced, "The four marriageable daughters of Mr. Calvin C. Pardee, the millionaire coal operator, will divide something like $12,000,000. They occupy a palatial mansion on West Walnut Lane. The eldest daughter, Miss Estelle Pardee, is engaged to a minister and will be married during the coming season." See also Class Secretary, *First Annual Record of the Class of Eighty-Six of Princeton College for 1886–87* (Philadelphia: American Printing House, 1887), 16.
59. "Dr. Erdman's Remarkable Career"; Homrighausen, "In Memoriam, Charles Erdman," 38.
60. Homrighausen, "In Memoriam, Charles Erdman," 36.
61. E. D. Warfield to Charles R. Erdman, 6 January 1906, Erdman Papers.

62. *Dictionary of American Biography*, s.v. "Erdman, Charles Rosenbury," 195.

63. Charles R. Erdman, "Modern Practical Theology," *New York Observer*, 3 January 1907, pp. 17–18.

64. *Dictionary of American Biography*, s.v. "Erdman, Charles Rosenbury," 195–96; "Pen Portraits of Church Leaders, Charles R. Erdman" *Christian Herald*, 20 November 1926, p. 994.

65. Sandeen, "Fundamentals," 72, n. 46; Sandeen, *Roots of Fundamentalism*, 223.

66. Erdman's visa described him as 5 feet 9 inches (Erdman Papers).

67. Homrighausen, "In Memoriam, Charles Erdman," 38–39; "Pen Portraits of Church Leaders," 994.

68. See Charles Erdman, *The Epistle of Paul to the Ephesians: An Exposition* (Philadelphia: Westminster, 1931), 98; and "Pen Portraits of Church Leaders," 994.

69. Charles R. Erdman, *The Pastoral Epistles of Paul: An Exposition* (Philadelphia: Westminster, 1923), 38, 40.

70. Charles R. Erdman, *The Spirit of Christ: Devotional Studies in the Doctrine of the Holy Spirit* (New York: George H. Doran, 1926; reprint, New York: Richard R. Smith, 1929), 49.

71. Sandeen, *Roots of Fundamentalism*, 176–80; Findlay, *Moody*, 341–43; Marsden, *Fundamentalism and American Culture*, 249, n. 36.

72. Marsden, *Fundamentalism and American Culture*, 77–79; Sandeen, *Roots of Fundamentalism*, 178–80. See also Gundry, *Love Them In*, 159–60; Findlay, *Moody*, 341–43, 408–9; W. J. Erdman, *Holy Spirit and Christian Experience*; idem, "The Holy Spirit and the Sons of God."

73. Charles R. Erdman, "Modern Spiritual Movements," in *Modern Spiritual Movements: Biblical and Theological Studies by Members of the Faculty of Princeton Theological Seminary* (New York: n.p., 1912), 365.

74. Erdman, *The Spirit of Christ*, 30.

75. Marsden, *Fundamentalism and American Culture*, 78; Erdman, *Spirit of Christ*, 41. For the similar views of Moody see Daniels, *Moody*, 399–402.

76. Erdman, *Spirit of Christ*, 43, 30, 47.

77. Ibid., 76–80. For a useful summary of the understanding of Scripture in the Westminster Confession, see Rogers and McKim, *Authority and Interpretation*, 200–218.

78. *New York Times*, 26 April 1925, p. 9. Given Erdman's premillennial roots, he may well have adhered to a strict doctrine of biblical inerrancy early in his career. I have not been able to locate any statements to this effect, however. In 1915 Erdman signed a "Back to Fundamentals" statement claiming "we believe pronounced and persistent emphasis should be placed on the integrity and authority of the Bible as the Word of God" (*Presbyterian*, 22 April 1915, p. 18). While this could have implied inerrancy, the language is certainly not explicit.

79. Erdman, *Spirit of Christ*, 79–80.

80. *New York Times*, 26 April 1925, p. 9.

81. Erdman, *Spirit of Christ*, 80–82, 85–86; cf. Rogers and McKim, *Authority and Interpretation*, 200–218.

82. Erdman, *Spirit of Christ*, 90–91.

83. Ibid., 100. For Machen's doctrine of the church, see Machen, *Christianity and Liberalism*, 157–80.

84. Ibid., 93. Erdman expressed this opinion in a discussion of "church unity," but the sentiment would seem to be the same for one or many denominations.

85. Ibid., 93. See also Charles R. Erdman, *The Gospel of Luke: An Exposition* (Philadelphia: Westminster, 1921), 102.

86. "America's Hope in God, Says Dr. Erdman," *Tulsa Tribune*, 17 January 1926, Erdman Papers.

87. See Charles R. Erdman, "The Church and Socialism" and "The Coming of Christ," in *The Fundamentals*, ed. Dixon, Meyer, and Torrey, 12:119, 11:98.

88. Charles R. Erdman, *The General Epistles: An Exposition* (Philadelphia: Westminster, 1919), 28.

89. Erdman, *Pastoral Epistles of Paul*, 107.

90. Erdman, *Spirit of Christ*, 11.

91. Erdman, *General Epistles*, 178. See also Charles Erdman, *The Lord We Love: Devotional Studies in the Life of Christ* (New York: George H. Doran, 1924), 65. Erdman believed that "The things which keep men from Christian faith are usually not intellectual difficulties, but secret sins, carelessness, or pride of intellect, self-indulgence or self-conceit" (Erdman, *Spirit of Christ*, 111).

92. "America's Hope in God, Says Dr. Erdman."

93. As noted earlier, William Erdman, though always a premillennialist, abandoned the central tenets of dispensationalist teaching around 1900 and was involved in a major schism among premillennialists because of this. See Sandeen, *Roots of Fundamentalism*, 210–24. As shall be discussed below, Charles Erdman, at least in his mature thought, also rejected dispensationalism. Among the major characters in this study Robert Speer, early on, also had premillennial leanings; but by the 1920s he seemed to have abandoned these views. See Robert E. Speer, "The Second Coming of Christ" (East Northfield, MA: A. P. Fitt, 1903); James A. Patterson, "Robert E. Speer and the Crisis of the American Protestant Missionary Movement: 1920–1937" (Ph.D. diss., Princeton Theological Seminary, 1980), 14, n. 30; and Chapter 8 below.

94. Erdman, "Coming of Christ," 87, 89. See also Charles Erdman, *The Return of Christ* (New York: George H. Doran, 1922), 27–33.

95. Erdman, *Return of Christ*, 70–72, 74–75. As noted above, Charles Erdman had assisted with the creation of the *Scofield Reference Bible*; but, as Sandeen implies, he had probably disavowed any strictly dispensationalist doctrine by this time (Sandeen, *Roots of Fundamentalism*, 223–24).

96. Erdman, *Return of Christ*, 75.

97. Ibid. For a neat comparison, see J. Gresham Machen, *God Transcendent*, 112.

98. Erdman, "Coming of Christ," 98–99.

99. Charles R. Erdman, *The Epistle of Paul to the Romans: An Exposition* (Philadelphia: Westminster, 1925), 7. Faith, Erdman claimed, was "belief founded upon evidence" (*Gospel of Luke*, 73). See also Erdman, *The Lord We Love*, 11, 125.

100. *New York Times*, 26 April 1925, p. 9.

101. Charles Erdman, *The Acts: An Exposition* (Philadelphia: Westminster, 1920), 132.

102. Erdman, "Church and Socialism," 116.

103. Charles R. Erdman, "Making the Nation Christian," *Presbyterian*, 26 May 1921, p. 8.

104. Charles R. Erdman, "Bible Teachings about Education," *Presbyterian*, 21 April 1921, p. 12. See also Charles R. Erdman, "Making the Social Order Christian," *Presbyterian*, 9 June 1921, p. 12.

105. Erdman, "Making the Nation Christian," 8.

106. Charles R. Erdman, "Rest and Recreation," *Presbyterian*, 28 April 1921, p. 12. See also Marsden, *Fundamentalism and American Culture*, 35.

107. Charles R. Erdman, "The Lord of the Sabbath," *The Lord's Day Leader*, pp. 10, 12 (clipping in Erdman Papers).

108. Charles R. Erdman, "Review: The Social Task of the Church," *Presbyterian*, 16 June 1921, p. 12.

109. "America's Hope in God, Says Dr. Erdman."

110. "Religious Education World's Greatest Need, Erdman Says," *Ohio State Journal*, 10 February 1926 (in Erdman Papers); Erdman, "Bible Teachings about Education," 12.

111. Charles R. Erdman, "Temperance Lessons—(World's Temperance Sunday)," *Presbyterian*, 23 October 1919, p. 14.

112. Charles R. Erdman, "How To Be Clean," *The Westminster Teacher*, pp. 473–74 (clipping in Erdman Papers). See also Charles R. Erdman, *Your Bible and You* (Philadelphia: Winston, 1950), 2. Despite these strong feelings, Erdman's enthusiasm for Prohibition seems to have waned a bit by the mid-1920s. See "No Peril in Jazz Age, Says Divine," *New Orleans States*, 9 November 1926(?) (in Erdman Papers).

113. Charles R. Erdman, "Strong Drink in a Nation's Life," *Presbyterian*, 20 October 1921, p. 12.

114. "Dr. Thompson Is Urged As Presbyterian Moderator," *Denver Post*, 15 Febuary 1926 (in Erdman Papers). See also "No Peril in Jazz Age, Says Divine" and "America's Hope in God, Says Dr. Erdman." Macartney claimed, in contrast, "We may talk as we please, that revolt is here in our midst, and no honeyed phrases in eulogy of the youth of our day, or in statements that it was always thus, can disguise the reach and power of the present casting off of restraint" ("The Rights of God," *Presbyterian*, 11 April 1929, p. 6).

115. Erdman, "Review: The Social Task of the Church," 12. See also "America's Hope in God Says Dr. Erdman"; "Dr. Thompson Is Urged As Presbyterian Moderator"; "Young People Are Indifferent, Moderator Says," *Oklahoma City Times* (in Erdman Papers).

116. "Selfishness Is Enemy of Sabbath," *Princeton Herald* (in Erdman Papers).

117. "America's Hope In God, Says Dr. Erdman"; Erdman, "Strong Drink in a Nation's Life," 12.

118. Preston W. Slosson, *The Great Crusade and After: 1914–1928* (New York: Macmillan, 1935), 95, 97–99, 113–18, 122–26. The vast concern of Presbyterians over the lawlessness of the nation, particularly in respect to Prohibition, can be perceived by even a cursory examination of *The Presbyterian* in 1926–1927. See, e.g., 21 January 1926, p. 5; 28 January 1926, p. 5; 29 April 1926, pp. 4–5; 13 May 1926, pp. 4–5; 30 June 1927, p. 12; 29 September 1927, p. 5. See also Leuchtenburg, *Perils of Prosperity*, 217; Carter, *Decline and Revival of the Social Gospel*, 129.

119. *Presbyterian*, 10 June 1926, p. 17.

120. "Young People Are Indifferent, Moderator Says."

121. Carter, *Decline and Revival of the Social Gospel*, 37–38, 129.

122. *New York Times*, 21 May 1925, p. 2.

123. Rian, *Presbyterian Conflict*, 69–70.

124. Charles R. Erdman to Clarence E. Macartney, 14 April 1925, Macartney Papers.

125. Rian, *Presbyterian Conflict*, 71–72.

126. See, e.g., *New York Times* 6 April 1925, p. 1; *Christian Work*, 18 April 1925, p. 486.

127. Nykamp, "Power Struggle," 369. Though Erdman's ouster was not simply the result of his feud with Machen, Machen was strongly opposed to Erdman's continuing service as student advisor and was, in fact, the one who moved that Robert D. Wilson replace him. The press reports, though distorted, were not, therefore, entirely mistaken (*Minutes of GA*, 1927, 1:93).

128. Nykamp, "Power Struggle," 371–72.

129. "Presbyterian Press Association Later Presbyterian Conservatives Association," p. 56, Erdman Papers.

130. *New York Times*, 26 April 1925, p. 9.

131. *New York Times*, 27 April 1925, p. 3.

132. Nykamp, "Power Struggle," 357.

133. Machen, *God Transcendent*, 106–7.

134. J. Gresham Machen, "The Present Situation in the Presbyterian Church," *Presbyterian*, 14 May 1925, pp. 7–8.

135. Ibid., 8.

136. *New York Times*, 21 May 1925, p. 2.

137. "Dr. Erdman Again Outlines Position," *Trenton Times* (in Erdman Papers).

138. *New York Times*, 21 May 1925, p. 1.

139. See "Californian Is Chosen As Chief Rival of Erdman," *Ohio State Journal*, 21 May 1925 (in Macartney Papers).

140. These similarities were clearly revealed the following year when Erdman

endorsed Thompson to succeed him in the moderatorial chair. See "Dr. Thompson Is Urged As Presbyterian Moderator," Erdman Papers.

141. Henry S. Coffin to Charles R. Erdman, 6 April and 2 May 1925, Erdman Papers.

142. Charles R. Erdman to Henry S. Coffin, 5 May 1925, Erdman Papers.

143. *New York Times*, 22 May 1925, p. 5.

144. Sunday wrote a letter stating, "There could be no finer selection for Moderator" than Erdman ("Californian Is Chosen As Chief Rival of Erdman," Macartney Papers). Bryan's candidate, W. O. Thompson, withdrew from consideration before the election (*New York Times*, 22 May 1925, p. 5).

145. *New York Times*, 22 May 1925, p. 1.

146. Quirk, "Auburn *Affirmation*," 280; Nykamp, "Power Struggle," 394; "Erdman Installed by Presbyterians," unidentified newspaper clipping, Erdman Papers.

147. *Minutes of GA*, 1925, 1:28, 83–88.

148. Henry S. Coffin to Dorothy Coffin, 24 May 1925, Coffin Papers.

149. Noyes, *Coffin*, 174–75.

150. *Minutes of GA*, 1925, 1:84–85, 87–88.

151. *Presbyterian Banner*, 17 May 1923, 5, quoted in Loetscher, *Broadening Church*, 127.

152. Nichols, "Leader of Liberal Presbyterianism," 52.

153. *Minutes of GA*, 1925, 1:88.

154. Charles Erdman, "The Special Commission of 1925," *Presbyterian Magazine*, August 1925 (in Erdman Papers); Nykamp, "Power Struggle," 405.

155. Loetscher, *Broadening Church*, 128.

156. Ibid., 128.

157. Henry S. Coffin to Morgan Noyes, 4 June 1925, Coffin Papers.

158. New York Times, 27 May 1925, p. 1; quote in Nykamp, "Power Struggle," 410.

159. Nykamp, "Power Struggle," 394.

160. Quoted in Nykamp, "Power Struggle," 410.

161. Coffin, untitled sermon, *Summer Monthly*, 3 July 1925, p. 3 (in Coffin Papers).

162. Ibid., 4.

163. Ibid., 5–6.

164. Levine, *Defender of the Faith*, 329–30. The evolution controversy and Scopes trial are also addressed in Leslie H. Allen, ed., *Bryan and Darrow at Dayton: The Record and Documents of the "Bible–Evolution Trial"* (New York: Russell & Russell, 1925); Coletta, *William Jennings Bryan*; Norman Furniss, *The Fundamentalist Controversy, 1918–1931* (New Haven: Yale University Press, 1954); Willard B. Gatewood, ed., *Controversy in the Twenties: Fundamentalism, Modernism, and Evolution* (Nashville: Vanderbilt University Press, 1969); Ray Ginger, *Six Days or Forever? Tennessee Versus John Thomas Scopes* (Boston: Beacon, 1958); Gail Kennedy, ed., *Evolution and Religion*; and Szasz, *Divided Mind*.

165. Ibid., 328–30.
166. Quoted in Gatewood, *Controversy in the Twenties*, 332.
167. J. Gresham Machen to William J. Bryan, 2 July 1925, Machen Papers.
168. Macartney, "Wisconsin As I Remember Her," 17.
169. Coletta, *William Jennings Bryan*, 3:240.
170. Arthur G. Hays. "The Scopes Trial," in *Evolution and Religion*, ed. Kennedy, 35–36.
171. Levine, *Defender of the Faith*, 341–42; Gatewood, *Controversy in the Twenties*, 334.
172. Levine, *Defender of the Faith*, 346–48.
173. See Russell D. Owen, "The Meaning of the Scopes Trial," in *Controversy in the Twenties*, ed. Gatewood, 350.
174. Levine, *Defender of the Faith*, 351.
175. Ibid.
176. See Marsden, *Fundamentalism and American Culture*, 188–89.
177. Clarence E. Macartney, "The Great Commoner: William Jennings Bryan," *Presbyterian and Herald and Presbyter*, 8 October 1925, pp. 14, 18.
178. Szasz, *Divided Mind*, 124–25; Marsden, *Fundamentalism and American Culture*, 189.
179. J. Gresham Machen to Malcolm [Lockhart], 21 December 1925, Machen Papers.
180. J. Gresham Machen to F. E. Robinson, 25 June 1927, quoted in Stonehouse, *Machen*, 429.
181. Erdman, "The Special Commission of 1925," Erdman Papers; Bryan and Bryan, *Memoirs*, 50.
182. Letters from Machen, 28 June and 16 July 1925, quoted in Nykamp, "Power Struggle," 415.
183. Loetscher, *Broadening Church*, 130.
184. Ibid., 129.
185. "The Written and Verbal Statements of Rev. J. Gresham Machen, D.D., Rev. Henry Sloane Coffin, D.D., Rev. William Adams Brown, D.D., Rev. Clarence E. Macartney, D.D." Presented to the special commission of 1925 of the General Assembly of the Presbyterian Church in the U.S.A., Atlantic City, 1925, mimeograph, p. 1, Machen Papers (hereafter, "1925 Commission"; different parts of this report were taken from the Machen and Speer Papers).
186. 1925 Commission, 35–36, Speer Papers.
187. Ibid., 16.
188. Ibid., 17.
189. Loetscher, *Broadening Church*, 130.
190. Charles R. Erdman, *The Power of the Spirit* (Philadelphia: General Assembly of the Presbyterian Church, 1926).
191. *Christian Century*, 17 June 1926, p. 785; "Dr. Thompson Is Urged As Presbyterian Moderator," Erdman Papers.
192. Henry S. Coffin to Dorothy Coffin, 28 May 1926, Coffin Papers.
193. *Presbyterian*, 10 June 1926, p. 8.

194. *Minutes of GA*, 1926, 1:63, 67–72.
195. Ibid., 1:78.
196. Ibid., 1:79.
197. Ibid., 1:80, 79.
198. Ibid., 1:82–84.
199. Loetscher, *Broadening Church*, 132.
200. *Minutes of GA*, 1926, 1:86.
201. *Time*, 7 June 1926, p. 24.
202. *Christian Century*, 17 June 1926, pp. 788–89; *New York Times*, 1 June 1926, pp. 1, 11.
203. *Christian Century*, 17 June 1926, p. 789.
204. *Literary Digest*, 26 June 1926, p. 28. See also *New York Times*, 1 June 1926, p. 1.
205. *Christian Century*, 17 June 1926, p. 789.
206. *Report of the Special Commission of 1925 to the General Assembly of the Presbyterian Church in the U.S.A.* (Philadelphia: Office of the General Assembly, 1927), 20–21.
207. Loetscher, *Broadening Church*, 134.

Chapter 7

1. Rian, *Presbyterian Conflict*, 68–76; John W. Hart, "The Controversy within the Presbyterian Church, U.S.A., in the 1920's with Special Emphasis on the Reorganization of Princeton Theological Seminary" (Princeton University, 1978 typescript), 54–58, 61–64. Hart's work has been most helpful in the following discussion of the Princeton controversy.
2. *Minutes of GA*, 1926, 1:174.
3. Rian, *Presbyterian Conflict*, 67; Hart, "Controversy," 75. See also J. Gresham Machen, "The Action of the Presbytery of New Brunswick," *Presbyterian*, 1 March 1928, p. 14; and C. W. Hodge, "The Historical Position of Princeton Seminary," *Presbyterian*, 1 March 1928, pp. 27–28.
4. Hart, "Controversy," 75. See also J. Gresham Machen to Rockwell S. Brank, 16 April 1925, and J. Gresham Machen to Reid Dickson, 10 March 1925—Machen Papers.
5. Hart, "Controversy," 65.
6. J. Gresham Machen to Clarence E. Macartney, 6 February 1926, Machen Papers.
7. Hart, "Controversy," 66.
8. Macartney, *Autobiography*, 198.
9. *First Church Life*, 27 April 1952, p. 9, Macartney Papers.
10. Stonehouse, *Machen*, 384. See "Dr. Macartney Gets Call Here," *Chronical Telegraph* (Pittsburgh), 1 February 1927, Macartney Papers.
11. Stonehouse, *Machen*, 384–85. Quoted in Stonehouse, *Machen*, 386. That this was not a passing thought is confirmed by the reiteration of the exact

sentiment in a letter to Jr.o. Gibson Inkster on 12 May 1926. See J. Gresham Machen to Jno. Gibson Inkster, 12 May 1926, Machen Papers.

12. *Minutes of GA,* 1926, 1:174–75.

13. *New York Times,* 3 June 1926, p. 4.

14. Ibid.

15. See Carter, *Decline and Revival of the Social Gospel,* 128–29; Joseph R. Gusfield, *Symbolic Crusade: Status Politics and the American Temperance Movement,* 2d ed. (Urbana: University of Illinois Press, 1986), 107, 117; Robert M. Miller, *American Protestantism and Social Issues, 1919–1939* (Chapel Hill: University of North Carolina Press, 1958), 18–19, 52–53, 57–58.

16. Gusfield, *Symbolic Crusade,* 7–8; See also pp. 110, 122–26.

17. Stonehouse, *Machen,* 387.

18. J. Gresham Machen to Clarence E. Macartney, 24 May 1926, Machen Papers.

19. Clarence E. Macartney to J. Gresham Machen, 21 May 1926, Machen Papers.

20. *Presbyterian,* 10 June 1926, p. 17. See also *New York Times,* 3 June 1926, p. 1; Stonehouse, *Machen,* 389.

21. *Presbyterian,* 24 June 1926, p. 16; see also p. 17.

22. J. Gresham Machen to Francis Patton, 11 July 1926, Machen Papers. On Machen's refusal to comment publicly, see *New York Times,* 3 June 1926, p. 4.

23. *New York Times,* 3 June 1926, p. 4.

24. *R°port of the Special Committee To Visit Princeton Theological Seminary to the General Assembly of the Presbyterian Church in the U.S.A.* (Philadelphia: Office of the General Assembly, 1927), 4 (hereafter, *Special Committee*).

25. Ibid., 5–6.

26. Ibid., 8.

27. Hart, "Controversy," 76–77; *Special Committee,* 60–82.

28. *Special Committee,* 68, 75.

29. *Special Committee,* 51, 55.

30. *Special Committee,* 56; "Transcripts of the Hearings by the General Assembly Special Committee To Visit Princeton Theological Seminary, Jan. 5–6, 1927," 192, Machen Papers.

31. Hart, "Controversy," 78.

32. Ibid., 78–80; *Special Committee,* 106–19.

33. J. Gresham Machen, "Statement by J. Gresham Machen Submitted to the Committee Appointed by Action of the General Assembly of 1926" (n.p.: J. Gresham Machen, 1926), 22, quoted in Hart, "Controversy," 80.

34. Machen, "Statement," 117, quoted in Hart, "Controversy," 80.

35. Rian, *Presbyterian Conflict,* 63–67.

36. Ibid., 61–63.

37. Hart, "Controversy," 69–71.

38. *Special Committee,* 92, 96; Hart, "Controversy," 72.

39. *Special Committee,* 47–49, 50.

40. *Minutes of GA,* 1927, 1:19. See also chap. 8 below.

41. *New York Times*, 26 May 1927, p. 15.
42. Loetscher, *Broadening Church*, 144–45.
43. *New York Times*, 31 May 1927, p. 23; *Minutes of GA*, 1927, 1:87, 133–34.
44. *New York Times*, 31 May 1927, p. 23. The quote is a summary by the reporter.
45. J. Gresham Machen to K. C. Hill, 14 July 1927, Machen Papers, quoted in Ronald T. Clutter, "The Reorientation of Princeton Theological Seminary 1900–1929" (Th.D. diss., Dallas Theological Seminary, 1982), 196.
46. *New York Post*, 29 September 1927, quoted in Stonehouse, *Machen*, 430.
47. J. Gresham Machen, "The Attack upon Princeton Seminary: A Plea for Fair Play" (n.p.: J. Gresham Machen, 1927), 5, 16, 20–21, 28 (in Machen Papers).
48. Ibid., 26–27.
49. Ibid., 33–35.
50. Ibid., 38–39.
51. Clutter, "Reorientation," 205–11.
52. Clarence E. Macartney, "Shall Princeton Pass?" *Presbyterian Banner*, 5 January 1928, pp. 5–6.
53. *Presbyterian*, 3 May 1928, p. 21.
54. See George L. Haines, "The Princeton Theological Seminary, 1925–1960" (Ph.D. diss., New York University, 1966), 74–92; and below in this chapter.
55. *Minutes of GA*, 1928, 1:33. See also Rian, *Presbyterian Conflict*, 78.
56. *Presbyterian*, 24 May 1928, p. 12. Other reports estimate the signatories numbering as high as eleven thousand (Stonehouse, *Machen*, 435).
57. The only mention of the petition in the *Minutes of GA*, 1928, is acknowledgment of its reception in vol. 1 p. 33. Stonehouse suggests that the petition "may have influenced [the assembly's] decision to postpone action for another year" (*Machen*, 435).
58. *Minutes of GA*, 1928, 1:225–50; quote is from p. 41; *New York Times*, 27 May 1928, p. 21.
59. *New York Times*, 27 May 1928, p. 21.
60. *Minutes of GA*, 1928, 1:59. See also Hart, "Controversy," 99.
61. Hart, "Controversy," 100–101.
62. Ibid., 103.
63. Loetscher, *Broadening Church*, 146.
64. *Minutes of GA*, 1929, 1:78.
65. Quoted in Stonehouse, *Machen*, 439–40. Macartney also addressed the assembly on this issue. For his speech see *Presbyterian*, 6 June 1929, p. 23.
66. Marsden, "J. Gresham Machen, History, and Truth," 169.
67. *New York Times*, 28 May 1929, p. 35.
68. *Minutes of GA*, 1929, 1:133–34.
69. Hart, "Controversy," 108. See also Roark, "J. Gresham Machen and His Desire To Maintain a Doctrinally True Presbyterian Church," 119–21.
70. Quoted in Stonehouse, *Machen*, 442.

71. Stonehouse, *Machen*, 442–43.

72. Hart, "Controversy," 108; *Presbyterian*, 27 June 1929, p. 12. There was also at this time discussion of an independent board of missions which would come to fruition in 1933. See *Presbyterian*, 20 June 1929, p. 12.

73. J. Gresham Machen to Mary Gresham Machen, n.d., quoted in Stonehouse, *Machen*, 442.

74. Rian, *Presbyterian Conflict*, 88.

75. *Presbyterian*, 3 October 1929, p. 8, quoted in Rian, *Presbyterian Conflict*, 88.

76. J. Gresham Machen to Arthur Machen, 14 July 1929, Machen Papers. In this letter Machen noted that Schall had been pastor of the Presbyterian Church in Macon, Georgia.

77. Quoted in Stonehouse, *Machen*, 448. See *Presbyterian*, 2 July 1929, p. 16 for more on this organizational meeting.

78. "Refuses Position on Seminary Board," *Philadelphia Evening Public Ledger*, 18 October 1929, Macartney Papers.

79. J. Gresham Machen to Arthur W. Machen, Jr., 14 July 1929, Machen Papers.

80. J. Gresham Machen to A. W. Machen, n.d. in file "1928–29, A. W. Machen Jr.," Machen Papers.

81. "Refuses Position on Seminary Board," Macartney Papers.

82. Machen, "Christianity and Culture," 7.

83. See chap. 8 below.

84. Stonehouse, *Machen*, 449–51.

85. Ibid., 454, 460; Hart, "Controversy," 110.

86. Stonehouse, *Machen*, 456.

87. Machen, "Attack upon Princeton Seminary," 26.

88. Machen, *What Is Christianity?* 231–32.

89. See Robert L. Kelly, *Theological Education in America: A Study of One Hundred Sixty-One Theological Schools in the United States and Canada* (New York: George H. Doran, 1924), 82, 84, 87, 88, 90–91, 100; William Adams Brown, *The Education of American Ministers*, vol. 1. *Ministerial Education in America: Summary and Interpretation* (New York: Institute of Social and Religious Research, 1934), 4, 6–12, 81–84, 120–28; Luther A. Weigle, "A Survey of Contemporary Theological Education," *Bulletin of the American Association of Theological Schools* 5 (September 1926): 11–12.

90. Kelly, *Theological Education*, 88.

91. Ibid., 296–97, 88, 344.

92. *Charter and Constitution of Westminster Theological Seminary* (Philadelphia, May 1930), 15, quoted in Hart, "Controversy," 111.

93. Machen, *What Is Christianity?* 232–33.

94. *Presbyterian*, 3 October 1929, p. 10. This quote is a paraphrase of Wilson's remarks as reported by those attending the meeting.

95. Ibid., 10.

96. Ibid., 26.

97. Machen, *What Is Christianity?* 226. Somewhat ironically, while announcing these high academic standards Machen felt called to explain that the school would not be a Bible college. "We are not conducting a school for layworkers at Westminster Seminary," he said, "useful though such a school would be" (Machen, *What Is Christianity?* 226).

98. *Presbyterian*, 22 August 1929, p. 24.

99. *Presbyterian*, 3 October 1929, p. 26.

100. Machen, *What Is Christianity?* 231, 226–30.

101. Hart, "Controversy," 111.

102. Machen, *What Is Christianity?* 224, 230; idem, *Christianity and Liberalism*, 16.

103. Machen, *What Is Christianity?* 136–37, 230, 232; idem, "Attack upon Princeton Seminary," 35.

104. Machen, *God Transcendent*, 57.

105. Machen, *What Is Christianity?* 22.

106. Machen, "Christianity and Culture," 7.

107. Machen, *What Is Christianity?* 129, 251–52. See also Machen, *What Is Christianity?* 169; idem, "Christianity and Culture," 14–15.

108. Arthur M. Byers, Jr., *Biographical Catalogue of Princeton Theological Seminary* (Princeton: Princeton Theological Seminary, 1977), lxv, lxvii–lxviii, lxxv.

109. Haines, "Princeton," 80–82.

110. Olmstead, *History of Religion*, 574, quoted in Haines, "Princeton," 81. Olmstead also notes the guest professorships of Emil Brunner and Josef Hromadka in 1938 and 1939, respectively (Olmstead, *History of Religion*, 574).

111. *Minutes of GA*, 1934, 1:114–16.

112. Rian, *Presbyterian Conflict*, 99.

Chapter 8

1. J. Gresham Machen to Rev. Henry G. Martin, 8 January 1925, Machen Papers. See also Patterson, "Speer," 138–39. For accounts of conservative suspicions of mission work earlier in the decade, see Patterson, "Speer," 128–33 and Loetscher, *Broadening Church*, 107.

2. Robert E. Speer to J. Gresham Machen, 4 April 1929, Speer Papers.

3. Loetscher, *Broadening Church*, 133–36; J. Gresham Machen to Robert E. Speer, 4 May 1929, Speer Papers.

4. Quoted in Charles R. Erdman to Robert E. Speer, 6 September 1928, Speer Papers.

5. J. Gresham Machen, "Can Evangelical Christians Support Our Foreign Board?" typed manuscript, April 1929, 2–6, Speer Papers; Patterson, "Speer," 139.

6. Robert E. Speer, *Are Foreign Missions Done For?* (New York: Board of Foreign Missions of the Presbyterian Church U.S.A., 1928), 1.

7. Machen, "Can Evangelical Christians," 7–10.
8. Ibid., 7; Patterson, "Speer," 140–41.
9. Machen, "Can Evangelical Christians," 8.
10. Ibid., 11.
11. Ibid., 12.
12. Robert E. Speer to J. Gresham Machen, 30 April 1929, 1–2, 7–10, Speer Papers. See also Patterson, "Speer," 129–30.
13. Robert E. Speer to J. Gresham Machen, 30 April 1929, 16.
14. Ibid., 17–18.
15. Ibid., 20.
16. Wheeler, *Speer*, 32.
17. Ibid., 22–23, 25–29.
18. Ibid., 22–23, 26–30, 32.
19. Ibid., 32–33; see also p. 35.
20. Wheeler, *Speer*, 36–37, 39, 41–42; Homrighausen, "In Memoriam, Charles Erdman," 36.
21. Wheeler, *Speer*, 42, 46; Patterson, "Speer," 5.
22. Patterson, "Speer," 5.
23. Wheeler, *Speer*, 38. Patterson notes that Speer, in a letter to his father from Princeton in 1886, "expressed his wish to hear Professors Tucker, Harris, and Moore of Andover Seminary preach at Princeton" (Patterson, "Speer," 6, n. 9). This is not to imply that at this early stage in Speer's career, he had necessarily or in any systematic way adopted all of the doctrines taught by these men. It is, however, to suggest that at this point in his life Speer was introduced to liberal theology and found it and at least some of its proponents appealing.
24. Robert E. Speer to Robert M. Speer, 27 September 1885, Speer Papers, quoted in Patterson, "Speer," 6.
25. Robert E. Speer to Robert M. Speer, 9 October 1885, Speer Papers, quoted in Patterson, "Speer," 6.
26. Wheeler, *Speer*, 49.
27. Patterson, "Speer," 6.
28. Patterson, "Speer," 8–9.
29. Robert E. Speer to Robert M. Speer, 27 March 1887, Speer Papers, quoted in Patterson, "Speer," 9. This explicit emphasis on the future fate of the heathen as a missionary motive seems to have waned in Speer's later thought. While he did not deny that questions of eternal destiny were important, he also claimed that "no man is lost for not accepting a Saviour of whom he has never heard." It appears, therefore, that Speer accepted the Andover doctrine of "future probation." The "supreme argument for foreign missions," Speer asserted, ". . . is Christ Himself, and what he reveals and signifies" (Robert E. Speer, *Christianity and the Nations* [New York: Fleming H. Revell, 1910], 33, 17). See also R. Pierce Beaver, "Missionary Motivation through Three Centuries," in *Reinterpretation in American Church History*, ed. Jerald C. Brauer (Chicago: University of Chicago Press, 1968), 129–33, 144–45.
30. Patterson, "Speer," 12.

31. Ibid., 13–14, 20, 32; Wheeler, *Speer*, 60, 104, 138. Speer spoke at the student's meeting at Keswick in 1890 (Sherwood Eddy, *Pathfinders of the World Missionary Crusade* [New York: Abingdon-Cokesbury, 1945], 267). As Patterson notes, Speer's interest in premillennialism declined in his later years ("Speer," 14, n. 30).

32. Robert E. Speer, "D. L. Moody," Address to the Northfield (MA) Schools on Founder's Day, 1931, Speer Papers quoted in Patterson, "Speer," 12.

33. Patterson, "Speer," 15, 18.

34. Ibid., 16; Hopkins, *John R. Mott*, 83.

35. *Annual Report* (New York: Board of Foreign Missions of the Presbyterian Church in the U.S.A., 1892), 6, quoted in Patterson, "Speer," 22.

36. Eddy, *Pathfinders*, 263.

37. Wheeler, *Speer*, 70–85, 92, 103–22, 184; Eddy, *Pathfinders*, 265.

38. Patterson, "Speer," 185; John A. Mackay, "The Missionary Statesman," *Princeton Seminary Bulletin* 42 (Summer 1948): 10.

39. Wheeler, *Speer*, 180–81; John F. Piper, Jr., "Robert E. Speer, Christian Statesman in War and Peace," *Journal of Presbyterian History* 47 (September 1969): 218. Notably, Speer had serious reservations about the ill-fated Inter-Church World Movement (Wheeler, *Speer*, 175–76).

40. Robert E. Speer, "Unity in the Mission Field," in *The Problem of Christian Unity*, ed. Frederick Lynch (New York: Macmillan, 1921), 65.

41. Patterson, "Speer," 24.

42. Ibid., 26; Wheeler, *Speer*, 176; Eddy, *Pathfinders*, 267.

43. Eddy, *Pathfinders*, 267.

44. Robert E. Speer, "Paul, the Great Missionary Example," in *The Student Missionary Enterprise: Addresses and Discussions of the Second International Convention of the Student Volunteer Movement for Foreign Missions*, ed. Max W. Moorhead (Boston: T. O. Metcalf, 1894[?]), 12.

45. Ibid., 14.

46. In the course of his busy schedule Speer somehow found time to author or edit some sixty-seven books. A voracious reader, consuming on average seventy-five books a year during his working years, he borrowed ideas wherever he found them (Wheeler, *Speer*, 9, 14). Claude Welch claims that Horace Bushnell, who, as shall be seen, had a profound influence on Speer, was also a difficult theologian to classify (Welch, *Protestant Thought*, 1:144).

47. Patterson, "Speer," vi; Sandeen, "Fundamentals," 68; *Dictionary of American Biography*, ed. Garrity, Suppl. 4, "1946–1950," s.v. "Speer, Robert Elliott."

48. William R. Hutchison, "Modernism and Missions: The Liberal Search for an Exportable Christianity, 1875–1935," in *Missionary Enterprise in China and America*, ed. Fairbank, 128–29; Handy, *Christian America*, 113.

49. Patterson, "Speer," 14; Sandeen, *Roots of Fundamentalism*, 180; Robert E. Speer, "The Challenge of Missions," in *Victory in Christ: A Report of the Princeton Conference, 1916* (Philadelphia: Board of Managers of Princeton Conference, 1916), 209–18; idem, "Second Coming of Christ."

50. See Robert E. Speer, "God in Christ the Only Revelation of the Fatherhood of God" and "Foreign Missions; or, World-Wide Evangelism" in *The Fundamentals*, ed. Dixon, Meyer, and Torrey, 3:61–75, 12:64–84.

51. Hutchison, "Modernism and Missions," 128–29.

52. See Wheeler, *Speer*, 263–64; Patterson, 34, n. 79; and ch. 9 below.

53. Speer, *Some Living Issues*, 136; Wheeler, *Speer*, 155–61.

54. See *Dictionary of American Biography*, ed. Garrity, Suppl. 4, "1946–1950" s.v. "Speer, Robert Elliott."

55. Sydney E. Ahlstrom, "Horace Bushnell," in *A Handbook of Christian Theologians*, ed. Dean G. Peerman and Martin E. Marty (New York: New American Library, 1965), 36.

56. Ibid., 37–38; Barbara Cross, *Horace Bushnell, Minister to a Changing America* (Chicago: University of Chicago Press, 1958), 1–4, 10–12.

57. H. Shelton Smith, ed., *Horace Bushnell* (New York: Oxford University Press, 1965), 3, 106.

58. See Ahlstrom, "Horace Bushnell," 36–39; Smith, *Bushnell*, 106.

59. See, e.g., Conrad Cherry, ed., *Horace Bushnell: Sermons* (New York: Paulist, 1985), 1; and Horace Bushnell, *God in Christ: Discourses Delivered at New Haven, Cambridge, and Andover with a Preliminary Dissertation on Language* (London: Richard D. Dickinson, n.d.), 304.

60. Bushnell, *God in Christ*, 304.

61. Horace Bushnell, *Nature and the Supernatural As Together Constituting the One System of God* (New York: Charles Scribner, 1871), 320.

62. Horace Bushnell, *Building Eras in Religion* (New York: Charles Scribner's Sons, 1881), 389.

63. Bushnell, *Building Eras*, 459, 425, 444.

64. Ibid., 456.

65. See Welch, *Protestant Thought*, 1:259–61.

66. Smith, *Bushnell*, 97–101.

67. Bushnell, *Building Eras*, 456.

68. Bushnell, *God in Christ*, 286–87, 338–39, 356.

69. Speer, *Some Living Issues*, 31; idem, *When Christianity Was New* (New York: Fleming H. Revell, 1939), 29; idem, *Christian Realities* (New York: Fleming H. Revell, 1935), 44–45. The essay Speer referred to was "The Character of Jesus Forbids His Possible Classification with Men," and the sermon was "Our Duty To Live to God on Common Occasions and in Small Things." The designation of Speer as an "Apostle of Christian Unity" was by Samuel M. Cavert (quoted in Wheeler, *Speer*, 181).

70. Quoted in Robert E. Speer to J. Gresham Machen, 30 April 1929, Speer Papers. See also Speer, *Some Living Issues*, 136; and Wheeler, *Speer*, 184–87.

71. Bushnell, *God in Christ*, 304; Robert E. Speer, *Missionary Principles and Practice: A Discussion of Christian Missions and of Some Criticisms upon Them* (New York: Fleming H. Revell, 1902), 122. See also Robert E. Speer, *The Finality of Jesus Christ* (New York: Fleming H. Revell, 1933), 288; and idem, *The Deity of Christ* (New York: Fleming H. Revell, 1909), 6. In *The Finality of Jesus Christ* Speer claims, "Christianity is . . . not a doctrine, or a method, or

a philosophy, or a theology—except derivatively. It is a Person—Christ—and a life in and from that Person" (Speer, *Finality*, 288). In *The Deity of Christ* Speer acknowledges his debt to Bushnell on matters of Christology, writing, "I believe, first of all, in the deity of our Lord Jesus Christ because of His *character*; for it seems to me, in the great language of Horace Bushnell, that 'the character of Jesus forbids His possible classification with men.' The argument of the whole volume, 'Nature and the Supernatural,' is concentrated by Bushnell, in that one chapter, 'The Character of Jesus Forbidding His Possible Classification with Men'" (Speer, *The Deity of Christ*, 13).

72. Speer, *Christian Realities*, 18, 21, 27, 23–24.

73. Robert E. Speer, *A Young Man's Questions* (New York: Fleming H. Revell, 1903), 31.

74. Speer, "Paul, the Great Missionary Example," 12. See also Speer, *Christian Realities*, 50, 52, 57.

75. Robert E. Speer, *The Gospel and the New World* (New York: Fleming H. Revell, 1919), 236.

76. Speer, *Finality*, 205.

77. Speer, *Seeking the Mind of Christ*, 53–54.

78. Speer, *Deity of Christ*, 26; idem, *Gospel and the New World*, 239–41; idem, "Paul, the Great Missionary Example," 12.

79. Speer, *Christian Realities*, 45.

80. Speer, *Some Living Issues*, 141–42.

81. Speer, *Christianity and Nations*, 337.

82. Speer, "Unity in the Mission Field," 67. See also Speer, *Gospel and the New World*, 241.

83. Speer, *Some Living Issues*, 136. See also Speer, *Gospel and the New World*, 191.

84. Ibid., 136, 78.

85. Speer, *Gospel and the New World*, 230, 234, 231–32.

86. See, e.g., Fosdick, "Shall the Fundamentalists Win?" 174–75.

87. Robert E. Speer to J. Gresham Machen, 30 April 1929, p. 7 (in Speer Papers).

88. Though social intimacy does not necessarily entail theological intimacy, there is probably more than a little theological significance in the fact that Speer and Coffin were "life-long friends" and retired to the same town. Coffin helped conduct Speer's funeral service and led the graveside ceremony (Wheeler, *Speer*, 263–64; Patterson, "Speer," 34, n. 79).

89. Speer, *Gospel and the New World*, 241.

90. Speer, "Unity in the Mission Field," 81.

91. Ibid., 67–68. See also Speer, *Some Living Issues*, 82.

92. Quoted in Wheeler, *Speer*, 181.

93. Speer, *Principles and Practice*, 540. See also James A. Patterson, "Robert E. Speer, J. Gresham Machen, and the Presbyterian Board of Foreign Missions," *American Presbyterians: Journal of Presbyterian History* 64 (Spring 1986): 59. On Bushnell's similar thoughts concerning the necessity of conflict in the early church, see Bushnell, *God in Christ*, 320–22.

94. Speer, *Principles and Practice*, 540; idem, *The Church and Missions* (New York: George H. Doran, 1926), 149.

95. See Wheeler, *Speer*, 219.

96. Speer, "Challenge of Missions," 211, 214.

97. Speer, "Unity in the Mission Field," 69.

98. Patterson, "Speer," 26; Piper, "Robert E. Speer," 223. See also Speer, "Challenge of Missions," 214.

99. Missions were, to Speer, *the* basic function of the church. See Speer, *Christian Realities*, 227.

100. John F. Piper, Jr., *The American Churches in World War I* (Athens: Ohio University Press, 1985), 195, 182.

101. Robert E. Speer, *The War and the Religious Outlook* (New York: Association, 1919), 27, quoted in Piper, *American Churches*, 182–83.

102. Speer, *Gospel and the New World*, 58.

103. See, e.g., Speer, *Principles and Practice*, 43; idem, *Christianity and Nations*, 394; Piper, *American Churches*, 51. This section owes a good deal to Piper, "Robert E. Speer," esp. 218–25; and John F. Piper, "Robert E. Speer on Christianity and Race," *Journal of Presbyterian History* 61 (Summer 1983): 227–47.

104. Speer, *Gospel and the New World*, 22, 21.

105. Ibid., 98; see also p. 146.

106. Speer, *When Christianity Was New*, 102; idem, *Gospel and the New World*, 299.

107. Piper, "Christianity and Race," 228.

108. Robert E. Speer, *Race and Race Relations: A Christian View of Human Contacts* (New York: Fleming H. Revell, 1924), 343. On prevailing views of race relations, see Piper, "Christianity and Race," 231–32. See also Piper, "Robert E. Speer," 221–24. Speer opposed Hitler's racist philosophy on the same grounds (*When Christianity Was New*, 103–34).

109. Robert E. Speer, "Missionary Convictions," Northfield talk, 3 July 1898, Speer Papers, quoted in Piper, "Christianity and Race," 230.

110. Speer, *Gospel and the New World*, 70.

111. See Piper, "Christianity and Race," 233, 244.

112. Piper, "Christianity and Race," 229. Piper also notes the importance of John 10:16 for Speer on this issue.

113. Ibid., 229. See Robert E. Speer, *Of One Blood: A Short Study of the Race Problem* (New York: Council of Women for Home Missions & Missionary Education Movement of the United States and Canada, 1924). This work was an abridged version of Speer, *Race and Race Relations*.

114. Speer, *Of One Blood*, 1.

115. Piper, "Christianity and Race," 229.

116. John F. Piper, Jr. to author, 5 February 1988; H. McKennie Goodpasture, "Robert E. Speer's Legacy," *Occasional Bulletin of Missionary Research* 2 (April 1978): 38.

117. Speer, *Principles and Practice*, 457. See also Speer, *Church and Missions*, 221; idem, *Some Living Issues*, 202.

118. Speer, *Some Living Issues*, 193, 195–97.

119. Ibid., 202–3. See also Robert E. Speer, *The Principles of Jesus Applied to Some Questions of Today* (New York: Fleming H. Revell, 1902), 84; idem, *Church and Missions*, 221.

120. Robert E. Speer, "Christianity and International Relations," in *Christianity and Modern Thought*, ed. Ralph H. Gabriel (New Haven: Yale University Press, 1924), 180, 183, 185, 188–94. See also Speer, *Some Living Issues*, 208; idem, *Gospel and the New World*, 29.

121. Speer, *Principles of Jesus*, 115.

122. Robert E. Speer, *The Unfinished Task of Foreign Missions* (New York: Fleming H. Revell, 1926), 343. This aspect of Speer's thought seems to have remained constant throughout his life. See Speer, *Principles of Jesus*, 225; idem, *Christian Realities*, 161–62; idem, *The New Opportunity of the Church* (New York: Macmillan, 1919), 13.

123. Speer, *Church and Missions*, 220–21.

124. Speer, *Some Living Issues*, 270.

125. Speer, *Gospel and the New World*, 25–26. See also Piper, "Robert E. Speer," 218–21, 224–25.

126. Ibid., 137.

127. See Speer, *Principles and Practice*, 39; idem, *Some Living Issues*, 114–15.

128. Robert E. Speer, "Our Country and National Missions," *Presbyterian Magazine* 33 (1927): 642, quoted in Patterson, "Speer," 30.

129. Patterson, "Speer," 29–31. On temperance and Sabbatarianism see Speer, *A Young Man's Questions*, 91–101, 70–81. On religion in the home see Speer, *When Christianity Was New*, 9–33.

130. See Speer, *Principles of Jesus*, 115; idem, *Finality*, 225.

131. Patterson, "Speer," 80–87; William R. Hutchison, *Errand to the World: American Protestant Thought and Foreign Missions* (Chicago: University of Chicago Press, 1987), 158; William Ernest Hocking et al., *Re-Thinking Missions: A Laymen's Inquiry after One Hundred Years* (New York: Harper & Brothers, 1932), xi.

132. Patterson, "Speer," 90; Hutchison, *Errand*, 158–59.

133. Hutchison, "Modernism and Missions," 127.

134. Hocking, *Re-Thinking Missions*, 49, 20, 32–33, 44, 47.

135. Ibid., 25, 35, 64–65, 89, 26.

136. Patterson, "Speer," 94–98.

137. Hutchison, "Modernism and Missions," 127–28; idem, *Errand*, 165; Patterson, "Speer," 96–98.

138. *Christianity Today* 3 (December 1932): 20.

139. Hutchison, *Errand*, 166–67; J. Gresham Machen, "Modernism and the Board of Foreign Missions of the Presbyterian Church in the U.S.A." (n.p.: J. Gresham Machen, 1933), 12–18 (in Machen Papers).

140. Pearl S. Buck, "The Laymen's Mission Report," *Christian Century*, 23 November 1932, pp. 1434, 1436–37.

141. Hutchison, *Errand*, 167; Pearl S. Buck, "Is There a Case for Foreign Missions?" *Harper's* 166 (January 1933): 148–49, 152, 150.

142. Buck, "Is There a Case for Foreign Missions," 151.

143. Hutchison, *Errand*, 169; Patterson, "Speer," 153–54.

144. See Patterson, "Speer," 86, n.17, 99.

145. Robert E. Speer, *"Re-Thinking Missions" Examined: An Attempt at a Just Review of the Report of the Appraisal Commission of the Laymen's Foreign Missions Inquiry* (New York: Fleming H. Revell, 1933), 7, 49, 50, 56, 14–25, 29–31.

146. Ibid., 29–31.

147. Ibid., 59–60, 63–64.

148. Machen, "Modernism and Missions," 1, 6–18.

149. Ibid., 58–60. Machen leveled similar charges against Speer in a review of Speer's *Some Living Issues* ("Dr. Machen Surveys Dr. Speer's New Book," *Christianity Today* 1 [October 1930]: 9–11, 15); and in idem, "Dr. Robert E. Speer and His Latest Book," *Christianity Today* 4 [May 1933]: 15–16, 22–26, where he notes the "underlying confusion" in Speer's mind.

150. Machen, "Modernism and Missions," 62–63. See also Machen, "Dr. Robert E. Speer and His Latest Book," 25.

151. Speer, *Principles and Practice*, 119.

152. See, e.g., Speer, *Some Living Issues*, 136; idem, *Christian Realities*, 134–35.

153. Speer, *Some Living Issues*, 267–70.

154. Machen, "Modernism and Missions," 63. See also Machen, "Dr. Robert E. Speer and His Latest Book," 25.

155. Ibid., 9–10, 12.

156. Patterson, "Speer," 149.

157. Clarence E. Macartney, "'Renouncing Missions' or 'Modernism Unmasked'," *Presbyterian*, 26 January 1933, p. 6.

158. *Christianity Today* 3 (April 1933): 23.

159. Charles R. Erdman to the Session of the First Presbyterian Church, Pittsburgh, 23 March 1933, Speer Papers. Though this letter went out over Erdman's signature it was drafted by Speer and another staff member of the board. See Charles R. Erdman to Robert E. Speer, 25 March 1933, Speer Papers; *Christianity Today* 3 (April 1933): 22.

160. Charles R. Erdman to the Session of the First Presbyterian Church, Pittsburgh, 23 March 1933, Speer Papers.

161. *Christianity Today* 3 (April 1933): 23. See also *Christianity Today* 4 (May 1933): 36. For Macartney's statements on Pearl Buck, see *Christianity Today* 4 (May 1933): 34–36.

162. *Christianity Today* 3 (April 1933): 19–21.

163. "A Statement by Mr. Robert E. Speer to the Presbytery of New Brunswick at Its Meeting in Trenton, NJ, April 11, 1933," Speer Papers.

164. Ibid., 8.

165. Ibid., 15.

294

Notes

166. *Christianity Today* 3 (April 1933): 23; *Christianity Today* 4 (May 1933):
31–34.
167. See *Christianity Today* 4 (May 1933): 34–36; Patterson, "Speer," 153–
55.
168. *Christianity Today* 4 (June 1933): 10–12.
169. Ibid., 13.
170. Machen wrote, "The objective of the whole movement to my mind was
from the beginning the forming of the new Board, since there was not one
chance in a thousand that any nominee of the Bible-believing party in the church
would be elected by the General Assembly" (J. Gresham Machen to Clarence
E. Macartney, 5 June 1933, Machen Papers).
171. See Clarence E. Macartney to J. Gresham Machen, telegram, 27 May
1933, Machen Papers; J. Gresham Machen to Clarence E. Macartney, 5 June
1933, Machen Papers.
172. Rian, *Presbyterian Conflict*, 146.
173. Speer, *"Re-Thinking Missions" Examined*, 59–60.
174. Speer, *Gospel and the New World*, 19.
175. Speer, *Principles and Practice*, 540.
176. Speer, *Some Living Issues*, 270.
177. Speer, "Christianity and International Relations," 194.
178. Speer, *Gospel and the New World*, 98.
179. Speer, "Christianity and International Relations," 184–85.
180. Speer, *Gospel and the New World*, 25–26.
181. Piper, "Robert E. Speer," 223.
182. See Speer, *Principles and Practice*, 39; Patterson, "Speer," 12–13.

Chapter 9

1. *Minutes of GA*, 1934, 1:110, 114–15; Rian, *Presbyterian Conflict*, 151–52.
2. Clarence Macartney, "Presbyterians, Awake!" *Presbyterian*, 19 July 1934,
p. 8.
3. *Presbyterian Tribune*, 1 November 1934, quoted in Rian, *Presbyterian
Conflict*, 170.
4. J. Gresham Machen, "Statement to the Special Committee of the Presbytery of New Brunswick" (Philadelphia: J. Gresham Machen, 1934), 10,
14–15.
5. Rian, *Presbyterian Conflict*, 175–76, 184; *Christianity Today* 5 (May 1935):
292–93.
6. Clarence E. Macartney to J. Gresham Machen, 26 June 1935, Machen
Papers.
7. J. Gresham Machen to Clarence Macartney, 28 June 1935, Machen Papers.
Though Machen's response to Macartney was cordial, his frustrations with his
former ally came through in a letter to his sister-in-law, when he described

Macartney as "a very distressing man" (J. Gresham Machen to Mrs. Arthur W. Machen, 4 July 1935, Machen Papers).

8. Ibid.

9. "Covenant of the Constitutional Covenant Union," quoted in Rian, *Presbyterian Conflict*, 219.

10. *Christianity Today* 6 (February 1936): 193–95. The immediate cause of this ultimatum was some editorial statements by Samuel G. Craig (editor of *Christianity Today* and a trustee of Westminster) that questioned the wisdom of the independent board and the Constitutional Covenant Union. See Rian, *Presbyterian Conflict*, 97–100, 220–21; Stonehouse, *Machen*, 496–97; *Christianity Today* 6 (September 1935): 73–74.

11. Clarence E. Macartney to the Faculty, Westminster Theological Seminary, 11 November 1935, Machen Papers. See also the faculty response in Faculty to Clarence E. Macartney, 23 November 1935, Machen Papers; and Rian, *Presbyterian Conflict*, 300–301.

12. See "Minutes of the Meeting of the Board of Trustees of Westminster Theological Seminary Held January 7, 1936," Machen Papers; *Christianity Today* 6 (February 1936): 193–96.

13. *Christianity Today* 6 (February 1936): 195.

14. See Clarence E. Macartney to Dr. Edmonds, n.d., box 1935–36, Machen Papers. Unlike Craig, Macartney believed that the independent board was not unconstitutional (J. Gresham Machen to Clarence E. Macartney, 9 May 1936, Machen Papers).

15. Rian, *Presbyterian Conflict*, 212.

16. J. Gresham Machen to Clarence E. Macartney, 9 May 1936, Machen Papers.

17. Ibid.

18. *Minutes of GA*, 1936, 1:83–101, 138–42; Rian, *Presbyterian Conflict*, 227.

19. J. Gresham Machen, "The Church of God," *Presbyterian Guardian* 2 (June 1936): 98, quoted in Dallas M. Roark, "J. Gresham Machen: The Doctrinally True Presbyterian Church," *Journal of Presbyterian History* 43 (June 1965): 124.

20. Rian, *Presbyterian Conflict*, 237–43.

21. Stonehouse, *Machen*, 506–8.

22. *Presbyterian Guardian* 3 (February 13, 1937): 187.

23. Homrighausen, "In Memoriam, Charles Rosenbury Erdman," 36.

24. Wheeler, *Speer*, 251.

25. Speer wrote a number of books and lectured widely in his retirement in addition to serving as president of the Princeton Board of Trustees from 1937 until his death in 1947. Charles Erdman held the office of president of the Board of Foreign Missions until 1941 and carried on an active preaching ministry almost until his death in 1960 (Board of Trustees of Princeton Seminary, "Robert E. Speer Memorial Minute," *Princeton Seminary Bulletin* (Summer 1948): 14; "Dr. Erdman Dies; Funeral Thursday," *Princeton Herald*, 11 May 1960 [in Erdman Papers]).

26. Noyes, *Coffin*, 180, 191–98.
27. Ibid., 222. Coffin's biographer claims that "Coffin's liberalism remained basically unchanged" but then goes on to state, "Although he did not specifically give up old beliefs or adopt new ones, a new accent came into his preaching and writing during the Thirties and Forties, which was not unrelated to the contemporary trend in theological thought" (Noyes, *Coffin*, 221–22). Though Coffin did not specifically renounce any of his former beliefs, his "new accent" indicates a significant change. Nevertheless, see Coffin's impassioned defense of liberalism in Henry S. Coffin, *Religion Yesterday and Today* (Nashville: Cokesbury, 1940), 143.
28. Henry S. Coffin, *God Confronts Man in History* (New York: Charles Scribner's Sons, 1947), 122. For an early manifestation of this alteration see Henry S. Coffin, *God's Turn* (New York: Harper & Brothers, 1934), 7.
29. See, e.g., Coffin, *Some Christian Convictions*, 122; idem, *A More Christian Industrial Order*, 81.
30. Coffin, *God Confronts Man in History*, 54.
31. Coffin, *Yesterday and Today*, 61–63.
32. Ibid., 105–7.
33. Ibid., 52, 172.
34. The phrase is William Hutchison's. See Hutchison, *Modernist Impulse*, 2.
35. Coffin, *Yesterday and Today*, 171–72.
36. Coffin, *Social Rebuilding*, 14, 36. See also Coffin, *Ten Commandments*, 7.
37. Henry S. Coffin, *Communion through Preaching: The Monstrance of the Gospel* (New York: Charles Scribner's Sons, 1952), 108.
38. Coffin, *Yesterday and Today*, 32–33.
39. Coffin, *God Confronts Man in History*, 87.
40. Ibid., 118–19.
41. Macartney, "Warm Hearts," 315, 317–18. See also Clarence E. Macartney, "The Opportunity of the 149th General Assembly," *Presbyterian*, 27 May 1937, p. 1.
42. Ibid., 317.
43. "Dr. Macartney Dies after Long Illness," *Pittsburgh(?) Sun Telegraph*, 20 February 1959 (in Macartney Papers).
44. *General Assembly Daily News*, 21 May 1947, p. 3 (in Macartney Papers); Paul C. Johnston to Clarence E. Macartney, 21 July 1937, Macartney Papers; Kurtz, "Macartney," 132–33.
45. *Christianity Today* 2 (May 1931): 19–20.
46. *Presbyterian Guardian*, 6 July 1936, pp. 163–64; *Christianity Today* 8 (July 1937): 49–50.
47. *Christianity Today* 8 (July 1937): 49.
48. Rian, *Presbyterian Conflict*, 262–69.
49. Kurtz, "Macartney," 138–39.
50. Macartney, *Autobiography*, 211–12. See also "Business Men's Religious

Club Grows from 12 to 1600 Members," unidentified newspaper clipping, 16 March 1946, Macartney Papers; and Russell, *Voices*, 197.

51. Kurtz, "Macartney," 137.

52. See Kurtz, "Macartney," xi; "A Great Man Has Fallen," *News–Tribune*, undated clipping, Macartney Papers.

53. Macartney, "A Man under Authority," Macartney Papers; "Clarence Edward Macartney, M.A., D.D., LL.D., Litt.D." 5 April 1952, Macartney Papers.

54. Nancy M. Rademacher to author, 12 February 1988.

55. See Kurtz, "Macartney," 432; J. Clyde Henry to Robert Lamont, 31 December 1956, Macartney Papers.

56. Hirschfeld, "Baltimore," 32.

57. Machen, *Christianity and Liberalism*, 15–16.

58. Coffin, "The Claims of the Church upon Christians," in *University Sermons*, 75.

59. Bryan, "Applied Christianity," 12.

60. Charles Erdman, "Making the Nation Christian," 8; Patterson, "Speer," 30–31. On Speer's view of the mission of America see also Speer, *Gospel and the New World*, 150–51; and Patterson, "Speer," 169–74.

61. Macartney, "America, Her Great Leaders, and God," Macartney Papers; Clarence E. Macartney, "Bought with a Price," 29 May 1932, Macartney Papers.

62. Macartney, "Bought with a Price."

63. Sandeen, *Roots of Fundamentalism*, 172, 251, 254, 260.

64. Ibid., 170.

65. Marsden, *Fundamentalism and American Culture*, 4, 33.

66. Machen, *Christianity and Liberalism*, 18.

67. *New York Times Magazine*, 28 November 1926, p. 18.

68. Bryan, *Heart to Heart Appeals*, 128.

69. Erdman, *Spirit of Christ*, 11.

70. Speer, *Gospel and the New World*, 236.

71. Speer, *Christian Realities*, 23.

72. Edwin Seligman, ed. *Encyclopedia of the Social Sciences*, (New York: Macmillan, 1937), s.v. "Fundamentalism." This section follows Marsden, *Fundamentalism and American Culture*, 212–21.

73. Furniss, *Fundamentalist Controversy*, 39; Robert Handy, "Fundamentalism and Modernism in Perspective," *Religion in Life* 24 (Summer 1955): 393; Hofstadter, *Anti-Intellectualism*, 130.

74. Bryan, "Modern Arena," 3. See also Bryan, "Menace of Darwinism," 7.

75. Marsden, "J. Gresham Machen, History, and Truth," 157–58, 164, 166, 162.

76. Machen, *What Is Faith?* 249.

77. See Marsden, *Fundamentalism and American Culture*, 214–16.

78. Marsden, *Fundamentalism and American Culture*, 214–15.

79. See, e.g., Loetscher, *Broadening Church*, 117; Edward J. Carnell, *The*

Case for Orthodox Theology (Philadelphia: Westminster, 1959), 114; Roark, "J. Gresham Machen: The Doctrinally True Presbyterian Church," 126; Kihong Kim, "Presbyterian Conflict in the Early Twentieth Century: Ecclesiology in the Princeton Tradition and the Emergence of Presbyterian Fundamentalism" (Ph.D. diss., Drew University, 1983), 211.

80. Machen, *What Is Christianity?* 113.
81. Coffin, *Some Christian Convictions*, 186; idem, *University Sermons*, 75.
82. Robert E. Speer, "The Church a Missionary Society," *Presbyterian*, 28 January 1937, p. 1.
83. Warfield, *Selected Shorter Works*, ed. Meeter, quoted in Rogers and McKim, *Authority and Interpretation*, 329.
84. Machen, *What Is Christianity?* 162, 251.
85. Ibid., 169.
86. Todd, "Heritage", 20.
87. McFeeters, *Covenanters in America*, 38, 154–61.
88. Bryan and Bryan, *Memoirs*, 34.
89. Szasz, "Three Fundamentalist Leaders," 182; Bryan, "Applied Christianity," 11.
90. Smith, "Bryan and the Social Gospel," 53.
91. Erdman, "Bible Teachings about Education," 12.
92. "Young People Are Indifferent Moderator Says," unidentified newspaper clipping, Erdman Papers.
93. See Speer, "Unity in the Mission Field," 67; Coffin, *Social Rebuilding*, 32.
94. Compare, e.g., Coffin, *Some Christian Convictions*, 203; Speer, *Gospel and the New World*, 98; idem, *Some Living Issues*, 261–77.
95. Leonard Sweet develops this kind of critique in "The 1960s: The Crises of Liberal Christianity and the Public Emergence of Evangelicalism," in *Evangelicalism and Modern America*, ed. George M. Marsden (Grand Rapids: William B. Eerdmans, 1984): 29–45.

Epilogue

1. See, for example, Milton J Coalter, John M. Mulder, and Louis Weeks, ed., *The Presbyterian Predicament: Six Perspectives* (Louisville, KY: Westminster/John Knox Press, 1990); William R. Hutchison, ed., *Between the Times: The Travail of the Protestant Establishment in America, 1900–1960* (New York: Cambridge University Press, 1989); Roof and McKinney, *American Mainline Religion*; Michaelsen and Roof, ed., *Liberal Protestantism*; Dean Hoge and David Roozen, ed., *Understanding Church Growth and Decline: 1950–1978* (New York: Pilgrim Press, 1979); Robert Wuthnow, *The Restructuring of American Religion* (Princeton: Princeton University Press, 1988); Robert Wuthnow, *The Struggle for America's Soul: Evangelicals, Liberals, and Secularism* (Grand Rapids: William B. Eerdmans, 1989). The Lilly Endowment is largely responsible for supporting this research.

2. Donald E. Miller, "Constituencies for Liberal Protestantism: A Market Analysis," in Michaelsen and Roof, *Liberal Protestantism*, 202–3; Roof and McKinney, *American Mainline Religion*, 161, 175–76; Benton Johnson, "Liberal Protestantism: End of the Road?", *The Annals of the American Academy of Political and Social Science* 480 (July 1985): 42; Hoge and Roozen, *Understanding Church Growth*, 328–29.

3. See Dean M. Kelley, *Why Conservative Churches Are Growing: A Study in Sociology of Religion* (San Francisco: Harper & Row, 1972), x, xi, 84, 95; Roof and McKinney, *American Mainline Religion*, 20–21.

4. Dean R. Hoge, *Division in the Protestant House: The Basic Reasons Behind Intra-Church Conflict* (Philadelphia: Westminster Press, 1976), 126.

5. John McClure, "Changes in the Authority, Method, and Message of Presbyterian Preaching in the Twentieth Century," in *The Confessional Mosaic: Presbyterians and Twentieth-Century Theology*, ed. Milton J Coalter, John M. Mulder, and Louis Weeks (Louisville, KY: Westminster/John Knox Press, forthcoming 1990).

6. Benton Johnson, "On Dropping the Subject: Presbyterians and Sabbath Observance in the Twentieth Century," in *Presbyterian Predicament*, ed. Coalter, Mulder, and Weeks, 107.

7. John M. Mulder and Lee S. Wyatt, "The Predicament of Pluralism: The Study of Theology in Presbyterian Seminaries Since the 1920s," in *The Pluralistic Vision: Presbyterians and Mainstream Protestant Education and Leadership*, ed. Milton J Coalter, John M. Mulder, and Louis Weeks (Louisville, KY: Westminster/John Knox Press, forthcoming 1991).

8. James Moorhead, "Redefining Confessionalism: American Presbyterians in the Twentieth Century," in *Confessional Mosaic*, ed. Coalter, Mulder, and Weeks; David B. McCarthy, "The Emerging Importance of Presbyterian Polity," in *The Organizational Revolution: Presbyterians and American Denominationalism*, ed. Milton J Coalter, John M. Mulder, and Louis Weeks (Louisville, KY: Westminster/John Knox Press, forthcoming 1991).

9. Roof and McKinney, *American Mainline Religion*, 170; Wade Clark Roof and William McKinney, "Denominational America and the New Religious Pluralism," *The Annals of the American Academy of Political and Social Science* 480 (July 1985): 35.

10. Leonard Sweet, "The Modernization of Protestant Religion in America," in *Altered Landscapes, Christianity in America: 1935–1985*, ed. David W. Lotz (Grand Rapids: William B. Eerdmans, 1989), 37.

11. The Orthodox Presbyterian Church (formerly the Presbyterian Church of America), which has maintained a strict view of doctrine, has grown from 12,867 in 1965 to only 19,094 in 1987 (see Whitman, *Yearbook of American Churches, 1968*, 205; Jacquet, *Yearbook of American Churches, 1989*, 243).

12. Loetscher, *Broadening Church*, 135.

13. *Minutes of G.A.*, 1967, 1:129.

14. *Minutes of G.A.*, 1988, 1:851.

15. Loetscher, *Broadening Church*, 156.

Bibliography

Primary Sources

Archives

Henry Sloane Coffin Papers, Burke Library, Union Theological Seminary in the City of New York, New York, New York.

Charles R. Erdman Papers, Speer Library, Princeton Theological Seminary, Princeton, New Jersey.

Clarence E. Macartney Papers, McCartney Library, Geneva College, Beaver Falls, Pennsylvania.

J. Gresham Machen Papers, Montgomery Library, Westminster Theological Seminary, Philadelphia, Pennsylvania.

Department of History, Presbyterian Church (U.S.A.), Philadelphia, Pennsylvania.

Robert E. Speer Papers, Speer Library, Princeton Theological Seminary, Princeton, New Jersey.

Publications of the General Assembly of the Presbyterian Church in the U.S.A.

Minutes of the General Assembly of the Presbyterian Church in the U.S.A. 2 vols. Philadelphia: Office of the General Assembly, 1892, 1893, 1922–1937, 1967, 1988.

Report of the Special Commission of 1925 to the General Assembly of the Presbyterian Church in the U.S.A. Philadelphia: Office of the General Assembly, 1927.

Report of the Special Committee To Visit Princeton Theological Seminary to the General Assembly of the Presbyterian Church in the U.S.A. Philadelphia: Office of the General Assembly, 1927.

Books

Adams, Henry. *The Education of Henry Adams: An Autobiography.* Cambridge: Riverside, 1918; reprint, Boston: Houghton Mifflin, 1946.

301

Bryan, William J. *The Bible and Its Enemies: An Address Delivered at the Moody Bible Institute of Chicago.* Chicago: Bible Institute Colportage Association, 1921.

————. *Heart to Heart Appeals.* New York: Fleming H. Revell, 1917.

————. *In His Image.* New York: Fleming H. Revell, 1922.

————. *The Prince of Peace.* New York: Barse & Hopkins, n.d.

————. *Speeches of William Jennings Bryan,* 2 vols. New York: Funk & Wagnalls, 1909.

Bryan, William J., and Mary B. Bryan. *The Memoirs of William Jennings Bryan.* Philadelphia: Winston, 1925.

Bushnell, Horace. *Building Eras in Religion.* New York: Charles Scribner's Sons, 1881.

————. *God in Christ: Discourses Delivered at New Haven, Cambridge, and Andover with a Preliminary Dissertation on Language.* London: Richard D. Dick., n.d.

————. *Nature and the Supernatural As Together Constituting the One System of God.* New York: Charles Scribner, 1871.

Coffin, Henry S. *Communion through Preaching: The Monstrance of the Gospel.* New York: Charles Scribner's Sons, 1952.

————. *The Creed of Jesus and Other Sermons.* New York: Charles Scribner's Sons, 1907.

————. *God Confronts Man in History.* New York: Charles Scribner's Sons, 1947.

————. *God's Turn.* New York: Harper & Brothers, 1934.

————. *A Half Century of Union Theological Seminary: 1896–1945, An Informal History.* New York: Charles Scribner's Sons, 1954.

————. *In a Day of Social Rebuilding: Lectures on the Ministry of the Church.* New Haven: Yale University Press, 1918.

————. *Joy in Believing: Selections from the Spoken and Written Words and the Prayers of Henry Sloane Coffin.* Ed. Walter Russell Bowie. New York: Charles Scribner's Sons, 1956.

————. *A More Christian Industrial Order.* New York: Macmillan, 1920.

————. *The Portraits of Jesus Christ in the New Testament.* New York: Macmillan, 1932.

————. *Religion Yesterday and Today.* Nashville: Cokesbury, 1940.

————. *Social Aspects of the Cross.* New York: Hodder & Stoughton, 1911.

————. *Some Christian Convictions: A Practical Restatement in Terms of Present-Day Thinking.* New Haven: Yale University Press, 1915.

————. *The Ten Commandments with a Christian Application to Present Conditions.* New York: Hodder & Stoughton, 1915.

————. *University Sermons.* New Haven: Yale University Press, 1914.

————. *What To Preach.* New York: Harper & Brothers, 1926.

Dixon, Amzi C., Louis Meyer, and Reuben A. Torrey, eds. *The Fundamentals: A Testimony to the Truth.* 12 vols. Chicago: Testimony, 1910–1915.

Erdman, Charles R. *The Acts: An Exposition.* Philadelphia: Westminster, 1920.

————. *D. L. Moody: His Message for To-day.* New York: Fleming H. Revell, 1928.

————. *The Epistle of Paul to the Ephesians: An Exposition.* Philadelphia: Westminster, 1931.

————. *The Epistle of Paul to the Romans: An Exposition.* Philadelphia: Westminster, 1925.

————. *The General Epistles: An Exposition.* Philadelphia: Westminster, 1919.

————. *The Gospel of Luke: An Exposition.* Philadelphia: Westminster, 1921.

————. Introduction to *Dwight L. Moody,* by Dwight L. Moody. New York: Fleming H. Revell, 1949.

————. *The Lord We Love: Devotional Studies in the Life of Christ.* New York: George H. Doran, 1924.

————. *The Pastoral Epistles of Paul: An Exposition.* Philadelphia: Westminster, 1923.

————. *The Return of Christ.* New York: George H. Doran, 1922.

————. *The Spirit of Christ: Devotional Studies in the Doctrine of the Holy Spirit.* New York: George H. Doran, 1926; reprint, New York: Richard R. Smith, 1929.

————. *Your Bible and You.* Philadelphia: Winston, 1950.

Erdman, William J. *The Holy Spirit and Christian Experience.* New York: Gospel, 1909.

————. *Notes on the Revelation.* Ed. Charles R. Erdman. New York: Fleming H. Revell, 1930.

Fosdick, Harry E. *As I See Religion.* New York: Harper & Brothers, 1932.

————. *The Living of These Days: An Autobiography.* New York: Harper & Brothers, 1956.

Herrmann, Wilhelm. *The Communion of the Christian with God.* Ed. Robert T. Voelkel. Trans. J. Sandys Stanyon. New York: G. P. Putnam's Sons, 1906; reprint, Philadelphia: Fortress, 1971.

Hocking, William E., et al. *Re-Thinking Missions: A Laymen's Inquiry after One Hundred Years.* New York: Harper & Brothers, 1932.

Hodge, Charles. *What Is Darwinism?.* New York: Scribner, Armstrong, 1874.

Macartney, Clarence E. *The Christian Faith and the Spirit of the Age.* New York: American Tract Society, 1940.

————. *The Faith Once Delivered.* New York: Abingdon-Cokesbury, 1952.

————. *Great Women of the Bible.* New York: Abingdon-Cokesbury 1942.

————. *The Greatest Men of the Bible.* New York: Abingdon, 1941.

————. *The Greatest Questions of the Bible and of Life.* New York: Abingdon-Cokesbury, 1948.

————. *Lincoln and His Generals.* Philadelphia: Dorrance, 1925; reprint, Freeport, NY: Books for Libraries, 1970.

————. *Lincoln and the Bible.* New York: Abingdon-Cokesbury, 1949.

————. *The Making of a Minister: The Autobiography of Clarence E. Macartney.* Ed. J. Clyde Henry. Great Neck: Channel, 1961.

————. *Putting on Immortality.* New York: Fleming H. Revell, 1926.

———. *Things Most Surely Believed: A Series of Sermons on the Apostles' Creed.* Nashville: Cokesbury, 1930.

———. *Twelve Great Questions about Christ.* New York: Fleming H. Revell, 1923; reprint, Grand Rapids: Baker Book House, 1956.

———. *What Jesus Really Taught.* New York: Abingdon, 1958.

Machen, Arthur W., Jr., ed. *Letters of Arthur W. Machen with Biographical Sketch.* Baltimore: Arthur W. Machen, 1917.

Machen, J. Gresham. *The Christian Faith in the Modern World.* New York: Macmillan, 1936.

———. *The Christian View of Man.* New York: Macmillan, 1937.

———. *Christianity and Liberalism.* New York: Macmillan, 1923; reprint, Grand Rapids: William B. Eerdmans, 1946.

———. *God Transcendent and Other Selected Sermons.* Ed. Ned Stonehouse. Grand Rapids: William B. Eerdmans, 1949.

———. *What Is Christianity?* Ed. Ned B. Stonehouse. Grand Rapids: William B. Eerdmans, 1951.

———. *What Is Faith?* New York: Macmillan, 1925.

Speer, Robert E. *Are Foreign Missions Done For?* New York: Board of Foreign Missions of the Presbyterian Church U.S.A., 1928.

———. *The Christian Man, the Church, and the War.* New York: Macmillan, 1918.

———. *Christian Realities.* New York: Fleming H. Revell, 1935.

———. *Christianity and the Nations.* New York: Fleming H. Revell, 1910.

———. *The Church and Missions.* New York: George H. Doran, 1926.

———. *The Deity of Christ.* New York: Fleming H. Revell, 1909.

———. *The Finality of Jesus Christ.* New York: Fleming H. Revell, 1933.

———. *The Gospel and the New World.* New York: Fleming H. Revell, 1919.

———. *Missionary Principles and Practice: A Discussion of Christian Missions and of Some Criticisms upon Them.* New York: Fleming H. Revell, 1902.

———. *The New Opportunity of the Church.* New York: Macmillan, 1919.

———. *Of One Blood: A Short Study of the Race Problem.* New York: Council of Women for Home Missions & Missionary Education Movement of the United States and Canada, 1924.

———. *The Principles of Jesus Applied to Some Questions of Today.* New York: Fleming H. Revell, 1902.

———. *Race and Race Relations: A Christian View of Human Contacts.* New York: Fleming H. Revell, 1924.

———. *"Re-Thinking Missions" Examined: An Attempt at a Just Review of the Report of the Appraisal Commission of the Laymen's Foreign Missions Inquiry.* New York: Fleming H. Revell, 1933.

———. *Seeking the Mind of Christ.* New York: Fleming H. Revell, 1926.

———. *Some Living Issues.* London: Marshall, Morgan, & Scott, 1930.

———. *The Unfinished Task of Foreign Missions.* New York: Fleming H. Revell, 1926.

———. *The War and the Religious Outlook.* New York: Association Press, 1919.

————. *When Christianity Was New.* New York: Fleming H. Revell, 1939.

————. *A Young Man's Questions.* New York: Fleming H. Revell, 1903.

Chapters in Edited Volumes

Beecher, Henry W. "The Two Revelations." In *Evolution and Religion: The Conflict between Science and Religion in Modern America*, ed. Gail Kennedy, 14–21. Boston: D. C. Heath, 1957.

Bryan, William J. "God and Evolution." In *Evolution and Religion: The Conflict between Science and Religion in Modern America*, ed. Gail Kennedy, 23–29. Boston: D. C. Heath, 1957.

Coffin, Henry S. "Why I Am a Presbyterian." In *Twelve Modern Apostles and Their Creeds*, Gilbert K. Chesterton et al., 53–71. New York: Duffield, 1926; reprint, Freeport, NY: Books for Libraries, 1968.

Erdman, Charles R. "The Church and Socialism." In *The Fundamentals: A Testimony to the Truth*, ed. Reuben A. Torrey. 12:108–19. Chicago: Testimony, 1910–15.

————. "The Coming of Christ." In *The Fundamentals: A Testimony to the Truth*, ed. Reuben A. Torrey. 11:87–99. Chicago: Testimony, 1910–15.

————. "Modern Spiritual Movements." In *Modern Spiritual Movements: Biblical and Theological Studies by Members of the Faculty of Princeton Theological Seminary*, 357–92. New York: n.p., 1912.

Erdman, William J. "The Holy Spirit and the Sons of God." In *The Fundamentals: A Testimony to the Truth*, ed. Louis Meyer. 10:64–78. Chicago: Testimony, 1910–15.

————. "The Holy Spirit in Relation to Christ." In *The Holy Spirit in Life and Service*, ed. Amzi C. Dixon, 102–5. New York: Fleming H. Revell, 1895.

Fosdick, Harry E., "A Reply to Mr. Bryan in the Name of Religion." In *Evolution and Religion: the Conflict between Science and Religion in Modern America*, ed. Gail Kennedy, 23–29. Boston: D. C. Heath, 1957.

————. "*Shall the Fundamentalists Win?*" In *American Protestant Thought in the Liberal Era*, ed. William R. Hutchison, 170–82. Lanham: University Press of America, 1968.

Hodge, Archibald A., and Benjamin B. Warfield. "Inspiration." In *The Princeton Theology, 1812–1921*, ed. Mark A. Noll, 218–32. Grand Rapids: Baker Book House, 1983.

McGiffert, Arthur C. "The Historical Study of Christianity." In *American Protestant Thought in the Liberal Era*, ed. William R. Hutchison, 69–80. Lanham: University Press of America, 1968.

Machen, J. Gresham. "Christianity in Conflict." In *Contemporary American Theology: Theological Autobiographies*, ed. Vergilius Ferm, 1:245–74. New York: Round Table, 1932.

Speer, Robert E. "The Challenge of Missions." In *Victory in Christ: A Report of the Princeton Conference, 1916*, 209–18. Philadelphia: Board of Managers of Princeton Conference, 1916.

————. "Christianity and International Relations." In *Christianity and Modern*

Thought, ed. Ralph H. Gabriel, 179–96. New Haven: Yale University Press, 1924.

———. "Foreign Missions or World-wide Evangelism." In *The Fundamentals: A Testimony to the Truth*, ed. Reuben A. Torrey 12:64–84. Chicago: Testimony, 1910–1915.

———. "God in Christ the Only Revelation of the Fatherhood of God." In *The Fundamentals: A Testimony to the Truth*, ed. Amzi C. Dixon 3:61–75. Chicago: Testimony, 1910–1915.

———. "Paul, the Great Missionary Example." In *The Student Missionary Enterprise: Addresses and Discussions of the Second International Convention of the Student Volunteer Movement for Foreign Missions*, ed. Max W. Moorhead, 2–18. Boston: T. O. Metcalf, 1894(?).

———. "Unity in the Mission Field." In *The Problem of Christian Unity*, ed. Frederick Lynch, 62–83. New York: Macmillan, 1921.

Articles

Bledsoe, Albert. "Chivalrous Southrons." *Southern Review* 6 (July 1869): 96–110.

Bryan, William J. "Applied Christianity." *Commoner* 19 (May 1919): 11–12.

———. "Brother or Brute." *Commoner* 20 (November 1920): 11–12.

———. "But Where Are the Nine." *Commoner* 20 (September 1920): 7–11.

———. "The Fundamentals." *Forum* 70 (July 1923): 1665–80.

———. "The Menace of Darwinism." *Commoner* 21 (April 1921): 5–8.

———. "The Modern Arena." *Commoner* 21 (June 1921): 3–4.

———. "World-wide Prohibition." *Commoner* 21 (October 1921): 7–10.

Buck, Pearl S. "Is There a Case for Foreign Missions?" *Harper's* 166 (January 1933): 143–55.

———. "The Laymen's Mission Report." *Christian Century*, 23 November 1932, pp. 1434–37.

Coffin, Henry S. "Freedom in the Presbyterian Church," *Christian Century*, 19 May 1927, pp. 620–22.

Erdman, Charles R. "Bible Teachings about Education," *Presbyterian*, 21 April 1921, p. 12.

———. "Dr. Erdman Speaks in Self-Defense." *Presbyterian Advance*, 22 January 1925, p. 24.

———. "Making the Nation Christian." *Presbyterian*, 26 May 1921, p. 8.

———. "Making the Social Order Christian." *Presbyterian*, 9 June 1921, p. 12.

———. "Modern Practical Theology." *New York Observer*, 3 January 1907, pp. 17–18.

———. "Rest and Recreation." *Presbyterian*, 28 April 1921, p. 12.

———. "Review: The Social Task of the Church." *Presbyterian*, 16 June 1921, p. 12.

———. "The Special Commission of 1925." *Presbyterian Magazine* (August 1925). In Erdman Papers.

———. "Strong Drink in a Nation's Life." *Presbyterian*, 20 October 1921, 12.

———. "Temperance Lessons—(World's Temperance Sunday)." *Presbyterian*, 23 October 1919, 14.

Fosdick, Harry E. "The Trenches and the Church at Home." *Atlantic Monthly* 123 (January 1919): 22–33.

Hodge, Caspar W. "The Historical Position of Princeton Seminary." *Presbyterian*, 1 March 1928, pp. 27–28.

Macartney, Clarence E. "Another Gospel Which Is Not Another." *Presbyterian*, 23 January 1930, pp. 7–9.

———. "The Authority of the Holy Scriptures." *Princeton Theological Review* 23 (1925): 389–96.

———. "Birth Control and the Presbyterian Church." *Presbyterian*, 7 May 1931, p. 26.

———. "A Christian's Difficulty with Evolution." *Presbyterian*, pt. 1, 3 June 1937, pp. 8–9; pt. 2, 10 June 1937, pp. 5–6; pt. 3, 17 June 1937, pp. 6–7.

———. "Come before Winter." *Presbyterian Life*, 13 October 1951, 8–11.

———. "Dr. Clarence Macartney Answers the President." *Presbyterian*, 24 October 1935, 4–5.

———. "Dr. Clarke and the Presbyterian Standards." *Presbyterian*, 13 March 1924, pp. 6–9.

———. "The Fall of Germany and the Vindication of the Moral Order." *Presbyterian*, 4 September 1919, p. 11.

———. "The Great Commoner: William Jennings Bryan." *The Presbyterian and Herald and Presbyter*, 8 October 1925, pp. 14, 18–19.

———. "The Heroism of the Ministry in the Hour of Christianity's Peril." *Princeton Theological Review* 20 (July 1922): 361–74.

———. "Historical Address Delivered at the General Assembly on Last Tuesday, June 1, by Dr. Clarence E. Macartney." *Presbyterian*, 3 June 1926, pp. 7, 10–11.

———. "In the House of My Friends." *Presbyterian*, 6 March 1919, pp. 10–11, 31.

———. "The Irrepressible Conflict." *Presbyterian*, 14 February 1924, pp. 6–9.

———. "The Moderator's Message." *Presbyterian*, 8 January 1925, pp. 10–11, 23.

———. "A New Kind of Christianity." *Presbyterian Banner*, 3 July 1919, pp. 7–8.

———. "The Opportunity of the 149th General Assembly." *Presbyterian*, 27 May 1937, p. 1.

———. "The Overture on Divorce." *Presbyterian*, 19 May 1921, pp. 7–8.

———. "The Overture on Divorce." *Presbyterian Banner*, 17 January 1929, 11–12.

———. "The Presbyterian Church at the Cross Roads." *Presbyterian*, 19 February 1925, 6–7.

———. "Presbyterians, Awake!" *Presbyterian*, 19 July 1934, pp. 8–9, 13.

———. "Renouncing Missions; or, Modernism Unmasked." *Presbyterian*, 26 January 1933, p. 6.

———. "The Rights of God." *Presbyterian*, 11 April 1929, pp. 5–8.

———. "Shall Princeton Pass?" *Presbyterian Banner*, 5 January 1928, 5–6.

———. "Shall Unbelief Win? An Answer to Dr. Fosdick." pt. 1. *Presbyterian*, 13 July 1922, pp. 8–10, 26

———. "Shall Unbelief Win? An Answer to Dr. Fosdick." pt. 2. *Presbyterian*, 20 July 1922, pp. 8–10.

———. "The State of the Church." *Princeton Theological Review* 23 (April 1925): 177–92.

———. "Their Name Liveth Forevermore." *Presbyterian*, 14 July 1927, pp. 6–7.

———. "Two Years of Prohibition in Philadelphia." *Presbyterian*, 16 March 1922, 9–10, 26.

———. "Warm Hearts and Steady Faith." *Christian Century*, 8 March 1939, pp. 315–19.

———. "The Worship of the Beast; or, The Renaissance of Paganism." *Christian Statesman* 58 (April 1924): 30–36.

Machen, J. Gresham. "The Action of the Presbytery of New Brunswick." *Presbyterian*, 1 March 1928, pp. 13–15, 26.

———. "Apology and Polemic in the New Testament." *Presbyterian*, 13 September 1923, pp. 10–11.

———. "Christianity and Culture." *Princeton Theological Review* 11 (1911): 1–15.

———. "A Debate: Is the Teaching of Dr. Harry Emerson Fosdick Opposed to the Christian Religion? Yes." *Christian Work*, 13 December 1924, pp. 686–88.

———. "Does Fundamentalism Obstruct Social Progress?—The Negative." *Survey Graphic*, 1 July 1924, pp. 391–92, 426–27.

———. "Dr. Machen Replies to Dr. Erdman." *Presbyterian*, 5 February 1925, pp. 20–21.

———. "Dr. Machen Surveys Dr. Speer's New Book." *Christianity Today* 1 (October 1930): 9–11, 15.

———. "Dr. Merrill in the World's Work." *Presbyterian*, 7 February 1924, pp. 6–7.

———. "Dr. Robert E. Speer and His Latest Book." *Christianity Today* 4 (May 1933): 15–16, 22–26.

———. "An Earnest Plea for Christian Freedom—and Honesty!" *Lookout*, 2 March 1924, 6.

———. "History and Faith." *Princeton Theological Review* 5 (July 1915): 337–51.

———. "Liberalism or Christianity." *Princeton Theological Review* 20 (January 1922): 93–117.

———. "The Parting of the Ways." *Presbyterian*, pt. 1, 17 April 1924, pp. 7–9; pt. 2, 24 April 1924, pp. 6–7. Reprint in Machen Papers.

———. "The Present Situation in the Presbyterian Church." *Presbyterian*, 14 May 1925, pp. 6–8.

———. "Religion and Fact." *Real Issue*, 15 April 1924, pp. 3–4.

———. "Sermon on the Present Issue in the Church." *Presbyterian*, 24 January 1924, pp. 16–18.

———. "What Fundamentalism Stands for Now, Defined by a Leading Exponent of Conservative Reading of the Bible and the Word of God." *New York Times*, 21 June 1925, sec. 9, p. 1.

Patton, Francis. "A Theological Seminary." *Princeton Theological Review* 14 (January 1916): 72–81.

"Pen Portraits of Church Leaders, Charles R. Erdman." *Christian Herald*, 20 November 1926, p. 994.

Speer, Robert E. "The Church a Missionary Society." *Presbyterian*, 28 January 1937, p. 1.

Weigle, Luther A. "A Survey of Contemporary Theological Education." *Bulletin of the American Association of Theological Schools* 5 (September 1926): 11–18.

Pamphlets and Sermons

Coffin, Henry S. "Freedom in the Presbyterian Pulpit," New York: Jacobs, 1925.

———. "The Practical Aims of a Liberal Evangelicalism," 18 May 1915. In Coffin Papers.

———. "The Religious Opportunity of the Present Social Awakening." In *Some Social Aspects of the Gospel: An Address and A Sermon*, by Henry S. Coffin and Francis Brown. New York: Union Theological Seminary, 1912.

———. "What Liberal Presbyterians Are Standing for." *Summer Monthly*, 5 June 1925, pp. 3–6. In Coffin Papers.

Erdman, Charles R. "The Power of the Spirit." Philadelphia: General Assembly of the Presbyterian Church, 1926.

Fosdick, Harry E. "The Farewell Sermon of Harry Emerson Fosdick to the First Presbyterian Church of New York," 1925.

Macartney, Clarence E. "America, Her Great Leaders, and God," 25 November 1943.

———. "Awake, O America!" 30 June 1935.

———. "Bought with a Price," 29 May 1932.

———. "The Christian Home," 14 May 1939.

———. "The Destroyer of Souls," 16 October 1949.

———. "The Great Defection," n.p., n.d.

———. "The Great Revolt against Rationalism in the Presbyterian Church." Philadelphia: Wilber Hanf, n.d.

———. "Is America on the Road to Ruin?" 28 January 1945.

———. "The Sabbath," 15 May 1952.

———. "A Son's Tribute to His Mother." Philadelphia: Wilber Hanf, n.d.

McCartney, Catherine R. "A Word to Mothers." Chicago: Ruby I. Gilbert, n.d. In Macartney Papers.

Machen, J. Gresham. "Additional Statement by J. Gresham Machen Concerning the Personal Relations between the Rev. Professor Charles R. Erdman, D.D., and J. Gresham Machen." N.p.: J. Gresham Machen, 1926.

———. "The Attack upon Princeton Seminary: A Plea for Fair Play." N.p.: J. Gresham Machen, 1927.

———. "Modernism and the Board of Foreign Missions of the Presbyterian Church in the U.S.A.." N.p.: J. Gresham Machen, 1933.

———. "Statement by J. Gresham Machen Submitted to the Committee Appointed by Action of the General Assembly of 1926." N.p.: J. Gresham Machen, 1926.

———. "Statement to the Special Committee of the Presbytery of New Brunswick." Philadelphia: J. Gresham Machen, 1934. In Machen Papers.

Speer, Robert E. "The Second Coming of Christ." East Northfield, MA: A. P. Fitt, 1903.

Todd, G. Hall. "He Being Dead Yet Speaketh." In "Tributes to Clarence Edward Noble Macartney," 10 March 1957. In Macartney Papers.

———. "The Heritage from Clarence Edward Macartney." In "Tributes to Clarence Edward Noble Macartney, 1879–1957: Minister of the Arch Street Presbyterian Church, Philadelphia, Penn. 1914–1927," pp. 15–24, 1979(?). In Macartney Papers.

Periodicals

Christian Century, 1922–1938.
Christianity Today, 1–8 (1930–1937).
The Commoner, 19–23 (1919–1923).
New York Times, 1922–1936.
The Presbyterian, 1919–1937.
Presbyterian Advance, 1922–1934.
Presbyterian Guardian, 1936–1937.

Secondary Sources

Books

Ahlstrom, Sydney E. *A Religious History of the American People*. New Haven: Yale University Press, 1972.

———. *Theology in America: The Major Protestant Voices from Puritanism to Neo-Orthodoxy*. Indianapolis: Bobbs-Merrill, 1967.

Allen, Frederick L. *Only Yesterday: An Informal History of the Nineteen-Twenties*. New York: Harper & Brothers, 1931.

Allen, Leslie H., ed. *Bryan and Darrow at Dayton: The Record and Documents of the "Bible–Evolution Trials."* New York: Russell & Russell, 1925.

Anderson, Robert M. *Vision of the Disinherited: The Making of American Pentecostalism.* New York: Oxford University Press, 1979.

Armstrong, Maurice, Lefferts A. Loetscher, and Charles A. Anderson, eds. *The Presbyterian Enterprise: Sources of American Presbyterian History.* Philadelphia: Westminster, 1956.

Atherton, Lewis. *Main Street on the Middle Border.* Bloomington: Indiana University Press, 1954.

Barrus, Ben M., Milton L. Baughn, and Thomas H. Campbell, eds. *A People Called Cumberland Presbyterians.* Memphis: Frontier, 1972.

Beecher, Willis J. *Index of Presbyterian Ministers: 1706–1881.* Philadelphia: Presbyterian Board of Publication, 1883.

Bozeman, Theodore Dwight. *Protestants in an Age of Science: The Baconian Ideal and Antebellum American Religious Thought.* Chapel Hill: University of North Carolina Press, 1977.

Brown, William A. *The Education of American Ministers.* Vol. 1, *Ministerial Education in America: Summary and Interpretation.* New York: Institute of Social and Religious Research, 1934.

Byers, Arthur M., Jr. *Biographical Catalogue of Princeton Theological Seminary.* Princeton: Princeton Theological Seminary, 1977.

Carnell, Edward B. *The Case for Orthodox Theology.* Philadelphia: Westminster, 1959.

Carter, Paul L. *The Decline and Revival of the Social Gospel: Social and Political Liberalism in American Protestant Churches, 1920–1940.* Ithaca: Cornell University Press, 1954.

———. *The Twenties in America.* New York: Thomas Y. Crowell, 1968.

Cauthen, W. Kenneth. *The Impact of American Religious Liberalism.* New York: Harper & Row, 1962.

Cherny, Robert W. *A Righteous Cause: The Life of William Jennings Bryan.* Boston: Little, Brown, 1985.

Cherry, Conrad., ed. *Horace Bushnell: Sermons.* New York: Paulist, 1985.

Clark, Thomas D., and Albert O. Kirwan. *The South since Appomattox: A Century of Regional Change.* New York: Oxford University Press, 1967.

Class Secretary. *First Annual Catalogue of the Class of Eighty-Six of Princeton College for 1886–87.* Philadelphia: American Printing House, 1887.

Clements, Kendrick A. *William Jennings Bryan: Missionary Isolationist.* Knoxville: University of Tennessee Press, 1982.

Cole, Stewart G. *The History of Fundamentalism.* New York: Richard R. Smith, 1931.

Coletta, Paolo E. *William Jennings Bryan.* 3 vols. Lincoln: University of Nebraska Press, 1964–1969.

Commager, Henry S. *The American Mind: An Interpretation of American Thought and Character since the 1880s.* New Haven: Yale University Press, 1950.

Coray, Henry. *J. Gresham Machen: A Silhouette.* Grand Rapids: Kregel, 1981.

Copeland, Robert M. *Spare No Exertions: 175 Years of the Reformed Presbyterian Theological Seminary.* Pittsburgh: Reformed Presbyterian Theological Seminary, 1986.

Coulter, E. Merton. *The South during Reconstruction, 1865–1877.* Baton Rouge: Louisiana State University Press, 1947.

Cross, Barbara. *Horace Bushnell: Minister to a Changing America.* Chicago: University of Chicago Press, 1958.

Curtis, Richard K. *They Called Him Mr. Moody.* Garden City: Doubleday, 1962.

Daniels, William H., ed. *Moody: His Words, Work, and Workers.* New York: Nelson & Phillips, 1877.

Degler, Carl N. *The Age of the Economic Revolution: 1876–1900.* 2d ed. Glenview: Scott, Foresman, 1977.

Dictionary of American Biography, Ed. Allen Johnson and others. New York: Charles Scribner's Sons, 1928–1937.

———. Supplement Two. Ed. Robert Schuyler. New York: Charles Scribner's Sons, 1958.

———. Supplement Four. Ed. John A. Garrity and Edward T. James. New York: Charles Scribner's Sons, 1974.

Eddy, Sherwood. *Pathfinders of the World Missionary Crusade.* New York: Abingdon-Cokesbury, 1945.

Ellis, David M., James A. Frost, Harold C. Syrett, and Harry J. Carman. *A Short History of New York State.* Ithaca: Cornell University Press, 1957.

Evans, Frederick, ed. *After Twenty Five Years: Class Record of 1886.* Princeton: Princeton University Press, 1911.

Fairbank, John, ed. *The Missionary Enterprise in China and America.* Cambridge: Harvard University Press, 1974.

Farmer, James O. *The Metaphysical Confederacy: James Henley Thornwell and the Synthesis of Southern Values.* Macon: Mercer University Press, 1986.

Ferm, Vergilius, ed. *Contemporary American Theology: Theological Autobiographies.* 2 vols. New York: Round Table, 1932.

Findlay, James F., Jr. *Dwight L. Moody, American Evangelist: 1837–1899.* Chicago: University of Chicago Press, 1969.

Flower, Elizabeth, and Murray G. Murphey. *A History of American Philosophy.* New York: G. P. Putnam's Sons, 1977.

Fowler, Dorothy G. *A City Church: The First Presbyterian Church in the City of New York, 1716–1976.* New York: The First Presbyterian Church, 1981.

Furniss, Norman F. *The Fundamentalist Controversy, 1918–1931.* New Haven: Yale University Press, 1954.

Gabriel, Ralph H. *The Course of American Democratic Thought.* 2nd ed. New York: John Wiley & Sons, 1956.

Gaston, Paul M. *The New South Creed: A Study in Southern Myth Making.* New York: Alfred A. Knopf, 1970.

Gatewood, Willard B., ed. *Controversy in the Twenties: Fundamentalism, Modernism, and Evolution*. Nashville: Vanderbilt University Press, 1969.

Ginger, Ray. *Six Days or Forever? Tennessee Versus John Thomas Scopes*. Boston: Beacon, 1958.

Glad, Paul W. *The Trumpet Soundeth: William Jennings Bryan and His Democracy, 1896–1912*. Lincoln: University of Nebraska Press, 1960.

———, ed. *William Jennings Bryan: A Profile*. New York: Hill & Wang, 1968.

Gould, Joseph E. *The Chautauqua Movement: An Episode in the Continuing American Revolution*. New York: State University of New York, 1961.

Grave, S. A. *The Scottish Philosophy of Common Sense*. Oxford: Clarendon, 1960.

Gundry, Stephen N. *Love Them In: the Proclamation Theology of D. L. Moody*. Chicago: Moody, 1976.

Gusfield, Joseph R. *Symbolic Crusade: Status Politics and the American Temperance Movement*. 2d ed. Urbana: University of Illinois Press, 1986.

Handlin, Oscar. *The Uprooted*. 2d ed. Boston: Little, Brown, 1973.

Handy, Robert T. *A Christian America: Protestant Hopes and Historical Realities*. Rev. ed. New York: Oxford University Press, 1981.

———. *A History of Union Theological Seminary in New York*. New York: Columbia University Press, 1986.

———, ed. *The Social Gospel in America, 1870–1920: Gladden, Ely, Rauschenbusch*. New York: Oxford University Press, 1954.

Harris, Theodore F. *Pearl S. Buck: A Biography*. New York: John Day, 1969.

Harrison, Harry P., and Karl Detzer. *Culture under Canvas: The Story of Tent Chautauqua*. New York: Hastings House, 1958.

Hatch, Carl E. *The Charles A. Briggs Heresy Trial: Prologue to Twentieth-Century Liberal Protestantism*. New York: Exposition, 1969.

Hatch, Nathan O., and Mark Noll, eds. *The Bible in America: Essays in Cultural History*. New York: Oxford University Press, 1982.

Hirschfeld, Charles. *Baltimore, 1870–1900: Studies in Social History, Johns Hopkins University Studies in Historical and Political Science*, Series 59, no. 2. Baltimore: Johns Hopkins University Press, 1941.

Hoge, Dean R. *Division in the Protestant House: The Basic Reasons Behind Intra-Church Conflict*. Philadelphia: Westminster, 1976.

Hoge, Dean R. and David Roozen, eds. *Understanding Church Growth and Decline: 1950–1978*. New York: Pilgrim, 1979.

Hoffecker, W. Andrew. *Piety and the Princeton Theologians: Archibald Alexander, Charles Hodge, and Benjamin Warfield*. Grand Rapids: Baker Book House, 1981.

Hofstadter, Richard. *The Age of Reform: From Bryan to F.D.R.* New York: Alfred A. Knopf, 1955.

———. *The American Political Tradition and the Men Who Made It*. New York: Random House, 1948.

———. *Anti-Intellectualism in American Life*. New York: Alfred A. Knopf, 1962.

———. *Social Darwinism in American Thought*. Philadelphia: University of Pennsylvania Press, 1944; reprint, Boston: Beacon, 1955.

Hollifield, E. Brooks. *The Gentlemen Theologians: American Theology in Southern Culture, 1795–1860*. Durham: Duke University Press, 1978.

Hopkins, C. Howard. *John R. Mott, 1865–1955: A Biography*. Grand Rapids: William B. Eerdmans, 1979.

———. *The Rise of the Social Gospel in American Protestantism: 1865–1915*. New Haven: Yale University Press, 1940.

Hopper, Orion C. *Biographical Catalogue of Princeton Theological Seminary, 1815–1954*. Princeton: Princeton Theological Seminary, 1955.

Hordern, William E. *A Layman's Guide to Protestant Theology*. Rev. ed. New York: Macmillan, 1968.

Horner, Charles. *Strike the Tents: The Story of the Chautauqua*. Philadelphia: Dorrance, 1954.

Hovenkamp, Herbert, *Science and Religion in America, 1800–1860*. Philadelphia: University of Pennsylvania Press, 1978.

Hudson, Winthrop. *Religion in America: An Historical Account of the Development of American Religious Life*. 3d ed. New York: Charles Scribner's Sons, 1981.

Hutchison, William R. *Errand to the World: American Protestant Thought and Foreign Missions*. Chicago: University of Chicago Press, 1987.

———. *The Modernist Impulse in American Protestantism*. Cambridge: Harvard University Press, 1976; reprint, New York: Oxford University Press, 1982.

———, ed. *American Protestant Thought in the Liberal Era*. Lanham: University Press of America, 1968.

———, ed. *Between the Times: The Travail of the Protestant Establishment in America, 1900–1960*. New York: Cambridge University Press, 1989.

Jacquet, Constant H., Jr, ed. *Yearbook of American Churches, 1972*. Nashville: Abingdon, 1972.

———, ed. *Yearbook of American and Canadian Churches, 1989*. Nashville: Abingdon, 1989.

Kelley, Brooks M. *Yale: A History*. New Haven: Yale University Press, 1974.

Kelley, Dean M. *Why Conservative Churches Are Growing: A Study in Sociology of Religion*. San Francisco: Harper & Row, 1972.

Kelly, Robert L. *Theological Education in America: A Study of One Hundred Sixty-One Theological Schools in the United States and Canada*. New York: George H. Doran, 1924.

Kennedy, Gail. *Evolution and Religion: The Conflict between Science and Religion in Modern America*. Boston: D. C. Heath, 1957.

Koenig, Louis W. *Bryan: A Political Biography of William Jennings Bryan*. New York: G. P. Putnam's Sons, 1971.

Leuchtenburg, William. *The Perils of Prosperity: 1914–32*. Chicago: University of Chicago Press, 1958.

Levine, Laurence. *Defender of the Faith: William Jennings Bryan, the Last Decade, 1915–1925.* New York: Oxford University Press, 1965.

Link, Arthur S., ed. *The First Presbyterian Church of Princeton: Two Centuries of History.* Princeton: First Presbyterian Church, 1967.

Livingstone, David N. *Darwin's Forgotten Defenders: The Encounter between Evangelical Theology and Evolutionary Thought.* Grand Rapids: William B. Eerdmans, 1987.

Loetscher, Lefferts. *The Broadening Church: A Study of Theological Issues in the Presbyterian Church since 1869.* Philadelphia: University of Pennsylvania Press, 1954.

———, ed. *Twentieth Century Encyclopedia of Religious Knowledge.* Grand Rapids: Baker Book House, 1955.

McAllister, David. *A Manual for Christian Civil Government.* Allegheny, PA: Christian Statesman, 1898.

McFeeters, James C. *The Covenanters in America: The Voice of Their Testimony on Present Moral Issues.* Philadelphia: Spangler & Davis, 1892.

McKelvey, Blake. *The Urbanization of America, 1860–1915.* New Brunswick: Rutgers University Press, 1963.

MacLaren, Gay. *Morally We Roll Along.* Boston: Little, Brown, 1938.

Marsden, George M. *The Evangelical Mind and the New School Presbyterian Experience: A Case Study of Thought and Theology in Nineteenth-Century America.* New Haven: Yale University Press, 1970.

———. *Fundamentalism and American Culture: The Shaping of Twentieth Century Evangelicalism, 1870–1925.* New York: Oxford University Press, 1980.

———. *Reforming Fundamantalism: Fuller Seminary and the New Evangelicalism.* Grand Rapids: William B. Eerdmans, 1987.

———, ed. *Evangelicalism and Modern America.* Grand Rapids: William B. Eerdmans, 1984.

May, Henry. *The End of American Innocence: A Study of the First Years of Our Own Time, 1912–1917.* New York: Alfred A. Knopf, 1959; reprint, New York: Oxford University Press, 1959.

———. *The Enlightenment in America.* New York: Oxford University Press, 1976.

———. *Protestant Churches and Industrial America.* New York: Harper & Brothers, 1949.

Mead, Frank. *Handbook of Denominations in the United States.* 5th ed. Nashville: Abingdon, 1970.

Meyer, Donald B. *The Protestant Search for Political Realism, 1919–1941.* Berkeley: University of California Press, 1960.

Miller, Robert M. *American Protestantism and Social Issues, 1919–1939.* Chapel Hill: University of North Carolina Press, 1958.

———. *Harry Emerson Fosdick: Preacher, Pastor, Prophet.* New York: Oxford University Press, 1985.

Mills, C. Wright. *Sociology and Pragmatism: the Higher Learning in America.* New York: Paine Whitman, 1964.

Moody, William R. *D. L. Moody.* New York: Macmillan, 1931.

Moore, R. Laurence, *Religious Outsiders and the Making of Americans.* New York: Oxford University Press, 1986.

Mosier, Richard D. *Making the American Mind: Social and Moral Ideas in the McGuffey Readers.* New York: Russell & Russell, 1965.

Nichols, Robert H. *Presbyterianism in New York State: A History of the Synod and Its Predecessors.* Philadelphia: Westminster, 1963.

Noll, Mark A., ed. *The Princeton Theology, 1812–1921: Scripture, Science, and Theological Method from Archibald Alexander to Benjamin Warfield.* Grand Rapids: Baker Book House, 1983.

Noyes, Morgan Phelps. *Henry Sloane Coffin: The Man and His Ministry.* New York: Charles Scribner's Sons, 1964.

Olmstead, Clifton. *History of Religion in the United States.* Englewood Cliffs: Prentice Hall, 1960.

Osterweis, Rollin G. *The Myth of the Lost Cause, 1865–1900.* Hamden: Archon, 1973.

———. *Romanticism and Nationalism in the Old South.* New Haven: Yale University Press, 1949.

Owens, Hamilton. *Baltimore on the Chesapeake.* Garden City: Doubleday, Doran, 1941.

Patterson, James T. *America in the Twentieth Century: A History.* New York: Harcourt Brace Jovanovich, 1976.

Peck, George T. *A Noble Landmark of New York; The Fifth Avenue Presbyerian Church: 1808–1958.* New York: Van Rees, 1960.

Persons, Stow, ed. *Evolutionary Thought in America.* New Haven: Yale University Press, 1950.

Piper, John F., Jr. *The American Churches in World War I.* Athens: Ohio University Press, 1985.

Pollock, John C. *Moody: A Biographical Portrait of the Pacesetter in Modern Mass Evangelism.* New York: Macmillan, 1963.

Reformed Presbyterian Church in North America. *Reformation Principles Exhibited by the Reformed Presbyterian Church in the United States of America.* New York: Osborn & Buckingham, 1835.

Rian, Edwin. *The Presbyterian Conflict.* Grand Rapids: William B. Eerdmans, 1940.

Rogers, Jack B., and Donald K. McKim. *The Authority and Interpretation of the Bible: An Historical Approach.* San Francisco: Harper & Row, 1979.

Roof, Wade Clark, and William McKinney. *American Mainline Religion: Its Changing Shape and Future.* New Brunswick: Rutgers University Press, 1987.

Rudolph, Frederick. *The American College and University: A History.* New York: Random House, 1962.

Russell, C. Allyn. *Voices of American Fundamentalism: Seven Biographical Studies.* Philadelphia: Wesminster, 1976.

Sandeen, Ernest R. *The Roots of Fundamentalism: British and American Millenarianism, 1800–1930*. Chicago: University of Chicago Press, 1970.

Schlesinger, Arthur M. *The Rise of the City: 1878–1898*. New York: Macmillan,
1933.

Seligman, Edwin, ed. *Encyclopedia of the Social Sciences*. New York: Macmillan, 1937.

Singal, Daniel J. *The War Within: From Victorian to Modernist Thought in the
South, 1919–1945*. Chapel Hill: University of North Carolina Press, 1982.

Slosson, Preston W. *The Great Crusade and After: 1914–1928*. New York: Macmillan, 1935.

Smith, Gary S. *The Seeds of Secularization: Calvinism, Culture, and Pluralism
in America: 1870–1915*. Grand Rapids: Christian University Press, 1985.

Smith, H. Shelton, ed. *Horace Bushnell*. New York: Oxford University Press,
1965.

Smith, H. Shelton, Robert T. Handy, and Lefferts A. Loetscher, eds. *American
Christianity: An Historical Interpretation with Representative Documents*.
2 vols. New York: Charles Scribner's Sons, 1960–1963.

Smith, Willard H. *The Social and Religious Thought of William Jennings Bryan*.
Lawrence, KS; Coronado, 1975.

Stonehouse, Ned. *J. Gresham Machen: A Biographical Memoir*. Grand Rapids:
William B. Eerdmans, 1954.

Szasz, Ferenc Morton. *The Divided Mind of Protestant America, 1880–1930*.
University: University of Alabama Press, 1982.

Taylor, William R. *Cavalier and Yankee: The Old South and American National
Character*. New York: George Braziller, 1961.

Thompson, Ernest T. *Presbyterians in the South*. 3 vols. Richmond: John Knox,
1963–1973.

Trinterud, Leonard. *The Forming of an American Tradition: A Re-examination
of Colonial Presbyterianism*. Philadelphia: Westminster, 1949.

VanderStelt, John C. *Philosophy and Scripture: A Study in Old Princeton and
Westminster Theology*. Marlton, NJ: Mack, 1978.

Vander Velde, Lewis G. *The Presbyterian Churches and the Federal Union:
1861–1869*. Cambridge: Harvard University Press, 1886.

Veysey, Laurence R. *The Emergence of the American University*. Chicago:
University of Chicago Press, 1965.

Vincent, John H. *The Chautauqua Movement*. Boston: Chautauqua, 1886.

Wacker, Grant. *Augustus H. Strong and the Dilemma of Historical Consciousness*. Macon: Mercer University Press, 1985.

Watt, Hugh, A. Mitchell Hunter, and W. A. Curtis. *New College, Edinburgh:
A Centenary History*. Edinburgh: Oliver & Boyd, 1946.

Weber, Timothy P. *Living in the Shadow of the Second Coming: American
Premillennialism, 1875–1982*. Enl. ed. Grand Rapids: Zondervan, 1983.

Weisenburger, Francis P. *Ordeal of Faith: The Crisis of Church-Going America,
1865–1900*. New York: Philosophical Library, 1959.

Welch, Claude. *Protestant Thought in the Nineteenth Century*. 2 vols. New Haven: Yale University Press, 1972–1985.

318   *Bibliography*

Wells, David, ed. *Reformed Theology in America: A History of Its Modern Development*. Grand Rapids: William B. Eerdmans, 1985.

Wertenbaker, Thomas J. *Princeton: 1746–1896*. Princeton: Princeton University Press, 1946.

Westerhoff, John H. III. *McGuffey and His Readers: Piety, Morality, and Education in Nineteenth-Century America*. Nashville: Abingdon, 1978.

Wheeler, W. Reginald. *A Man Sent from God: A Biography of Robert E. Speer*. Westwood: Fleming H. Revell, 1956.

White, Morton. *Social Thought in America: The Revolt against Formalism*. New York: Viking, 1949; reprint, New York: Oxford University Press, 1976.

Whitman, Lauris B., ed. *Yearbook of American Churches: Information on All Faiths in the U.S.A., Edition for 1968*. New York: National Council of Churches, 1968.

Wiebe, Robert H. *The Search for Order: 1877–1920*. New York: Hill & Wang, 1967.

Williams, Daniel D. *The Andover Liberals: A Study in American Theology*. New York: King's Crown, 1941.

Wilson, Charles R. *Baptized in Blood: The Religion of the Lost Cause, 1865–1920*. Athens: University of Georgia Press, 1980.

Woodward, C. Vann. *Origins of the New South, 1877–1913*. Baton Rouge: Louisiana State University Press, 1951.

Wuthnow, Robert. *The Restructuring of American Religion*. Princeton: Princeton University Press, 1988.

———. *The Struggle for America's Soul: Evangelicals, Liberals, and Secularism*. Grand Rapids: William B. Eerdmans, 1989.

Chapters in Edited Volumes

Ahlstrom, Sydney E. "Horace Bushnell." In *A Handbook of Christian Theologians*, ed. Dean G. Peerman and Martin E. Marty, 36–48. New York: New American Library, 1965.

Beaver, R. Pierce. "Missionary Motivation through Three Centuries." In *Reinterpretation in American Church History*, ed. Jerald C. Brauer, 113–51. Chicago: University of Chicago Press, 1968.

Carter, Paul A. "The Fundamentalist Defense of the Faith." In *Change and Continuity in Twentieth-Century America: The 1920s*, ed. John Braeman, Robert H. Bremner, and David Brody, 179–214. Columbus: Ohio State University Press, 1965.

Fein, Albert. "Centennial New York, 1876." In *New York: The Centennial Years, 1676–1976*, ed. Milton Klein, 75–120. Port Washington, NY: Kennikat, 1976.

Garber, Paul L. "A Centennial Appraisal of James Henley Thornwell." In *A Miscellany of American Christianity*, ed. Stuart C. Henry, 95–137. Durham: Duke University Press, 1963.

Hall, David D. "The Victorian Connection." In *Victorian America*, ed. Daniel W. Howe, 81–94. Philadelphia: University of Pennsylvania Press, 1976.

Hoffecker, W. Andrew, "Benjamin B. Warfield." In *Reformed Theology in America: A History of Its Modern Development*, ed. David F. Wells, 60–86. Grand Rapids: William B. Eerdmans, 1985.

Hofstadter, Richard. "The Revolution in Higher Education." In *Paths of American Thought*, ed. Arthur M. Schlesinger, Jr. and Morton White, 269–90. Boston: Houghton Mifflin, 1963.

Howe, Daniel D. "Victorian Culture in America." In *Victorian America*, ed. Daniel D. Howe, 3–28. Philadelphia: Univeristy of Pennsylvania Press, 1976.

Hutchison, William R. "Modernism and Missions: The Liberal Search for an Exportable Christianity, 1875–1935." In *The Missionary Enterprise in China and America*, ed. John K. Fairbank, 110–31. Cambridge: Harvard University Press, 1974.

Johnson, Benton. "On Dropping the Subject: Presbyterians and Sabbath Observance in the Twentieth Century." In *The Presbyterian Predicament: Six Perspectives*, ed. Milton J Coalter, John M. Mulder, and Louis Weeks, 90–108. Louisville, KY: Westminster/John Knox Press, 1990.

Lerner, Max. "The Triumph of Laissez-faire." In *Paths of American Thought*, ed. Arthur Schlesinger, Jr. and Morton White, 147–66. Boston: Houghton Mifflin, 1963.

McCarthy, David B. "The Emerging Importance of Presbyterian Polity." In *The Organizational Revolution: Presbyterians and American Denominationalism*, ed. Milton J Coalter, John M. Mulder, and Louis Weeks. Louisville, KY: Westminster/John Knox Press, forthcoming 1991.

McClure, John. "Changes in the Authority, Method, and Message of Presbyterian Preaching in the Twentieth Century." In *The Confessional Mosaic: Presbyterians and Twentieth-Century Theology*, ed. Milton J Coalter, John M. Mulder, and Louis Weeks. Louisville, KY: Westminster/John Knox Press, forthcoming 1990.

McKinney, William, and Wade Clark Roof. "Liberal Protestantism: A Sociodemographic Perspective." In *Liberal Protestantism: Realities and Possibilities*, ed. Robert S. Michaelsen and Wade Clark Roof, 37–50. New York: Pilgrim, 1986.

Marsden, George M. "A Case of the Excluded Middle: Creation Versus Evolution in America." In *Uncivil Religion: Inter-Religious Hostility in America*, ed. Robert N. Bellah and Frederick E. Greenspahn, 132–55. New York: Crossroad, 1987.

———. "The Collapse of American Evangelical Academia." In *Faith and Rationality: Reason and Belief in God*, ed. Alvin Plantinga and Nicholas Wolterstorff, 219–64. Notre Dame: University of Notre Dame Press, 1983.

———. "The Era of Crisis: From Christendom to Pluralism." In *Eerdmans' Handbook to Christianity in America*, ed. Mark A. Noll, Nathan O.

Hatch, George M. Marsden, David F. Wells, and John D. Woodbridge, 277–387. Grand Rapids: William B. Eerdmans, 1983.

Miller, Donald E. "Constituencies for Liberal Protestantism: A Market Analysis." In *Liberal Protestantism: Realities and Possibilities*, ed. Robert S. Michaelsen and Wade Clark Roof, 201–19. New York: Pilgrim, 1986.

Moorhead, James. "Redefining Confessionalism: American Presbyterians in the Twentieth Century." In *The Confessional Mosaic: Presbyterians and Twentieth-Century Theology*, ed. Milton J Coalter, John M. Mulder, and Louis Weeks. Louisville, KY: Westminster/John Knox Press, forthcoming 1990.

Mulder, John M. and Lee S. Wyatt. "The Predicament of Pluralism: The Study of Theology in Presbyterian Seminaries Since the 1920s." In *The Pluralistic Vision: Presbyterians and Mainstream Protestant Education and Leadership*, ed. Milton J Coalter, John M. Mulder, and Louis Weeks. Louisville, KY: Westminster/John Knox Press, forthcoming 1991.

Nichols, Robert H. "Leader of Liberal Presbyterianism." In *This Ministry: The Contribution of Henry Sloane Coffin*, ed. Reinhold Niebuhr, 39–58. New York: Charles Scribner's Sons, 1946.

Noyes, Morgan P. "Parish Minister." In *This Ministry: The Contribution of Henry Sloane Coffin*, ed. Reinhold Niebuhr, 1–22. New York: Charles Scribner's Sons, 1946.

Persons, Stow. "Religion and Modernity, 1865–1914." In *Religion in American Life*, vol. 1, *The Shaping of American Religion*, ed. James W. Smith and A. Leland Jameson, 369–401. Princeton: Princeton University Press, 1961.

Phillips, Clifton J. "The Student Volunteer Movement and Its Role in China Missions, 1886–1920." In *The Missionary Enterprise in China and America*, ed. John K. Fairbank, 91–109. Cambridge: Harvard University Press, 1974.

Rogers, Max G. "Charles Augustus Briggs: Heresy at Union." In *American Religious Heretics: Formal and Informal Trials*, ed. George H. Shriver, 89–147. Nashville: Abingdon, 1966.

Smith, Morton. "The Southern Tradition." In *Reformed Theology in America: A History of Its Modern Development*, ed. David F. Wells, 189–207. Grand Rapids: William B. Eerdmans, 1985.

Sweet, Leonard I. "The 1960's: The Crises of Liberal Christianity and the Public Emergence of Evangelicalism." In *Evangelicalism and Modern America*, ed. George M. Marsden, 29–45. Grand Rapids: William B. Eerdmans, 1984.

————. "The Modernization of Protestant Religion in America." In *Altered Landscapes, Christianity in America: 1935–1985*, ed. David W. Lotz, 19–41. Grand Rapids: William B. Eerdmans, 1989.

Tinder, Donald. "Foreign Missions, 1865–1930." In *Eerdmans' Handbook to Christianity in America*, ed. Mark A. Knoll, Nathan O. Hatch, George M. Marsden, David F. Wells, and John D. Woodbridge, 299–302. Grand Rapids: William B. Eerdmans, 1983.

Wacker, Grant A. "The Demise of Biblical Civilization." In *The Bible in America: Essays in Cultural History*, ed. Nathan O. Hatch and Mark A. Noll, 121–38. New York: Oxford University Press, 1982.

Wells, David F. "Charles Hodge." In *Reformed Theology in America: A History of Its Modern Development*, ed. David F. Wells, 36–59. Grand Rapids: William B. Eerdmans, 1985.

Articles

Ahlstrom, Sydney E. "The Scottish Philosophy and American Theology." *Church History* 24 (September 1955): 257–72.

Ames, John T. "Cumberland Liberals and the Union of 1906." *Journal of Presbyterian History* 52 (Spring 1974): 3–18.

Board of Trustees of Princeton Seminary, "Robert E. Speer Memorial Minute." *Princeton Seminary Bulletin* 42 (Summer 1948): 13–15.

Bozeman, Theodore D. "Science, Nature, and Society: A New Approach to James Henley Thornwell." *Journal of Presbyterian History* 50 (June 1972): 307–25.

Buchanan, John G. "Robert E. Speer, the Man." *Princeton Seminary Bulletin* 42 (Summer 1948): 5–8.

Clutter, Ronald T. "The Reorganization of Princeton Theological Seminary Reconsidered." *Grace Theological Journal* 7, no. 2 (1986): 179–201.

Coletta, Paolo E. "The Youth of William Jennings Bryan—Beginnings of a Christian Statesman." *Nebraska History* 31 (March 1950): 1–24.

Faculty of Princeton Theological Seminary, "Robert E. Speer Memorial Minute," *Priceton Seminary Bulletin* 42 (Summer 1948): 15–17.

Garber, Paul L. "James Henley Thornwell: Presbyterian Defender of the Old South." *Union Seminary Review* 54 (February 1943): 93–116.

Genovese, Eugene D. "James Thornwell and Southern Religion." *Southern Partisan* (Summer 1987): 17–21.

Goodpasture, H. McKennie. "Robert E. Speer's Legacy." *Occasional Bullentin of Missionary Research* 2 (April 1978): 38–41.

Handy, Robert. "Fundamentalism and Modernism in Perspective." *Religion in Life* 24 (1955): 381–94.

Hart, Darryl G. "The Princeton Mind in the Modern World and the Common Sense of J. Gresham Machen." *Westminster Theological Journal* 46 (1984): 1–25.

Hart, John W. "Princeton Theological Seminary: The Reorganization of 1929." *Journal of Presbyterian History* 58 (Summer 1980): 124–40.

Homrighausen, Elmer G., Charles T. Fritsch and Bruce M. Metzger. "In Memoriam, Charles Rosenbury Erdman, July 20, 1866–May 10, 1960." *Princeton Seminary Bulletin* 54 (November 1960): 36–39.

Johnson, Benton. "Liberal Protestantism: End of the Road?" *The Annals of the American Academy of Political and Social Science* 480 (July 1985): 39–52.

Kerr, Hugh T. "In Memoriam: Robert E. Speer." *Theology Today* 5 (April 1948): 93–97.

Loewenberg, Bert J. "The Controversy over Evolution in New England." *New England Quarterly* 8 (June 1935): 232–57.

———. "Darwinism Comes to America: 1859–1900." *Mississippi Valley Historical Review* 28 (December 1941): 339–68.

———. "The Reaction of American Scientists to Darwinism." *American Historical Review* 38 (July 1933): 687–701.

Mackay, John A. "The Missionary Stateman." *Princeton Seminary Bulletin* 42 (Summer 1948): 10–13.

———. "Robert Elliott Speer: A Man of Yesterday and Today." *Princeton Seminary Bulletin* 60 (June 1967): 11–21.

Maddex, Jack P. "From Theocracy to Spirituality: The Southern Presbyterian Reversal on Church and State." *Journal of Presbyterian History* 54 (Winter 1976): 438–57.

Marsden, George M. "J. Gresham Machen, History, and Truth." *Westminster Thological Journal* 42 (Fall 1979): 157–75.

———. "The New School Heritage and Presbyterian Fundamentalism." *Westminster Theological Journal* 32 (May 1970): 129–47.

Muller, Richard A. "Henry Boynton Smith: Christocentric Theologian." *Journal of Presbyterian History* 61 (Winter 1983): 429–44.

Nichols, Robert H. "Fundamentalism in the Presbyterian Church." *Journal of Religion* 5 (January 1925): 14–36.

Niebuhr, Reinhold. "Minute on the Death of Dr. Coffin." *Union Seminary Quarterly Review* 10 (January 1955): 5–7.

Patterson, James A. "Robert E. Speer, J. Gresham Machen, and the Presbyterian Board of Foreign Missions." *American Presbyterians: Journal of Presbyterian History* 64 (Spring 1986): 58–68.

Piper, John F., Jr., "Robert E. Speer: Christian Statesman in War and Peace." *Journal of Presbyterian History* 47 (September 1969): 201–25.

———. "Robert E. Speer on Christianity and Race." *Journal of Presbyterian History* 61 (Summer 1983): 227–47.

Quirk, Charles E. "Origins of the Auburn Affirmation." *Journal of Presbyterian History* 53 (Summer 1975): 120–42.

———. "A Statistical Analysis of the Signers of the Auburn Affirmation." *Journal of Presbyterian History* 43 (September 1965): 182–96.

Roark, Dallas. "J. Gresham Machen: The Doctrinally True Presbyterian Church." *Journal of Presbyterian History* 43 (June & September 1965): 124–38, 174–81.

Roof, Wade Clark and William McKinney. "Denominational America and the New Religious Pluralism." *The Annals of the American Academy of Political and Social Science* 480 (July 1985): 24–38.

Sandeen, Ernest. "The Fundamentals: The Last Flowering of the Millenarian–Conservative Alliance." *Journal of Presbyterian History* 47 (March 1969): 55–73.

———. "The Princeton Theology: One Source of Biblical Literalism in American Protestantism." *Church History* 31 (September 1962): 307–21.
———. "Toward a Historical Interpretation of the Origin of Fundamentalism." *Church History* 36 (March 1967): 66–83.
Smith, Gary S. "Calvinists and Evolution: 1870–1920." *Journal of Presbyterian History* 61 (Fall 1983): 335–52.
Smith, H. Shelton. "The Church and the Social Order in the Old South As Interpreted by James H. Thornwell." *Church History* 7 (June 1938): 115–24.
Smith, Willard H. "William Jennings Bryan and the Social Gospel." *Journal of American History* 53 (June 1966): 41–60.
Szasz, Ferenc M. "William Jennings Bryan, Evolution, and the Fundamentalist–Modernist Controversy." *Nebraska History* 56 (Summer 1975): 259–78.
Tait, L. Gordon. "Evolution: Wishart, Wooster, and William Jennings Bryan." *Journal of Presbyterian History* 62 (Winter 1984): 306–21.

Theses and Dissertations

Clutter, Ronald T. "The Reorientation of Princeton Theological Seminary 1900–1929." Th.D. diss., Dallas Theological Seminary, 1982.
Davis, Dennis R. "Presbyterian Attitudes toward Science and the Coming of Darwinism in America, 1859–1929." Ph.D. diss., University of Illinois at Urbana–Champaign, 1980.
Farra, Harry E. "The Rhetoric of Reverend Clarence Edward Macartney: A Man under Authority." Ph.D. diss., Pennsylvania State University, 1970.
Haines, George L. "The Princeton Theological Seminary, 1929–1960." Ph.D. diss., New York University, 1966.
Hart, Darryl G. "*Doctor fundamentalis*: An Intellectual Biography of J. Gresham Machen, 1881–1937." Ph.D. diss., Johns Hopkins University, 1988.
Hart, John W. "The Controversy within the Presbyterian Church, U.S.A., in the 1920s with Special Emphasis on the Reorganization of Princeton Theological Seminary." Senior thesis, Princeton University, 1978.
Jeschke, Channing R. "The Briggs Case: The Focus of a Study in Nineteenth-Century Presbyterian History." Ph.D. diss., University of Chicago, 1966.
Johnson, Deryl F. "The Attitudes of the Princeton Theologians toward Darwinism and Evolution from 1859–1929." Ph.D. diss., University of Iowa, 1968.
Kim, Ki-hong. "Presbyterian Conflict in the Early Twentieth Century: Ecclesiology in the Princeton Tradition and the Emergence of Presbyterian Fundamentalism." Ph.D. diss., Drew University, 1983.
Kurtz, Arnold. "A Rhetorical Analysis of the Preaching of Dr. Clarence Edward Macartney, Twentieth Century Exponent of the Traditional Orthodoxy." Ph.D. diss., Michigan State University, 1966.
Livingstone, William D. "The Princeton Apologetic As Exemplified by the

Work of Benjamin B. Warfield and J. Gresham Machen." Ph.D. diss., Yale University, 1948.

Nelson, John. "The Rise of the Princeton Theology." Ph.D. diss., Yale University, 1935.

Nykamp, Delwin G. "A Presbyterian Power Struggle: A Critical History of Communication Strategies Employed in the Struggle for Control of the Presbyterian Church, U.S.A., 1922–1926." Ph.D. diss., Northwestern University, 1974.

Patterson, James A. "Robert E. Speer and the Crisis of the American Protestant Missionary Movement, 1920–1937." Ph.D. diss., Princeton Theological Seminary, 1980.

Quirk, Charles E. "The Auburn *Affirmation*: A Critical Narrative of the Document Designed To Safeguard the Unity and Liberty of the Presbyterian Church in the United States of America in 1924." Ph.D. diss., University of Iowa, 1967.

Roark, Dallas. "J. Gresham Machen and His Desire To Maintain a Doctrinally True Presbyterian Church." Ph.D. diss., State University of Iowa, 1963.

Smith, Gary S. "Calvinism and Culture in America, 1870–1915." Ph.D. diss., Johns Hopkins University, 1981.

Szasz, Ferenc M. "Three Fundamentalist Leaders: The Roles of William Bell Riley, John Roach Straton, and William Jennings Bryan, in the Fundamentalist–Modernist Controversy." Ph.D. diss., University of Rochester, 1969.

Weston, William J. "The Emergence of the Idea of Religious Pluralism within the Presbyterian Church in the U.S.A., 1890–1940." Ph.D. diss., Yale University, 1988.

Index